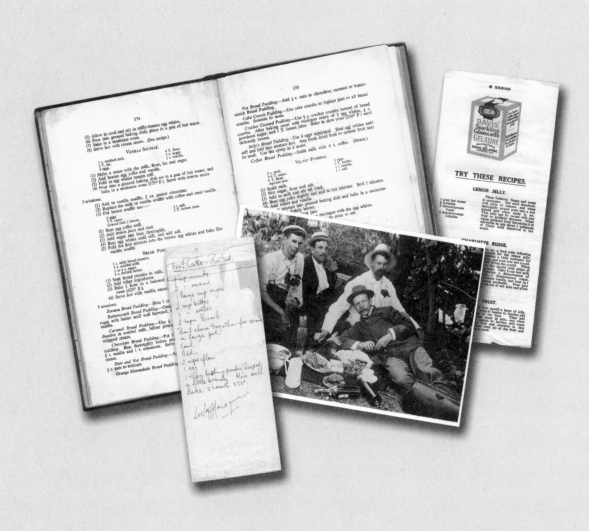

TRULY DELICIOUS

TRULY DELICIOUS

350 memorable recipes rediscovered for today's South African families

READER'S DIGEST

TRULY DELICIOUS
SOUTH AFRICAN EDITORIAL TEAM

Project Editor: Pat Kramer
Art Director: Stuart Nix, Square Edge Design
Proofreaders: Anne Wevell, Judy Beyer
Production Manager: Grant Moore
High-resolution scanning: Craig Meyer

Recipe consultant: Marina Searle-Tripp

Photographer: Henrique Wilding

Published by Heritage Publishing (Pty) Ltd, a licensee of
The Reader's Digest Association, Inc., 10 Mill Street,
Newlands 7708
http://www.readersdigest.co.za

First published 2003

ISBN 1-919750-46-0

Reproduction done by Imvakalelo Repro cc
Printed and bound in the Far East

LIKE GRANDMA USED TO MAKE
AUSTRALIAN EDITORIAL TEAM

Project Editor: Jenni Bruce
Art Direction: Margaret Cook and Mark Thacker
Designer: Katrina Beltran-Rehberg
Editor: Lynn Cole
Research Editor: Alistair McDermott
Picture Researcher: Joanna Collard
Researchers: Catherine Grillo, Maud Kernowski,
Milada Rehakova
Editorial Assistant: Karen Hardie
Proofreader: Tracy Rutherford
Indexer: Garry Cousins
Production Controller: Louise Mitchell

CONTRIBUTORS

Consultant for Australia: Meg Thomason
Consultant for New Zealand: Julie Biuso
Recipes Researchers and Testers: Pat Alburey,
Valerie Barrett, Julie Biuso, Janelle Bloom, Jackie Burrow,
Maxine Clark, Petra Jackson, Angela Kingsbury, Neal Martin,
John Palmer, Brenda Ratcliffe, Jennie Reekie, Jeni Wright
Photographers: Martin Brigdale, Laurie Evans, Howard Jones,
Gregory McBean, Vernon Morgan, Pia Tryde, Peter Williams
Home Economists: Maxine Clark, Justine Poole,
Jane Suthering, Carla Tomasi, Berit Vinegrad
Stylists: Carolyn Fienberg, Róisin Neild, Georgina Rhodes,
Lesley Richardson, Helen Trent
Illustrations: Steven Bray, Rodney Shackell

Picture facing title page: Fresh fruit fool, recipe page 218

Meals that memories are made of...

Rediscover food as you remember it – food as it ought to taste. Sometimes it is good to return to old-fashioned cooking with meals of deceptive simplicity that are nourishing and satisfying, as well as delicious. This is the kind of cooking you make time for, the kind that is a joy to create, a delight to serve and a pleasure to eat with family and friends. This is the food that Grandma used to make.

In the past, our mothers and grandmothers would build up a stock of recipes from friends and magazine clippings, rejecting those that didn't work, eagerly preserving those that did and handing these tried and trusted recipes from generation to generation. Many a favourite steaming broth, a secret way of cooking lamb with herbs or a featherlight sponge cake has found its way onto our tables in this way.

Much of the food that we eat today has, over the generations, been influenced by cooks from all around the world. Many ingredients and recipes that we now cook regularly were exciting, new and 'foreign' to our adventurous grandmothers who tried them out as 'something different'. They added them to their own lists of favourites, creating new family traditions, while still keeping alive the recipes from their past.

Here, garnished with tips, contemporary short cuts and fascinating anecdotes, we have selected more than 350 of these traditional recipes – succulent Loin of Pork with Sage and Onion Stuffing, hearty Bean Soup, Grilled Sole and many more, plus breads, biscuits, cakes and jams galore. This unique treasury of old-fashioned recipes and tips, reworked for today's kitchens, will enable you to recreate meals that memories are made of ... the flavour of an age that knew what cooking was all about.

The Editors

Contents

STARTERS, SOUPS & SNACKS

EGGS & CHEESE

PASTA, GRAINS & RICE

POULTRY & GAME

VEGETABLES & SALADS

DESSERTS & BEVERAGES

BREADS, CAKES & BISCUITS

JAMS, PICKLES & PRESERVES

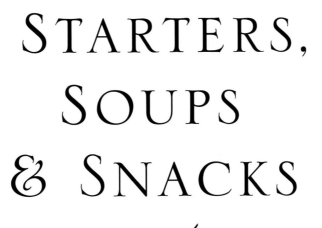

STARTERS,
SOUPS
& SNACKS

SALMON PINWHEELS

1 bunch watercress

375 g cream cheese

8 long, thin slices white
   bread, cut lengthways from
   a large sandwich loaf

500 g smoked salmon or
   salmon trout, thinly sliced

Lemon juice, to sprinkle

Freshly ground black pepper

PREPARATION TIME: 20 minutes

CHILLING TIME: overnight

MAKES: 40 pinwheels

CHICKEN & ANCHOVY
TRIANGLES

500 g cooked chicken,
   finely chopped

60 g tinned anchovy fillets,
   drained and finely chopped

2 tablespoons capers,
   finely chopped

8 tablespoons mayonnaise,
   homemade (p.306)
   or bought

Freshly ground black pepper

1 small, crisp lettuce

10 thin slices brown bread

10 thin slices white bread

125 g butter, softened

PREPARATION TIME: 25 minutes

CHILLING TIME: 3–4 hours

MAKES: 40 triangles

ASPARAGUS ROLLS

10 spears fresh asparagus

10 thin slices brown bread,
   cut from a large loaf

125 g butter, softened

2 teaspoons finely grated
   lemon rind

Pinch of cayenne pepper

PREPARATION TIME: 30 minutes

COOKING TIME: 10 minutes

CHILLING TIME: 3–4 hours

MAKES: 20 rolls

Tea Sandwiches

*For a formal afternoon tea, offer these tasty little mouthfuls
with a selection of cakes and a pot of tea.*

SALMON PINWHEELS

Prepare these the day before serving. Trim and finely chop the watercress and mix it with the cream cheese. Trim the crusts from the bread and, using a rolling pin, gently roll each slice to make it thin and flexible. Spread each slice evenly with the cream cheese mixture, then cover with a thin layer of salmon, trimming to fit where necessary. Sprinkle the lemon juice over the salmon and season with the pepper. Starting from a short end, roll up each slice tightly like a Swiss roll. Wrap each roll tightly in plastic wrap and refrigerate overnight. Just before serving, unwrap, cut each roll into five slices and arrange on a serving dish.

CHICKEN & ANCHOVY
TRIANGLES

Make these 3–4 hours ahead. Put the chopped chicken, anchovies, capers and mayonnaise in a bowl, season to taste with black pepper and mix well together. Trim and shred the lettuce. Spread each slice of bread thinly with butter, then spread the chicken mixture evenly over each brown slice. Sprinkle the shredded lettuce on the chicken and top with the white slices. Stack the sandwiches together, wrap in plastic

wrap and chill for 3–4 hours. Just before serving, unwrap, trim off the crusts, cut each sandwich into four triangles and arrange on a serving dish.

ASPARAGUS ROLLS

Make these delicate rolls 3–4 hours ahead. Trim the asparagus spears and peel to halfway up each spear if they are tough. Bring lightly salted water to a simmer in a frying pan. Place the asparagus in the pan in a single layer, cover with a lid and poach for about 5 minutes or until tender. Remove the spears carefully from the pan, put them into a colander and rinse under cold water. Drain well and allow to cool.

Remove the crusts from the bread and, using a rolling pin, lightly roll each slice to make it thinner. Blend the butter, lemon rind and cayenne pepper together and spread the mixture evenly over each slice of bread. Cut each slice and each asparagus spear in half crossways. Lay a piece of asparagus crossways on each slice of bread, trimming to fit, if necessary. Roll up tightly, wrap in plastic wrap and chill for 3–4 hours. Just before serving, unwrap, cut each asparagus roll in half diagonally and arrange the pieces on a serving dish.

Blini with 'Caviar'

These very small pancakes originate from Russia and Poland.
The use of buckwheat flour and fresh yeast makes all the difference.

Dissolve the sugar in the warm milk and use 2 tablespoons of the liquid to mix the yeast to a smooth, thin paste in a large, warmed mixing bowl. Stir in the remaining milk. Add about two-thirds of the flour and the salt and whisk to make a smooth batter. Cover with plastic wrap and stand in a warm place to rise for an hour.

Add the remaining flour and the butter to the batter, and beat well. The mixture should have the consistency of thick cream; if it is too stiff, add a little extra warm milk. Fold the egg white into the batter. Cover and allow to rise again for 30 minutes.

Meanwhile, put the onions in a serving bowl. Spoon the sour cream and 'caviar' into two serving bowls. Wash the lemon, cut it into segments and arrange them in another bowl. Chill until you are ready to serve.

Brush the inside of a large, heavy-based frying pan with oil and heat it until it exudes a slight haze. Cook three blini at a time, allowing a full tablespoon of batter for each. Fry gently for about 2 minutes until the surface has just dried out and is a mass of small holes, then turn the blini over to brown on the other side for about 2 minutes. Cover the cooked blini with foil and keep warm until you are ready to serve.

When serving, place two or three blinis on each plate and pass around the bowls of chopped onion, sour cream (or crème fraîche), 'caviar' and lemon wedges.

VARIATION

For different flavours, try the blinis with thinly sliced smoked salmon or salmon trout, or chopped hard-boiled eggs and snipped chives.

¼ teaspoon sugar
1 cup warm milk (you may need a little more)
15 g fresh yeast
225 g buckwheat or wholewheat flour
Pinch of salt
25 g butter, melted
1 egg white, whisked until stiff
2 onions, coarsely chopped
1 cup sour cream or crème fraîche
1 small jar (about 100 g) black lumpfish 'caviar'
Lemon wedges
Sunflower oil for frying

PREPARATION TIME: 25 minutes
RISING TIME: 1½ hours
COOKING TIME: 20 minutes
SERVES: six

Fresh yeast can be obtained at your local supermarket's bakery and any leftover yeast can be frozen for later use. Buckwheat flour is kept in the supermarket's refrigerators. Leftover buckwheat flour should be stored in your own refrigerator.

Seafood Cocktails

Discover for yourself just how good these classic starters are.
They are once again enjoying the popularity they deserve.

THE COCKTAIL SAUCE
⅓ cup pouring cream
⅓ cup tomato sauce
2–3 drops Tabasco sauce
3 teaspoons lemon juice
Salt and cayenne pepper

PRAWN COCKTAIL
3 iceberg lettuce leaves,
    shredded
32 medium, cooked prawns,
    peeled and deveined,
    tails left intact
1 quantity cocktail sauce
    (see above)
Cayenne pepper to garnish
Lemon wedges, to serve

MIXED SEAFOOD
COCKTAIL
3 iceberg lettuce leaves,
    shredded
16 medium, cooked prawns,
    peeled and deveined,
    tails left intact
1 cooked crayfish tail, diced
250 g cold, poached kingklip,
    flaked
1 quantity cocktail sauce
    (see above)
Cayenne pepper to garnish
Lemon wedges, to serve

FOR EACH COCKTAIL
PREPARATION TIME: 10 minutes
SERVES: four

To prepare the cocktail sauce, combine the cream, tomato sauce, Tabasco sauce and lemon juice in a small bowl and mix well. Season to taste with salt and cayenne pepper. Cover and refrigerate until ready to serve.

PRAWN COCKTAIL
Arrange the shredded lettuce in the base of four individual serving bowls (preferably glass). Top with the prawns. Drizzle with the cocktail sauce and sprinkle with cayenne pepper. Serve with lemon wedges.

MIXED SEAFOOD COCKTAIL
Arrange the shredded lettuce in four serving bowls (preferably glass). Top the lettuce in each bowl with four prawns, and the crayfish and kingklip pieces. Drizzle with the cocktail sauce and sprinkle with salt and cayenne pepper. Serve with lemon wedges.

A VICTORIAN COCKTAIL
This elaborate 'Bouquet of Prawns' was among the suggestions in Mrs Beeton's famous Book of Cookery and Household Management, *first published in 1860.*

Seafood Pâté and Mousse

Two starters which can both be made in advance. In fact, the smoked snoek pâté can be frozen and then thawed in the refrigerator when needed.

SMOKED SNOEK PÂTÉ

Blend the snoek, cottage cheese, spring onions and melted butter in a food processor (or pound the ingredients together) until smooth. Add lemon juice and chilli powder to taste (remember, this fish is salty, so only add salt if necessary). Spoon into small dishes or ramekins and chill until ready to serve. Garnish with herbs and lemon slices and serve with Melba toast, bread, toast or crackers.

SALMON MOUSSE

Drain the salmon, discard any skin and large bones and flake the fish. Sprinkle the gelatine over the cold water in a small heat-proof dish, then dissolve it over a saucepan of simmering water, stirring until the liquid is clear. Blend the salmon, cucumber, celery and lemon juice in a food processor until smooth. Stir in the mayonnaise, salt, Tabasco and créme fraîche, strain in the dissolved gelatine and mix well together. Taste and adjust seasoning. Spoon the mousse into 6 small moulds (coated with non-stick cooking spray) and refrigerate until set.

Mix the ingredients for the sauce (retain a little cucumber for garnishing) in a food processor until smooth. Check the seasoning and chill well.

Turn the moulds out onto individual plates, loosening the edges with a small spatula. Garnish with the chopped cucumber and serve with the cucumber sauce.

VARIATION

Use 350 g smoked salmon trout fillets instead of tinned salmon and replace the celery with 1 tablespoon chopped fresh dill. Garnish with dill sprigs and serve with Melba toast and lemon wedges.

SMOKED SNOEK PÂTÉ

250 g smoked snoek, boned and flaked
250 g smooth cottage cheese
2 spring onions, chopped
2 tablespoons melted butter
1 tablespoon lemon juice
Chilli powder
Herbs and lemon slices to garnish

PREPARATION TIME: 20 minutes
CHILLING TIME: 25 minutes
SERVES: six

SALMON MOUSSE

2 tins red salmon (about 210 g each)
1 tablespoon gelatine
4 tablespoons cold water
¼ English cucumber, peeled and finely diced
1 stick celery, diced
1 tablespoon lemon juice
4 tablespoons mayonnaise
¼ teaspoon salt
A few drops Tabasco sauce
125 ml crème fraîche

FOR THE CUCUMBER SAUCE

½ English cucumber, peeled and finely diced
1 cup natural yoghurt or crème fraîche
1 small onion, finely chopped
A squeeze of lemon juice
Salt and freshly ground black pepper

PREPARATION TIME: 30 minutes
CHILLING TIME: 4 hours
SERVES: six

EGG ROLLS

7 eggs, hard-boiled

7 tablespoons mayonnaise, homemade (p.306) or bought

1 teaspoon anchovy essence

Freshly ground black pepper

10 cocktail rolls (about 8 cm long), or 20 slices baguette, 1 cm thick

90 g butter, softened

Small bunch watercress

PREPARATION TIME: 30 minutes

MAKES: 20 pieces

SHRIMP ROLLS

10 cocktail rolls, or 20 slices baguette, 1 cm thick

2 tablespoons olive oil

1 teaspoon lemon juice

1 tablespoon mayonnaise, homemade (p.306) or bought

200 g cooked, peeled and deveined shrimps, chopped (reserve some for garnish)

60 g cream cheese (low-fat, if possible)

1 small, crisp lettuce, trimmed and finely shredded

Cayenne pepper

Fresh dill and reserved peeled shrimps, to garnish

PREPARATION TIME: 25 minutes

COOKING TIME: 2 minutes

MAKES: 20 pieces

MUSHROOM & HAM SCONES

150 g butter

300 g button mushrooms, wiped and chopped

3 tablespoons dry sherry

2 tablespoons chopped parsley

Salt and freshly ground black pepper

8 thin slices ham

10 cheese scones (p.251)

Fresh parsley, to garnish

PREPARATION TIME: 30 minutes

COOKING TIME: 10–15 minutes

MAKES: 20 pieces

Easy Canapés

*Eggs, shrimps, and ham and mushrooms make
delicious toppings for an array of finger food.*

EGG ROLLS

Shell and finely chop the eggs, put them into a bowl, carefully mix in the mayonnaise and anchovy essence and season well with the pepper. Cut each roll, if using, in half horizontally and spread the rolls or baguette slices with butter. Spread the egg mixture on top and garnish with watercress.

SHRIMP ROLLS

Cut each roll, if using, in half horizontally, then lightly toast the cut sides, or one side of the baguette slices. Allow to cool. Mix the oil, lemon juice and mayonnaise together, add the shrimps and stir until evenly coated. Spread the cream cheese over the toasted surfaces, sprinkle on some lettuce, then spoon on the shrimp mixture. Sprinkle with cayenne pepper and garnish with shrimps and a sprig of dill.

MUSHROOM & HAM SCONES

Melt 60 g of the butter in a frying pan. Add the mushrooms, sherry and chopped parsley and cook over medium heat for 10–15 minutes, or until the mushrooms are soft and all the liquid has evaporated. Remove from the heat, season to taste with salt and pepper and leave to cool.

Using a 5 cm plain round cutter, stamp out 20 rounds from the ham and set aside. Finely chop the remaining ham, including the trimmings, and stir into the mushrooms.

Cut the scones in half horizontally. Spread each half lightly with some of the remaining butter, place a round of ham on each and spoon on the mushroom mixture.

Garnish the mushroom and ham scones with sprigs of parsley and arrange attractively on a serving dish.

Creamy Mornays

Sliced or halved hard-boiled eggs are baked in a creamy cheese sauce.
For a sharper flavour, replace some of the Cheddar with grated Gruyère and Parmesan.

CREAMY MORNAYS

Boil the eggs in water for 10–12 minutes. Drain, cool under cold running water and shell the eggs. Halve them lengthways and arrange them, cut side down, in a shallow oven-proof or gratin dish.

To make the sauce, melt the butter, stir in the flour and cook for 1–2 minutes without browning. Gradually stir in the milk and bring to the boil, stirring continually to make a smooth sauce. Season well.

Remove from the heat and add half the cheese and the mustard. Stir until the cheese has melted, and pour the sauce over the eggs. Sprinkle with the crumbs (mixed with the remaining cheese) and bake for 30 minutes.

To add colour, sprinkle with paprika and parsley sprigs just before serving.

Serve with crusty bread or hot buttered toast. The addition of cooked rice and a green salad will turn this into a main course.

VARIATION

Make a bed of mashed potato or creamed spinach, lay the egg halves on top, then spoon over the sauce.

ASPARAGUS MORNAY

Proceed as for eggs mornay, replacing the eggs with asparagus spears. If using fresh asparagus, first cook the spears by lying them flat in a large pan and poaching in gently boiling, salted water for 5 minutes, or until just tender. Remove the spears carefully from the pan, put them into a colander and rinse under cold water to halt the cooking. Drain well.

EGGS MORNAY
8 extra large eggs

1 quantity mornay sauce (see below)

Paprika and parsley sprigs to garnish

FOR THE MORNAY SAUCE
50 g butter

50 g flour

2 cups milk

Salt and freshly ground black pepper

250 g mature Cheddar cheese, grated

1 teaspoon prepared mustard

½ cup breadcrumbs

ASPARAGUS MORNAY
2 bunches fresh asparagus, trimmed (enough to serve four), or 1 x 340 g tin asparagus spears, drained

1 quantity mornay sauce (see above)

Paprika and parsley sprigs, to garnish

FOR EACH MORNAY

PREPARATION TIME: 25 minutes

COOKING TIME: 40 minutes

SERVES: four

Cook hard-boiled eggs for 10 minutes in boiling water. Remove the eggs from the pot and plunge them into cold water immediately. Peel underwater and allow to cool. This will prevent a dark ring from forming around the yolk.

Bread Tartlets

These delicious mouthfuls are quick and easy for even a novice cook to prepare. You can vary the fillings – hard-boiled egg and bacon, or spinach and cheese are other possibilities. The crisp cases (without the filling) can be stored in an airtight container for a couple of days.

FOR THE BREAD CASES
24 slices day-old white bread
60 g butter, melted

FOR THE SAUCE
1 cup milk
1 small bay leaf
2 thin slices onion
5 black peppercorns
1 small stick celery, sliced
30 g butter
1½ tablespoons plain flour
Salt and freshly ground
   white pepper

FOR THE FILLING
Any of the following: 200 g
   button mushrooms, thinly
   sliced and cooked; 200 g
   cooked chicken, diced;
   grated cheese; halved
   cherry tomatoes; chopped,
   grilled red pepper; tinned
   tuna, drained and flaked;
   tinned asparagus, chopped
¼ cup chopped chives or
   parsley, to garnish

PREPARATION TIME: 15 minutes
COOLING TIME: 15 minutes
COOKING TIME: 27 minutes
MAKES: 24 tartlets

To prepare the bread cases, preheat the oven to 180°C. Use a rolling pin to flatten each slice of bread to a thickness of 1–2 mm. Use a 7 cm round cutter to cut one round from each piece of bread. Lightly brush both sides of the bread with melted butter and then press into 24 small tartlet pans. Bake in the preheated oven for 10–12 minutes, or until light golden.

To make the sauce, combine the milk, bay leaf, onion, peppercorns and celery in a small, heavy-based saucepan. Heat on medium heat until bubbles form around the edge of the saucepan. Remove from the heat and stand at room temperature for 15 minutes to cool. Strain and reserve the milk, discarding the contents of the sieve.

Melt the butter in a small saucepan until hot and bubbling. Add the flour and stir constantly for 1 minute. Remove from the heat and add the strained milk in a slow, steady stream, whisking constantly to avoid the sauce becoming lumpy. Return the saucepan to the heat and cook, stirring constantly on medium-high heat until the sauce comes to the boil and thickens. Stir in the filling you have chosen. Season to taste with salt and white pepper.

Spoon about 1 tablespoon of the filling into each bread case and return to the oven to bake for a further 5 minutes, or until they are warmed through. Sprinkle with chopped chives or parsley and serve immediately.

Chicken Liver Pâté

This richly flavoured pâté is a wonderful standby for when guests drop in. It can also be served in individual pots with triangles of hot toast as a first course.

600 g chicken livers
1 medium onion
100 g butter, chopped
2 cloves garlic, crushed
1 bay leaf
1 tablespoon fresh thyme
   leaves
2-3 tablespoons brandy or port
Salt and freshly ground
   black pepper
Clarified butter (p.311)
   (optional)
Additional fresh thyme
   leaves, to garnish

PREPARATION TIME: 10 minutes
COOKING TIME: 20 minutes
COOLING TIME: 20 minutes
CHILLING TIME: overnight
SERVES: ten to twelve

Trim any discoloured spots, fat and membrane from the chicken livers. Wash the trimmed livers and pat dry with paper towels. Peel and finely chop the onion.

Melt the butter in a large frying pan over medium heat until it is foaming. Add the onion and garlic and cook, stirring often, until the onion is soft.

Add the livers, bay leaf, thyme and brandy or port. Cook for 10 minutes, or until the livers are just cooked through. Remove from the heat and cool for 20 minutes.

Remove the bay leaf and spoon the liver mixture into a food processor. Process until smooth and season to taste with salt and pepper. Spoon the pâté into ramekins or a pâté pot and cover with plastic wrap, pressing it directly onto the surface of the pâté to prevent it from discolouring. Alternatively, pour a layer of melted clarified butter over the surface of the pâté.

Chill the pâté overnight in the refrigerator. To serve, sprinkle the top with fresh thyme leaves and provide fresh, crusty bread or crackers to accompany.

FACING PAGE: *Bread tartlets*

CURRIED ONION DIP

1 cup sour cream (smetena)

½ cup mayonnaise,
   homemade (p.306)
   or bought

2 large spring onions with
   tops, finely chopped

½ teaspoon curry powder

1 clove garlic, peeled
   and crushed

PREPARATION TIME: 10 minutes

CHILLING TIME: 1 hour

MAKES: 1½ cups

LIME & HONEY DIP

250 g cream cheese, at room
   temperature

½ cup plain Greek yoghurt

2 tablespoons honey

2 tablespoons milk

1 tablespoon lime juice

1 teaspoon vanilla essence

Pinch of ground mace
   or grated nutmeg

¼ teaspoon grated lime rind

PREPARATION TIME: 10 minutes

CHILLING TIME: 1 hour

MAKES: about 1⅓ cups

YOGHURT AND CUCUMBER

1 cup plain Greek yoghurt

½ cup chopped English
   cucumber

Salt

1 clove garlic, crushed

1 tablespoon olive oil

1 tablespoon lemon juice

Salt and freshly ground black
   pepper to taste

PREPARATION TIME: 1 hour

CHILLING TIME: 1 hour

MAKES: about 1⅓ cups

Delectable Dips

Creamy dips were standard fare at cocktail parties in the 1950s. They were usually served with plain crackers or potato chips, but you might also like to serve them with pita triangles or a platter of sliced fresh vegetables.

CURRIED ONION DIP

Mix all the ingredients together in small bowl. Cover and refrigerate for at least 1 hour. (This dip will keep for 2 days.)

LIME & HONEY DIP

Beat the cream cheese in a small bowl with an electric mixer. Add the yoghurt, honey, milk, lime juice, vanilla and mace and beat until creamy. Stir in the lime rind. Cover and refrigerate for at least 1 hour. (This dip will keep for 2 days.) You can serve this dip with an assortment of fresh fruits.

YOGHURT AND CUCUMBER DIP

Drain any whey from the yoghurt to ensure a thick yoghurt. Turn the cucumber into a colander, salt it, weight it down and leave to drain. After about an hour mix the yoghurt and cucumber together. Then add the rest of the ingredients and season. Chill for an hour. Use on the same day.

Instead of making pinwheel savouries, add most of the onion, bacon and cheese to the dry ingredients and mix to a dough with milk. Knead lightly and shape into scones. Top with a few pinches of onion, bacon and cheese, and bake as for pinwheel savouries.

Pinwheel Savouries

These crisp and tasty savouries are good for a light lunch with a salad. Alternatively, make mini ones and serve them with drinks.

Preheat the oven to 250°C. Sift the flour and salt into a large mixing bowl. Rub the butter into the flour until the mixture resembles fine breadcrumbs. Add the milk and mix quickly to a stiff dough.

Knead lightly on a floured surface until smooth and roll into a rectangle about 30 cm long by 20 cm wide. Distribute the onion, bacon and cheese on top of the dough. Roll into a long sausage, dampening the edge of the dough with a little water. Cut into small rounds and transfer to a baking sheet lined with baking paper. Bake for about 12 minutes, or until golden and crisp, and serve piping hot.

2 cups self-raising flour
½ teaspoon salt
2½ tablespoons butter, softened
⅔ cup milk
1 small onion, peeled and finely chopped
100 g (2–3 rashers) streaky bacon, rind removed, finely chopped
1 cup loosely packed grated Cheddar cheese

PREPARATION TIME: 20 minutes
COOKING TIME: 12–15 minutes
MAKES: 12 scones

Mushroom Pancakes

Served with a green salad, mushroom pancakes make a fine light lunch or snack.

FOR THE PANCAKES
1 cup plain flour
Pinch of salt
1 egg
1¼ cups milk (or half milk,
    half water)
2 tablespoons vegetable oil,
    for frying

FOR THE SAUCE
Bouquet garni (p.310)
1 slice onion
2½ cups milk
45 g butter
⅓ cup plain flour
Salt and freshly ground
    black pepper
4 tablespoons chopped fresh
    parsley
½ cup grated Cheddar cheese

FOR THE FILLING
60 g unsalted butter
1 large onion, peeled
    and chopped
750 g button mushrooms,
    wiped and chopped
2 tablespoons dry sherry
Salt and freshly ground
    black pepper

PREPARATION TIME: 1¼ hours
COOKING TIME: 30 minutes
SERVES: four

To prepare the pancakes, sift the flour and salt into a bowl. Make a well in the centre, add the egg and gradually whisk in the milk until the batter is smooth. Pour into a measuring jug and set aside for at least 30 minutes while you prepare the sauce and filling.

To prepare the sauce, add the bouquet garni and onion to the milk and bring to the boil. Remove from the heat, cover and stand for 30 minutes to infuse the flavours.

Meanwhile, prepare the filling. Melt the butter in a medium saucepan, add the onion and cook until soft. Add the mushrooms and sherry, cover and cook for 30 minutes, stirring occasionally. Uncover and cook for a further 15 minutes, or until most of the liquid has evaporated. Remove the pan from the heat, season the filling to taste, cover and set aside.

To cook the pancakes, heat 1 teaspoon of the oil in an 18 cm nonstick frying pan until a faint haze is given off. Stir the batter and pour in one-eighth. Tilt the pan so that it coats the base evenly, then cook over medium heat for 1–2 minutes, or until the underside is golden. Turn the pancake over and cook the second side for a minute more. Tip the pancake onto a plate and cover with a sheet of greaseproof paper. Make seven more pancakes in this way, interleaving them with greaseproof paper.

Preheat the oven to 200°C. To finish off the sauce, melt the butter in a medium saucepan, stir in the flour and cook over medium heat for 1 minute. Strain the infused milk and gradually add to the pan, stirring continuously until the sauce comes to the boil and thickens. Reduce the heat and cook for 2–3 minutes. Remove from the heat, season to taste and stir in the chopped parsley.

Lightly oil a shallow ovenproof dish. Spoon some of the mushroom mixture onto the centre of each pancake, roll up and place, folded side down, in the dish. Pour the sauce over the rolls, sprinkle with cheese and cook in the centre of the oven for about 30–40 minutes, or until golden brown and bubbling.

VARIATION

Seafood Pancakes: Mix a tin of drained, mashed tuna or salmon with 125 g savoury cottage cheese. Add a squeeze of lemon juice, salt and freshly ground black pepper to the mixture.

Instead of rolling the pancakes, you can also sandwich open pancakes with the filling of your choice to form a 'cake'. Place in an ovenproof dish, pour over the sauce, sprinkle with breadcrumbs and bake until golden. Cut into wedges for serving.

BEEFY GOODNESS IN A CUBE
In 1847 German chemist, Baron Justus van Liebig, developed a method to extract the goodness of beef. Originally used in hospitals as a health-boosting drink, it only appeared on the market 14 years later. A worker used the symbol 'OXO' to distinguish consignments of different meat types headed for the beef extract factory and the name stuck. Oxo cubes first appeared in 1910.

An avocado is ripe if it feels a little soft when held in your hand. To help ripen an avocado, put it in a paper bag with a ripe banana or apple and store in an airy spot.

Avocado Vinaigrette

As a starter, the sumptuous avocado needs very little embellishment.

To make the vinaigrette, combine the olive oil, white wine vinegar, Dijon mustard and salt and pepper to taste in a screwtop jar. Shake well to combine. Taste and adjust the seasoning, if necessary.

Cut the avocados in half lengthways and gently twist the halves to separate. To remove the seed, insert a sharp knife into it, then twist and lift it out.

Brush the cut surfaces with lemon juice and place the avocado halves on a serving plate. Shake the dressing again and drizzle it evenly over the avocado halves. Serve with buttered toast triangles.

FOR THE VINAIGRETTE
½ cup olive oil
2 tablespoons white wine vinegar
1 teaspoon Dijon mustard
Salt and freshly ground black pepper

FOR THE AVOCADOS
2 firm, ripe avocados
1 tablespoon lemon juice
Toasted bread, buttered and cut into triangles, to serve

PREPARATION TIME: 5 minutes
SERVES: four

FOR THE MEATBALLS

400 g lean minced beef
½ cup soft breadcrumbs
   (p.310)
¼ cup finely chopped onion
¼ cup grated carrot
2 tablespoons finely
   chopped fresh parsley
2 tablespoons milk
½ teaspoon dried
   marjoram leaves
¼ teaspoon salt
Pinch of ground sage
Pinch of freshly ground
   black pepper
1 egg, lightly beaten

FOR THE SAUCE

½ cup apple juice
⅓ cup firmly packed dark
   brown sugar
¼ cup red wine vinegar
   or apple cider vinegar
4 teaspoons cornflour
1½ tablespoons soya sauce
1 clove garlic, peeled
   and crushed

PREPARATION TIME: 20 minutes
COOKING TIME: 23 minutes
MAKES: 18 meatballs

You can make the meatballs and the sauce a day ahead. Refrigerate them separately, then reheat the meatballs in the sauce just ahead of serving time.

Cocktail Meatballs

Be sure to supply cocktail forks or toothpicks and napkins when you serve these herbed meatballs with their sweet-and-sour sauce.

Preheat the oven to 180°C. To prepare the meatballs, mix the beef in a large bowl with the breadcrumbs, onion, carrot, parsley, milk, marjoram, salt, sage, pepper and lightly beaten egg. Shape the mixture into a 2,5-cm-thick rectangle and cut into 18 pieces. Roll each piece into a ball. Place the meatballs in a large baking pan and bake for 15–20 minutes, or until the meatballs are no longer pink. Drain on paper towels.

Meanwhile, prepare the sauce. Whisk the apple juice, brown sugar, vinegar, cornflour, soya sauce and garlic together in a medium saucepan. Bring to the boil, stirring frequently, and cook for 2 minutes, or until thickened. Stir the meatballs into the sauce and simmer for 3 minutes, or until heated through.

To serve, place the meatballs in a small chafing dish or shallow serving dish and provide cocktail forks or toothpicks.

Cream Cheese Log with Ham

This chilled log is easy to prepare and makes a handsome appetiser for serving with drinks.

Beat the cream cheese, mayonnaise and horseradish in a small bowl with an electric mixer until creamy. Stir in the cheese, ham and pimientos. Shape the mixture into a log 20 cm long. Wrap the log in plastic wrap and refrigerate for at least 2 hours (it will keep for 2 days). Spread the chives on wax paper. Unwrap the log and carefully roll it in the chives, until it is completely coated. Rewrap the log in plastic wrap and refrigerate until serving time.

Serve the log with Melba toast.

250 g smooth cream cheese, softened
¼ cup mayonnaise, homemade (p.306) or bought
1 teaspoon drained prepared horseradish
½ cup grated Emmenthal cheese
100 g ham, finely chopped
1 tablespoon drained tinned pimientos or peppadews, chopped
½ cup finely chopped chives
Melba toast (p.312), to serve

PREPARATION TIME: 20 minutes
CHILLING TIME: 2 hours
SERVES: twelve as an appetiser

Quiche Lorraine

*Although the original Quiche Lorraine did not include cheese,
this is the version that became popular in the 1950s.
A quiche is perfect for lunch or for a first course at dinner.*

FOR THE PASTRY CASE

Shortcrust pastry, homemade
(p.311) or bought

1 egg, lightly beaten

FOR THE FILLING

4 rashers streaky bacon,
rind removed

60 g Swiss or Gruyère
cheese, grated

2 eggs

1 teaspoon plain flour

Pinch of grated nutmeg

Pinch of cayenne pepper

1/2 teaspoon salt

1/2 cup cream

1/2 cup milk

20 g butter, melted

PREPARATION TIME: 45 minutes

COOKING TIME: 30 minutes

SERVES: four to six

Roll out the pastry to line a 23 cm, fluted, loose-bottomed flan tin. Brush the inside of the pastry case with the egg. Chill the pastry case while making the filling.

Preheat the oven to 200°C. Grill the bacon lightly and chop. Place the bacon and cheese in the pastry case in layers. Beat the eggs, flour, nutmeg, cayenne, salt, cream, milk and melted butter together and pour over the bacon and cheese. Bake for 10 minutes, then reduce the heat to 180°C and bake for a further 20 minutes, or until a knife comes out clean. To serve, cut the quiche into wedges.

VARIATIONS

Blue-Cheese Quiche: You can vary this recipe by replacing the bacon and cheese filling with a blue-cheese filling. Prepare the pastry case as for Quiche Lorraine and then make the filling while the case chills.

In a small bowl, toss 1 tablespoon plain flour with 1/2 cup grated Swiss cheese and 1/2 cup crumbled blue cheese. Spread in the pastry case. In a medium bowl, whisk 3 eggs with 1 cup milk, 1/4 cup finely chopped chives and a pinch each of salt and pepper. Pour over the cheese mixture in the pastry case. Bake the quiche, uncovered, for 20–30 minutes, or until the centre is set. To serve, cut into wedges.

Cheddar Quiche: This recipe can also be made with a Cheddar filling, or a mixture of Swiss and Cheddar. Prepare as for blue-cheese quiche, substituting 1/2 cup grated Cheddar cheese for the blue cheese and 1/4 cup finely chopped onion for the chopped chives.

Cheese Straws

*You can store these crisp nibbles in an airtight container
to have on hand for when friends drop in for drinks.*

Melted butter, for greasing

60 g butter, chopped

3/4 cup finely grated tasty
Cheddar cheese

1/4 cup finely grated
Parmesan cheese

3/4 cup plain flour, sifted

1/2 teaspoon ground sweet
paprika

Pinch of cayenne pepper

1/2 teaspoon salt

1 tablespoon cold water

1 egg, lightly beaten

PREPARATION TIME: 15 minutes

CHILLING TIME: 1 hour 10 minutes

COOKING TIME: 12 minutes

MAKES: 32 straws

Preheat the oven to 180°C. Brush two flat baking trays with melted butter and line with nonstick baking paper. (The butter will prevent the paper from moving around on the tray.)

Cream the butter and the Cheddar and Parmesan cheeses together in a medium bowl until well combined. Add the flour, paprika, cayenne pepper, salt and water and mix with a wooden spoon until the dough comes together in a ball. Turn the dough out on a lightly floured surface and press into a square. Wrap the dough in greaseproof paper and place in the refrigerator for 1 hour to chill.

Roll the dough out between two sheets of nonstick baking paper into a 24 x 20 cm rectangle 5 mm thick. Trim the edges of the pastry. Cut the dough into straws 10 cm long by 15 mm wide. Place the straws on the prepared trays, allowing a little room between each straw. Refrigerate the trays for 10 minutes, or until the dough is firm.

Brush the cheese straws with lightly beaten egg and bake for 10–12 minutes, or until the straws are light golden and firm to the touch. (Halfway through the cooking time, swap over the top and bottom trays in the oven.) Allow the cheese straws to cool on the baking trays for 5 minutes before transferring them to a wire rack to cool completely.

FACING PAGE: Quiche Lorraine

Club Sandwich

This is one of the world's favourite sandwiches, perfect for a satisfying, nourishing light meal at any time of day.

4 rashers streaky bacon, rind removed, halved

12 slices white or wholewheat sandwich bread, toasted

½ cup mayonnaise

8 lettuce leaves

1 large tomato, thinly sliced

250 g thinly sliced, cooked chicken breast

8 pimiento-stuffed green olives (optional)

8 tiny sweet gherkins (optional)

PREPARATION TIME: 15 minutes

COOKING TIME: 5 minutes

SERVES: four

Cook the bacon in a frying pan over medium heat until crisp. Drain the cooked bacon on paper towels and set aside.

Spread one side of each slice of bread with some of the mayonnaise. Place a lettuce leaf on the mayonnaise on four slices of the bread. Top each with some of the sliced tomato and bacon. Add another slice of bread to each, with the mayonnaise side up. Top with the remaining lettuce leaves. Divide the chicken among the sandwiches and top with the remaining bread, with the mayonnaise side down. Cut the sandwiches in half diagonally. Thread an olive and a gherkin (if using) onto each of eight wooden picks and poke a pick into each sandwich half.

Samoosas
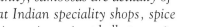

Although associated with the Cape Malay community, samoosas are actually of Indian origin. Samoosa pastry can be purchased at Indian speciality shops, spice shops and Muslim butcheries, but why not try this version using phyllo pastry?

MEAT FILLING

Cook the meat with the turmeric, salt, garlic, ginger, coriander leaves and chillies. When the mixture is nearly dry, add the onions and cook until the liquid has evaporated. Stir frequently to prevent the meat from forming lumps. Add the ghee or butter. The final product should be fine and dry (like breadcrumbs). Allow to cool, then add the spring onions and garam masala.

VEGETABLE FILLING

Heat the oil, add the onion and sauté until it becomes transparent. Mix the carrots, rice and mashed potato together and add them to the onions, then stir and cook until they are crumbly (remove from the heat as soon as they reach this stage; do not overcook). Add the garam masala, turmeric and salt; cook for a few more minutes, stirring to blend. Remove from the heat and allow to cool. Then add the rest of the ingredients. Stir well to mix.

ASSEMBLING AND COOKING

Allow the filling to cool before it is used.

Cut the sheet of phyllo pastry lengthways into 4 x 8 cm-wide strips. Brush with ghee or melted butter. Allow 1 tablespoon for each samoosa. Make a triangular-shaped pocket at one end of the pastry, add the filling and then fold the long strip of dough over to seal the pocket. Brush all over with ghee or butter and bake in preheated oven at 180°C for 10 minutes or until crispy. Or fry in hot oil until golden, then drain well on paper towels.

Phyllo pastry (or samoosa pastry)

MEAT FILLING
500 g mutton, lamb or chicken, minced
½ teaspoon turmeric
1 teaspoon salt
1 teaspoon garlic and ginger paste, or 1 large clove garlic and an equivalent-sized piece of fresh ginger, pounded together
2 teaspoons well-chopped coriander (dhania) leaves
5 green chillies, well pounded
2 medium onions, finely chopped
1 tablespoon ghee (p.313) or butter
4 spring onions, finely chopped
½ teaspoon garam masala

VEGETABLE FILLING
3 tablespoons sunflower oil
1 large onion, grated
5 medium carrots, cooked and minced
150 g rice, cooked
1 medium potato, cooked and mashed
2 teaspoons garam masala
½ teaspoon turmeric
½ teaspoon salt
2 teaspoons garlic and ginger paste, or 2 large cloves garlic and an equivalent-sized piece of fresh ginger, pounded together
2 small to medium green chillies, pounded together
2 teaspoons well-chopped coriander (dhania) leaves
8 spring onions, chopped

FOR EACH RECIPE
PREPARATION TIME: 3 hours
COOKING TIME: 10 minutes
MAKES: 24 meat or vegetable samoosas

150 g streaky bacon, chopped

4 onions, finely chopped

3 leeks, finely chopped (white part only)

2 tablespoons oil

5 young carrots, diced

1 tablespoon butter

1 kg boneless venison, cut into cubes

2 tablespoons flour

500 ml beef stock, heated (p.304)

½ teaspoon ground cloves

1 teaspoon ground allspice

2 bay leaves

Salt and freshly ground black pepper

200 g button mushrooms, sliced

5 tablespoons port wine

125 ml sour cream (smetena)

Clarified butter

PREPARATION TIME: 30 minutes

COOKING TIME: 2 hours

CHILLING TIME: overnight

MAKES: one kilogram

LICENSED GAME DEALERS

The licensed game dealers, Lewis, Sims and Co. of Longmarket Street, Cape Town, carried a huge range of game and fish. Many people still had strong connections with the country and could hunt their own game.

Venison Pâté

Hunting was a popular pasttime in the 1920s and 1930s. These days most people have to buy their venison from the butcher.

Place the bacon, onions and leeks in a large saucepan and sauté gently in a little oil over a medium heat until the onions are transparent, then add the carrots and sauté for another 2–3 minutes. Remove the mixture and put set side.

Heat the rest of the oil and butter in the same saucepan and fry the meat, a few pieces at a time, until it is well browned. (Add more oil and butter if needed.) Remove the meat from the saucepan and stir in the flour. Slowly add the stock, scraping the bits from the bottom of the saucepan and bring to a boil. Return the meat and bacon and vegetable mixture to the saucepan. Add the ground cloves, allspice, bay leaves and seasoning.

Reduce the heat and simmer for 1 hour or until meat is tender when tested.

Add the mushrooms to the meat and simmer for another 30 minutes. Remove the saucepan from the heat and let the mixture cool. Remove the bay leaves. Blend in batches in a food processor. Add the port and sour cream and adjust the seaoning. Pour in to a terrine or individual ramekins and cover the pâté with a layer of clarified butter (see p.311). Refrigerate.

The pâté improves if left for a day or two. Serve with Melba toast or wholewheat bread, pickles and a green salad.

Grilled Black Mussels

Mussels have long been 'free from the sea' favourites with South Africans. Remember that there are regulations controlling their collection.

Preheat the oven to 200°C. Soak the mussels in fresh water for one or two hours and scrub the shells thoroughly.

Place the mussels in the oven for 10 minutes (to open), then remove them, discard the empty half-shells and remove the 'beards'. Arrange the mussels in the half shell on a baking tray. Mix the butter, garlic and parsley to form a soft paste and place 1 teaspoon on each mussel. Sprinkle with breadcrumbs (if used) and place them under a grill until golden-brown.

Serve with hot, crusty French bread.

If using tinned mussels, skip the first part of the recipe. Remove the mussels from the tin, rinse gently, open and discard the empty half-shells. Add crushed garlic and grill.

60 fresh mussels (or sufficient tinned mussels on the shell)

250 g butter, softened

1 large clove garlic, crushed

3 tablespoons finely chopped parsley

1 slice white bread, crumbed (optional)

SOAKING TIME: 2 hours

PREPARATION TIME: 1 hour

COOKING TIME: 15 minutes

SERVES: six

HOMEGROWN PUMPKINS

The best-known pumpkin in South Africa is the Flat White Boer (Boerpampoen). These pumpkins are traditionally stored on the flat rooftops of farm outbuildings - a familiar sight along country roads.

45 g butter

750 g pumpkin (or butternut), peeled and diced

1 large onion, chopped

1 teaspoon curry powder

2 teaspoons chopped fresh ginger

2 cups chicken stock (p.305)

Finely grated rind and the juice of 1 orange

Salt and freshly ground black pepper

1 cup milk

½ cup cream

2 tablespoons chopped coriander (dhania) leaves for garnish

PREPARATION TIME: 20 minutes

COOKING TIME: 45 minutes

SERVES: six

Pumpkin Soup

Pumpkins and butternuts, sadly neglected vegetables for many years, have recently become popular once more. Try this hearty, rich, creamy soup that can be eaten as a starter or main meal.

Melt the butter in a large saucepan. Add the pumpkin, onion, curry powder and ginger, and cook over a very gentle heat until the onion is soft; this should take about 5 minutes. Add the stock, orange juice and rind and seasonings and bring to the boil.

Reduce the heat and simmer gently (covered) for about 30 minutes, or until the pumpkin is tender. Purée the soup in batches in a liquidiser or food processor. Return the purée to a cleaned saucepan. Add the milk and bring slowly to the boil, stirring constantly. Reduce the heat and simmer for 5 minutes. Check the seasoning, pour into a preheated tureen, stir in the cream and sprinkle with coriander. Serve immediately.

Serve with fresh, crusty bread.

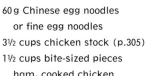

Chinese Noodle Soup

Once South Africans were introduced to Chinese food, quick and easy dishes such as this noodle soup soon found their way into Grandma's kitchen.

Cover the dried mushrooms with warm water in a small bowl and let stand for 30 minutes. Rinse well and squeeze to drain thoroughly. Slice thinly, discarding the stems.

In a large saucepan, cook the noodles according to the directions on the package. Drain well and set aside. In the same saucepan, bring the stock to the boil. Stir in the mushrooms, the pieces of meat, the sliced cabbage and the pepper. Lower the heat and simmer, covered, for 10 minutes.

To serve, place the noodles in soup bowls. With a slotted spoon, lift the mushroom mixture out of the soup and place on the noodles. Carefully pour the soup over. Garnish with spring onion and parsley.

6 dried mushrooms

60 g Chinese egg noodles or fine egg noodles

3½ cups chicken stock (p.305)

1½ cups bite-sized pieces ham, cooked chicken or cooked pork

1 cup thinly sliced Chinese cabbage or other cabbage

Pinch of black pepper

1 large spring onion, with top, finely sliced, to garnish

2 tablespoons chopped fresh parsley, to garnish

PREPARATION TIME: 15 minutes

STANDING TIME: 30 minutes

COOKING TIME: 15 minutes

SERVES: six

Dried mushrooms are sold in small packets and are now available in many supermarkets. They add an intense flavour to the soup. Keep leftover mushrooms properly wrapped and they will last indefinitely.

3 tablespoons olive oil

¾ teaspoon curry powder

1 onion, sliced

2 carrots, sliced

2 leeks, sliced

3 ripe tomatoes, skinned,
   seeded and chopped

3 litres fish stock (p.305)

1 cup dry white wine

3 cloves garlic

2 strips orange rind

A good pinch of saffron

Salt and freshly ground black
   pepper

6 small potatoes, peeled

1,5 kg linefish, skinned and
   filleted

FOR THE GARNISH

8 slices French bread

Garlic mayonnaise

50 g grated Gruyère cheese

3 tablespoons chopped
   parsley

PREPARATION TIME: 1 hour

COOKING TIME: 1¾ hours

SERVES: eight

Cape Fish Soup

*The saffron gives rich golden colour and a delicate almond-like flavour to the soup,
which is substantial enough to be a complete meal.*

Put the olive oil, curry powder and onion in a large saucepan and fry until the onion is translucent. Add the carrots and leeks. Heat until they are soft, then add the tomatoes, stock, white wine, garlic, orange rind, saffron, salt and pepper. Cover the saucepan and simmer gently for 1 hour, then add the potatoes and fish.

Bring to the boil, then reduce the heat and simmer for about 10 minutes. Remove most of the fish fillets and place on a platter. Cover with foil and keep warm. Allow the potatoes to cook for another 15 minutes. Remove the potatoes and set aside with the fish on the platter. Cool the soup, discard the orange rind and liquidise. Return the potatoes and fish to the soup.

Reheat and taste to correct the seasoning. Place a slice of crusty French bread in each soup bowl and top with a dollop of garlic mayonnaise and a spoonful of grated Gruyère cheese. Ladle the soup onto the bread, add a slice of fish, and sprinkle with parsley.

3 rashers streaky bacon with
   rinds removed, diced

1 large onion, peeled and
   chopped

2 medium carrots, peeled and
   chopped

500 g dried split peas, washed

2,5 litres vegetable stock
   (p.304) or chicken stock
   (p.305)

Salt and pepper

1 teaspoon Worcestershire
   sauce

Croûtons to garnish (p.310)

Finely chopped mint to
   garnish

PREPARATION TIME: 15 minutes

COOKING TIME: 2¼ hours

SERVES: six

Split Pea Soup with Bacon

*This dish of dried peas and cured pork was first made in England in the Middle
Ages. It is a marvellous soup to come home to on a cold winter day, and,
more importantly, it is quite economical.*

Put the bacon in a large, heavy-based saucepan and cook over gentle heat until the fat runs out. Add the onion and carrots and cook gently until the fat has been absorbed.

Add the peas to the pan with the stock. Bring to the boil, season lightly with salt and pepper, cover and allow to simmer for about 2 hours, or until the split peas are sufficiently soft mushy – they must be mushy.

Pass through a sieve or food processor, taste and add the salt and pepper as needed. Add the Worcestershire sauce and reheat. Serve topped with croûtons (see p.310) and mint.

VARIATION

A meaty ham bone can be used instead of the bacon. When the peas are cooked, removed the bone from the soup, take off the meat, chop it and return the chopped meat to the soup.

FACING PAGE: *Split pea soup with bacon*

To rid leeks of grit after chopping and slicing, rinse them in a colander under running water and drain well.

Cock-a-Leekie

You can serve cock-a-leekie with the chicken in it, or serve the soup first with a spoonful of rice, followed by the chicken as the main course.

1 small chicken with giblets, cleaned (discard the liver)
1 onion, unpeeled, washed and quartered
2 carrots, unpeeled, washed and chopped
Bouquet garni (p.310)
8 peppercorns
1 teaspoon salt
12 dried prunes (optional)
2 litres water
6 leeks, trimmed and thinly sliced
2 spring onions, trimmed and thinly sliced
Salt and pepper

PREPARATION TIME: 30 minutes
COOKING TIME: 2¼ hours
CHILLING TIME: about 4 hours
SERVES: four to six

Place the chicken with its giblets in a large, heavy-based saucepan. Add the onion, carrots, bouquet garni, peppercorns, salt and prunes (if using) to the pan and cover with the water.

Bring the liquid very slowly to the boil, skim off any white scum and then simmer for about 1¼ hours until the chicken is tender. Strain off the stock into a large bowl, leave it to cool and then chill it in the refrigerator until the fat has hardened on the surface. Lift off the fat carefully with a slotted spoon and reserve 2 tablespoons of it.

Reserve the prunes (if used) but discard the vegetables, chicken neck and heart, bouquet garni and peppercorns. When the chicken is cool enough to handle, remove the skin from it and cut the flesh into thin strips.

Heat the chicken fat in a large, heavy-based saucepan, add the leeks and spring onions and cook over a low heat for about 15 minutes until they are soft and transparent, and the butter has been absorbed. Add the stock (from which the fat has been removed), bring to the boil and add salt and pepper to taste.

Simmer the soup for about 15 minutes or until the leeks and onions are tender. Add the chicken strips and prunes (if used) and simmer for a further 10 minutes.

Lamb & Vegetable Soup

This satisfying soup makes a warming and economical meal.

Remove any excess fat and gristle from the lamb. Heat the lard or oil in a large saucepan, add the meat and cook over high heat until evenly browned. Remove from the pan with a slotted spoon and drain on paper towels.

Add the onions, turnips, carrots and potatoes to the pan and cook gently, stirring a few times, for 10 minutes. Return the lamb to the pan and add the water and bouquet garni. Increase the heat and bring to the boil, then immediately reduce the heat to low and skim any scum from the surface. Cover and simmer for 1½ hours, or until the meat is tender.

Using a slotted spoon, lift the meat from the saucepan and transfer it to a plate. Season the soup to taste with salt and black pepper, increase the heat and add the sliced leeks. When the soup is gently boiling again, cover the saucepan, reduce the heat and leave to simmer for a further 30 minutes.

Meanwhile, remove all the meat from the bones and cut it into small cubes. Return it to the soup for the last 10 minutes of cooking time. Skim any excess fat from the surface. Remove and discard the bouquet garni. If necessary, adjust the seasoning to taste.

Pour the soup into a large, heated tureen or six warmed serving bowls. Sprinkle the chopped parsley over the top and serve with good wholewheat bread.

1kg scrag end or middle neck of lamb, cut into pieces
15g lard or
1 tablespoon olive oil
2 medium onions, peeled and thinly sliced
2 small turnips, peeled and cut into small cubes
2 medium carrots, peeled and thinly sliced
2 small potatoes, peeled and cut into small cubes
2 litres water
Bouquet garni (p.310)
Salt and freshly ground black pepper
2 medium leeks, halved lengthways, washed and thickly sliced
4 tablespoons chopped fresh parsley

PREPARATION TIME: 40 minutes
COOKING TIME: 2¼ hours
SERVES: six

'PERFECTRIC' COOKWARE

The advent of electric stoves meant that pots and pans had to change with the times as well. The heavy old cast-iron ware used on anthracite stoves was no longer suitable. The new aluminium pots had heavy machine-flat bases which were designed to 'save electricity by transmitting every possible unit from the hot plate to the contents of the pan'. A play on the words 'perfect' and 'electric' resulted in 'Perfectric' cookware.

2,5 litres water

500 g lean brisket on the bone, cut into small pieces

6 carrots, sliced

1 onion, chopped

½ cup chopped celery

3 potatoes, peeled and quartered

250 g pearl barley

1 tablespoon salt

½ teaspoon white pepper

2 beef stock cubes

PREPARATION TIME: 20 minutes

COOKING TIME: 3 hours

SERVES: eight

Brisket & Barley Soup

This soup needs to simmer for a long time to allow the flavours to mingle.

Put the water in a large pot and place the brisket in it. Bring to the boil, then remove the scum. Add the carrots, onion, celery, potatoes, barley, salt and pepper. Reduce the heat, cover with a lid and simmer gently for about 3 hours. Stir in the stock cubes and taste for seasoning.

FROM POTS TO STOVES

The giant electrical goods company Defy can trace its origins back to the humble three-legged cast-iron pot. When the Durban pot manufacturer turned to making stoves, it linked up with the Falkirk Iron Company of Scotland and became the Durban Falkirk Iron Company. In 1932 the company switched to manufacturing electric stoves, but the name had to be shortened to fit the stove's image. The initials D.F.I. (for Durban Falkirk Iron) were suggested, but when it was realised that phonetically they produced the word DEFY, the name was deemed perfect.

To give the soup a greener hue, process it with a few tablespoons of chopped, fresh parsley or watercress.

Leek & Potato Soup

You can give this popular soup a smooth finish by adding a liaison of egg yolks and cream. In summer, made without the liaison, it is invigorating if chilled for several hours and served icy cold.

Use a large knife to cut off the tops of the leeks, then shave off any tough parts and remove any coarse outer leaves. Trim off the roots and cut each leek in half lengthways. Rinse thoroughly under running water and slice thinly.

Melt the butter in a large saucepan, then add the leeks. Toss them in the butter for 3–5 minutes, then lay the potatoes on top. Don't stir the potatoes through the leeks because they can stick to the bottom of the pan. Cover the pan with a lid and cook on very low heat for about 20 minutes.

Stir in the salt, then add the water and hot milk. Bring the soup just to boiling point, stirring often, then immediately turn the heat to low. Partly cover with a lid and cook very gently for 20 minutes more. Purée, in batches, in a food processor or blender, and return the soup to the cleaned pan.

To give the soup a smooth finish, prepare the liaison. Blend the egg yolks and cream in a small bowl and add a ladleful of the hot soup. Pour this, stirring, into the soup and set the pan on medium heat. Keep stirring until the soup thickens slightly (do not allow it to boil or it will curdle).

If you are not using the liaison, reheat the soup until it is piping hot. Ladle into bowls and garnish with a little chopped parsley, a few snipped chives or watercress.

For a change, sizzle a few rashers of bacon, rind removed and finely chopped, and sprinkle on top of the soup before serving.

FOR THE SOUP
4 medium leeks
50 g butter
4 medium potatoes, peeled and thinly sliced
1½ teaspoons salt
4 cups water
2 cups milk, heated
Chopped fresh parsley, snipped chives or watercress to garnish

FOR THE LIAISON (OPTIONAL)
2 egg yolks
3 tablespoons cream

PREPARATION TIME: 20 minutes
COOKING TIME: 45 minutes
SERVES: six to eight

Refrigerate the cooked chicken legs left over after preparing this dish. Serve them the next day with salad or make them into croquettes or a small pie.

Creamy Chicken Soup

You can serve this appealing soup as a main course or for a weekend lunch or supper.

2 litres chicken stock (p.305)

1,5 kg chicken, rinsed and
  dried with paper towels

1 bunch parsley, with stalks,
  roughly chopped

3 medium leeks, trimmed,
  washed and cut into
  fine strips

4 egg yolks

½ cup pouring cream

Salt and freshly ground black
  pepper or ground allspice

2 tablespoons finely chopped
  fresh parsley to garnish

PREPARATION TIME: 45 minutes

COOKING TIME: 1½ hours

SERVES: six as a starter
  or four as a main course

Put the stock, chicken, parsley and two-thirds of the leeks into a large saucepan. Bring to the boil, reduce the heat, skim any scum from the surface, then cover and simmer for 1 hour, or until the chicken is tender.

Transfer the cooked chicken to a plate and set aside. Skim the fat from the surface of the soup. Reserve the legs of the chicken – they are not needed for the soup. Remove the skin from the breast, then take the meat off the carcass and cut it into thin strips. Return the meat to the pan and heat gently.

Whisk the egg yolks in a bowl with the cream, then gradually stir in three ladlefuls of the soup. Stir the egg and cream mixture into the soup, season to taste with the salt and black pepper or ground allspice and heat gently, stirring until the soup thickens slightly – do not let it boil as it will curdle.

Cook the remaining leek in boiling water for 1 minute and drain well. Pour the soup into a heated tureen or bowls and sprinkle with the leek and the chopped parsley. Serve with Melba toast (see p.310).

Scotch Broth

As its name suggests, this hearty soup came to this part of the world with Scottish immigrants.

3 tablespoons pearl barley

1 tablespoon yellow split peas

1 kg neck or shoulder of lamb, cut into pieces

2,5 litres water

Bouquet garni (p.310)

Salt and freshly ground black pepper

3 medium carrots, peeled and diced

2 small swedes, peeled and diced

1 small leek, trimmed and washed, white part finely chopped, green part reserved

3 tablespoons chopped fresh parsley, to garnish

Cover the pearl barley and yellow split peas with cold water in a bowl and leave to soak overnight. Next day, put the lamb in a large saucepan, cover with the water and bring to the boil. Reduce the heat and skim the scum from the surface.

Drain the barley and split peas and add them to the saucepan with the bouquet garni and salt and pepper to taste. Cover and simmer for 1 hour, skimming occasionally. Stir in the carrots and swedes and simmer for 15 minutes. Add the white parts of the leeks and simmer for a further 15 minutes. Remove the pan from the heat, cool the soup and refrigerate overnight. Next day, remove the solidified fat from the surface of the soup. Discard the bouquet garni. Lift out the lamb, remove the meat from the bones, cut it into small pieces and return it to the soup.

Finely slice the reserved green parts of the leek and stir them into the soup with the parsley. Reheat until boiling. Season to taste with salt and black pepper and serve piping hot with crusty bread.

PREPARATION TIME:
Day 1, overnight soaking
Day 2, 40 minutes

COOKING TIME: 1½ hours

CHILLING TIME: overnight

SERVES: four

SOUTH AFRICA'S SPECIAL OUMA

During World War II, the name Ouma Smuts (wife of the South African prime minister, Jan Smuts) became synonymous with 'support for the boys up North'. The Victory Cookery Book was just one of her projects and contained recipes sent in from all over the country. The first edition was published in 1940 and the 7th in 1955, after her death. During the war all proceeds went to the South African Gifts and Comforts Fund for the troops.

Tomato Soup

Both fresh and tinned tomatoes are used in this soup, the fresh ones for their sunny flavour, the tinned ones for depth.

30 g butter or 2 tablespoons oil

2 rashers bacon, rind removed, chopped

1 large onion, peeled and chopped

1 large carrot, scrubbed and chopped

1 medium celery stick, trimmed and chopped

2 large tomatoes, chopped

1 x 410 g tin whole tomatoes

4 cups chicken stock (p.305) or vegetable stock (p.304)

1 blade mace

1 sprig each fresh thyme, parsley and rosemary

½ teaspoon celery seeds

10 black peppercorns

½ cup pouring cream

Small fresh rosemary sprigs, to garnish

PREPARATION TIME: 30 minutes

COOKING TIME: 1 hour

SERVES: four

Melt the butter in a large saucepan, add the bacon, onion, carrot and celery and cook, without browning, over low heat for about 5 minutes. Add the fresh tomatoes, the tinned tomatoes with their juice and the stock. Bring to the boil, stirring occasionally.

Put the mace, herbs, celery seeds and peppercorns in the centre of a square of muslin. Tie each pair of opposite corners together to form a bag, then add to the soup. Reduce the heat, cover and simmer for about an hour, or until the vegetables are soft. Remove the spice bag and pass the soup through a nylon sieve into a bowl.

Alternatively, first cool the soup, then purée it in a food processor or blender before passing it through a sieve into a clean saucepan.

To serve, reheat the soup and pour it into a warmed tureen or bowls. Pour a little cream on top and garnish with fresh rosemary sprigs.

Oxtail Soup

Full of goodness and flavour, this is a soup to relax with after a hard day's work.

1,5 kg oxtail (1 large oxtail)

30 g dripping or vegetable oil

2 large carrots, roughly chopped

1 medium onion, peeled and roughly chopped

2 sticks celery, roughly chopped

Bouquet garni (p.310)

4 rashers bacon or bacon bones

2 litres water or beef stock (p.304)

1 large carrot, extra, peeled and diced

1 medium onion, extra, peeled and finely chopped

2 sticks celery, extra, diced

Juice of ½ lemon

½ cup chopped fresh parsley

Salt and freshly ground black pepper

PREPARATION TIME:
Day 1, 30 minutes
Day 2, 15 minutes

CHILLING TIME: overnight

COOKING TIME:
Day 1, 5 hours
Day 2, 20 minutes

SERVES: six

Pat the oxtail dry with paper towels and remove as much visible fat as possible. Using a sharp, heavy knife, cut the oxtail into sections (or ask your butcher to do this for you). Place the oxtail in a stockpot and cover with plenty of cold water. Cover with a lid and bring to the boil over medium heat. Turn the heat off and allow the oxtail to stand for 20 minutes. Strain, discarding the water. Place the oxtail on a clean chopping board and pat dry with paper towels.

Melt the dripping (or heat the oil) in the stockpot over medium-high heat. Cook the oxtail, in batches, for 4–5 minutes on each side, or until browned. Remove the meat and set aside. Add the carrots, onion and celery and cook, stirring constantly, until lightly browned. Return the oxtail to the pot, along with the bouquet garni and bacon or bacon bones. Add the water or stock, making sure the oxtail is completely covered. Bring to the boil slowly, skimming any excess fat from the surface. Cover with a lid and simmer over very low heat for 4 hours, checking every hour that the oxtail is still covered with liquid.

Remove the oxtail to a chopping board. Strain the stock into a large heatproof bowl and refrigerate overnight. Discard the contents of the strainer. Remove the meat from the bones and shred. Refrigerate the meat overnight.

Remove the solidified fat from the surface of the soup and return the soup to the stockpot with the oxtail meat and the extra carrot, onion and celery. Bring to the boil over medium heat and cook for 20 minutes, or until the vegetables are tender. Just before serving, stir in the lemon juice and parsley and season to taste with salt and pepper. Ladle into warm bowls and serve with crusty bread.

FACING PAGE: *Tomato soup*

If you are not able to soak the beans overnight, cover with water and bring to the boil. Remove from the heat and allow to stand covered for an hour. Then drain.

500 g dried brown or sugar beans
1 tablespoon oil
1 large onion, chopped
3 leeks, sliced
1 large ripe tomato, diced
500 g shin of beef
500 g beef marrow bones (optional)
Salt and freshly ground black pepper
2 litres water
Croûtons (p.310) and chopped parsley to garnish

SOAKING TIME: 12 hours
PREPARATION TIME: 15 minutes
COOKING TIME: 2¼ hours
SERVES: six

Bean Soup

Bean soup is thought to have originated in Germany and then spread to Holland and beyond. It is the perfect soup for a cold winter's day.

Soak the beans in water for 12 hours (or overnight), then wash and drain them. Heat the oil in a large saucepan and sauté the onion, leeks and diced tomato until tender.

Place the meat and marrow bones on the bed of vegetables and season with salt and pepper. Add the beans. Cover with 2 litres of water and bring to the boil. Skim off foam as it rises to the surface. Reduce the heat and simmer, partially covered, for 2 hours or until the beans are tender. Purée about half of the beans and return to the soup (or mash roughly with a potato masher).

Remove marrow bones and flake the meat. Return meat to the soup. Reheat and adjust seasoning. Serve with croûtons or chopped parsley (If using marrow bones, serve separately on slices of hot toast.)

Minestrone

*Italian grandmas had no definite rules for what went into minestrone.
It just had to be hearty, with plenty of vegetables, white beans and pasta or rice.*

Heat the oil in a large saucepan over medium-high heat. Add the onion and garlic and cook for 5 minutes, or until the onion is tender. Stir in the beef stock, beans, tomatoes, cabbage, carrots, origanum, basil and salt and pepper to taste. Bring to the boil. Stir in the vermicelli. Lower the heat and simmer, covered, for 15 minutes, or until the pasta and vegetables are tender. Stir in the courgette pieces. Cook, uncovered, for 3 minutes more.

Serve the minestrone with grated Parmesan cheese, passed separately in a small bowl.

1 tablespoon olive oil
1 large onion, peeled and chopped
2 cloves garlic, peeled and crushed
3½ cups beef stock (p.304)
1 x 440g tin cannellini beans, drained
1¾ cups chopped tomatoes, or 1 x 410g tin whole tomatoes, undrained and cut up
2 cups coarsely shredded cabbage
2 large carrots, thinly sliced
1 teaspoon each dried origanum leaves and basil leaves
Salt and freshly ground black pepper
60g vermicelli or thin spaghetti, broken
1 small courgette, halved lengthways and sliced
Grated Parmesan cheese, to serve

PREPARATION TIME: 20 minutes
COOKING TIME: 30 minutes
SERVES: eight

You can use almost any vegetables that you have to hand in this soup — red kidney beans, potatoes, swedes, cauliflower, celery, spring onions, green beans and peas all work well.

1 kg smoked haddock

1 medium onion, peeled
   and sliced

2 cups milk

2 cups water

4 small floury potatoes,
   peeled and diced

Salt

1 small leek, trimmed,
   washed and sliced

1¼ cups pouring cream

1 egg yolk

Freshly ground black pepper

3 tablespoons chopped
   fresh parsley

60 g butter (optional)

PREPARATION TIME: 30 minutes

COOKING TIME: 35 minutes

SERVES: four

Smoked Fish Soup

*This nourishing dish has been carried around the world
by Scottish settlers, who called it Cullen Skink –
the word 'skink' means a stew-like soup.*

Place the fish in a shallow pan with the onion, milk and water and bring to the boil. Reduce the heat, cover the pan and poach gently for about 10 minutes. Strain the fish liquid through a large sieve into a saucepan and reserve, discarding the onion. Remove the skin and bones from the fish, flake the flesh and set aside.

Meanwhile, boil the potatoes in salted water for 10–15 minutes, or until tender. Drain and mash well. Whisk the mashed potatoes into the fish liquid, stir in the leek and bring to the boil. Reduce the heat, cover the pan and simmer for 10–15 minutes, or until the leek is tender.

Whisk the cream and egg yolk together and stir into the soup. Reheat gently, stirring until slightly thickened – do not boil or the soup will curdle. Stir in the flaked fish and season to taste with pepper only. Stir in the chopped parsley and heat through for 2–3 minutes.

Serve the soup piping hot in warmed bowls. If desired, dot with knobs of butter that melt and run over the surface of the soup.

A PIQUANT FISH SPREAD

Peck's Anchovette is still made according to the original recipe devised by Harry Peck in 1891 - fresh fish, salted anchovies and a special mix of spices. During the 1930s the spread became very popular in South Africa, but the supply was interrupted by World War II. Imports resumed in 1947 and in the 1960s an Anchovette factory was built at Saldanha Bay on the Cape West Coast.

Mulligatawny Soup

The name of this soup is derived from the Tamil milakutanni, *which means 'pepper water', an indication of both its spicy flavour and its origin in Madras.*

Put the beef into a large saucepan with the chicken carcass or cooked drumsticks, dried mango and stock. Put all the spices, the coconut, lemon rind, garlic, chilli and bay leaf in the centre of a square of muslin. Tie each pair of opposite corners together to form a bag, then lightly crush the contents with a rolling pin. Add to the saucepan and bring to the boil. Reduce the heat, skim the scum from the surface, partly cover and simmer for 1 hour.

Strain the stock through a sieve into a large clean saucepan and discard the contents of the sieve. In a separate bowl, whisk up the egg whites and shells until just foamy and add to the stock, then whisk over medium heat,

without allowing the liquid to boil, for about 10 minutes, or until a thick, grey-white crust has formed. Once this crust has formed, stop whisking and allow the stock to come back up to the boil and the crust to rise up the sides of the pan – do not allow the soup to boil over the top of the crust.

Remove the pan from the heat and allow the contents to subside for about 10 minutes. Line a large sieve with a double thickness of muslin. Carefully strain the soup through the lined sieve into a clean saucepan, holding back the crust until last. The soup should now look very clear. Stir in the Madeira, season to taste with salt and pepper, reheat and serve.

Traditionally, this soup is garnished with rice. After serving, add two tablespoons of rice to each bowl of soup, keeping the rice in neat little heaps.

750 g shin of beef, trimmed of fat and cut into small cubes
1 leftover cooked chicken carcass or 4 chicken drumsticks, cooked and skinned
¼ cup (60 g) dried mango
2 litres chicken stock (p.305) or beef stock (p.304)
4 teaspoons each coriander seeds and cardamom pods
2 teaspoons cumin seeds
2 teaspoons fenugreek seeds
1 tablespoon black peppercorns
1½ tablespoons desiccated coconut
Thinly peeled rind of 1 lemon
2 cloves garlic, peeled and crushed
1 small fresh green chilli or 2 small dried chillies
1 bay leaf
2 egg whites
2 egg shells, washed and crushed
3 tablespoons Madeira
Salt and freshly ground black pepper

PREPARATION TIME: 30 minutes
COOKING TIME: 1 hour 20 minutes
SERVES: four

700 g ripe tomatoes

225 g fresh breadcrumbs

5 tablespoons olive oil

1 cucumber, peeled and
chopped

2 green peppers with cores
and seeds removed,
chopped

2 large cloves garlic, peeled

¼ cup red wine vinegar

600 ml water

1 tablespoon tomato paste

Salt and freshly ground black
pepper

12 ice cubes

FOR THE
ACCOMPANIMENTS

2 slices white bread, prepared
as croûtons (p.310)

2 hard-boiled eggs, shelled
and chopped (p.17)

6 spring onions, trimmed and
finely sliced

½ small cucumber, peeled and
finely diced

1 small red pepper, seeds
removed and finely chopped

PREPARATION TIME: 30 minutes

CHILLING TIME: 1 hour

SERVES: six

Gazpacho

*This is a light version of the famous Andalusian soup, traditonally made in an
earthenware bowl from ingredients pounded together with a pestle and mortar.*

Skin the tomatoes, remove the cores and seeds
and chop the flesh. Place the breadcrumbs in a
liquidiser, switch it on and gradually pour in
the olive oil. Continue blending for about
1 minute, or until all the oil has been absorbed
by the bread. Add the tomatoes and continue
liquidising until the mixture is reduced to a
smooth paste, then transfer to a bowl.

Place the cucumber, green peppers and
garlic in the liquidiser and blend for about
1 minute, or until they have been reduced to a
smooth purée. Combine with the puréed
tomatoes and stir in the vinegar, water and
tomato paste. Taste and add salt and pepper if
necessary. Cover the bowl and chill the soup
in a refrigerator for at least 1 hour.

Serve cold in shallow soup bowls, with
two ice cubes added to each. Serve the
accompaniments in separate bowls.

Chilled Cucumber Soup

The walnuts in this soup add an unexpected texture and flavour.
This is the perfect dish for a hot summer's day buffet.

1 large (500 g) English
    cucumber
Salt and pepper
2 cups natural yoghurt
½ cup cream
1 clove garlic, crushed
2 tablespoons olive or
    sunflower oil
2 tablespoons white wine
    vinegar
50 g walnuts, chopped

PREPARATION TIME: 10 minutes
STANDING TIME: 30 minutes
CHILLING TIME: 2 hours
MAKES: four cups (1 litre)

Peel the cucumber and dice into tiny cubes. Put these on a flat dish, sprinkle lightly with salt and leave standing for 30 minutes. Rinse the cucumber cubes in a colander under cold running water and then drain thoroughly.

In a bowl, blend the yoghurt with the cream, the crushed garlic, the olive or sunflower oil and the vinegar, and season to taste with salt and pepper.

Fold in the cucumber and just over half the chopped walnuts; blend thoroughly and then chill in the refrigerator for about 2 hours. For a smoother texture, blend briefly in a food processor.

Spoon the chilled soup into individual bowls, sprinkle the remaining chopped walnuts on top and serve with thin slices of crisp Melba toast or wedges of pita bread.

ICE DELIVERY

Before the use of electric fridges (which became widespread in the 1930s) the housewife relied on ice for all her chilling needs. The sight of the delivery man with a huge cube of ice on his shoulder was common, as were special ice boxes to store the ice and ice crushers to make crushed ice.

EGGS &
CHEESE

2 cups cake flour

Salt and freshly ground
   black pepper

125 g butter

About 4 tablespoons
   cold water

1 tablespoon vegetable oil

2 small onions, peeled
   and coarsely chopped

¾ cup crumbled or coarsely
   grated mature Cheddar
   cheese, or other sharp,
   crumbly cheese

¾ cup coarsely grated mild
   Cheddar, or other mellow,
   firm cheese

½ cup coarsely grated
   Gruyère cheese

½ cup finely grated fresh
   Parmesan cheese

3 tablespoons coarsely
   snipped chives

4 eggs

1¼ cups milk

2–3 medium, firm
   tomatoes, sliced

PREPARATION TIME: 40 minutes

COOKING TIME: 50–60 minutes

SERVES: six

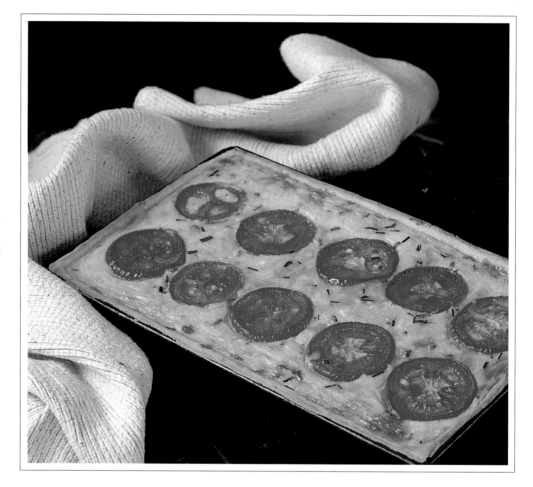

Tomato, Onion & Cheese Tart

A rectangular tart looks stylish and cuts into neat squares for serving.

Preheat the oven to 220°C. Sift the flour and a pinch of salt into a bowl. Rub in the butter until the mixture resembles fine breadcrumbs. Mix in enough water to make a firm dough. Roll out the dough on a lightly floured surface to an oblong a bit larger than a 28 x 18 x 4 cm baking tin. Line the tin with the dough and trim the edges, leaving about 1 cm above the top of the tin. Fold over the excess dough and press lightly with your fingertips to make a rim. Line the pastry case with crumpled greaseproof paper, fill with baking beans and bake blind for 10 minutes.

Meanwhile, heat the oil in a small pan and cook the chopped onions on low heat for about 10 minutes, or until soft and golden brown. Take the tart case out of the oven, remove the paper and baking beans and reduce the oven temperature to 180°C.

Spread the onions evenly over the bottom of the pastry case. Combine the four cheeses and the snipped chives and spread over the onions. Beat the eggs and milk together and season with salt and pepper. Pour the liquid over the cheese and chive mixture and decorate the top with tomato slices.

Bake the filled tart in the centre of the oven for 35–40 minutes, or until the pastry is golden brown and the filling is lightly set. Serve the tart warm, cut in squares.

Egg Salad & Devilled Eggs

Two old favourites – both are based on hard-boiled eggs and both are very easy to make. The eggs can be boiled in advance and the dish put together at the last minute.

EGG SALAD

Boil the eggs for 10–12 minutes, then cool under cold running water. Shell the eggs and halve them lengthways.

Wash the greens and remove the tough stalks. Dry the leaves thoroughly before arranging them in a shallow salad bowl. Arrange the egg halves side by side, cut side down, over the greens.

Just before serving, spoon the mayonnaise over the eggs and garnish the tops with strips of anchovy. Sprinkle with parsley or chives and serve immediately.

DEVILLED EGGS

Cut one-third from the top of each egg and set aside, then cut a thin sliver from the bottom of each to expose the yolk. Scoop out the yolks and set the whites aside. Press the yolks through a nylon sieve into a bowl, add the butter, anchovy essence, a little cayenne pepper and the cream cheese and beat together until smooth.

Spoon the mixture into a piping bag fitted with a small star nozzle. Place a few bean sprouts in each egg, then pipe a swirl of egg mixture on top. Replace the reserved tops and sprinkle with a little cayenne pepper.

Toss the watercress and lettuce with the remaining sprouts. Arrange on a serving dish with the radishes and nestle the eggs among the leaves.

Whisk the dressing ingredients together and spoon over the salad. Serve immediately.

EGG SALAD

6-8 eggs

1 crisp butter lettuce

1 bunch tender young spinach or watercress

200 ml well-flavoured homemade mayonnaise (p.306)

6-8 anchovies, drained and thinly sliced

1 tablespoon freshly chopped parsley or 6 fresh chives, snipped

PREPARATION TIME: 20 minutes
COOKING TIME: 10 minutes
SERVES: four

DEVILLED EGGS

8 eggs, hard-boiled and shelled

45 g butter, melted

1 teaspoon anchovy essence

Cayenne pepper

185 g cream cheese

1 punnet fine bean sprouts

1 bunch watercress, trimmed

6 cos lettuce leaves, finely shredded

6 radishes, trimmed and thinly sliced

FOR THE DRESSING

4 tablespoons olive oil

2 teaspoons lemon juice

½–1 teaspoon wholegrain mustard

PREPARATION TIME: 40 minutes
COOKING TIME: 10 minutes
SERVES: four

Poached Eggs with Cheese Sauce

Here is an idea for a quick and simple but colourful way of serving poached eggs.

8 thick slices white bread from a small loaf

125 g butter

4 tomatoes, quartered

1/4 cup plain flour

1 1/4 cups warm milk

Salt and freshly ground black pepper

1/2 cup finely grated mature Cheddar cheese

1 tablespoon white wine vinegar

8 very fresh eggs, free-range if possible

1 tablespoon snipped fresh chives, to garnish

PREPARATION TIME: 20 minutes

COOKING TIME: 15 minutes

SERVES: four

Using a large, plain, round pastry cutter, stamp out a round from the centre of each slice of bread. Toast the rounds on both sides and use 30 g of the butter to spread them on one side. Divide the tomatoes equally among four heatproof plates, placing them on the side, and dot with 60 g of the butter. Place two rounds of buttered toast on each of the four plates and keep warm.

Melt the remaining butter in a saucepan, stir in the flour and cook, without browning, on low heat for 1 minute. Gradually stir in the milk, season with the salt and pepper to taste and bring to the boil, stirring until the sauce has thickened. Reduce the heat and continue to cook for 2–3 minutes longer. Add the grated cheese and stir until it has melted. Remove the sauce from the heat and keep it warm.

Fill a large frying pan with water, add the vinegar and 1/2 teaspoon of salt and bring to the boil. Break two eggs, each into a separate cup. Stir the water, then carefully tip in the eggs, one at a time. Cover and cook on low heat for 2–3 minutes, or until the whites are set. Lift the eggs out with a slotted spoon, drain them on paper towels and keep warm.

Cook the remaining eggs quickly in the same way and put one on each piece of toast. Spoon some cheese sauce over each egg and grill, in two batches if necessary, for 2 minutes, or until they are lightly browned. Sprinkle the tomatoes with chives and serve at once.

French-Toasted Cheese Sandwiches

These luscious hot sandwiches make a splendid snack with a glass of wine.

FOR THE SANDWICHES

20 g butter

1/2 cup chopped fresh mushrooms

1/4 cup chopped onion

Pinch of black pepper

8 slices white sandwich bread

90 g Swiss or Cheddar cheese, sliced

90 g mozzarella cheese, sliced

Extra butter, for frying

FOR THE EGG COATING

2 eggs

4 tablespoons milk

1/2 teaspoon salt

PREPARATION TIME: 10 minutes

COOKING TIME: 12 minutes

SERVES: four as a main dish

To prepare the sandwiches, melt the butter over medium heat in a medium frying pan. Add the mushrooms, onion and pepper and cook until the vegetables are tender. Remove from the pan.

For each sandwich, layer a slice of bread, a slice of Swiss or Cheddar cheese, some of the mushroom-onion mixture, a slice of mozzarella cheese and another slice of bread.

To prepare the egg coating, whisk the eggs, milk and salt together in a shallow bowl. Dip the sandwiches in the egg mixture to coat on both sides. Wipe the frying pan and melt a little butter in it and swirl to cover the base. Add two sandwiches and brown on one side over medium heat. Add a little more butter and turn the sandwiches over to brown the second side. Keep warm while you cook the remaining two sandwiches in the same way.

VARIATION

Cream Cheese Sandwiches: Follow the same method as for the French-toasted cheese sandwiches, replacing the sandwich ingredients with 1/3 cup cream cheese, 1/4 cup finely grated carrot, 1/4 cup finely chopped walnuts and 8 slices raisin bread.

Place the cream cheese, carrot and walnuts in a small bowl and combine well. Spread half of the raisin bread slices with the cream cheese mixture. Top the filling with the remaining slices of bread.

Whisk together the ingredients for the egg coating, dip the sandwiches in the egg mixture to coat on both sides, and fry as for the French-toasted cheese sandwiches.

FACING PAGE: *Poached eggs with cheese sauce*

Eggs Baked with Cream

Baked eggs make a delicious breakfast, brunch or supper dish – in fact, they are perfect any time you want a quick, simple meal.

15g butter, softened

Salt and freshly ground
  black pepper

4 eggs

⅔ cup thick cream

Herbs of your choice,
  cracked black pepper
  or cayenne pepper,
  to garnish (optional)

PREPARATION TIME: 5 minutes

COOKING TIME: 10 minutes

SERVES: four as a starter

Preheat the oven to 180°C. Spread the softened butter over the bases and around the sides of four individual cocottes or ramekin dishes to coat them. Season the insides of the dishes well with salt and freshly ground black pepper. Crack an egg into each dish, then spoon 3 tablespoons of the cream over the top of each. Place on a baking tray and bake for 8–10 minutes, or until the whites are set but the yolks are still quite soft.

Garnish as desired and serve at once with slices of crusty bread or hot, buttered toast.

AN ABUNDANCE OF CHICKENS

Although eggs could be purchased at the shop, backyards during Grandma's day often featured a chicken 'hok'. Magazines and newspapers of the time carried numerous advertisements for chicken feed, brooding boxes and other equipment needed to rear chickens successfully and The Poultry Annual *dispensed advice on raising 'toothsome table poultry'.*

Creamy Scrambled Eggs, Mushrooms & Asparagus

Include this dish in your menu when a leisurely breakfast is the order of the day.

Melt 30 g of the butter over low heat in a nonstick frying pan. Add the mushrooms, cover and cook on low heat for 10 minutes, or until they are just softened. Steam the asparagus spears for 5–8 minutes, or until tender.

Meanwhile, beat the eggs with the cream in a mixing bowl and season to taste with salt and freshly ground white pepper. Melt the remaining butter in a heavy-based saucepan. Add the egg and cream mixture and stir gently over low heat until the eggs are just beginning to set. Remove from the heat and keep the eggs warm while toasting the bread. Cut the toast into triangles and arrange in a toast rack.

Spoon the scrambled eggs onto individual, warmed serving plates. Arrange the mushrooms and asparagus spears alongside the eggs. Sprinkle the eggs with chives and serve immediately with the triangles of toast and a dish of butter.

45 g butter

4 large flat, brown mushrooms, wiped

1 bunch asparagus spears, cut ends trimmed

8 eggs

½ cup pouring cream

Salt and freshly ground white pepper

4 medium slices white bread

1 tablespoon snipped fresh chives

PREPARATION TIME: 15 minutes
COOKING TIME: 10 minutes
SERVES: four

Potato & Bacon Omelette

For this delectable brunch or supper dish, you can cook the onion and potato ahead of time and reheat them when you make the omelette.

3 rashers bacon, rind
   removed, chopped

1 medium onion, chopped

3 medium potatoes, peeled,
   cooked and diced

7 eggs

¼ cup milk

½ teaspoon thyme leaves

1 tablespoon chopped parsley

½ teaspoon salt

¼ teaspoon black pepper

PREPARATION TIME: 10 minutes

COOKING TIME: 20 minutes

SERVES: six

Cook the chopped bacon over medium heat in a medium frying pan until it is crisp. Remove the bacon, reserve the drippings in the pan and set the bacon aside.

Add the onion to the pan and cook, stirring often, on low heat for 8–10 minutes, or until tender. Add the potatoes, increase the heat to medium and cook, pressing down from time to time with a spatula until browned underneath. Turn over, breaking up the cake as you go, and cook for a further 5 minutes.

Whisk the eggs in a large bowl with the milk, herbs, salt and pepper. Pour the egg mixture over the potatoes and onion. Cook over medium heat, without stirring, until set on the bottom and around the edge. (Use the spatula constantly to lift the cooked edge so the uncooked eggs flow to the bottom.) Cook for 3 minutes more, or until the eggs are almost set. Cover and cook for 1 minute, or until the eggs are set but still moist. Sprinkle with the cooked bacon and serve cut in wedges.

Cheese Omelette with Tomato Butter

The addition of tomato butter with Worcestershire sauce gives extra flavour to this omelette.

45 g butter

1 small onion, peeled
   and finely chopped

4 eggs

2 tablespoons water

1 tablespoon finely chopped
   fresh parsley

Generous pinch of fresh
   or dried thyme

Salt and cayenne pepper

1 medium tomato, peeled,
   seeded and chopped

¼ teaspoon Worcestershire
   sauce

¾ cup finely grated white
   mature firm cheese

Parsley sprigs, to garnish

PREPARATION TIME: 20 minutes

COOKING TIME: 10 minutes

SERVES: two

Set 30 g of the butter aside and divide the remainder into three equal pieces. Melt one piece in a small frying pan, add the onion and cook gently until softened. Put the onion into a bowl with the eggs, water, chopped parsley, thyme, salt and cayenne pepper. Whisk well and set aside.

Melt the reserved 30 g butter in the same small frying pan and, when foaming, add the chopped tomato and Worcestershire sauce. Reduce the heat to very low and cook until the tomato is soft, then keep warm.

In a small omelette pan, melt another of the small pieces of butter until it begins to sizzle, then quickly pour in half of the egg mixture and stir with a fork, over high heat, until all the butter is absorbed by the egg. Stop stirring and cook for about 30 seconds, or until the egg is almost set, but still very moist on top. Sprinkle half the cheese over the omelette, fold into three, turn out onto a hot plate and keep warm while making another omelette in the same way.

Spoon half the hot tomato butter over each omelette, garnish with the parsley sprigs and serve immediately with crusty bread and a green salad, if desired.

VARIATIONS

Cheese Omelette with Anchovy Butter: Add either 2 finely chopped anchovy fillets or ¼ teaspoon anchovy essence to the butter in place of the tomato.

Ham and Cheese Omelette: Reduce the amount of cheese and add 30 g of well-flavoured ham, finely chopped, to the omelette. Serve with hot tomato butter.

FACING PAGE: *Cheese omelette with tomato butter*

FOR THE PASTRY CASE

1½ cups plain flour

Pinch of salt

Pinch of mustard powder

90 g butter

⅓ cup finely grated mature
   Cheddar cheese

1 egg yolk

About 1 tablespoon cold water

FOR THE FILLING

30 g butter

¼ cup plain flour

⅔ cup milk

1½ cups finely grated mature
   Cheddar cheese

2 egg yolks

4 tablespoons thick cream

Freshly ground black pepper

FOR THE TOPPING

3 egg whites

Pinch of salt

Pinch of cayenne pepper

¼ cup finely grated mature
   Cheddar cheese

1 tablespoon fine soft brown
   breadcrumbs (p.310)

PREPARATION TIME: 30 minutes

CHILLING TIME: 30 minutes

COOKING TIME: 45 minutes

SERVES: four to six

Cheese Flan

*Served with a green salad, this would make a lovely centrepiece
for a vegetarian meal.*

To make the pastry case, sift the flour, salt and mustard into a bowl and rub in the butter with your fingers until the mixture resembles fine breadcrumbs. Mix in the cheese and then gradually mix in the egg yolk and water to form a stiff dough. Knead the dough on a lightly floured surface until smooth, then roll it out and line a 23 cm flan tin. Trim the edge and prick well all over the base with a fork. Refrigerate for 30 minutes.

Meanwhile, heat the oven to 220°C. Line the pastry case with crumpled greaseproof paper, fill with baking beans and bake blind for 10 minutes. Remove the paper and baking beans and bake in the centre of the oven for 10–15 minutes more, or until lightly browned.

When the pastry case has been cooking for about 15 minutes, start to make the filling. Melt the butter in a saucepan, stir in the flour and cook over low heat for 1 minute. Gradually stir in the milk and bring to the boil, stirring continuously until the sauce becomes very thick. Add the finely grated Cheddar cheese and stir over medium heat until the cheese melts and the mixture becomes smooth, but take care not to overheat. Remove the pan from the heat, beat in the egg yolks, one at a time, then stir in the cream. Season well with black pepper.

Remove the pastry case from the oven and fill it with the cheese sauce. Whisk the egg whites for the topping with salt and cayenne pepper until very stiff. Quickly spoon the mixture over the cheese filling to cover it completely. Sprinkle the top first with cheese, then with breadcrumbs, and return the flan to the oven. Bake for 15 minutes, or until golden brown on top. Serve hot, with a green salad.

Stand the cooked flan on an upturned bowl to allow the side of the flan tin to drop and the flan to be removed easily.

CHILDREN'S FAVOURITE

In 1916, Chicago businessman James L. Kraft invented a method to pasteurise and emulsify cheese. By halting the natural maturing of cheese during processing, he had discovered a method for storing cheese indefinitely. In advertisements such as this one from 1933, Kraft cheese was specifically marketed as suitable for children.

Potted Cheese

Here's a marvellous way to turn workaday cheese into a spirited, celebratory snack.

Beat the grated cheese with the butter, mace, paprika and Tabasco sauce and season to taste with black pepper. Finally, beat in the dry Madeira or sherry. Press the mixture into four ²/₃ cup ramekins or small pots and smooth the surface. Melt the clarified butter and carefully spoon it over the potted cheese to cover completely. Refrigerate for at least 1 hour and serve with crusty bread or a selection of savoury biscuits, or with celery sticks.

The potted cheese will keep, refrigerated, for about a week.

2 cups finely grated mature
   Cheddar or any firm cheese
125 g butter, softened
½ teaspoon ground mace
½ teaspoon paprika
Few drops Tabasco sauce
Freshly ground black pepper
2 tablespoons dry Madeira
   or sherry
125 g clarified butter (p.311)

PREPARATION TIME: 15 minutes

SERVES: eight as a starter or cheese course, four as a light lunch or supper

60 g butter

1 teaspoon mustard powder

1 teaspoon Worcestershire
   sauce

Freshly ground black pepper

2 egg yolks

½ cup soft white
   breadcrumbs (p.310)

2 cups finely grated
   mature Cheddar or
   other firm cheese

4 tablespoons light beer

4 large thick slices
   wholewheat or white bread

Sliced gherkins, celery
   leaves and sliced tomato,
   to garnish

PREPARATION TIME: 30 minutes

COOKING TIME: 5 minutes

SERVES: four

100 YEARS OF MARMITE

*It took a while to convince the
public to eat a product made from
spent brewer's yeast. German
chemist Justus van Lieberg
discovered that spent yeast
(a by-product of beer brewing)
could be made into a vegetarian
concentrated food product which
closely resembled meat extract. In
1902 the Marmite Food Co. Ltd.
was formed at Burton-on-Trent in
England, conveniently close to the
Bass Brewery. The cautious public
was eventually won over when
vitamins were discovered in 1912
and Marmite was found to be very
rich in B vitamins. 'Marmite' is the
French word for a stock pot which
is pictured on the label, and is the
shape of the Marmite jar itself.*

Welsh Rarebit

*Welsh rarebit makes a perfect quick snack or light lunch; for a
delicious change, fry the bread in bacon fat instead of toasting it.*

Melt the butter in a small saucepan and add
the mustard, Worcestershire sauce, pepper, egg
yolks, breadcrumbs and cheese. Stir continuously over low heat until the cheese has just
melted. Do not allow the mixture to bubble or
it will become stringy. Stir in the beer, remove
from the heat and cool for 15 minutes.

Toast the bread on both sides, under a hot
grill, until golden brown. Spread the cheese
mixture on one side of each slice of toast and
grill for 1–2 minutes, or until bubbling and
lightly browned. Serve the rarebit at once,
garnished with sliced gherkins, celery leaves
and tomato slices.

VARIATION

Buck Rarebit: For buck rarebit, you will also
need 4 eggs, for poaching (see p.54). Make as
for Welsh rarebit, but serve each slice with a
poached egg on top.

Cheese Soufflé

A cheese soufflé never fails to impress your family or friends.

Preheat the oven to 190°C. Butter a 1,5 litre soufflé dish. Melt the butter in a medium saucepan over medium heat, stir in the flour and cook on low heat for 1 minute. Gradually add the milk and bring to the boil, stirring all the time until very thick and smooth. Remove the saucepan from the heat and stir in the grated Cheddar cheese, salt, pepper and mustard or nutmeg. Leave to cool slightly, then beat in the egg yolks, one at a time.

Whisk the egg whites in a clean, grease-free bowl until they are stiff and glossy, but not dry. Add 2–3 tablespoons of the whisked whites to the cheese sauce and stir in to thin the sauce to a consistency similar to that of the whisked egg whites. Gently fold the remaining whisked egg whites into the sauce.

Pour the mixture into the prepared soufflé dish. Sprinkle with Parmesan cheese and bake in the centre of the oven for about 30 minutes, or until it is well risen, golden and just set. Do not open the door during cooking time. Serve the soufflé immediately, either as a starter or with a salad for a light lunch or supper.

30 g butter
¼ cup plain flour
⅔ cup milk
¾ cup finely grated mature Cheddar or other firm cheese
¼ teaspoon salt
¼ teaspoon freshly ground black pepper
¼ teaspoon mustard powder or grated nutmeg
4 eggs, separated
3 tablespoons grated Parmesan cheese

PREPARATION TIME: 20 minutes
COOKING TIME: 30 minutes
SERVES: four as a starter, two as a light meal

Eggs Benedict

This egg dish is an international favourite. The dish was created for Mr Legrande Benedict at Delmonico's restaurant in New York in 1893.

6 extra-large eggs

3 English muffins or soft, round rolls, or 6 slices bread

Butter for spreading

6 slices cooked ham

FOR THE HOLLANDAISE SAUCE

175 g butter

1 tablespoon white wine vinegar

2 tablespoons lemon juice

3 egg yolks

½ teaspoon caster sugar

Salt and freshly ground black pepper

PREPARATION TIME: 15 minutes

COOKING TIME: 40 minutes

SERVES: six

First make the sauce. Put the butter into a small saucepan over a gentle heat and leave it to melt slowly. Put the vinegar and lemon juice into a second saucepan and bring to the boil. Blend the egg yolks, sugar and a little salt in a liquidiser or food processor, gradually adding the lemon juice, vinegar and pepper.

When the butter starts to boil, pour it very slowly (with the liquidiser still switched on) into the yolk mixture until all the butter has been added and the sauce has thickened. Turn the sauce into a basin and keep it warm by standing the basin in a saucepan of hot water.

To poach the eggs, bring a frying pan of water to the boil. Reduce to a simmer and slip in 3 eggs for poaching, one at a time. When they are set to your liking (about 3 minutes),

lift them out with a slotted spoon and leave to drain well on a plate lined with paper towels. Poach the remaining eggs in the same way.

Meanwhile, split and toast the muffins, rolls or bread and spread them with butter. Top each with a slice of ham and a poached egg. Spoon over warm Hollandaise sauce and serve.

To make the Hollandaise sauce with a whisk, see p.307.

Eggs Florentine

This famous dish consists of eggs nestled in a bed of spinach and covered with a cheese sauce.

1 kg fresh spinach, washed

Salt and freshly ground black pepper

45 g butter

8 eggs

40 g grated Parmesan cheese

FOR THE CHEESE SAUCE

55 g butter

40 g flour

2 cups milk

Salt and pepper

150 g Cheddar or Gruyère cheese, grated

1 teaspoon French mustard (optional)

PREPARATION TIME: 40 minutes

COOKING TIME: 20 minutes

SERVES: four

Heat the oven to 190°C. Cook the spinach with about 100 ml water until tender, then drain well. Chop it roughly and season.

Melt 30 g of the butter, stir in the spinach and allow to heat through. Turn the spinach and butter mixture into a buttered, shallow gratin or baking dish and spread evenly over the base.

To make the sauce, melt the butter, stir in the flour and cook for 1–2 minutes without browning. Gradually beat in the milk and bring to the boil, stirring all the time to make a smooth sauce. Season and stir in the grated cheese and mustard (if used). Cook over a gentle heat for 1 minute.

Make 8 depressions in the spinach with the back of a spoon. Gently break an egg into each one, season and spoon over the sauce.

Sprinkle with Parmesan cheese and dot with the remaining 15 g butter. Bake for 15–20 minutes. Serve with crusty bread.

FACING PAGE: *Eggs Florentine (back) and eggs Benedict (front)*

FOR THE HOT TOMATO RELISH

1 tablespoon olive oil

½ red pepper, seeded
   and finely chopped

1 small onion, peeled
   and finely chopped

1 clove garlic, peeled
   and crushed

1 x 410g tin diced tomatoes

1 tablespoon Worcestershire
   sauce

1 tablespoon tomato sauce

Dash of Tabasco sauce

½ teaspoon dried marjoram

1 tablespoon wholegrain
   mustard

2 teaspoons soft, dark
   brown sugar

Salt and freshly ground
   black pepper

FOR THE HERBY SCOTCH EGGS

650g pork sausage meat

1 tablespoon chopped
   fresh parsley

1 teaspoon chopped fresh sage

2 teaspoons tomato paste

Salt and freshly ground
   black pepper

6 eggs, hard-boiled and shelled

3 tablespoons plain flour

2 eggs, beaten

1 cup fine dried white
   breadcrumbs (p.310)

Vegetable oil, for deep-frying

PREPARATION TIME: 45 minutes

COOKING TIME: 1 hour

SERVES: six

Herby Scotch Eggs with Hot Tomato Relish

Served warm or cold, Scotch eggs are a popular addition to a picnic spread.

To make the hot tomato relish, heat the oil in a saucepan, add the red pepper, onion and garlic and cook until soft but not browned. Stir in the diced tomatoes, Worcestershire sauce, tomato sauce, Tabasco sauce, marjoram, mustard and sugar and add salt and pepper to taste. Bring the mixture to the boil, reduce the heat and simmer, stirring from time to time, for 30–40 minutes, or until thick and pulpy.

To make the herby Scotch eggs, put the sausage meat into a bowl. Add the parsley, sage, tomato paste and salt and pepper to taste and mix well. Divide the mixture into six equal pieces. Dry the hard-boiled eggs with paper towels and roll them in a little flour until evenly coated. With floured hands, take a piece of sausage meat and flatten it into a round. Place an egg in the centre and wrap the sausage meat around it, pinching the join together. Shape neatly and set aside. Repeat with the remaining eggs. Lightly coat all the eggs with the remaining flour, then with the beaten egg and breadcrumbs.

Half-fill a deep pan with oil and heat until the temperature reaches 190°C on a fat-frying thermometer, or until a piece of bread dropped into the oil browns in 20–30 seconds. Fry the eggs, in batches, for 10–15 minutes, or until they are golden brown. (Reheat the oil between batches.) Using a slotted spoon, transfer the eggs to paper towels. When the eggs are cooked, cover them loosely with foil and keep them warm in the oven.

To serve, cut the eggs in half and arrange the halves on a serving dish. Serve with the hot tomato relish.

THROUGH A GLASS CLEARLY

A significant kitchen revolution was the invention of attractive, heatproof kitchenware that could be brought from oven to table. Much of the credit goes to the German Otto Schott who mixed boron oxide with silica to make a glass that could resist rapid changes in temperature. However, it was Corning, a U.S. company, that first marketed it and called it Pyrex.

Curried Eggs

This simple Indian dish consists of hard-boiled eggs doused with a curry sauce with onions and tomatoes. It is a superb light meal.

Boil the eggs for 10–12 minutes, cool under cold running water, and shell. Set aside.

To make the sauce, heat the oil in a pan and add the chopped chillies and curry leaves (if used). Brown for 10 seconds, then add the onion and stir the mixture well. Cook for 3 minutes.

Pour the grated tomato into the pan and add the remaining spices and salt. Stir, cover the pan and simmer for 20 minutes, or until the vegetables are soft and blended with the spices. Cut the eggs in half lengthways and arrange in the pan. Cook for 3 minutes. Garnish with the coriander leaves and serve immediately.

Serve with a helping of white rice or hot roti and pickles.

8 eggs

2 tablespoons chopped coriander (dhania) leaves for garnish

FOR THE CURRY SAUCE

¼ cup sunflower oil

1-1½ green chillies, chopped

8 curry leaves, fresh or dried (optional)

2 onions, peeled and grated or finely chopped

4 tomatoes, halved and grated on coarse side of the grater

¾ teaspoon turmeric

1 teaspoon cumin seeds, crushed

2 teaspoons coriander seeds, crushed

1 teaspoon salt

PREPARATION TIME: 30-40 minutes
COOKING TIME: 30 minutes
SERVES: four to six

Pasta,
Grains
& Rice

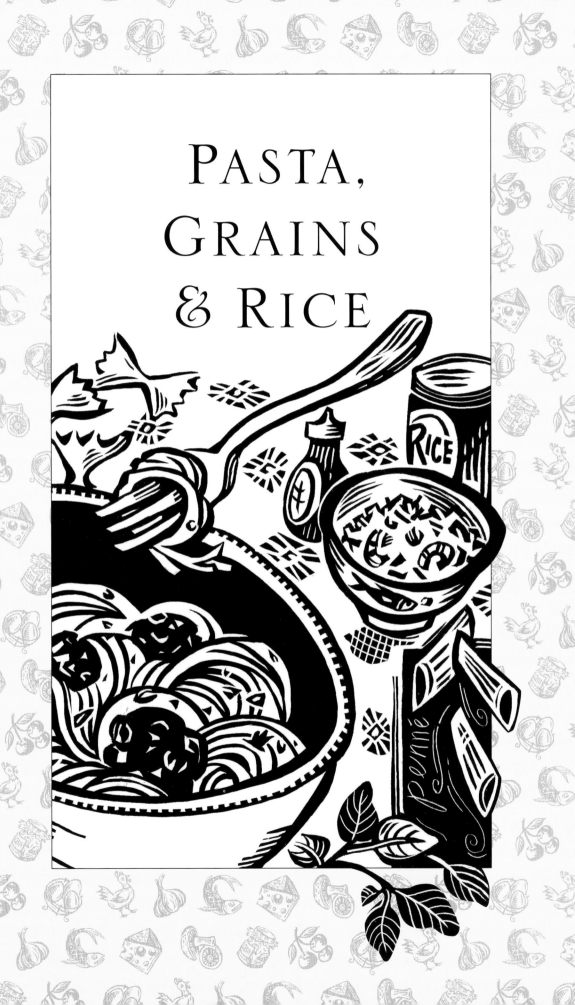

PORRIDGE

3 cups rolled oats (not instant
  - look in the health food
   section of the supermarket)
1/4 teaspoon salt
Cream, milk or buttermilk,
  to serve
Brown sugar, to serve

PREPARATION TIME: 5 minutes
SOAKING TIME: overnight
COOKING TIME: 10 minutes
SERVES: four

DRIED FRUIT COMPOTE

1/3 cup pitted dessert prunes
1/2 cup dried apple rings
1/2 cup each dried apricots,
  figs and peaches
1 orange, washed
1 lemon, washed
1 1/2 cups water
1 tablespoon clear honey
Pouring cream, to serve
  (optional)

PREPARATION TIME: 10 minutes
STANDING TIME: overnight
SERVES: four

Porridge & Dried Fruit Compote

Rolled oats, the steamed grain flattened between rollers,
has been making good breakfasts for generations.

PORRIDGE

Put the rolled oats into a bowl and cover with cold water; stand overnight. Next morning, put the oats into a heavy-based saucepan and add 1 1/2 cups water and the salt. Bring to the boil, stirring, then cover and reduce the heat. Cook on very low heat, stirring occasionally, for about 10 minutes.

Pour the porridge into a large, heated serving dish or individual bowls. Serve with the cream, milk or buttermilk and offer brown sugar, passed separately.

For a creamier porridge, replace some or all of the water with milk.

DRIED FRUIT COMPOTE

The day before, put the dried fruits into a stainless-steel or enamel saucepan. Using a zester, remove thin strips of rind from the orange and lemon and add to the fruits. Alternatively, peel the rinds thinly with a potato peeler and cut into fine shreds with a knife. Cut the orange and lemon in half, then squeeze out and strain the juice. Pour the fruit juice and water over the fruit, add the honey and heat gently until hot but not boiling. Remove from the heat, cover and stand overnight. Pour the compote into a serving bowl and serve with pouring cream, if desired.

THE CHAMPION ENERGY
BREAKFAST

*The familiar Jungle Oats package
was introduced to South African
homes in 1925 - and the design
has remained essentially the same
ever since. Daniel Bolton Redler
built his first mill in 1897, and
after much trial and tribulation,
the brand Tiger Oats was born.
Redlar was always quick to
investigate new machinery and
techniques, and the 'original
quick-cooking oat food' was an
instant success and has remained
so ever since.*

Kedgeree

*This famous Anglo–Indian dish was a popular Edwardian
breakfast dish from the days of the Raj.*

Put the fish into a wide, shallow pan and pour on the milk and 1 cup of the water. Scatter half the chopped celery and onion over the fish, add the mace and the peppercorns and bring slowly to the boil. Take off the heat immediately, cover and set aside.

Put the rice in a medium saucepan, cover with the remaining water and the salt. Bring to the boil, reduce the heat, cover the pan and simmer for about 20 minutes, or until all the water is absorbed and the rice is just tender. Remove the pan from the heat.

Melt the butter in a large frying pan, add the remaining celery and onion and fry over low heat, stirring, for about 5 minutes, or until they are soft but not coloured. Mix in the curry powder or garam masala and fry, stirring, for 1–2 minutes, or until the mixture has become fragrant. Remove from the heat.

Take the fish out of the poaching liquid and strain, discarding the flavourings but reserving the liquid. Flake the fish into large pieces, removing and discarding the skin and any bones. Return the frying pan to medium heat, add the cooked rice and mix with the curried celery and onion, then add the cream and season to taste with pepper. Stir until heated through, then add the flaked fish and toss very gently so that it mixes in but does not break up.

Remove from the heat and fork in the parsley and a little of the reserved poaching liquid to moisten. Season to taste. Serve in a heated serving dish with the eggs arranged on top. Garnish with the chopped parsley.

1 kg smoked haddock

1¼ cups milk

4½ cups water

4 celery sticks, trimmed
and chopped

2 medium onions, peeled
and chopped

2 blades of mace

A few black peppercorns

2 cups basmati rice, rinsed

½ teaspoon salt

30 g butter

4 teaspoons mild curry
powder or garam masala

1¼ cups thick cream

Freshly ground black pepper

5 tablespoons finely chopped
fresh parsley

4 eggs, hard-boiled, shelled
and quartered lengthways

Chopped fresh parsley,
to garnish

PREPARATION TIME: 20 minutes

COOKING TIME: 35 minutes

SERVES: eight

Lamb Pilaf

You can substitute chicken or prawns for the lamb in this great rice dish.

2 cups basmati or
    long-grain rice

3 tablespoons peanut oil

2 medium onions, peeled,
    halved and finely sliced

1 cinnamon stick

4 cardamom pods, crushed

10 black peppercorns, crushed

Salt and freshly ground
    black pepper

3½ cups beef stock (p.304)
    or chicken stock (p.305)

400 g lean, boneless lamb
    (rump, fillet or thick
    chump chops)

1 tablespoon oil, extra

½ cup toasted slivered
    almonds or cashew nuts,
    to garnish

PREPARATION TIME: 15 minutes

COOKING TIME: 30 minutes

SERVES: four to five

Place the rice in a fine strainer and rinse under cold running water until the water runs clear. Drain the rice well.

Heat the oil over medium heat in a wide (about 20 cm), heavy-based saucepan or casserole dish. Add the onion and cook gently, stirring occasionally, until the onion is soft. Add the cinnamon stick, cardamom pods and peppercorns and cook for a further 2 minutes, or until the spices give off a pleasant aroma. Add the rinsed rice and salt to the spice mixture and stir over medium heat for 2 minutes, or until the rice is coated with the mixture.

Meanwhile, bring the stock to the boil in another saucepan. Stir the boiling stock into the rice mixture. Reduce the heat to low, cover the saucepan with a tight-fitting lid and simmer for 18 minutes. Remove the saucepan from the heat and stand for 5 minutes without lifting the lid.

While the rice is cooking, brush the lamb with extra oil and cook under a preheated grill or pan-fry until it is cooked to your liking. Remove the lamb to a chopping board, cover with foil and rest for 3 minutes before cutting into small cubes.

Gently stir the lamb into the pilaf, using a fork to separate the grains of rice. Season to taste with salt and pepper. Spoon the pilaf into serving bowls. Garnish with toasted almonds or cashew nuts. Serve immediately.

Vary the spicing by adding one or two whole cloves, a pinch of saffron or a little turmeric.

KEEPING COOL

The Portway Cooler was advertised in the Family Magazine and Farmer's Review *in 1923. The entire cooler was covered with fabric which was kept damp by water dripping from the water tank on top. As the water evaporated, it absorbed the heat from the surrounding air, keeping the food in the 'fridge' cool.*

4 cups water

½ teaspoon salt

2 cups long-grain rice

⅓ cup olive oil

2½ tablespoons red wine vinegar

1 teaspoon Dijon mustard

Salt and freshly ground black pepper

1 cup fresh or frozen peas

400 g ham, cut into bite-sized cubes

6 spring onions, finely sliced on the diagonal

6 medium radishes, cleaned and finely sliced

3 sticks celery, finely sliced on the diagonal

1 tablespoon chopped fresh mint

2 tablespoons chopped fresh parsley

½ cup mayonnaise, homemade (p.306) or good quality bought

2 tablespoons chopped fresh chives

PREPARATION TIME: 20 minutes

COOLING TIME: 20 minutes

COOKING TIME: 22 minutes

SERVES: six

Ham & Rice Salad

The secret of a flavoursome rice salad is to dress the rice with a good vinaigrette while it is still warm, so that it absorbs the flavours, then add the mayonnaise last, for a creamy texture.

Bring the water to the boil in a medium, heavy-based saucepan. Stir in the salt and rice. Reduce the heat to low, cover the saucepan with a tight-fitting lid and cook for about 20 minutes, or until the liquid is absorbed and the rice is just tender. Remove from the heat. Remove the lid to allow the steam to escape. Gently fluff the rice with a fork to separate the grains. Cover with the lid again and stand for 10 minutes, or until the rice is lukewarm.

Whisk the olive oil in a bowl with the red wine vinegar, Dijon mustard and salt and pepper until well combined. Pour the dressing over the warm rice and stir gently with a fork. Set the rice aside to cool completely.

Bring a small saucepan of salted water to the boil. Add the peas and cook until they are bright green and tender. Drain the peas and refresh them under cold running water. Pat dry with paper towels.

Spoon the rice into a serving bowl. Add the peas, ham, spring onion, radish, celery, mint and parsley and mix until the vegetables are evenly distributed. Fold in the mayonnaise and season to taste with salt and pepper. Sprinkle with the chives just before serving.

3 cups water

½ teaspoon salt

1½ cups long-grain rice

¼ cup peanut oil

3 eggs, lightly beaten

1 onion, peeled and
finely chopped

1 clove garlic, peeled
and crushed

1 small fresh red chilli,
seeded and finely chopped

250 g pork fillet, diced

250 g chicken thigh fillet, diced

250 g small, cooked,
peeled prawns or shrimps

1 small carrot, peeled
and grated

¼ small Chinese cabbage,
finely shredded

PREPARATION TIME:
Day 1, 5 minutes
Day 2, 15 minutes

CHILLING TIME: overnight

COOKING TIME:
Day 1, 20 minutes
Day 2, 15 minutes

SERVES: four

FOR THE SAMBAL GORENG TERUNG

2 medium aubergines

1 teaspoon salt

1 tablespoon lemon juice

1 small onion, peeled and
sliced

2 tablespoons sunflower oil

1 teaspoon ground coriander

1 teaspoon brown sugar

1 dried red chilli, crushed

2 teaspoons shrimp paste

PREPARATION TIME: 15 minutes

COOKING TIME: 10 minutes

FOR THE SAMBAL KETIMUM

1 large cucumber

½ dried red chilli, crushed

50 ml vinegar

1 teaspoon salt

50 ml water

PREPARATION TIME: 10 minutes

Nasi Goreng

Quickly prepared and spiked with many flavours, this Indonesian classic became popular with our more adventurous Grandmas. Nasi Goreng is, in fact, only one component of a larger range of dishes which make up the rijstafel. Piled onto one large platter with a few sambals, it is a splendid dish for a buffet.

Bring the water to the boil in a medium, heavy-based saucepan. Stir in the salt and rice. Reduce the heat to low, cover the saucepan with a tight-fitting lid and cook for about 20 minutes, or until all the liquid is absorbed and the rice is tender. Remove from the heat. Spread the rice on a tray lined with baking paper and allow to cool. Cover with plastic wrap and refrigerate overnight.

Next day, heat 1 tablespoon of oil in a large, deep, frying pan. Add the eggs and tilt the pan so the eggs cover the base of the frying pan to form a thin omelette. Cook for 1–2 minutes, or until the omelette is just set. Slide the omelette onto a chopping board and roll up. Allow to cool, then thinly slice.

Meanwhile, heat the remaining oil, add the onion, garlic and chilli and cook, stirring often, for 1–2 minutes. Add the pork and cook for 5 minutes. Add the chicken and cook for a further 5 minutes, or until the pork and chicken are cooked through.

Add the rice and prawns and fry until the rice is heated through. Stir in the carrot and Chinese cabbage and cook for a further 1–2 minutes, or until the cabbage wilts.

To serve, spoon the rice onto a platter or into bowls and scatter with the omelette slices. Serve with sambal goreng terung (peppery aubergine) and sambal ketimum (spicy cucumber) and sauces such as peanut sauce or sweet and sour sauce.

SAMBAL GORENG TERUNG

Slice the aubergines (with the skin) into 1 cm thick slices. Sprinkle with the salt and lemon juice.

Sauté the onion in the oil. Add the coriander, brown sugar, chilli and shrimp paste. Place the aubergine slices in this mixture, turn to coat and sauté for about 10 minutes in an open pan until cooked. A little water may be added to speed up the cooking and prevent burning. Be careful not to reduce the aubergine to a pulp.

SAMBAL KETIMUM

Peel and slice the cucumber. Mix all the other ingredients together and add to the cucumber. Spicy cucumber is an important dish as it cools the palate.

SETTING THE TABLE

Traditionally knives are not used at a *rijstafel*. Set a dessert spoon (right hand side) and two forks – one on either side of the dinner plate. A tall, frosty glass of beer is a popular accompaniment.

FACING PAGE: *Nasi goreng*

To prevent spaghetti or any other pasta from becoming soft and sticky, always cook it in plenty of water — 1 litre for each portion of pasta and 1 litre for the pot.

500 g chicken livers
2 tablespoons olive oil
1 onion, peeled and finely chopped
2 cloves garlic, peeled and chopped
250 g lean minced beef
250 g lean minced pork
1 x 800 g tin whole tomatoes
½ cup beef stock (p.304)
2½ tablespoons tomato paste
2 bay leaves
Salt and freshly ground black pepper
750 g dried spaghetti
1 tablespoon fresh chopped origanum or 1 teaspoon dried origanum
20 g butter
Grated Parmesan cheese, to serve

PREPARATION TIME: 15 minutes
COOKING TIME: 1 hour 10 minutes
SERVES: six to eight

Spaghetti Bolognaise

This nourishing dish is a particular favourite with children.

Trim any discoloured spots, fat and membrane from the chicken livers. Wash the livers and then pat them dry with paper towels. Roughly chop the livers.

Heat the oil in a large frying pan over medium heat. Add the chicken livers, onion, garlic, and beef and pork mince. Cook, stirring frequently with a wooden spoon to break up the mince, until the meat is brown. Add the tomatoes and juice, the stock and the tomato paste. Stir until well combined, breaking up the tomatoes with a wooden spoon. Add the bay leaves and bring the sauce to the boil. Reduce the heat to low, cover the frying pan with a lid and simmer on very low heat, for 1 hour, or until the sauce is thick and rich. Stir the sauce from time to time during cooking to prevent the meat from sticking.

Bring a large saucepan of salted water to the boil. Add the spaghetti and cook, uncovered, stirring from time to time, for 10–12 minutes, or until the pasta is *al dente*. Drain. (Be careful not to overcook the pasta.)

Remove and discard the bay leaves from the sauce. Stir in the origanum. Remove from the heat, season to taste with salt and pepper. Stir in the butter.

To serve, turn the cooked, drained pasta into a heated bowl and top with the sauce. Sprinkle with a little of the Parmesan cheese and pass the remaining cheese separately.

Bolognaise sauce is traditionally made with this combination of chicken livers, beef mince and pork mince. If you prefer to omit the chicken livers, however, you can double the amount of minced beef and pork.

Macaroni Cheese

One of the great comfort foods, macaroni cheese makes splendid eating when prepared with a blend of good cheeses.

Salt
1½ cups macaroni
60 g butter
½ cup plain flour
4 cups milk or a mixture of milk and thick cream
¼ teaspoon mustard powder
Pinch of cayenne pepper
1 cup grated mature Cheddar cheese
1 cup grated Gruyère cheese
½ cup grated Parmesan cheese
2 tomatoes, sliced
Celery leaves, to garnish

PREPARATION TIME: 25 minutes
COOKING TIME: 40 minutes
SERVES: six

Preheat the oven to 200°C. Bring a large saucepan of lightly salted water to the boil. Add the macaroni and cook, uncovered, at a rolling boil for about 12 minutes, or as directed on the packet.

Meanwhile, melt the butter in a saucepan, stir in the flour and cook on low heat for 1 minute. Gradually stir in the milk, or the milk and cream. Bring to the boil over medium heat, stirring continuously until the mixture thickens. Remove the pan from the heat and season the sauce to taste with mustard powder,

salt and cayenne pepper. Add the Cheddar and Gruyère cheeses to the sauce and stir until the cheeses have melted.

Drain the macaroni well, then mix into the sauce and pour into a large, shallow ovenproof dish. Sprinkle the Parmesan cheese on top and cook in the centre of the oven for 35 minutes, or until the top is golden and bubbling.

Arrange the tomato slices on top and return to the oven for 5 minutes. Garnish with celery leaves and serve with a celery, walnut and watercress salad.

THE PREVALENCE OF PASTA

'Give him a macaroni dish this evening' urged the above advertisement in 1935. Both the founders of Fatti's and Moni's pasta products arrived in South Africa in the late 1800s - Guiseppe Moni from Italy and Luigi Fatti from Argentina, and both set up shop in Johannesburg selling pasta and other mainly Italian delicatessen products. The intense price rivalry which followed continued until the two families reached an agreement and formed the United Macaroni Company in 1925.

125 g flat noodles

1 tablespoon olive or
    vegetable oil

1 medium onion, chopped

1 medium green pepper,
    chopped

1 stick celery, sliced

⅓ cup plain flour

Pinch of black pepper

3½ cups milk

½ cup grated Swiss cheese or
    sharp Cheddar

2 tins tuna packed in oil,
    drained and flaked

⅓ cup grated Parmesan
    cheese

PREPARATION TIME: 20 minutes

COOKING TIME: 40 minutes

SERVES: four

Tuna & Noodle Casserole

*Tinned tuna first appeared some years after World War II
and quickly became popular for dishes such as this casserole,
which were ideal for family meals or informal entertaining.*

Preheat the oven to 180°C. Cook the noodles according to the directions on the package. Drain, rinse and drain again; return to the saucepan and cover.

Meanwhile, heat the oil over medium heat in a large saucepan. Add the onion, green pepper and celery and cook for 5 minutes, or until the vegetables are tender. Stir in the flour and black pepper. Add the milk and cook, stirring constantly, for 10 minutes, or until the mixture is thickened and bubbly. Add the Swiss cheese, stirring until melted. Stir in the cooked noodles and then carefully stir in the tuna.

Spoon the tuna and noodle mixture into a lightly greased 20 x 20 x 5 cm baking dish. Top with grated Parmesan cheese and bake for 25 minutes, or until heated through.

Try using tinned salmon or cooked chicken instead of tuna for this casserole and garnish it with quartered hard-boiled eggs.

Spaghetti & Meatballs

This is a useful 'standby' dish to have in your repertoire since both the meatballs and tomato sauce freeze perfectly and can be reheated successfully in the microwave.

To make the meatballs, combine the minced beef, breadcrumbs, chopped onion, lemon rind, Parmesan cheese, egg and salt and pepper to taste in a medium bowl. Use your hands to mix until well combined. With wet hands, shape the mixture into small balls. Place on a tray, cover with plastic wrap and chill in the refrigerator for 20 minutes.

Heat the olive oil in a frying pan over medium-high heat. Add half the meatballs and cook, turning occasionally, until the meatballs are browned. Remove to a plate and repeat with the remaining meatballs. Wipe the frying pan clean with paper towels.

To make the tomato sauce, heat the olive oil over medium heat. Add the onion and garlic and cook until the onion is soft and translucent. Stir in the tomato paste and cook for 1 minute. Add the tomatoes and their juice, the sugar and the water and bring to the boil. Reduce the heat to medium-low and add the meatballs, spooning the tomato mixture over the meatballs so they are covered. Cover the frying pan with a lid and cook, stirring occasionally, for 10 minutes, or until the meatballs are cooked through and the sauce has thickened. Stir in the origanum, and season to taste with salt and pepper.

Bring a large saucepan of salted water to the boil. Add the spaghetti and cook, uncovered, stirring occasionally, for 10–12 minutes, or until *al dente*. Drain. To serve, scoop the spaghetti onto a large platter or into individual bowls and spoon over the meatballs and sauce.

FOR THE MEATBALLS
500 g minced beef

1 cup soft breadcrumbs (p.310)

1 small onion, peeled and finely chopped

Finely grated rind of 1 lemon

2½ tablespoons finely grated Parmesan cheese

1 egg

Salt and freshly ground black pepper

2 tablespoons olive oil

FOR THE TOMATO SAUCE
2 tablespoons olive oil

1 onion, peeled and finely chopped

1 clove garlic, peeled and chopped

2½ tablespoons tomato paste

1 x 800 g tin diced or crushed tomatoes

Pinch of caster sugar

½ cup water

1 tablespoon chopped fresh origanum or 1 teaspoon dried origanum

Salt and freshly ground black pepper

400 g dried spaghetti

PREPARATION TIME: 20 minutes

CHILLING TIME: 20 minutes

COOKING TIME: 25 minutes

SERVES: four

FOR THE LASAGNE
250 g precooked lasagne
 sheets
90 g mozzarella cheese,
 thinly sliced
¼ cup grated Parmesan
 cheese

FOR THE MEAT SAUCE
4 tablespoons olive oil
1 onion, peeled and chopped
2 cloves garlic, peeled
 and crushed
1 carrot, peeled and chopped
1 stick celery, chopped
500 g lean minced beef
2 rashers (about 60 g) lean
 bacon, rind removed and
 chopped or 4 slices (about
 60 g) prosciutto, chopped
½ cup dry red wine
1 x 410 g tin chopped tomatoes
1 teaspoon dried origanum
¼ teaspoon freshly grated
 nutmeg
Salt and freshly ground
 black pepper

FOR THE BÉCHAMEL
SAUCE
1½ cups milk
1 slice onion
Bouquet garni (p.310)
50 g butter
4 tablespoons plain flour
Salt and freshly ground
 black pepper

PREPARATION TIME: 40 minutes

STANDING TIME: 10 minutes

COOKING TIME: 30 minutes for
 meat sauce; 40 minutes to
 bake lasagne

SERVES: four to six

Lasagne

*You can make both sauces ahead of time and warm them over hot water
or in a microwave when needed.*

To make the meat sauce, heat the oil in a wide saucepan and cook the onion, garlic, carrot and celery on low heat until soft. Increase the heat to medium, stir in the beef and bacon, breaking up any lumps with two forks, and cook, stirring, until the meat changes colour. Add the wine, tomatoes, origanum and nutmeg, cover and simmer for 30 minutes. Season the sauce to taste with salt and pepper.

To make the béchamel sauce, heat the milk to simmering point with the onion and bouquet garni, then remove from the heat and stand for 10 minutes to infuse. Heat the butter in a small saucepan, stir in the flour and cook, stirring, for 3 minutes. Remove from the heat and allow to cool a little. Strain the warm milk and stir it into the flour mixture until blended. Stir on low heat until the sauce boils and thickens. Season with salt and pepper.

Preheat the oven to 180°C. Grease a shallow, rectangular ovenproof dish. Spread a layer of meat sauce on the base of the dish and top with a layer of béchamel sauce. Add a layer of mozzarella, then a layer of pasta. Repeat these four layers until the dish is full, ending with béchamel sauce. Sprinkle with Parmesan cheese and bake for 40 minutes, or until the lasagne is hot and bubbling. Stand for 10 minutes before serving. Serve with a green salad and crusty bread.

Chicken Biriani

Biriani is a savoury dish of meat or fish and rice, which sometimes includes lentils and eggs. Garnish with hard-boiled egg slices and serve with cool cucumber raita.

1 chicken (1,5 kg)

Salt

6 tablespoons sunflower oil or ghee (p.313)

1 large onion, chopped or sliced into rings

2 cm piece fresh ginger

2 cloves garlic

½ teaspoon cumin seeds

1 teaspoon coriander

¼ teaspoon cayenne pepper

A few fresh coriander or bay leaves

1 large tomato, skinned and grated

⅓ cup sour milk (smetena)

4 small potatoes, cut into quarters

250 g rice

A few cardamom seeds

2 cloves

A pinch of saffron

1 cup boiling water

2 hard-boiled eggs, sliced

Coriander leaves (dhania) to garnish

PREPARATION TIME: 30 minutes

COOKING TIME: 2 hours

SERVES: six

Cut the chicken into small pieces, salt and put aside. Heat 4 tablespoons of the oil or ghee and sauté the onion in it until golden. Pound the ginger, garlic, cumin seeds, coriander, cayenne pepper and fresh coriander or bay leaves in a mortar, add to the onions and cook for 4 minutes over a very low heat.

Add the chicken and cook for another 7 minutes. Next, add the tomato and sour milk, and let the chicken simmer slowly for 30 minutes. Fry the potatoes in the remaining 2 tablespoons of hot oil and add them to the chicken mixture. In the meantime, cook the rice with salt, cardamom and cloves until almost cooked. Then strain.

Spoon a layer of rice into a large, heavy-bottomed saucepan, followed by a layer of the chicken mixture. Repeat, ending with a layer of rice.

Dissolve the saffron in the boiling water and pour over the rice. Cover the saucepan with a tight-fitting lid and cook over a very low heat until the rice is done. Do not remove the lid until you are ready to serve.

CUCUMBER RAITA

Peel the cucumber and cut into small cubes. Arrange in a colander and sprinkle with salt. Leave to stand for 1 hour. Then drain the cucumber and pat dry with a paper towel.

Stir the crushed garlic into the yoghurt with the mint, lemon juice and a pinch of cayenne pepper. Pour the mixture over the cucumber, mix well and chill for 30 minutes.

FOR THE CUCUMBER RAITA

1 English cucumber

1 tablespoon salt

1 clove garlic, peeled and crushed

150 ml natural yoghurt

2 tablespoons freshly chopped mint

2 tablespoons lemon juice

A pinch of cayenne pepper

PREPARATION TIME: 5-10 minutes

STANDING TIME: 1 hour

CHILLING TIME: 30 minutes

SERVES: six

FISH & SHELLFISH

FOR THE FISH

1,5 kg whole fish, cleaned and
    scaled

Olive oil

Salt and freshly ground
    black pepper

Lemon wedges, to serve

FOR THE HERB
STUFFING

30 g butter

1 onion, peeled and
    finely chopped

3 teaspoons finely grated
    lemon rind

2 tablespoons chopped
    fresh parsley

1 tablespoon fresh
    thyme leaves

1 tablespoon chopped
    fresh dill

2 cups soft breadcrumbs
    (p.310)

Salt and freshly ground
    black pepper

PREPARATION TIME: 20 minutes

COOKING TIME: 55 minutes

SERVES: four

Whole Baked Fish with Herb Stuffing

A fish baked whole always looks spectacular.

Preheat the oven to 180°C. Rinse the fish and pat dry with paper towels.

To make the herb stuffing, melt the butter in a medium frying pan. Add the onion and cook until it is soft and translucent. Remove from the heat and transfer to a mixing bowl. Add the lemon rind, parsley, thyme leaves, dill and breadcrumbs and season to taste. Mix well to combine the stuffing.

Cut three slashes, each 1 cm deep, into the thickest part of the fish on both sides. Brush both sides of the fish with olive oil and season with salt and pepper. Loosely fill the cavity with the stuffing (do not overfill as the stuffing

will expand during cooking, causing the flesh to split). Close the cavity and secure with wooden toothpicks.

Select a shallow ovenproof dish that is large enough to contain the fish and pour in enough olive oil to thinly cover the base. Place the fish in the prepared dish and cover tightly with two sheets of foil.

Bake the whole fish in the preheated oven for 45–50 minutes, or until the fish is cooked when tested at the thickest part – the flesh should be opaque and flake easily when tested with a fork. Serve the baked fish immediately with lemon wedges.

A GOOD CATCH

The fishing village of Hermanus in the Cape was renowned for its fishing from the rocks. In the 1920s a Mr Selkirk caught fish weighing a total of 267 kilograms in just one afternoon! Here Mr Alan Guthrie displays a kabeljou weighing 45 kilograms which he caught off the rocks at Mossel River, Hermanus.

Trout with Almonds

This traditional French dish is popular worldwide. It is the perfect dish for an elegant lunch or dinner party. Use local trout which is of excellent quality and is freely available.

Preheat the oven to 180°C. Clean the trout through the gills and wash them thoroughly. (Or ask your fishmonger to do this for you.) Sprinkle with salt and pepper and put aside.

Spread the almonds on an oven tray and place them in the preheated oven. Roast until golden-brown, turning from time to time, and put aside.

Meanwhile, dredge the fish with flour and shake off any surplus flour. Melt half the butter in a large frying pan and add half the oil. Fry 3 trout over a medium heat for 6 minutes on each side. Place on a heated serving dish and scatter with the roasted almonds. Keep warm while frying the remaining trout (using the rest of the butter and oil). Scatter these with almonds and sprinkle lemon juice over the trout.

VARIATION

Bake the trout in a well-greased pan at 200°C for 15–20 minutes. Baste with melted butter and lemon juice, and sprinkle with browned almonds when cooked.

One large trout weighing about 850 g will need to be baked for about 35 minutes and will serve 4 people.

6 trout, each 180-200 g
Salt and freshly ground black pepper
100 g flaked almonds
Flour for dredging
¾ cup clarified butter (p.311)
¼ cup sunflower oil
Juice of 1 lemon

PREPARATION TIME: 12 minutes
COOKING TIME: 25 minutes
SERVES: six

4 trout, each about 350 g,
    gutted and washed
Salt and freshly ground
    black pepper
1 large lemon, cut into 8 slices
4 sprigs fennel or tarragon
    (optional)
12–16 sheets newspaper

PREPARATION TIME: 10 minutes
COOKING TIME: 25–30 minutes
SERVES: four

Trout Cooked in Newspaper

Wet newspaper conserves moisture and succulence by effectively steaming these fish, particularly when they are cooked over an open fire.

Trout can be cooked in newspaper either in the oven or on a braai.

Preheat the oven to 200°C, or light the fire. Season the trout well with salt and pepper and put two slices of lemon and a sprig of fennel or tarragon, if using, inside each one.

Lay each fish on three layers of newspaper and wrap, tucking in the ends of the paper carefully. Soak the wrapped fish in cold water until thoroughly wet. Place the parcels in the oven or on the braai and cook, turning once halfway through the cooking time, for 25–30 minutes, or until the paper is dry.

Serve the trout in the paper and cut it open with scissors at the table. The skin will peel off with the paper, leaving a perfectly cooked, moist and succulent fish.

VARIATIONS

Kabeljou: A whole kabeljou can also be cooked in newspaper very successfully. To cook a larger fish, weighing about 1,5 kg, in the same way, increase the amount of wet paper and the cooking time in proportion to the size of the fish.

Fish Cooked in Seaweed: Very large fish can be wrapped in seaweed and cooked on a kettle braai or an open fire. Depending on the type of seaweed, wrap about eight layers of seaweed around the fish and cook for about an hour, or until just cooked through.

Any whole fish, for example kabeljou or yellowtail, can be cooked in newspaper using this method.

FROM FISHING TO FROZEN FOODS GIANT

In 1910 George Irvin and Charles Johnson started a fishing company based in Cape Town harbour. Together they pioneered the trawling industry in South Africa, expanding until Irvin and Johnson became the leading supplier of fish to the nation. Meanwhile, in the United States Clarence Birdseye had developed a method of freezing food for retail purposes. Irvin and Johnson ventured into this market, introducing their first frozen product - hake fillets - in 1952. Today I & J has over 800 product lines.

Fish Pie

This large pie made with a fish, egg and parsley sauce makes a filling meal. Use whatever fish is available and add prawns or mushrooms to turn the pie into a special meal.

Preheat the oven to 180°C. Wipe the fish and place in a large saucepan or oven-proof casserole. Sprinkle with dill or fennel seeds, salt and pepper. Pour over the milk and then add the onion stuck with cloves. Cover and simmer, or bake at 180°C, for 10–15 minutes, or until the fish flakes easily.

Increase the oven temperature to 200°C.

Meanwhile, drain off and keep the milk. Cool the fish, discard the skin and bones, and flake the flesh into a shallow litre-sized pie or gratin dish.

Rinse out the saucepan and melt the butter, stir in the flour and cook for 1 minute without browning. Slowly add the strained milk, stirring continually to make a smooth sauce.

Season well, and if the sauce is too thick, add a little more milk to give it a coating consistency. Pour it over the fish. Top with the sliced eggs and parsley.

To make the topping, boil the potatoes for 20–25 minutes, or until they are really tender. Mash and beat them with the sour cream or milk, butter, nutmeg and seasoning.

Spread the mashed potato evenly over the fish mixture. Brush the top of the potatoes with the beaten egg.

Bake at 200°C for 20 minutes, or brown under the grill.

VARIATIONS

Instead of brushing the potatoes with egg, dot with butter and sprinkle with grated cheese.

Top with puff pastry instead of potato, for a less filling version, and bake until golden and puffy.

For a special meal, replace some of the fish with 125–200g cooked prawns and/or 200g sliced, sautéed mushrooms.

---

750 g white fish or smoked haddock
½ teaspoon dill or fennel seeds
Salt and freshly ground black pepper
1½ cups milk
1 small onion stuck with 4 cloves
75 g butter
50 g flour
3 hard-boiled eggs, sliced
1 tablespoon parsley

FOR THE TOPPING
9 medium potatoes, peeled and halved
½ cup sour cream (smetana) or milk
50 g butter
Nutmeg, freshly grated
Salt and pepper
1 egg, beaten

PREPARATION TIME: 30 minutes
COOKING TIME: 1 hour
SERVES: four

Grilled Calamari

800 g fresh calamari or 600 g
  frozen calamari

½ cup clarified butter (p.311)

Juice of 1 lemon

Salt and freshly ground black
  pepper

PREPARATION TIME: 20 minutes

COOKING TIME: 5 minutes

SERVES: six

*If you are using fresh calamari, try to choose young ones as they are more tender.
Frozen calamari should be allowed to thaw completely before cooking.*

Preheat the oven to 200°C. Clean the calamari and slice the body into 1 cm rings. Cut the tentacles into bite-sized pieces. Brush well with a mixture of the lemon juice and clarified butter.

Turn on the grill in the preheated oven and place the calamari on a well-oiled grid. Grill until the calamari turns white and singes slightly (about 5 minutes). Sprinkle with salt and pepper and serve.

This dish can be served on a bed of rice – savoury rice is particularly good. To add colour to the presentation of the calamari, serve with a salad of mixed vegetables.

VARIATION

Add peri-peri spice to the lemon butter mixture and use olive oil in the place of the butter.

Serve with lemon wedges and a green salad.

GARLIC PRAWNS

1 cup olive oil

10 small cloves garlic,
  peeled and finely chopped

Salt and freshly ground
  black pepper

24 medium prawns (about
  1 kg), defrosted if you are
  using frozen prawns)

⅔ cup white wine

1 tablespoon lemon
  or lime juice

⅓ cup chopped fresh parsley

PREPARATION TIME:
  Day 1, 15 minutes
  Day 2, 5 minutes

MARINATING TIME: overnight

COOKING TIME: 8 minutes

SERVES: four

PRAWNS PERI-PERI

36 large or 60 small prawns,
  fresh or frozen

250 g butter

½ cup sunflower oil

4 cloves garlic, peeled and
  crushed

2 teaspoons peri-peri powder

Salt

PREPARATION TIME: 20 minutes

COOKING TIME: 15 minutes

SERVES: six

Two Prawn Classics

*Marinate the Garlic Prawns overnight with the garlic to ensure a pungent flavour;
baking them will keep them deliciously juicy. Vary the amount of peri-peri powder in
the Prawns Peri-Peri recipe to suit your taste.*

GARLIC PRAWNS

Combine the olive oil, garlic, salt and pepper in a medium bowl. Peel and devein the prawns, leaving the tails intact, and add to the garlic and oil mixture. Stir well to coat the prawns. Cover with plastic wrap and chill overnight.

The next day, preheat the oven to 220°C. Arrange the prawns in a single layer in an ovenproof dish or divide the prawns equally among four individual ovenproof bowls.

Add the white wine and lemon or lime juice to the marinade and whisk well to combine. Pour the mixture over the prawns and season to taste. Cover the dish with foil and bake in the preheated oven for 8 minutes, or until the prawns are cooked. Sprinkle with parsley and serve with fresh, crusty bread.

PRAWNS PERI-PERI

Defrost the prawns if they are frozen. Devein them (leaving them in their shells with the heads and tails intact). Rinse the prawns and pat dry with paper towels. Melt the butter with the oil in a large pan and then add the garlic and peri-peri powder. Swirl the ingredients around to mix well.

Fry the prawns (a few at a time) for 3 minutes and then place them in a serving dish in the oven warmer. Add salt to the remaining liquid (to taste) and then pour some of this sauce over the prawns just before serving.

Serve on a bed of hot rice with a green salad and any leftover sauce in a jug.

FACING PAGE: *Garlic prawns*

4 medium potatoes, peeled
   and quartered

Salt and cayenne pepper

30 g butter

2 x 210 g tins red salmon,
   drained

1 egg, beaten

2 tablespoons capers, chopped

3 tablespoons finely chopped
   fresh parsley

2 cups fine dried white
   breadcrumbs (p.310)

2 eggs, extra, beaten

Vegetable oil, for frying

Lemon wedges, to garnish

PREPARATION TIME: 40 minutes

CHILLING TIME: 2–2½ hours

COOKING TIME: 24 minutes

SERVES: six

Fish Cakes

Fish cakes can be either a special-occasion dish or an everyday meal. It all depends on the presentation and accompaniments.

Boil the potatoes in salted water until they are soft. Mash the cooked potatoes well in a bowl with the butter.

Drain the salmon, remove and discard the skin and bones, and flake the flesh. Add the salmon, egg, capers and parsley to the potato, season well and mix together. Allow to cool, then cover and refrigerate for 1–2 hours.

Divide the salmon mixture into 12 equal portions and, with lightly floured hands, shape each portion into a flat cake. Put the breadcrumbs into a shallow dish or onto a baking tray. Pour the extra beaten egg into a shallow dish.

Dip the fish cakes in the beaten egg, then in the breadcrumbs, making sure they are evenly coated all over. Reshape the fish cakes, put them on a plate and chill well.

Heat a little of the oil in a frying pan and cook the fish cakes, in batches, over medium heat for 4 minutes on each side, or until crisp, golden and heated through. Drain on paper towels and arrange on a heated serving plate.

Garnish the fish cakes with lemon wedges and serve with tartare sauce (see p.306) and a tossed green salad.

VARIATION

Substitute some of the salmon with an equal amount of peeled, chopped cooked prawns for a more deluxe version.

Local fish, such as hake or yellowtail, can also be used.

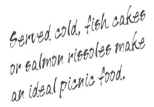

Served cold, fish cakes or salmon rissoles make an ideal picnic food.

Crayfish Classics

Crayfish, once so plentiful, is now a rare and expensive luxury. These two crayfish dishes are classics which are cooked all over the world.

CRAYFISH THERMIDOR

Twist off the crayfish legs and reserve. Remove the intestinal veins from the tails. Remove the meat from the tails and cut into bite-sized pieces. Rinse and dry the shells.

Preheat the grill. Melt the butter over medium heat in a frying pan. Add the mushrooms and onion and cook, stirring occasionally, for 3 minutes. Remove from the heat. Add the crayfish meat and set aside.

In a medium saucepan, whisk the cream with the flour, mustard, salt and cayenne pepper. Add the milk and cook on medium heat, whisking constantly, for 8 minutes, or until the sauce is thick and bubbling. Slowly stir about 1/2 cup of sauce into the egg yolks, then return this mixture to the saucepan. Cook the mixture, whisking constantly, for 3 minutes, or until it thickens (do not boil).

Stir in the crayfish-mushroom mixture and dry sherry and heat through. Spoon the hot crayfish mixture into the shells. Sprinkle the Parmesan cheese over the top and grill for 2–3 minutes, or until the cheese is melted and lightly browned. Serve immediately, garnished with the crayfish legs.

CRAYFISH MORNAY

Twist off the crayfish legs and reserve. Remove the intestinal veins from the tails. Remove the meat from the tails and cut into bite-sized pieces. Rinse and dry the shells.

Preheat the grill. Heat the mornay sauce gently in a heavy saucepan and fold the crayfish meat through. Spoon the mixture into the crayfish shells. Sprinkle with the Parmesan cheese and grill for 2–3 minutes, or until the cheese is melted and lightly browned. Serve immediately, garnished with crayfish legs.

CRAYFISH THERMIDOR

2 cooked crayfish, halved
   lengthways
20 g butter
1 cup sliced fresh mushrooms
1/4 cup finely chopped onion
3/4 cup pouring cream
2 tablespoons plain flour
1 teaspoon dry mustard
1/2 teaspoon salt
Pinch of cayenne pepper
3/4 cup milk
2 egg yolks, lightly beaten
3 tablespoons dry sherry
3 tablespoons grated
   Parmesan cheese

PREPARATION TIME: 20 minutes
COOKING TIME: 20 minutes
SERVES: four

CRAYFISH MORNAY

2 cooked crayfish, halved
   lengthways
1 quantity mornay sauce
   (p.307)
2 tablespoons grated
   Parmesan cheese

PREPARATION TIME: 20 minutes
COOKING TIME: 2–3 minutes
SERVES: four

Salad of Prawns

*Prawns are best treated very simply
so that the luxurious taste and texture come through.*

**FOR THE PRAWN
SALAD**

1 kg prawns

4 cups mixed salad leaves

1 avocado, halved, stone
   removed and flesh chopped

FOR THE DRESSING

½ cup olive oil

2 tablespoons lemon juice

1 teaspoon Dijon mustard

½ teaspoon caster sugar

1 clove garlic, peeled
   and crushed

Salt and freshly ground
   black pepper

PREPARATION TIME: 15 minutes
SERVES: four

Bring a large pot of salted water to the boil. Add the prawns and cook for 5 minutes or until the parwns change colour. Drain and devein.

To make the salad dressing, combine the olive oil, lemon juice, Dijon mustard, caster sugar, garlic and salt and pepper to taste in a screwtop jar. Shake well to combine.

Place the salad leaves in a large serving bowl. Add the avocado and prawns. Pour on the salad dressing and toss gently to combine.

Season to taste with salt and pepper and serve immediately.

Fish Meunière

*Meunière is a French term meaning 'in the style of the miller's wife', which refers to
fish coated with flour, cooked in butter, and served with parsley and lemon juice.*

800 g fish fillets

30 g flour

A pinch of salt

White pepper

Juice of 1 lemon

1 tablespoon chopped parsley

2 teaspoons chopped fresh
   chives or tarragon

50 g butter

1 tablespoon sunflower oil

PREPARATION TIME: 15 minutes
COOKING TIME: 20 minutes
SERVES: four

Wipe the fillets and pat them dry. Mix the flour with a little salt and pepper and use it to coat the fish: shake off the excess. Combine the lemon juice and herbs with salt and white pepper.

In a large frying pan, heat 20 g of the butter and the oil until it foams. Add a single layer of fish and cook over a medium-high heat for 1–3 minutes, until the fillets turn golden-brown (do not overcook or they will fall apart). Turn the fish and brown the other side. Transfer the fish to a serving dish and keep it warm while you fry the remaining fillets.

To make the sauce, wipe out the frying pan, put in the remaining butter and heat it until it turns nut-brown. Add the lemon juice-herb mixture, stirring to blend properly and pour the foaming mixture over the fish.

Scatter a handful of finely chopped parsley over the fish and serve with new potatoes, crisp sautéed potatoes or shoestring chips. Serve at once.

VARIATION

Lay the fillets side by side in a buttered oven-proof dish, dot with butter, and bake at 220°C, basting with butter every 5 minutes: they should be cooked in about 18 minutes.

Pour off the butter into a small pan, add 2 tablespoons of almond flakes and brown lightly, add a squeeze of lemon juice and pour over the fish.

FACING PAGE: *Salad of prawns*

CRAYFISH OR CRAWFISH

The terms 'crayfish', the rather old-fashioned 'crawfish', and 'rock lobster' are all used locally to refer to the same creatures. Strictly speaking, 'crayfish' should only be applied to freshwater crustaceans; 'crawfish' is the common name for marine crustaceans and 'rock lobster' is the most correct name of all.

250 g spicy Spanish (chorizo) Polish or Russian sausages, cut into big slices

3 tablespoons olive oil

8 portions chicken (legs and thighs)

250 g chicken livers

3 cloves garlic, crushed

1 large onion, peeled and chopped

1 green pepper, cut into strips

300 g rice

3 cups chicken stock (p.305)

½ teaspoon cayenne pepper

A good pinch of saffron

4 ripe tomatoes, skinned, seeded and thinly sliced

6 large prawns or 2 small cooked crayfish, cut into pieces

12 black mussels

1 red pepper, roasted, skin removed and cut into strips

White wine for moistening

100 g green peas (frozen or fresh), cooked

12 black olives and lemon wedges to garnish

PREPARATION TIME: 45 minutes
COOKING TIME: 1 hour
SERVES: eight

Paella

This is the best known Spanish dish outside Spain. It looks complicated, but is really quite easy to make and always impresses guests.

Heat the paella pan on the coals (or use an electric frying pan set on high). Fry the sausages until brown on both sides. Remove and put aside. Add oil to the pan and fry the chicken pieces until golden in colour; then remove from the heat.

Add the chicken livers and two cloves of crushed garlic, and lightly brown; then set aside. Add the onion and green pepper and fry until softened. Stir in the rice and cook until pale gold in colour. Pour in half of the chicken stock, add the cayenne pepper, saffron, tomatoes and the remaining garlic. Return the sausages, chicken and chicken liver to the pan, then the prawns or crayfish, mussels and roasted peppers.

Cook carefully, stirring frequently. Add the remaining stock and, if necessary, some wine.

Cook for about 30 minutes (or until the rice is tender). Stir in the green peas, taste and correct the seasoning. Garnish with the olives and lemon wedges.

VARIATION
Substitute cubed, firm fish and calamari rings for the crayfish and prawns. Mix the seafood according to your taste.

A packet of frozen seafood marinara mix can also be used.

Fish Bobotie

This is an interesting variation on meat bobotie. Serve it with white rice, blatjang, and cucumber sambal.

Preheat the oven to 140°C. Poach the fish in a small quantity of seasoned water to which 2 teaspoons of the lemon juice or vinegar have been added. Remove the fish from this stock, cool and flake it. Enrich 1 cup of the stock with the milk powder and soak the bread in it.

Using a covered pan, sauté the onion in the butter until it is just transparent. Add the masala, sugar and the remaining lemon juice, and simmer, covered, for 5 minutes. Add this sauce to the flaked fish.

Remove the bread from the stock, squeeze out the stock (all of which should be kept for the custard), mash and add to the fish and the sauce. When the fish mixture has cooled, add one lightly whisked egg. Mix well and spoon the mixture into a buttered dish, smoothing it down well.

Stick the almonds at intervals into the surface, leaving the round ends protruding. Cut off the stems of the lemon leaves and twist the leaves into little cones. Insert them into the fish mixture at regular intervals, so that each serving has a leaf.

Whisk the remaining egg with the whole milk and the strained residue of liquid in which the bread was soaked. Pour this over a spoon onto the fish mixture so that the lemon leaves and almonds are not disturbed.

Place the baking dish in a pan of boiling water on the lower shelf of the oven. Bake until the custard is set – about 40 minutes.

1 kg white fish (hake or any other white fish)
Salt and freshly ground black pepper
6 teaspoons lemon juice or white vinegar
1 tablespoon fat-free milk powder
1 slice white bread, 2 cm thick, with crust
1 medium onion, peeled and finely chopped
2 teaspoons butter
4 teaspoons fish masala
2 teaspoons sugar
2 large eggs
12 blanched almonds
Fresh lemon leaves (do not substitute bay leaves)
½ cup whole milk

PREPARATION TIME: 45 minutes
COOKING TIME: 40 minutes
SERVES: six

THE EASTERN INFLUENCE

South African cuisine reflects many nationalities - British, Dutch, German, French, Indian and African are just a few. However, the influence of people brought to South African shores from Madagascar, Indonesia and southern India as slaves or political prisoners is huge. 'Malay' cooking introduced distinctive combinations of foods, herbs and spices. Bobotie and gesmoorde snoek are just two examples of dishes which are immediately associated with South Africa.

1 kg fresh snoek, cut into 6
  portions
100 g butter or margarine, cut
  into 6 pats
Salt and pepper
4 tablespoons lemon juice
6 squares of greaseproof
  paper
12 squares of brown paper
Fennel for garnish

PREPARATION TIME: 30 minutes
COOKING TIME: 50 minutes
SERVES: six

Sandveld Snoek

*Wrapping the snoek up in paper parcels is an excellent way of braaing fresh snoek.
It keeps the fish moist and juicy.*

Wrap each piece of fish with a pat of butter, and seasoning and lemon juice, in greaseproof paper, tucking under the ends. Place these wrapped pieces on double thicknesses of brown paper (newspaper is sometimes used in the veld) and make a flat parcel of each, tucking the ends underneath.

Place the parcels on a grid about 20 cm below the grill or just above the coals – just far enough for the paper not to catch fire (the outer layer will become scorched). Cook for about 50 minutes, turning the parcels carefully.

Bring the parcels of fish to the table, and have kitchen scissors on hand to cut open the parcels to reveal the succulent portion of snoek in each little pool of savoury sauce.

Garnish the fish with fennel (if available) and serve with slices of fresh bread or baked potatoes and grape jam.

"THE MOST POPULAR FISH"

This Malay fish hawker is carrying snoek to his cart in Roggebaai (before the development of the Foreshore), Cape Town in about 1936. When the snoek were 'running' trucks or carts selling the fish were a common sight, while the strident blaring of the fish horn alerted customers near and far. Some expertise had to be shown in the selection of the fish to avoid 'pap' (soft) snoek. This is the most popular fish in Malay cookery.

Gesmoorde Snoek

Traditionally, dried and salted snoek was used for this dish. However, it is not readily available these days, so smoked snoek is used instead.

Fry the onions in hot oil until golden brown. Add the potatoes, turmeric and chillies, and sauté until the potatoes are lightly browned. Add about 2 tablespoons of water. Cover the pan and reduce the heat to low, and cook until the potatoes are done. Add the flaked snoek and heat through. Taste and season if necessary. Sprinkle with parsley and serve with boiled rice.

VARIATIONS
To speed up the cooking, precook the potatoes and add when you put the dish together.

Some people like to add the rice to the dish so that it also absorbs all the flavours.

A tin of crushed or chopped tomatoes can be added at the same time as the snoek.

3 medium onions, peeled and sliced
Oil for frying
3 medium potatoes, peeled and diced
½ teaspoon turmeric
2 red or green chillies, finely chopped
2 tablespoons water
750 g smoked snoek, boned and flaked (be sure to remove all the bones)
Salt and freshly ground black pepper
2 tablespoons chopped parsley

PREPARATION TIME: 20 minutes
COOKING TIME: 30 minutes
SERVES: four to six

Fish & Chips

Wrapped in newspaper or served on a china plate, this is one of the classic comfort foods.

FOR THE BATTER
2 cups self-raising flour

Pinch of salt

½ cup beer

1 cup cold water

FOR THE FISH & CHIPS
5 medium potatoes, peeled and washed

Vegetable oil, for deep-frying

4 large or 6 small fillets of kingklip, hake or other white fish

3 tablespoons flour, seasoned with salt and pepper

Lemon wedges, to garnish

PREPARATION TIME: 40 minutes

COOKING TIME: 25 minutes

SERVES: four

To make the batter, whisk the self-raising flour, salt, beer and water together until smooth (this can be done in a food processor, then the mixture transferred to a large bowl). Cover and stand for at least 30 minutes, or up to 2 hours.

Meanwhile, cut the potatoes into chips, about 5 mm thick. Put them in cold water for 5 minutes, to remove the excess starch, then drain well and pat dry on a clean tea towel. Half-fill a deep-fryer or large, deep saucepan with oil and heat to 195°C. Blanch the chips, in two batches, in the hot oil for 4–5 minutes, or until very pale golden. Remove from the oil, drain well on paper towels and set aside.

Allow the temperature of the oil to drop to 175°C. Coat the fish lightly in seasoned flour. Stir the batter vigorously and, using tongs, dip two fillets of fish into it. Lift out the fillets and allow the excess batter to drip back into the bowl. Carefully lower the fillets into the hot oil, submerging them with the tongs, and cook, turning once, for 4–5 minutes, or until crisp and golden.

Using a large wire skimmer or slotted spoon, lift the fillets out of the pan and drain on paper towels. Keep warm while dipping and frying the remaining fillets.

Increase the oil temperature to 200°C and fry the chips for 2–3 minutes more, or until crisp and golden. Drain well on paper towels. Arrange the fish and chips on heated plates and garnish with the lemon wedges. Pass some full-flavoured vinegar separately.

Oven-Fried Fish & Chips

Everybody loves a good piece of fried fresh fish. This method of cooking the fish will leave the fillets crispy and delicious without being too oily.

FOR THE CHIPS
6 large potatoes

⅓ cup sunflower oil or melted butter

Salt and vinegar

FOR THE FISH
1 kg firm fish fillets, sliced

Salt and freshly ground black pepper

Milk for dipping

Cornflake crumbs or dry breadcrumbs for coating the fish

2 tablespoons sunflower oil

PREPARATION TIME: 25 minutes

BAKING TIME: 50 minutes

SERVES: six

Preheat the oven to 250°C. Peel and wash the potatoes. Slice them up into chip shapes and soak for about 15 minutes in iced water. Drain and pat dry very thoroughly with paper towels, then arrange them in a single layer in a large baking tin.

Pour over the oil or butter and toss the chips around until they are well-coated. Bake for about 40 minutes, or until browned and tender. Place in the warming oven.

Wash and dry the fish and season with salt and pepper. Dip the fish fillets in milk and roll them in the crumbs. (The crumbed fish may be placed in the refrigerator for 15 minutes before baking to allow the crumbs to adhere to the fish fillets better.)

Arrange the fish in a well-oiled, shallow, ovenproof dish or baking tin. Drizzle with the cooking oil and bake for 10 minutes at 230°C without turning or basting. Serve immediately.

Season the chips with salt and vinegar just before serving and provide lemon wedges for squeezing over each serving.

FACING PAGE: *Fish & chips*

UNION CASTLE LINE

Thousands of South Africans travelled to and from Britain on the lavender-hulled Union Castle liners. The ships kept to a strict 14-day schedule and with little else to do for two weeks but take part in the ship's entertainment and eat, South Africans encountered a wide array of dishes - many for the first time. Pre-dinner cocktails were also an extremely popular way to pass the time. The passenger service ended in 1977.

FRIED SOLE

1 dressed sole
Salt
Flour for coating
4 tablespoons butter
1 tablespoon chopped parsley
Lemon

PREPARATION TIME: 5 minutes
COOKING TIME: 10 minutes
SERVES: one

GRILLED SOLE

4 skinned soles, each 300 g
Salt
¼ cup clarified butter (p.311)
Lemon butter (p.307)
1 lemon, thinly sliced, or
    quartered

PREPARATION TIME: 30 minutes
COOKING TIME: 10 minutes
SERVES: four

Sole - Grilled or Fried

Local sole is available throughout the year. West Coast soles can be as long as 80 cm and the flesh is firmer and more flavoursome than that of the smaller East Coast sole. Soles vary in size, but most cooks prefer a medium (300 g) fish as it fits easily into a frying pan and feeds one person adequately.

FRIED SOLE

Sprinkle the fish with salt, then coat lightly with flour. Heat half the butter in a frying pan. Fry for 5 minutes on each side until brown and cooked, turning once. Drain and put on a hot plate. Add the remaining butter and parsley to the pan. Swirl around until the butter is melted and add a squeeze of lemon juice. Pour over the fish and serve at once.

GRILLED SOLE

Brush the fish with butter and grill for about 5 minutes a side. The cooking time depends on the thickness of the sole. Sprinkle lightly with salt and serve topped with 2–3 pats of lemon butter. Garnish with lemon.

Curried Pickled Fish

Kabeljou, Cape salmon, yellowtail or kingklip are suitable for this dish.
Slice and sprinkle with salt then refrigerate overnight.

Preheat the oven to 160°C. Clean and fillet the fish (yellowtail's leathery skin must be removed). Pack the fish pieces, cut into oblongs about 4 cm x 6 cm, into a deep, oiled oven pan. Sprinkle the fish with salt and pepper, brush it over with a little sunflower oil and then bake it in the oven until it is cooked, about 30 minutes.

Mix the sugar, curry powder, turmeric, 4 teaspoons salt, vinegar and water in a large, flat-bottomed saucepan.

Add the onion rings, chillies, lemon leaves and allspice and cook these ingredients for 20–30 minutes – the onion rings must remain whole and not be allowed to become mushy. Just before removing the saucepan from the stove add the flour, mixed to a smooth paste with a little water. While stirring, bring the sauce to the boil, then simmer for 5 minutes to cook the flour.

Place the fillets of baked fish in layers in a dish and cover each layer completely with the warm curry sauce. Pour over the remaining sauce and allow to cool. Cover the dish and keep it in a cool place for 2–3 days.

2 kg dry-fleshed white fish
Salt and pepper
Sunflower oil
1 cup sugar
3 tablespoons medium-strength curry powder
1 tablespoon turmeric
3 cups malt vinegar
2 cups water
8 medium onions, peeled and sliced into 5 mm thick rings
2 red chillies, seeds removed and chopped
8 lemon leaves
1 tablespoon whole allspice
2-3 tablespoons flour

PREPARATION TIME: 45 minutes
COOKING TIME: 40 minutes
STANDING TIME: 2-3 days
SERVES: eight to ten

This dish will keep for up to a month in the refrigerator. Keep it in a glass container as the curry will discolour plastic.

MEATS

Roast Lamb Dinner

The beloved 'roast dinner' is as popular today as it has been for generations. The only difference is that we cook the lamb a little less than our grandmothers did, so that it remains juicy and pink.

1,8 kg leg of lamb
¼ cup olive oil
Freshly ground black pepper
2 cloves garlic, peeled and
    thinly sliced (optional)
6 potatoes, peeled
    and quartered
1 kg butternut, peeled,
    chopped and seeds
    removed, or sweet potatoes,
    peeled and cut into large
    chunks
Salt
1 tablespoon plain flour
1½ cups beef stock (p.304)
400 g green beans, topped
    and tailed, boiled, to serve
4 small carrots, peeled
    and thickly sliced on the
    diagonal, boiled, to serve

PREPARATION TIME: 20 minutes
COOKING TIME: 1¾ hours
SERVES: six

Preheat the oven to 220°C. Place the lamb in a large roasting pan and brush it all over with a little of the oil. Season well with pepper. If you are using the garlic, make 1-cm-deep slits with a small, sharp knife in the leg of lamb, and press a piece of garlic into each slit with your fingers. Roast the lamb for 15 minutes, then reduce the oven temperature to 180°C.

Meanwhile, place the potatoes and butternut or sweet potatoes on a board and brush with the remaining oil. Season with salt and pepper. Arrange the potatoes around the lamb and roast the lamb and potatoes for 30 minutes. Add the butternut or sweet potatoes to the roasting pan and roast for a further 40 minutes (for medium-cooked lamb). Transfer the lamb to a carving plate, cover loosely with foil and set aside to rest. Transfer the vegetables to a large, well-greased roasting pan. Increase the oven temperature to 230°C and return them to the oven for 10 minutes to crisp up.

Meanwhile, make the gravy. Skim off all but about 2 tablespoons of the fat from the juices remaining in the roasting pan. Place the pan on the stove over medium heat. Add the flour and cook, stirring with a wooden spoon and scraping the base of the pan to loosen any crisp bits, for 1–2 minutes, or until the flour just starts to brown. Gradually stir in the stock until well combined. Increase the heat to high and bring to the boil. Reduce the heat to medium-high and boil, uncovered, for 5 minutes, or until the gravy thickens.

Carve the lamb and serve with the butternut or sweet potatoes, potatoes, carrots, beans and gravy.

Pot Roast

Beef braised slowly in a flavoursome liquid of stock, vegetables and spices becomes wonderfully rich and succulent.

1–1,5 kg braising beef
    (aitchbone or topside),
    trimmed
1 tablespoon vegetable oil
20 g butter
1 large onion, peeled
    and chopped
2 large carrots, chopped
1 x 410 g tin diced tomatoes,
    undrained
½ cup beef stock (p.304)
2 bay leaves
½ teaspoon salt
½ teaspoon ground cumin
¼ teaspoon black pepper
½ cup sour cream (smetena)
2 tablespoons plain flour
Hot cooked noodles, to serve

PREPARATION TIME: 15 minutes
COOKING TIME: 2 hours 40 minutes
SERVES: six to eight

Preheat the oven to 180°C. Use string to tie the beef into a neat, compact shape. Heat the oil and butter in a flameproof casserole on top of the stove. Add the meat and cook on medium-high heat, turning it several times, for 6 to 10 minutes, or until it is well browned. Remove the meat, add the onion and carrot, cover and cook on low heat for 5 minutes.

Add the tomatoes, beef stock, bay leaves, salt, cumin and pepper. Return the meat to the casserole, cover and cook in the oven, basting occasionally with the liquid, for 2½ to 3 hours, or until tender. Transfer the meat to a platter; cover with foil and keep warm. Discard the bay leaves and skim the fat from the liquid.

In a small bowl, stir the sour cream and flour together; stir into the liquid in the casserole. Cook over medium heat, stirring constantly, for 3 minutes, or until thickened (do not boil). Serve the sauce with the sliced meat over hot cooked noodles.

VARIATION

Daube de Boeuf à la Provençale: Substitute 2 tablespoons olive oil for the vegetable oil and butter. Cook an extra sliced onion, 3 peeled and chopped cloves of garlic and 125 g diced bacon in the oil. Remove these before browning the meat, then return them to the pan and proceed with the pot roast recipe, using half red wine and half beef stock for the liquid and replacing the cumin with a bouquet garni (see p.310) that includes a strip of orange rind. Omit the sour cream and flour finish to the sauce.

FACING PAGE: *Roast lamb dinner*

TOMATO BREDIE

700 g shoulder of mutton, cut into pieces

2 tablespoons sunflower oil

2 onions, peeled and sliced

2 cloves garlic, crushed

½ cup beef stock (p.304) or red wine

2 cm piece of fresh ginger, peeled and finely chopped

4 cloves

2 cinnamon sticks

½ green or red chilli, seeded and chopped

700 g (about 4 large) ripe tomatoes, skinned and chopped

1 tablespoon tomato paste

2 teaspoons brown sugar

Salt and black pepper

3 potatoes, peeled and quartered

PREPARATION TIME: 1 hour

COOKING TIME: 2-2½ hours

SERVES: four

PUMPKIN BREDIE

1 kg dry pumpkin

2 tablespoons sunflower oil

700 g shoulder of mutton, cut into pieces

2 medium onions, peeled and sliced

1 cm piece fresh ginger, peeled and finely chopped

½ green or red chilli, seeded and chopped

1 clove garlic, crushed

2 cardamom seeds, pounded

2 coriander seeds, pounded

150-200 ml water, or half water and half white wine

1 tablespoon brown sugar

2,5 cm cinnamon stick

Salt and white pepper

1 tablespoon lemon juice or white wine

PREPARATION TIME: 45 minutes

COOKING TIME: 2-2½ hours

SERVES: four

Four Bredies

Bredies are virtually meals in themselves and need little more than a bowl of white rice as an accompaniment. Although salads, sambals and chutneys are often served with the bredie, take care not to eclipse the subtle flavours.

ABOUT BREDIES

Fat mutton rib is the traditional meat to use for bredies, the meat being cut into 6 cm squares. However, neck or best-end-of-neck chops are equally acceptable. The essence of making a tasty bredie is long, slow cooking for a complete marriage of flavours.

Traditionally mutton fat or butter is used for the braising of the meat and onions, but these recipes use a lighter sunflower oil. Purists can use butter or mutton fat.

Very little additional liquid is used in a bredie, the flavour deriving from the meat and vegetable juices. It is essential to shake or gently stir the bredie while cooking. The water or water and wine mixture should be used only to prevent the bredie from sticking to the pot. There should be no actual gravy.

TOMATO BREDIE

Heat the oil in a cast-iron pot or casserole and brown the meat, then set aside. Brown the onions and then return the meat with the garlic to the pot. Add a little of the stock or wine, cover and simmer very slowly for about ½ hour, shaking the pot occasionally and adding more stock to prevent the meat from sticking to the pot.

Skim off the excess fat. Sprinkle the spices over the meat and layer the tomatoes. Stir in the tomato paste, brown sugar and season. Scatter the potatoes on top. Cover and simmer on low heat for another 2 hours. (It can also be cooked, covered, in a low oven.) Remove the lid, and if sauce is not thick enough, simmer uncovered until the tomato sauce has thickened.

PUMPKIN BREDIE

Peel the pumpkin and cut into 5 cm cubes. Heat the oil and brown the meat in the pot with the onions, ginger, chilli, garlic, cardamom and coriander. Pour on a little of the water, or water and wine mixture, and cover. Simmer on a very low heat for 1½ hours, shaking from time to time and adding liquid when necessary.

Add the pumpkin, sugar, cinnamon stick, salt, pepper and a little extra liquid. Cover and simmer slowly, stirring carefully, or shaking from time to time, until the pumpkin is soft and the meat is tender (about 30 minutes).

There should be very little liquid, so watch the pot carefully and remove the cover to evaporate excess moisture if necessary.

Skim off any excess fat and add the lemon juice or white wine. Correct the seasoning.

GREEN BEAN BREDIE

Trim and cut the beans in diagonal pieces about 4 cm long.

Heat the oil and brown the meat a few pieces at a time, then set aside. Brown the onions and then return all the meat to the pot with the garlic, chilli, basil and nutmeg. Add a little of the water or water and wine mixture.

Cover and simmer very slowly (shaking occasionally) for 1½ hours until the meat is tender. Then add the beans, potatoes, sugar (if used), salt, pepper and a little more liquid, stirring the vegetables into the bredie. Cover and cook for 30 minutes.

Remove the lid and cook until the bredie is sufficiently dry, and the meat and vegetables are tender. Be careful when adding liquid after the beans have been added as they sometimes give off a lot of liquid themselves.

When the bredie is done, skim off any excess fat, add the lemon juice and season.

WATERBLOMMETJIE BREDIE

Trim the stalks from the waterblommetjie buds or flowers and wash well. Rinse and put into a bowl of water to which 1 tablespoon of salt has been added. Leave to soak for 2–3 hours (or overnight).

Heat the oil and brown the meat a few pieces at a time. Return all the meat to the pot and add the onions, garlic and chopped chilli. Stir until the onion is soft and brown.

FACING PAGE: *Tomato bredie*

Drain and rinse the waterblommetjie buds or flowers, and add to the meat with the chopped sorrel or lemon juice and the nutmeg. Add 100 ml or so of the wine, or water and wine mixture, place the potatoes on top, then cover and cook gently for 1½ to 2 hours, or until the meat is tender. Periodically add more liquid and shake the pot to prevent the meat from sticking to the bottom. Avoid stirring the bredie, as this can break up the flowers.

After 1½ to 2 hours, season the bredie. If there is too much moisture, cook uncovered until the consistency is right. Skim off any excess fat before serving and add the lemon juice.

GREEN BEAN BREDIE

300 g green beans

700 g shoulder of mutton, cut into pieces

2 tablespoons sunflower oil

2 medium onions, peeled and thinly sliced

1 clove garlic, crushed

½ green or red chilli, seeded and chopped

1 teaspoon dried basil or a handful of fresh chopped basil

¼ teaspoon grated nutmeg

200 ml water or half water and half wine

2 medium quartered potatoes

1 teaspoon sugar (optional)

Salt and black pepper

1 tablespoon lemon juice

PREPARATION TIME: 1 hour

COOKING TIME: 2-2½ hours

SERVES: four

WATERBLOMMETJIE BREDIE

1-2 bunches waterblommetjies

Salt and black pepper

2 tablespoons oil

700 g shoulder of mutton, cut into pieces

2 medium onions, peeled and sliced

1 clove garlic, crushed

½ green or red chilli, seeded and chopped

3 stalks wild sorrel, well-washed and finely chopped, or 4 teaspoons lemon juice

¼ teaspoon grated nutmeg

200 ml water or half water and half wine

1 large or 2 medium potatoes, peeled and quartered

1 teaspoon sugar (optional)

Salt and black pepper

1 tablespoon lemon juice

SOAKING TIME: 2-3 hours

PREPARATION TIME: 1 hour

COOKING TIME: 2-2½ hours

SERVES: four

FOR THE STEW

⅓ cup plain flour

¼ teaspoon salt

¼ teaspoon freshly ground
   black pepper

1 kg stewing steak, trimmed
   of fat and cut into
   2–3 cm cubes

4 tablespoons sunflower oil

4 medium carrots, peeled,
   halved crossways
   and quartered

3 medium onions, peeled
   and quartered

2 small turnips, peeled
   and diced

3¼ cups beef stock (p.304)

1 bay leaf

4 fresh thyme sprigs

FOR THE DUMPLINGS

1 cup self-raising flour

Pinch of salt

4 tablespoons butter

1 egg, beaten

1 tablespoon chopped parsley

About 4 tablespoons water

PREPARATION TIME: 30 minutes

COOKING TIME: 2½ hours

SERVES: four

*The secret of light
dumplings is to keep
them steaming on top of
the gently simmering
liquid and never to crowd
the pot.*

Beef Stew with Parsley Dumplings

Delicious, light dumplings give added flavour to this old favourite.

Sift the flour, salt and pepper onto a plate, add the beef in two batches and toss it well to coat thoroughly. Heat half the oil in a large saucepan until sizzling, add half the beef cubes and cook over medium heat, turning frequently, until evenly browned. Remove the meat from the saucepan with a slotted spoon and put on a plate. Fry the rest of the meat in the oil that is left in the saucepan, then add to the first batch.

Heat the remaining oil in the saucepan, add the carrots and onions and the diced turnips and cook, stirring frequently, until the onions have softened. Return the browned meat to the saucepan with any remaining flour and cook for 1 minute. Gradually stir in the beef stock, add the bay leaf and thyme and bring to the boil, stirring continuously. Reduce the heat to very low, and simmer the stew, covered, for 2 hours, stirring occasionally.

To make the dumplings, sift the flour with the salt. Rub in the butter. Beat the egg with the parsley and stir in. Add enough water to form a soft dough. With floured hands, divide the dough into eight to ten equal portions and roll each lightly into a ball. Add the dumplings to the gently simmering stew, spacing them well apart. Cover and cook the stew for a further 20 minutes, or until the dumplings have puffed up and are cooked through. Remove the bay leaf and thyme and serve immediately.

GRANDMA'S SPICE BOX

Spices to flavour curries, boboties, spicy soetkoekies and many other dishes were kept in a handy metal spice box. This interesting piece of kitchen history from the Joubert House Museum in Montagu has six wedge-shaped airtight boxes which fit together like the slices of a cake with a handy little grater in the middle for grating nutmeg or mace.

---

1 tablespoon sunflower oil

250 g boneless lamb, trimmed and cut into 2 cm cubes

1 medium onion, peeled and thinly sliced

2 tablespoons curry powder

2 cloves garlic, peeled and crushed

¼ cup plain flour

1½ cups chopped potato

1½ cups beef stock (p.304)

1 cup sliced celery

½ cup grated carrot

1 tablespoon firmly packed light brown sugar

1 teaspoon each dry mustard and ground ginger

½ teaspoon salt

¼ teaspoon crushed dried chilli flakes

Hot cooked rice, to serve

Boiled green peas, to serve

Cashews and/or peanuts, shredded coconut, raisins and chopped preserved ginger, to accompany

Lamb Curry

Earlier cooks in this part of the world knew little of authentic Indian curries, but their 'English-style' curries were, nevertheless, good eating.

Heat the oil in a large frying pan on medium-high heat. Add the meat, onion, curry powder and garlic and cook for 10 minutes, or until the meat is browned. Stir in the flour. Stir in the potato, beef stock, celery, carrot, brown sugar, mustard, ginger, salt and crushed chilli flakes. Bring to the boil. Reduce the heat and simmer, covered, for 30–40 minutes, or until the meat is tender.

Serve the curry with hot cooked rice and peas. Accompany with bowls of nuts, coconut, raisins and chopped preserved ginger.

PREPARATION TIME: 25 minutes

COOKING TIME: 45 minutes

SERVES: four

2 tablespoons butter or oil

1 onion, peeled and
    finely chopped

500 g lean minced beef

3 tablespoons plain flour

1/3 cup bought tomato sauce

1 tablespoon Worcestershire
    sauce

1 1/4 cups beef stock (p.304)

3 tablespoons chopped
    fresh parsley

Salt and freshly ground
    black pepper

2 x basic shortcrust pastry
    recipe (p.311), or ready-
    made frozen shortcrust
    pastry

1,5 x basic puff pastry recipe
    (p.311), or ready-made
    frozen puff pastry

1 egg, beaten

PREPARATION TIME: 20 minutes

COOLING TIME: 3 hours

COOKING TIME: 55 minutes

SERVES: four

Meat Pies

*The perfect meat pie has a base of shortcrust pastry for tenderness,
a puff pastry lid for crispness, and a well-flavoured filling.*

Heat the butter or oil in a medium frying pan. Add the onion and cook, stirring often, until the onion is soft. Add the minced beef, increase the heat to high and cook, stirring with a wooden spoon to break up any lumps for 6–8 minutes, or until the mince is brown. Sprinkle the flour over the meat and cook for 1 minute. Add the tomato sauce, Worcestershire sauce and beef stock. Bring to the boil, reduce the heat to medium and simmer, stirring occasionally to prevent the meat from sticking to the base of the pan, for 10 minutes, or until the sauce is thick. Stir in the parsley and season with salt and pepper. Remove from the heat and set aside to cool completely.

Preheat the oven to 200°C. Using a small plate about 17 cm in diameter as a guide, cut four circles from the shortcrust pastry and use them to line the base and sides of four 1-cup pie tins. Fill the pastry with the meat mixture – avoid spilling any on the edges.

Using the same plate as a guide, cut four circles from the puff pastry. Brush the shortcrust pastry edges of the pies with water to moisten and top with the puff pastry circles. Press the pastry edges together to secure. Trim the excess pastry with a sharp knife and crimp the edges. Cut a small cross in the centre of each pie and brush the top with beaten egg.

Bake the pies in the preheated oven for 10 minutes, reduce the oven temperature to 180°C and bake for a further 20 minutes, or until the pastry is puffed and golden.

Serve the pies immediately with creamy mashed potato and boiled green peas and pass some extra tomato sauce separately, if desired.

Heavenly Hamburgers

Hamburgers became hugely popular when American troops spread the word during World War II. Before that, we called minced beef patties 'rissoles' or 'frikkadels' and served them with gravy and vegetables.

1 thick slice white bread,
    crusts removed, soaked
    in 1/4 cup milk

500 g lean minced beef

1 onion, peeled and
    finely chopped

1 egg, beaten

1/4 teaspoon each salt and
    black pepper

1/4 cup plain flour seasoned
    with salt and black pepper

Vegetable oil, for frying

6 hamburger rolls, toasted

2 tomatoes, sliced

6 slices cooked or
    tinned beetroot

6 lettuce leaves

PREPARATION TIME: 10 minutes

COOKING TIME: 10 minutes

SERVES: six

Squeeze the bread almost dry, put it in a large bowl and mash with a fork. Add the beef, onion, egg, salt and pepper and mix together lightly. Divide the mixture into six equal portions, shape into patties and dust with the seasoned flour.

In a large frying pan, heat enough oil to come halfway up the patties and fry the patties for about 4 minutes on each side, or until cooked through. Drain on paper towels.

Serve the patties on the toasted rolls with the tomato and beetroot slices and lettuce leaves. You can spark up your hamburgers with other additions, such as fried onions, sliced Cheddar cheese, gherkins, a fried egg, fried bacon, mayonnaise and barbecue sauce (see p.307). Don't be afraid to ring the changes on your burgers, just don't make them so high that they're difficult to eat.

VARIATION

Rissoles: To prepare rissoles, add 2 teaspoons finely chopped fresh herbs, such as thyme, marjoram, parsley and origanum, to the hamburger mixture, form into rissoles and fry as for the hamburgers. When the rissoles are cooked, remove them from the frying pan and drain them on paper towels.

Pour off the fat from the pan, add 1 cup beef stock (see p.304) and boil briskly, stirring and scraping any browned residue off the bottom of the pan, until the sauce has thickened slightly. Return the rissoles to the pan, reheat briefly and serve them with mashed potato and a green vegetable.

FACING PAGE: *Meat pies (foreground)
and hamburgers (centre)*

4 steaks (fillet, entrecôte or
   rump) about 1,5 cm thick
3 tablespoons black
   peppercorns (or buy ready
   crushed pepppercorns)
2 tablespoons sunflower oil
50 g butter
Salt
2 tablespoons brandy
½ cup thick cream

PREPARATION TIME: 10 minutes

COOKING TIME: 5 minutes for
   rare steaks; 8-10 minutes for
   medium-rare steaks; 12
   minutes for well-done steaks

SERVES: four

Pepper Steak

*Pepper steak is a great South African favourite. Entrecôte and rump steak will need slight
tenderising before frying.*

Trim any gristle, untidy bits and excess fat
from the steaks (though a little fat left on
entrecôte and rump steaks helps to keep the
meat succulent). Tenderise the entrecôte and
rump steaks by placing them between 2 sheets
of wax paper and pounding them on both sides
with a wooden hammer before frying.

Crush the peppercorns coarsely in a mortar,
or use a rolling pin on a wooden board. Press
the ground pepper into the surface of the meat
on both sides.

Heat the sunflower oil in a heavy frying pan
until it is smoking hot, add half the butter and
cook the steaks over a high heat for 2 minutes,
sealing and browning on both sides.

Turn down the heat and cook for a further
3–10 minutes, according to taste. Do not cook
too many steaks at a time or the temperature
of the pan will be too low to seal the meat

properly. Transfer the steaks to a heated plate
with a slotted spoon and salt them lightly.
Keep them warm while you make the sauce.

Add the brandy to the pan juices, scrape in
all the crusty brown leftovers and bring to the
boil. Add the remaining butter and slowly stir
in the cream. Simmer to thicken the sauce
and season lightly to taste. Pour the sauce over
the steaks and serve immediately.

VARIATION

If you prefer a sauce which does not
incorporate cream, add 75 ml dry white wine
and 75 ml beef stock to the pan, heat it to
boiling point and scrape in the brown bits.
Then add 60 ml brandy, boil briskly for a
minute or so, and season to taste. Pour the
sauce over the steak and serve immediately.

*For a milder taste,
use tinned green
(Madagascar)
peppercorns instead
of black peppercorns.
Do not press them onto
the meat, but add 2-3
tablespoons to the sauce
together with the cream.*

IRELAND'S OFFERING

It was Irish immigrants and seamen who brought Irish stew to Liverpool, where it rapidly became as popular as in the old country. In Ireland, it was made with kid because no one would dream of killing a valuable sheep. Liverpudlians, however, firmly preferred mutton, and this is the version which has spread around the world.

Irish Stew

Any additions to the few ingredients in this dish would detract from the pure flavour and turn it into just another stew.

Arrange half the meat in the bottom of a medium, flameproof casserole and cover with half the onions followed by half the potatoes, seasoning each layer with salt and pepper and a little thyme. Repeat the layers, seasoning as before and finishing with potatoes. Pour over enough water to just cover the top layer.

Bring to the boil, reduce the heat, cover and cook very gently for 1½ hours, or until the meat and potatoes are tender. Check frequently to make sure that the water has not evaporated and add a little more, if necessary. Remove the lid and brown the top layer of potatoes under a hot grill. Serve with the traditional accompaniment of steamed red cabbage, if desired.

This stew can also be cooked in a moderate oven (180°C) for 2 hours.

1 kg sliced neck of lamb,
  trimmed of fat

4 medium onions,
  peeled and sliced

6 medium potatoes,
  peeled and sliced

½ teaspoon salt

Freshly ground black pepper

1 tablespoon chopped
  fresh thyme

2 cups water

Fresh thyme sprigs,
  to garnish

PREPARATION TIME: 20 minutes

COOKING TIME: 1½ hours

SERVES: four

Roast Leg of Pork with Apple Sauce

A succulent roast of pork and potatoes makes a magnificent treat for a family celebration or a winter dinner party. The sage and allspice in the apple sauce combine perfectly with the flavour of the pork to make it both aromatic and appetising.

FOR THE PORK

2,5–3 kg leg of pork
2–3 tablespoons olive oil
2 teaspoons salt
2 fresh rosemary sprigs, broken into small pieces

FOR THE POTATOES

8 medium potatoes, peeled and halved or quartered, depending on size, scored deeply all over with a fork
1 teaspoon salt
3/4 cup vegetable oil

FOR THE APPLE SAUCE

3 small cooking apples, peeled, cored and sliced
1 tablespoon water
1/4 teaspoon ground allspice
2 teaspoons soft brown sugar
4 dessert apples
3 tablespoons lemon juice
90 g butter
2 tablespoons chopped fresh sage

FOR THE GRAVY

2 tablespoons plain flour
2 cups chicken stock (p.305)
4 teaspoons redcurrant jelly
3 tablespoons dry sherry
Fresh sage sprigs, to garnish

PREPARATION TIME: 30 minutes
COOKING TIME: 3 hours
SERVES: eight

A sauce of apple purée flavoured with some diced tinned beetroot and a little horseradish is delicious on cold, leftover roast pork.

THE PORK

Preheat the oven to 200°C. Weigh the pork and calculate the cooking time, allowing 25 minutes per 500 g plus 25 minutes. Wipe the meat with paper towels. Using a very sharp knife, make diagonal scores in the skin across or vertically down 5–10 mm apart and about 3 mm deep. Put the meat in a roasting pan and, to encourage the skin to 'crackle', rub it all over with the olive oil, then rub in the salt and scatter with rosemary.

Roast the pork in the centre of the oven for 30 minutes to start the skin crisping, then reduce the oven temperature to 180°C. Cook, basting every 30 minutes with the fat from the bottom of the pan, until the meat is well done.

THE POTATOES

About 1 hour before the pork is due to come out of the oven, put the potatoes into a large saucepan, cover with cold water, add the salt and bring to the boil. Drain well, return to the pan and shake over high heat for 1–2 minutes until they are dry.

Pour the oil over the potatoes while they are still in the saucepan and coat well. Place the potatoes in a roasting pan on the shelf above the pork and roast for 1 1/4 hours, until crisp and golden. When the pork is cooked, remove it from the oven and leave it to rest in a warm place. Increase the oven temperature to 220°C and let the potatoes finish cooking.

THE APPLE SAUCE

About 30 minutes before the end of the pork's cooking time, put the apples into a small saucepan with the water, allspice and sugar. Cover and cook gently until soft and pulpy.

Remove from the heat and mash with a fork. Peel and core the dessert apples, cut in half horizontally and brush each half all over with the lemon juice. Melt the butter in a large frying pan, add the sage, then place the apple halves in the pan, cut sides up. Top each half with the apple sauce and baste well with the sage butter. Cover the pan and cook gently, basting occasionally, for 10 minutes, or until the apples are just softened. Remove from the heat and keep warm.

THE GRAVY

At the end of the calculated cooking time, pierce the pork with a skewer at the thickest part. The juices should run clear with no trace of pink. (If necessary, continue roasting until done.) Lift the cooked pork from the roasting pan onto a large, heated serving platter, cover loosely with foil and allow to stand while making the gravy.

Skim off all but 2 tablespoons of the fat from the roasting pan, then stir the flour into the fat and juices remaining in the pan. Cook over medium heat until well browned but not burned. Gradually add the chicken stock and bring to the boil, stirring continuously and scraping any browned residue off the bottom of the pan. Strain the gravy through a fine sieve into a saucepan, then blend in the redcurrant jelly and dry sherry, simmer for 5 minutes and season to taste.

TO SERVE

Arrange the apple halves around the pork, garnish with the sprigs of sage and serve with the roast potatoes and gravy. Buttered cabbage or green peas make a good accompaniment.

A smaller or larger joint of pork, such as a loin, shoulder or neck can be cooked in the same way. Your butcher will roll and tie it securely with kitchen string for you. Calculate the cooking time according to the weight of the joint.

FACING PAGE: *Roast leg of pork*

MAGIC MINCERS

Mechanical mincers started appearing in shops and catalogues in the 1850s. The design we know today was developed in the 1880s by a London ironmongery firm, Spong and Co. These hand mincers have a selection of attachments for mincing or slicing meat and vegetables. A small version was sold for use at the dinner table by those who had lost their teeth!

5 medium boiling potatoes,
   peeled and quartered

2/3 cup pouring cream
   or creamy milk

60 g butter

Salt and freshly ground
   black pepper

Freshly grated nutmeg

2 tablespoons vegetable oil

1 medium onion, peeled
   and chopped

1 clove garlic, peeled
   and crushed

2 teaspoons Worcestershire
   sauce

2 tablespoons bought
   tomato sauce

2 tablespoons chopped fresh
   mixed herbs (parsley,
   thyme, marjoram, mint)

500 g cooked lamb, trimmed
   of fat and minced

2/3 cup lamb gravy or beef
   stock (p.304)

PREPARATION TIME: 40 minutes

COOKING TIME: 45 minutes

SERVES: four

Shepherd's Pie

This is a favourite way to transform the leftovers from the weekend roast into a satisfying meal for all the family. Shepherd's pie is made with lamb, while cottage pie is made with beef.

Preheat the oven to 180°C. Boil or steam the potatoes until tender, then drain and mash well. Heat the cream or milk and half the butter in a saucepan and beat into the mashed potatoes. Season well with the salt, pepper and nutmeg. Cover and keep warm.

Heat the oil in a saucepan, add the onion and garlic and cook over medium heat for 5 minutes, or until soft and golden. Stir in the Worcestershire sauce, tomato sauce and herbs. Stir in the meat and gravy or stock. Transfer to an ovenproof dish and spoon the potatoes carefully over the surface. Smooth the potatoes, then fork the surface decoratively.

Dot the remaining butter over the top of the potato and bake the shepherd's pie in the centre of the oven for 45 minutes, or until golden brown and thoroughly heated through.

Bobotie

Bobotie is one of the best known South African dishes. Serve with fluffy white rice, apricot blatjang (chutney) and a cucumber or apple sambal.

Preheat the oven to 180°C. Soak the bread in milk and grease an ovenproof dish. Heat the oil and slowly cook the onion until soft, but not coloured. Add the curry powder and turmeric and cook for a minute. Remove from the heat and mix with the meat, vinegar or lemon juice, sugar, raisins, fruit chutney, grated lemon rind (if used), and one egg.

Squeeze the milk from the bread, reserving the milk, and mix with the mince. Season with salt and pepper. Spoon the mince mixture into the buttered dish. Stick the almonds and lemon leaves (twisted into little cones) into the meat. Bake for 30 minutes.

Lightly beat the remaining egg with the milk – add enough milk to make a full cup – and carefully pour onto the meat (over the back of a spoon). Return the dish to the oven and bake for a further 30 minutes, or until the custard has set and browned.

CUCUMBER SAMBAL

Sprinkle the grated cucumber with salt and allow to stand for at least 30 minutes to draw out the water. Squeeze out all the water. Add the chillies, garlic and mixed sugar and vinegar.

APPLE SAMBAL

Sprinkle the grated apples with the salt and leave to stand for at least 30 minutes to draw out some of the water, then drain thoroughly. Add the garlic and chillies.

1 slice white bread (3 cm thick)
1 cup milk
2 tablespoons sunflower oil
2 medium onions, chopped
1 tablespoon medium-strength curry powder
1 teaspoon turmeric
1 kg lean mince beef or lamb
2 tablespoons white vinegar or lemon juice
1 tablespoon sugar
75 g seedless raisins
3 tablespoons fruit chutney
Grated rind of 1 lemon (optional)
2 eggs
12 blanched almonds, halved
6 fresh lemon leaves

PREPARATION TIME: 30 minutes
COOKING TIME: 1¼ hours
SERVES: six

CUCUMBER SAMBAL

2 fresh cucumbers, peeled and coarsely grated
2 teaspoons salt
2 green chillies, seeded and sliced
1 clove garlic, crushed
1 teaspoon sugar
4 teaspoons vinegar

PREPARATION TIME: 15 minutes
STANDING TIME: at least 30 minutes
MAKES: 2 cups

APPLE SAMBAL

3 firm sour apples, coarsely grated
1 teaspoon salt
2 cloves garlic, crushed
2 green chillies, seeded and sliced

PREPARATION TIME: 15 minutes
STANDING TIME: at least 30 minutes
MAKES: 2 cups

8 best end neck of lamb,
divided into chops and
trimmed of excess fat

3 medium onions,
peeled and sliced

4 medium carrots,
peeled and sliced

Salt and freshly ground
black pepper

4 tablespoons chopped
fresh parsley

12 fresh oysters (optional)

5 medium potatoes, peeled
and thinly sliced

2 cups chicken stock (p.305)

1 tablespoon fresh
thyme leaves, or 1 teaspoon
dried thyme leaves

30 g butter

PREPARATION TIME: 30 minutes

COOKING TIME: 2½ hours

SERVES: four

Lancashire Hotpot

*In England this dish was traditionally made with oysters, although this
is very seldom seen nowadays.*

Preheat the oven to 180°C. Layer the lamb chops, onions and carrots in a large casserole, sprinkling each layer with salt, pepper and chopped parsley. Put the oysters (if used) on top and spoon over their juices. Arrange the potatoes, overlapping in a double layer, on top of the oysters. Pour over the stock and sprinkle with salt and pepper and the thyme.

Cover the casserole and cook the hotpot in the centre of the oven for 2 hours, then increase the temperature to 230°C. Remove the lid from the casserole, dot the potatoes with the butter and continue to cook, uncovered, for a further 30 minutes, or until the potatoes are golden brown. Serve immediately with steamed cabbage or spinach, if desired.

Mushrooms can be substituted for the oysters as a way of adding richness to the hotpot.

A cooked glazed ham will keep well, covered and refrigerated, for more than a week. It is best wrapped in clean muslin or cotton, which prevents the ham drying out but allows it to breathe. Greaseproof paper can also be used, but not plastic wrap.

Baked Ham with Pineapple & Mustard Glaze

Long before turkey became a Christmas dinner institution, there was baked ham. The ham can be prepared for glazing the day before, then covered and refrigerated.

Buy a pre-cooked ham on the bone. Allow plenty of time for the preparation – it is not difficult but it is a little messy. Strip off the brown skin, trying not to disturb the layer of creamy fat beneath it. Score the surface of the fat into small diamonds and stud each diamond with a clove. Line a large roasting pan with a double thickness of aluminium foil, bringing the foil over the edges of the pan. (This will catch drips of glaze falling off the ham and prevent flare-ups. It also means a clean roasting pan at the end of cooking time.) Put the ham in the pan, making sure the foil stays upright.

Preheat the oven to 225°C. Mix the glaze ingredients together, pour over the ham and put it in the oven. If you are glazing for appearance only, it will take about 45 minutes.

As parts of the fat take on enough colour, a rich golden brown with slightly charred edges, place small pieces of foil on top to deflect the heat. If you want to serve the ham hot, allow an hour longer for it to heat through (about 1½–1¾ hours in total), but lower the heat to 200°C after 1 hour. (You may need to protect the entire surface of the ham with foil after 50–60 minutes. The ham should be basted with the glaze every 20 minutes or so.)

Serve the ham hot or at room temperature. Use a long, thin-bladed knife to slice it. Cut the first slice vertically, down to the bone, in the centre of the leg, then slice at a slight angle on either side of this cut. This gives every slice of ham (until you get closer to the bone) a rim of glaze-encrusted fat.

FOR THE HAM
1 ham, cooked on the bone
Cloves
Aluminium foil

FOR THE GLAZE
1 cup runny honey
¼ cup pineapple juice
1 cup soft brown sugar
2 teaspoons Dijon mustard

PREPARATION TIME: about 1 hour
COOKING TIME: ¾–1¾ hours
SERVES: 20–25 (using a 7 kg ham)

Meat Loaf with Mushroom Sauce

*The meat and vegetables in this attractive luncheon loaf
provide many intriguing textures and flavours.*

6 baby carrots,
   halved lengthways
5 baby courgettes,
   halved lengthways
500 g minced lean beef
500 g minced pork
250 g bacon rashers, rind
   removed, chopped
1 cup soft breadcrumbs
   (p.310)
6 button mushrooms,
   wiped and chopped
Finely grated rind of ½ lemon
½ teaspoon ground mace
¼ teaspoon cayenne pepper
Salt
1 egg, beaten
¾–1 cup milk
30 g butter
6 button mushrooms,
   wiped and sliced
1 tablespoon plain flour
Fresh herbs, to garnish

PREPARATION TIME: 30 minutes
COOKING TIME: 1 hour
SERVES: six

Preheat the oven to 180°C. Line a loaf tin (20 x 10 x 6 cm) with nonstick baking paper, then arrange the carrot and courgette halves in an attractive pattern in the bottom of the tin.

Put the minced meat into a large bowl and add the bacon, breadcrumbs, chopped mushrooms, lemon rind, mace, cayenne, salt to taste and the egg. Mix together well and spoon the mixture carefully on top of the layer of vegetables in the loaf tin. Press down gently and smooth the top. Bake in the centre of the oven for 50 minutes to 1 hour, or until the point of a skewer inserted into the centre of the loaf is hot enough when removed to sting the back of your hand.

Remove the tin from the oven, pour the juices off carefully into a measuring jug and make up to 1¼ cups with milk. Run a knife round the sides of the loaf, place a serving dish over the tin and, holding the tin and dish together, reverse and bang on the work surface to drop the loaf out of the tin. Keep warm by covering with the tin while making the sauce.

Melt the butter in a saucepan and cook the sliced mushrooms for 2–3 minutes. Stir in the flour, cook for 1 minute, then gradually add the milk and cooking juice mixture. Bring to the boil, stirring continuously until thickened. Season the sauce to taste with salt and pepper, and simmer for 5 minutes.

Remove the tin and paper from the loaf and garnish with herbs – for example, sage looks good. Pour the sauce into a heated sauceboat and serve.

Frikkadels

*These tasty frikkadels, or savoury meat rissoles, can be made with minced beef on its own,
although the frikkadels will be coarser in texture.*

250 g minced topside
250 g minced lamb or mutton
   (not too fatty)
1 slice white bread, 4 cm
   thick
½ cup milk
1 extra-large egg
1 medium onion, peeled and
   grated
1 teaspoon ground coriander
   or 1 teaspoon grated
   nutmeg
1-2 teaspoons salt
¾ teaspoon freshly ground
   black pepper
Fine dried breadcrumbs
Sunflower oil for frying
3 ripe, firm tomatoes
½ cup boiling water

PREPARATION TIME: 20 minutes
STANDING TIME: 30 minutes
COOKING TIME: 40 minutes
SERVES: four

Mix the meats with a fork. Soak the bread in the milk and mash it, then mix well with all the other ingredients except the breadcrumbs, oil, tomatoes and water.

When well mixed, leave to stand for at least 30 minutes to let the flavours mingle. Remove small quantities of the mixture and lightly roll into 6 cm balls. Roll these in breadcrumbs, shake off the surplus and place the coated meatballs on a board.

Meanwhile, heat a little oil in a saucepan and lift the balls into the saucepan with a spatula. The frikkadels must not be deep-fried – there should be just sufficient oil to sear the bases. Cut two of the tomatoes into 1 cm slices and place a slice of tomato on each frikkadel and lightly dust it with breadcrumbs. Skin the remaining tomato, cut it into small pieces and drop the pieces into the saucepan between the frikkadels: they provide moisture for cooking. Add the boiling water, cover and simmer for 30–40 minutes.

To serve, lift the frikkadels onto a platter and pour over the gravy.

FACING PAGE: *Meat loaf with mushroom sauce*

NEARLY 200 YEARS OF HOT ENGLISH MUSTARD

Mustard dates back to Roman times, but had a coarse texture. In 1720 an Englishwoman - a Mrs Clements - started making and selling smooth mustard. George I's love of this new condiment made it wildly popular, and the stage was set for commercial production. Jeremiah Colman opened his mill in 1814 and produced a smooth, hot mustard which has become known worldwide as Hot English Mustard.

2 tablespoons olive oil

4 rashers bacon, rind removed

2 medium onions, peeled and thinly sliced

3 tablespoons plain flour

½ teaspoon salt

¼ teaspoon freshly ground black pepper

500 g lamb's liver (membrane removed), cut into 4 thin slices

30 g butter

16 large sage leaves

7 tablespoons Madeira

1¼ cups chicken stock (p.305)

PREPARATION TIME: 10 minutes

COOKING TIME: 15 minutes

SERVES: four

Lamb's Liver & Bacon with Sage & Madeira Sauce

This is not only a mouth-watering dish, it is also very easy to prepare and cook when you want to rustle up a meal quickly.

Heat 1 tablespoon of the oil in a large frying pan and fry the bacon rashers until lightly browned on both sides. Drain on paper towels and keep warm. Add the remaining oil to the pan and fry the onions until lightly browned, then push them to the side of the pan.

Meanwhile, mix the flour with the salt and pepper on a plate. Dip the liver, a slice at a time, in the seasoned flour until evenly coated, shaking off the excess. Add the butter to the pan and heat over medium heat until sizzling. Add the liver, sprinkle with half the sage leaves and fry for 2 minutes, or until lightly browned. Turn each piece and cook the other side, sprinkling with the remaining sage. Remove the liver from the pan and set aside.

Stir any remaining flour into the pan, pour in the Madeira and stir, scraping any browned residue off the bottom of the pan. Add the stock and bring to the boil, stirring occasionally. Return the liver to the pan, reduce the heat and simmer for 4–5 minutes, or until the liver is tender but still slightly pink.

Return the bacon to the pan and serve immediately with rice or mashed potatoes and a steamed green vegetable, if desired.

Sosaties

The hot flavour of this traditional Cape Malay dish can be lessened by reducing the chillies used.

1,5 kg leg of mutton, trimmed and cut into 2 cm cubes
250 g mutton fat (trimmed from the leg of mutton) cut into 1 cm cubes (or cubes of bacon)
1 cm piece of fresh ginger, scraped and finely chopped
2 cloves garlic, peeled and finely chopped
30 g butter
2 medium onions, peeled and finely chopped
125 ml water
125 ml red wine vinegar
1 tablespoon curry powder
1 tablespoon sugar
3 bay leaves, bruised
3 orange or lemon leaves, bruised
2 chillies, seeded and chopped
Salt

PREPARATION TIME: 45 minutes
MARINATING TIME: overnight
COOKING TIME: 10-15 minutes
SERVES: six

Put the meat and fat into a bowl with the ginger and garlic. Toss well so that all the meat pieces are coated with the ginger and garlic. Cover and set aside.

Heat the butter in a saucepan and add the onions. Stir-fry until soft and golden, then add the water, vinegar, curry powder and sugar. Bring to the boil and cook for 2 minutes. Leave until quite cold and then pour over the meat.

Add the bay leaves, orange or lemon leaves and chopped chillies and toss the meat well to coat evenly with the liquid. Cover and leave overnight in a cool place. Thread the cubes of meat onto 6–8 skewers, alternating pieces of meat with fat. A hot fire or grill is esssential for cooking the meat, but care must be taken not to overcook or burn the sosaties. Grill for 10–15 minutes, basting from time to time with the marinade. Salt the sosaties after cooking.

VARIATIONS

Dried apricots can be halved and threaded on the skewers with the meat. Plump them up by soaking in the marinade mixture as it cools (not with the meat). Pieces of onion can also be used.

If you don't want to use the traditional pieces of fat on the skewer, add 1/4 cup sunflower oil to the marinade and brush the sosaties with oil before grilling.

This marinade (with the oil added) can also be used on fish sosaties. Add some puréed apricots to the sauce for extra flavour.

BUTCHERS AND HEALTH STANDARDS

W.J. Lillywhite, family butcher in Bloemfontein around the beginning of the 20th century. After the appointment of meat inspectors in 1924, the display of carcasses on the street like this was banned. The Meat Industries Control Board, known as the Meat Board, was established in 1932 to control all aspects of the meat industry. The inspectors are still going strong, but the control board no longer exists.

Beef Braised with Stout

The use of a flour-and-water paste to seal the casserole is an old cooking technique that ensures no flavour or moisture is lost. For a lighter version, use lager instead of stout.

4 cups stout

2 medium onions, peeled and sliced

6 small young carrots, scraped and sliced, or 2 large carrots, peeled and cut into chunks

1,5 kg stewing steak, trimmed of fat and cut into bite-sized cubes

6 very small onions, peeled

125 g belly of pork, thickly sliced

A few thyme sprigs

6 parsley stalks

1 bay leaf

6 allspice berries, crushed

1 clove garlic, peeled and crushed

Salt and freshly ground black pepper

2 cups plain flour

2/3 cup water

PREPARATION TIME: 40 minutes

COOKING TIME: 3 hours

SERVES: six

Preheat the oven to 150°C. Bring the stout to the boil in a saucepan and boil vigorously until reduced to 1 cup. Cover the bottom of a heavy casserole with the sliced onions, then place the carrots on top, followed by the beef, whole onions and pork. Tie the herbs and allspice in a small square of muslin and bury this in the casserole with the garlic. Pour the hot reduced stout into the casserole. Season with a little salt and lots of pepper. Not much liquid will be visible at this stage.

In a small bowl, mix the flour to a smooth, pliable dough with the water. Roll the dough into a long sausage. Place the lid on the casserole, wet the edges with a little water and seal the join with the dough strip.

Cook the casserole in the centre of the oven for 3 hours. Remove the casserole from the oven and break the dough seal. Remove and discard the bag of herbs, stir the meat and vegetables together carefully and serve with potatoes and a green vegetable.

VARIATION

Carbonnade of Beef: Use beer instead of stout, omit the carrots, pork and allspice, and pour 1 cup beef stock (see p.304), flavoured with 1/2 teaspoon each of sugar and nutmeg and 1 teaspoon vinegar, over the ingredients before sealing the casserole with the dough. After discarding the dough seal and bag of herbs, cover the top of the casserole with baguette slices spread with Dijon mustard, pushing them down into the gravy. Cook uncovered for a further 30 minutes (the bread will float to the top and form a brown crust).

Veal Scaloppine with Mushroom Cream Sauce

When Italians opened their first restaurants, veal scaloppine became one of the most popular items on the menu. Home cooks soon discovered that it was an exquisite, simple dish for entertaining.

500 g boneless veal steak, cut into 5-mm-thick slices and trimmed

Salt and black pepper, to taste

2 tablespoons butter

1 1/2 cups sliced fresh mushrooms

1 small onion, peeled and sliced

3/4 cup chicken stock (p.305)

1/3 cup dry white wine

1 tablespoon lemon juice

1/2 teaspoon dried rosemary leaves

1 tablespoon chopped fresh parsley

PREPARATION TIME: 15 minutes

COOKING TIME: 15 minutes

SERVES: four

Cut the veal into serving pieces. Pound both sides of the meat with the flat side of a meat mallet until it is 3 mm thick. Sprinkle with salt and pepper. Melt the butter over medium heat in a large frying pan. Add two of the veal pieces and cook for 1–2 minutes on each side, or until tender. Transfer the veal to a platter; cover with foil and keep warm. Repeat with the remaining veal pieces.

Add the mushrooms and onion to the pan. Cook over medium heat, stirring frequently, for 4 minutes, or until tender. Stir in the stock, wine, lemon juice and rosemary, stirring and scraping any browned residue off the bottom of the pan. Bring to the boil and cook, uncovered, for 5 minutes, or until slightly thickened. Stir in the parsley and pour the sauce over the veal. Serve immediately.

VARIATION

Scaloppine with Lemon Sauce: Dust the flattened and seasoned veal lightly with flour before cooking in the butter, as described. When cooked, set aside on a platter, cover with foil and keep warm. Add 1/3 cup lemon juice and 2 tablespoons chopped parsley to the pan, remove from the heat and swirl in an extra tablespoon of butter bit by bit. Pour over the veal and serve immediately.

FACING PAGE: *Beef braised with stout*

30 g butter

2 medium onions,
    peeled and chopped

2 sticks celery, trimmed
    and chopped

1 tablespoon chopped
    fresh sage

2 small cooking apples,
    peeled, cored and chopped

2½ cups soft white
    breadcrumbs (p.310)

½ cup sultanas or chopped
    pitted dessert prunes

Salt and freshly ground
    black pepper

1 egg, beaten

1,5–1,8 kg loin of pork, boned,
    skin removed and reserved

2½ tablespoons plain flour

1¼ cups beef or vegetable
    stock (p.304)

⅓ cup red wine

4 teaspoons redcurrant jelly

Fresh sage and parsley
    sprigs, to garnish

Preparation time: 30 minutes

Cooking time: 2 hours

Serves: six

Loin of Pork with Sage & Onion Stuffing

For perfect crackling, remove the pork skin, rub it with salt and crisp it in a 230°C oven while you make the gravy. Cut or break the crackling into pieces and serve separately.

Preheat the oven to 190°C. Melt the butter in a frying pan, add the onions and cook on low heat until soft and golden. Put the onions into a bowl and add the celery, sage, chopped apples, breadcrumbs and sultanas or prunes. Season well, then mix in just enough beaten egg to bind the mixture together.

Make a deep horizontal cut the whole length of the thickest part of the loin, open out flat and season well with salt and pepper. Spread the stuffing evenly over the meat, then roll up and tie securely with fine kitchen string at 2–3 cm intervals along its entire length.

Put the meat in a roasting pan, cover with the reserved skin and cook in the centre of the oven, allowing 30 minutes per 500 g of meat. Remove the pork skin for the last 30 minutes of cooking time and baste the pork frequently with the pan juices until the meat is cooked and browned and the juices run clear when it is pierced with a skewer. Transfer the meat from the roasting pan to a heated serving platter and keep hot.

Skim off all but 1 tablespoon of the fat from the juices remaining in the roasting pan. Stir the flour into the juices and gradually stir in the stock and red wine. Bring to the boil, stirring continuously, then reduce the heat, stir in the redcurrant jelly, season to taste and cook for 5 minutes. Strain the gravy through a sieve into a heated gravy boat. Remove the string from the pork, garnish with sage and parsley and serve with the gravy, mashed potatoes and buttered red or green cabbage.

Roll any leftover stuffing into balls and cook alongside the loin for the last 20 minutes.

Crown Roast of Lamb

A crown roast is a splendid showpiece for a special dinner.
If you order it in advance, a butcher will prepare the crown for you.

Preheat the oven to 180°C. Put the veal or pork, the spring onions, parsley, thyme and garlic into a bowl, season well and mix. Fill the crown with the stuffing, then weigh it and calculate the cooking time, allowing 25 minutes per 500 g, plus 30 minutes.

Put the lamb into a roasting pan, rub all over with the oil, sprinkle with rosemary and season well. Cover the top half with foil and roast in the centre of the oven for the time calculated, basting occasionally. Remove the foil for the last 20 minutes to brown the top.

When the crown is uncovered, put all the vegetables into a wide frying pan with the butter, brown sugar and chicken stock or water. Season with salt and bring to the boil, then reduce the heat and cook gently, partly covered, until the vegetables are tender and

the liquid has almost evaporated – shake the pan often towards the end of the cooking time to prevent the vegetables from sticking to it. Remove from the heat, cover and keep hot.

Carefully transfer the crown from the roasting pan to a heated serving platter, cover and keep warm. To make the gravy, skim all but 2 tablespoons of fat from the roasting pan and stir in the flour and veal or chicken stock. Bring to the boil, stirring and scraping any browned residue off the bottom of the pan. Strain the gravy through a sieve into a saucepan and simmer for 5 minutes. Season to taste.

Trim the crown roast with cutlet frills and surround with the glazed vegetables. Serve with the hot gravy and buttered new potatoes. To carve, cut downwards between the bones and serve with a spoonful of the stuffing.

FOR THE CROWN ROAST

250 g minced veal or pork

3 spring onions, peeled and finely chopped

3 tablespoons chopped fresh parsley

1 tablespoon chopped fresh thyme

1 clove garlic, peeled and crushed

Salt and freshly ground black pepper

2 racks best end neck of lamb, 6 bones each, chined and prepared into a crown

3 tablespoons olive oil

2 teaspoons dried rosemary

3 tablespoons plain flour

2 cups veal or chicken stock (p.305)

FOR THE VEGETABLES

6 baby turnips, trimmed and washed

6 button onions, peeled

12 baby carrots, trimmed and washed

6 baby courgettes, washed and halved lengthways

60 g butter

2 tablespoons brown sugar

1¼ cups chicken stock (p.305) or water

PREPARATION TIME: 45 minutes

COOKING TIME: 1¾ hours

SERVES: six

FOR THE BEEF

3,5 kg beef prime rib, chined

4 tablespoons olive oil

1 teaspoon salt

¼ teaspoon freshly ground
    black pepper

1 teaspoon mustard powder

FOR THE ROAST POTATOES

8–10 medium baking potatoes
    (1 for each person), peeled
    and washed

1 teaspoon salt

Lard or vegetable oil,
    if required

FOR THE YORKSHIRE PUDDING

1½ cups plain flour

½ teaspoon salt

2 eggs

1¼ cups milk

FOR THE HORSERADISH SAUCE

4 teaspoons white
    wine vinegar

¾ teaspoon mustard powder

Salt and freshly ground
    white pepper

4 tablespoons finely grated
    peeled fresh horseradish,
    or bottled horseradish

1 cup pouring cream

FOR THE GRAVY

3 tablespoons plain flour

3¼ cups beef stock (p.304)

⅔ cup red wine

PREPARATION TIME: 45 minutes

COOKING TIME: 2 hours

SERVES: eight to ten

Roast Beef with Yorkshire Pudding

*Rich gravy, piquant sauce and roast potatoes join
the traditional combination of succulent roast beef and golden Yorkshire pudding.*

THE MEAT AND POTATOES

Preheat the oven to 220°C. Calculate the meat's cooking time, allowing 10–12 minutes per 500 g for rare meat, 15 minutes per 500 g for medium rare, and 20 minutes per 500 g for well done, all plus an extra 10–12 minutes. Put the beef, fat side up, in a large roasting pan and rub it all over with the oil. Mix the salt, pepper and mustard and rub evenly over the meat. Roast the meat in the centre of the oven for 20 minutes, reduce the temperature to 190°C and continue to cook for the remaining calculated time.

When the meat has been cooking for about 20 minutes, halve or quarter the potatoes, depending on their size, and place in a large saucepan. Cover with cold water, add the salt and bring to the boil. Drain well, return to the pan and shake over high heat for 1–2 minutes.

Remove the meat pan from the oven, spoon the fat from the bottom into a second pan and return the beef to the oven. If necessary, add extra lard or vegetable oil to the second pan to a depth of 5 mm. Heat on the shelf above the meat until the fat sizzles. Carefully add the potatoes, basting until well coated. Roast for about 1¼ hours, turning and basting them every 20 minutes, until they are crisp and golden.

THE BATTER

While the meat is roasting, make the Yorkshire pudding batter. Sift the flour and salt into a bowl, make a well in the centre and put the eggs and a third of the milk into the well. Stir with a wire whisk, gradually incorporating the flour from the sides to make a thick batter, then beat until very smooth. Gradually whisk in the rest of the milk. Cover the bowl and leave to stand for 1 hour.

THE HORSERADISH SAUCE

To make the horseradish sauce, put the wine vinegar, mustard, some salt and pepper and the horseradish into a small bowl and mix well. Whisk the cream until it holds a soft peak, then fold in the horseradish mixture, taking care not to overmix the sauce. Cover and refrigerate until required.

THE YORKSHIRE PUDDING

When the beef is cooked, transfer it to a heated serving dish, cover loosely with foil and allow it to rest while you cook the Yorkshire pudding.

If the potatoes are cooked, remove them from the oven and put them on a heated serving dish. Cover and keep hot. Otherwise, leave them to roast for a little longer while the oven heats up for the Yorkshire pudding.

For the Yorkshire pudding, use a 12-hole patty pan. Increase the oven temperature to 220°C. Take 4 tablespoons of fat from the meat pan and distribute it among the 12 patty holes. Place the patty pan in the centre of the oven and heat until the fat sizzles. Stir the Yorkshire pudding batter, distribute it evenly among the 12 patty holes and then cook for 10 minutes, or until puffed up and golden. (Alternatively, you can make the pudding in a 25 x 28 x 4 cm baking pan, cook it for about 20 minutes and then cut it into pieces.)

THE GRAVY

Meanwhile, make the gravy. Skim all but 2 tablespoons of fat from the meat pan. Stir in the flour and gradually add the stock and wine. Bring to the boil, stirring and scraping up the residue from the bottom of the pan. Strain into a saucepan and simmer, skimming off any fat that rises to the surface, for 5–10 minutes, or until slightly thickened. Season and pour into a heated gravy boat.

TO SERVE

Slice and serve the beef with portions of Yorkshire pudding, gravy, roast potatoes and horseradish sauce, thinned, if necessary, with a little pouring cream or milk. Pass freshly made English mustard separately.

Butterflied Leg of Lamb

1,5 kg leg of lamb, boned and opened up butterfly style
½ cup buttermilk
2 teaspoons coarse sea salt
¾ teaspoon freshly ground black pepper

FOR THE BASTING SAUCE

100 ml melted butter (do not substitute margarine)
2 cloves garlic, finely chopped or put through a garlic press
¾ teaspoon sugar
Juice of ½ lemon

PREPARATION TIME: 15 minutes
MARINATING TIME: 24 hours
COOKING TIME: about 1-1½ hours
SERVES: six to eight

Boning and flattening a leg of lamb has three advantages: it is easier to braai, easier to carve and will feed more people than a leg of lamb which still has a bone.

Place the meat in a glass dish with the buttermilk and turn it a couple of times to coat every part of the meat with the buttermilk. Leave to marinate for 24 hours in the refrigerator.

Next day, remove the meat from the buttermilk and dry it carefully with paper towels. Season it with the coarse sea salt and black pepper.

Make the basting sauce by mixing together the melted butter, garlic, sugar and lemon juice. Place the meat over moderately hot coals and cook for 15 minutes on one side until it is nicely browned, then turn it with a pair of tongs.

Baste the cooked side with the basting sauce. When the second side is nicely browned, turn the meat and baste this freshly cooked side. Do not overcook the meat – it must still be pink inside.

Cooking time varies from 1–1½ hours, depending on the thickness of the joint and the intensity of the heat. Carve the meat into thin slices and serve immediately on hot plates. Serve with baked potatoes or hot garlic bread and salads.

VARIATION

Add fresh herbs such as rosemary or mint to the basting sauce, or use a 'brush' made of sprigs of herbs for basting.

TO YOUR DOOR

Home delivery was the norm in Grandma's day. Butchers, for instance, had their established rounds, delivering meat to regular customers; department stores like Stuttafords had fleets of delivery vehicles. Where home delivery was out of the question, food could also be ordered by post. The Coast Trading Company, for example, offered to deliver salted snoek to any station in the Union.

Corned Beef & Carrots

Also known as silverside, this tasty meat is often served with dumplings.

Half-fill a very large saucepan with water and heat until lukewarm. Rinse the beef under cold water, drain, put into the pan and bring slowly to the boil. As soon as the water boils, lower the heat and skim the surface. Add the bouquet garni, onion and peppercorns. Partly cover and simmer for 1 hour.

While the beef is cooking, prepare the vegetables. Leave small carrots whole, but if you are using larger ones, cut them into 3 cm pieces. Cut the celery in half lengthways, then across into pieces about 5 cm long. Cut the leeks into 8 cm pieces. Halve or quarter the turnips and leave the onions whole.

When the beef has simmered for 1 hour, add the vegetables and continue cooking for 40–50 minutes, or until they are tender. Transfer the beef to a heated serving platter.

Remove the vegetables with a slotted spoon and arrange them around the meat. Cover the platter loosely with foil and keep hot. Reserve 3 cups of the beef stock.

To make the horseradish sauce, melt the butter in a saucepan, remove from the heat, and stir in the flour and horseradish. Stir the reserved 3 cups of beef stock gradually into the horseradish mixture and bring to the boil, stirring continuously. Reduce the heat, season the sauce to taste with pepper, stir in the lemon juice and simmer, stirring frequently, for 10 minutes. Stir in the cream and pour the sauce into a heated sauceboat.

Serve the beef and vegetables immediately with the horseradish sauce and hot prepared mustard, if desired. Any leftover corned beef can be used to make delicious sandwiches.

FOR THE CORNED BEEF & VEGETABLES

2 kg corned silverside
Large bouquet garni (p.310)
1 large onion, peeled and
    studded with 4 cloves
1 teaspoon black peppercorns
8 small carrots, peeled
1 head celery, trimmed
4 large leeks, green parts
    removed, washed
4 small turnips, peeled
8 medium onions, peeled

FOR THE HORSERADISH SAUCE

30 g butter
¼ cup plain flour
2 tablespoons grated fresh
    horseradish
Freshly ground black pepper
1 tablespoon lemon juice
⅓ cup pouring cream

PREPARATION TIME: 45 minutes
COOKING TIME: 2 hours
SERVES: eight

Serve a choice of condiments with the grill — English or Dijon mustard, tomato relish (p.292), bought tomato sauce, or a fruit chutney (p.298).

8 lamb kidneys, skinned,
    halved and cored, rinsed
    and dried with paper towels
8 lamb chops, trimmed
    of excess fat
8 beef fillet steaks, each
    about 125g, or 1kg rump
    steak, cut into 8 pieces
4 tablespoons olive oil
Salt and freshly ground
    black pepper
8 rashers streaky bacon,
    rind removed
8 pork sausages
8 tomatoes, halved
8 large, flat mushrooms,
    peeled

PREPARATION TIME: 40 minutes
COOKING TIME: 25 minutes
SERVES: eight

Mixed Grill

There is nothing complicated about cooking a mixed grill, but it does require your undivided attention until it goes to the table.

To prepare the meats, brush the kidneys, lamb chops and steaks with olive oil and season well with the salt and pepper. Put the bacon rashers on a board and stretch them with the back of a knife, cut in half, then roll up and thread the rolls on two skewers.

Preheat the stove's warming drawer. Heat a griddled frying pan or the stove's grill to high. Put two large, heatproof serving dishes into the warming drawer. Grill the ingredients in the following order, removing them as they are cooked and putting them on the dishes to keep hot in the warming drawer. First, grill the sausages and kidneys for 8–10 minutes,

turning frequently, then grill the lamb chops and bacon rolls for 5–6 minutes. Next grill the steaks for 2–3 minutes on each side. Finally, remove the rack from the grill pan (if it has a removable rack), add the tomatoes and mushrooms and brush with the hot fat remaining in the pan. Season to taste with salt and pepper and grill for 2–3 minutes.

Arrange the tomatoes and mushrooms on the dish with the meats. Skim all the fat from the juices remaining in the grill pan and spoon the juices over the meats.

If you are using a frying pan, keep the food warm in an oven set at 150°C.

Toad-in-the-Hole

A batter similar to that served with roast beef transforms the everyday sausage into a festive, yet economical, dish for the whole family.

To make the batter, sift the flour and salt into a bowl and make a well in the centre. Add the eggs and pour the milk into the well. Beat the eggs and milk together with a wooden spoon, gradually drawing in the flour from the sides of the bowl, until the batter is thick and smooth. Add the water gradually, stirring all the time, then beat the batter well for 1 minute. Cover the bowl and leave to stand for 1 hour.

Preheat the oven to 200°C. Heat the oil in a frying pan and cook the sausages until the fat is sizzling and the sausages are beginning to brown.

Pour 3 tablespoons of the oil from the pan into a roasting pan and heat in the oven. Transfer the sausages to the roasting pan and pour in the batter. Return the roasting pan to the oven and cook for a further 35–45 minutes, or until the batter is well risen and crisp and the sausages are cooked. Serve at once.

1½ cups plain flour
¼ teaspoon salt
2 eggs
¾ cup milk
¾ cup water
3 tablespoons sunflower oil
12 pork sausages (about 675 g)

PREPARATION TIME: 5 minutes
STANDING TIME: 1 hour
COOKING TIME: 50–60 minutes
SERVES: four

THE HOUSEWIFE'S FAVOURITE

The household name 'Bovril' is a combination of 'bo' from the Latin 'bos' meaning 'ox' and 'vril' the name given to the life force in the novel The Coming Race *written by Bulwer Lytton and published in 1871. The originator of the name was John Lawson Johnston of Edinburgh who began making Bovril commercially in the 1870s.*

Oxtail Braised with Red Wine

Cooked slowly in red wine, the meat in this recipe becomes so tender that it falls off the bone.

3 tablespoons plain flour

¼ teaspoon salt

¼ teaspoon freshly ground black pepper

1 oxtail (about 1 kg), cut into 8–10 pieces

30 g dripping or 2 tablespoons olive oil

2 large onions, peeled and sliced

3 small carrots, peeled and sliced

2 small swedes, peeled and diced

2 medium parsnips, peeled and diced

2 sticks celery, trimmed and sliced

1 large leek, trimmed, washed and sliced

⅔ cup red wine

1¼ cups water

Bouquet garni (p.310)

2 cups mixed very fine strips of carrot, parsnip, swede and celery, for the garnish

2 tablespoons chopped fresh parsley, to garnish

Preparation time: 30 minutes
Cooking time: 2½–3 hours
Serves: four

Preheat the oven to 150°C. Mix the flour, salt and pepper together on a plate, add the oxtail and coat well with the seasoned flour. Heat the dripping or oil in a large, flameproof casserole and fry the oxtail until browned all over, then remove it from the pan.

Add the vegetables and cook, stirring occasionally, over medium heat for 10 minutes. Increase the heat and fry briefly until lightly browned. Add the wine, stirring and scraping any browned residue off the bottom of the casserole. Add the water, bring to the boil, stirring, and remove from the heat.

Place the oxtail on top of the vegetables, tuck in the bouquet garni and cover the top with a butter wrapper (butter side down) or a piece of buttered greaseproof paper. Cook in the centre of the oven for 2½–3 hours, or until the oxtail is tender.

To serve, transfer the oxtail to a heated plate and keep warm. Using a slotted spoon, lift the vegetables out of the casserole and arrange them on a heated serving platter. Arrange the oxtail on top of the vegetables. Pour the red wine sauce over the meat and vegetables, cover the platter and keep warm.

Bring a small saucepan of water to the boil, add the vegetable strips for the garnish and boil for 1–2 minutes. Drain through a sieve and sprinkle the vegetable strips over the meat. Garnish with the chopped parsley and serve immediately.

Tripe & Onions

Tripe-lovers relish their favourite cooked simply and slowly and then served in a mustardy onion sauce, with hot buttered toast and crispy bacon on the side.

800 g parcooked honeycomb tripe

2 large onions, peeled

½ teaspoon salt

40 g butter

3 tablespoons plain flour

1½ cups milk

3 teaspoons mustard powder

3 tablespoons chopped fresh parsley

Pinch cayenne pepper

Hot buttered toast, to serve

Crispy bacon, to serve

Preparation time: 20 minutes
Cooking time: 50 minutes
Serves: four

Cut the tripe into 2 cm pieces. Cut 1 onion into 8 wedges. Place the tripe and onion wedges in a medium saucepan and cover with cold water. Stir in the salt. Cover with a lid and cook over low heat for 30 minutes, or until the tripe is tender. Drain, reserving 1 cup of the liquid and discarding the onion.

Meanwhile, finely chop the remaining onion. Melt the butter in a medium saucepan until hot and bubbling. Add the onion and cook until soft. Add the flour and stir constantly for 1 minute. Remove from the heat and add the combined milk and reserved 1 cup of cooking liquid in a slow, steady stream, whisking constantly to avoid the sauce becoming lumpy. Return the saucepan to the heat and cook, stirring constantly, on medium-high heat until the sauce comes to the boil and thickens.

Add the mustard, parsley and cayenne pepper and mix well to combine. Add the tripe, reduce the heat to low, cover the saucepan with a lid and cook, stirring occasionally, for 10 minutes, or until the tripe is heated through. Serve on warmed plates topped with crispy bacon and accompanied by slices of hot buttered toast.

FACING PAGE: *Oxtail braised with red wine*

Steak & Kidney Pie

This great classic, a favourite with English-speaking people around the world, is both a splendid family dish and a winner for entertaining as it can be made ahead and popped in the oven to reheat when needed.

4 tablespoons olive oil

1 onion, peeled and chopped

1 kg boneless chuck steak, trimmed and cut into 4 cm cubes

250 g ox kidney, skinned, cored and sliced

4 tablespoons plain flour, seasoned with salt and freshly ground black pepper

2½ cups beef stock (p.304)

2 cups Guinness

Bouquet garni (p.310)

125 g large, opened, flat mushrooms, wiped and quartered

625 g puff pastry, homemade (p.311) or bought

1 egg, beaten

PREPARATION TIME:
Day 1, 25 minutes, or 4 hours (mostly unattended) if making pastry
Day 2, 30 minutes

CHILLING TIME: overnight

COOKING TIME:
Day 1, about 3 hours
Day 2, 1 hour

SERVES: six

Heat 1 tablespoon of the oil in a heavy-based saucepan, add the onion and fry on low heat until softened, but not browned, then remove and put on a plate.

Heat the remaining oil in the pan and fry the steak and kidney in batches until evenly browned. Remove the meat as it browns and put it with the onion.

Stir the flour into the pan, then gradually stir in the stock and Guinness. Bring to the boil, stirring and scraping any brown residue off the bottom of the pan. Return the meat and onion to the pan, adding any juices left on the plate. Bring to the boil, add the bouquet garni, then reduce the heat, cover and simmer on the lowest possible heat for 2 hours, or until the meat is tender. Add the mushrooms and cook for 10 minutes more. Remove from the heat, cool and chill overnight. The next day, remove the bouquet garni, season the meat to taste and transfer it to a 1,25-litre pie

dish. Add enough of the meat juices to cover and reserve the remainder.

On a floured surface, roll out the pastry to 5 cm larger than the top of the pie dish. Trim off a strip 2–3 cm wide from around the edge.

Brush the edge of the pie dish with water, press the pastry strip onto it, then brush the strip with water. Cover the pie with the remaining pastry, pressing the edges together to seal. Trim and decorate the edge. Brush with the beaten egg and make a small hole in the centre of the pastry. Chill while heating the oven to 220°C.

Bake the pie for 25–30 minutes, then cover loosely with foil to prevent further browning. Reduce the oven temperature to 160°C, and cook for a further 20–25 minutes, or until the pastry is cooked. Reheat the reserved meat juices and serve separately with the pie. To reheat the pie, lay a sheet of foil loosely over the top to prevent it from overbrowning.

Crumbed Chops

This homely, old-fashioned way to serve lamb can be a gourmet treat if the meat is top quality and carefully trimmed, homemade fresh crumbs are used for the coating, and care is taken with cooking the chops. Ask your butcher for trimmed rib chops.

12 lamb rib chops, trimmed

½ cup plain flour, seasoned with salt and freshly ground black pepper

3 eggs

3 tablespoons milk

3 cups soft breadcrumbs (p.310)

Oil, for shallow-frying

PREPARATION TIME: 20 minutes

CHILLING TIME: 15 minutes

COOKING TIME: 20 minutes

SERVES: four

Trim any excess fat from the lamb chops. Put the seasoned flour on a flat plate. Beat the eggs and milk together with a fork in a shallow dish. Put the breadcrumbs on another flat plate. Coat both sides of each lamb chop in flour, shaking off any excess. Dip the chops in the egg mixture and then in breadcrumbs, pressing the breadcrumbs on with the palm of the hand to secure. Place the chops in a single layer on a tray, cover and refrigerate for 15 minutes (this will help to keep the bread-crumbs on during cooking).

Preheat the oven to 180°C. Heat the oil in a large frying pan on medium heat (the oil is

hot enough when a cube of bread dropped in begins to bubble immediately). Cook four chops at a time for 3–4 minutes on each side, or until the crumbs are light golden. Drain the chops on paper towels before transferring them to a baking tray.

Cook the chops in the preheated oven until they are done to your liking (roughly 5 minutes for medium-rare). Serve on warmed plates with mashed potato and steamed green beans, if desired.

FACING PAGE: *Steak and kidney pie*

FOR THE STUFFING

185 g minced pork

2/3 cup soft white
breadcrumbs (p.310)

Finely grated rind of 1/2 lemon

1 spring onion, trimmed
and finely chopped

1 tablespoon chopped
fresh parsley

1 tablespoon fresh thyme
leaves, or 1 teaspoon
dried thyme

1/4 teaspoon grated nutmeg

1/4 teaspoon salt

1/4 teaspoon freshly ground
black pepper

FOR THE BEEF OLIVES

4 slices of rump steak, each
about 125 g, fat removed,
beaten thin

4 rashers streaky bacon, rind
removed

1 tablespoon plain flour

1 tablespoon olive oil

15 g butter

2/3 cup dry white wine

2/3 cup chicken stock (p.305)

Salt and freshly ground
black pepper

Bouquet garni (p.310)

Fresh thyme sprigs,
to garnish

PREPARATION TIME: 30 minutes

COOKING TIME: 45–60 minutes

SERVES: four

When using veal for this recipe, you can make the flavour more delicate by using ham instead of bacon for the olives, and pork and veal mince instead of all pork for the stuffing.

Beef Olives

*Popular for centuries, beef olives offer a rich layering
of textures and flavours to tempt any appetite.*

Preheat the oven to 180°C. To make the stuffing, put all the ingredients in a bowl and mix well. Lay the slices of steak on a board and place a bacon rasher on top of each. Spread a quarter of the stuffing on top of the bacon rasher. Fold the sides in, roll up the steak and tie securely with clean, fine string or strong cotton. Roll them in the flour until evenly coated, then shake off the excess.

Heat the olive oil and butter in a frying pan and fry the beef olives until brown all over. Remove from the pan and put them into an ovenproof dish. Add any remaining flour to the frying pan and stir on low heat until slightly browned. Add the wine, stock, salt and pepper, and bring to the boil, stirring continuously. Pour the sauce over the beef olives and add the bouquet garni.

Cover and cook the beef olives in the centre of the oven for 45 minutes to 1 hour, or until tender. Discard the bouquet garni. Using a slotted spoon, transfer the beef olives to a plate. Remove the string or cotton, return the olives to the sauce and reheat, if necessary.

Garnish with thyme and serve hot with peas tossed in butter, chopped mint and ground black pepper, if desired. The olives can also be made with escalôpes of veal or pork.

THE BUTCHER'S STRIPES

The classic butcher's apron features wide blue stripes to hide the blood, for the customers' sake, and thin white stripes to act as a 'wash me' indicator. Although butchers today do little slaughtering and receive their carcasses already cleaned, the striped apron remains the symbol of their profession.

Wiener Schnitzel

Coating thin pieces of meat with flour before frying gives a delicious crusty finish and also protects the meat from drying out and becoming tough.

Pound the veal slices to flatten them evenly. Season with salt and pepper. Dip in the flour and shake off the surplus, then dip in the egg followed by the breadcrumbs. Press the crumbs onto the meat and chill in the refrigerator for at least an hour so that the crumb coating adheres during frying.

Fry in hot oil over a medium heat until golden-brown on both sides. Drain on paper towels and top each schnitzel with a slice of hard-boiled egg and a rolled caper-stuffed anchovy. Serve with lemon slices on the side.

VARIATIONS

Use skinned, filleted chicken breasts instead of the veal.

To make veal cordon bleu, sandwich a slice of baked ham and Gruyère cheese between 2 pounded schnitzels, then dip in the prepared breadcrumb coating.

8 thin slices leg of veal

Salt and freshly ground black pepper

Flour for coating

2 eggs, beaten

Fine dried breadcrumbs for coating

Sunflower oil

2 hard-boiled eggs, sliced

8 anchovy fillets, rolled and stuffed with capers

8 lemon wedges or slices

PREPARATION TIME: 15 minutes

CHILLING TIME: 1 hour

COOKING TIME: 10 minutes

SERVES: four

POULTRY & GAME

1,5 kg venison, cut into 2,5 cm
    cubes, with gristle removed
4 tablespoons seasoned flour
6 rashers bacon, trimmed and
    diced
2 tablespoons sunflower oil
12-15 pickling onions
200 g button mushrooms
4 carrots, scraped and cut
    into 1 cm pieces
2 sticks celery, trimmed and
    cut into 1 cm pieces
1 clove garlic, crushed
2 tablespoons chopped parsley
1 bay leaf
3/4 teaspoon dried thyme
3/4 teaspoon grated nutmeg
4 cloves
1 cinnamon stick
3/4 teaspoon cayenne pepper
2 cups red wine or beef stock
    or a mixture of both
2 tablespoons port (or red
    wine)
Salt and freshly ground black
    pepper
Cornflour (optional)
1/2 cup sour cream (smetena)
3 tablespoons finely chopped
    parsley for garnish

PREPARATION TIME: 30 minutes
COOKING TIME: 2 hours
SERVES: eight

Venison Casserole with Sour Cream

Thanks to the flourishing game-farming industry, venison is now available in supermarkets.

Dredge the meat with the seasoned flour, shaking off the excess. Fry the bacon in the oil in an oven-proof casserole until it is soft and starting to brown, then remove it with a slotted spoon and set aside. Lightly sauté the onions and mushrooms for 5 minutes, remove them with a slotted spoon, and set aside with the bacon.

Brown the meat, cooking a single layer at a time. When all the meat has been browned, return it to the casserole and add the carrots, celery, garlic, herbs and spices. Pour over the red wine (or wine and stock), cover the casserole and bring it to the boil.

Turn down the heat very low and cook on top of the stove until tender (about 1 hour). Stir from time to time to prevent sticking.

Add the onions, bacon and mushrooms, and cook for 20 minutes.

Add the port, correct the seasoning and thicken if necessary with a little cornflour mixed with water to a smooth paste. Remove the cinnamon stick and swirl in sour cream just before serving. Garnish with the parsley.

Mashed potatoes, chopped spinach or young green beans go well with this dish.

VARIATION
Instead of cooking the casserole on top of the stove, bake it in the oven at 150°C until tender (about 1 hour).

Ostrich Steaks with Red Wine Sauce

With special treatment, this ultra-lean meat becomes moist and succulent.

OSTRICH FILLET STEAKS

Heat a heavy cast-iron pan or, preferably, grid (with grooves to allow air circulation) until quite hot. Heat the butter and oil and fry the steaks in batches for 30–45 seconds on each side. Remove and place on a warmed serving plate. Season with salt and pepper.

Season then pour over the red wine sauce over the steaks. Serve immediately.

RED WINE SAUCE

Sauté the onion and garlic in the butter until brown. Stir in the flour. Pour in the wine and bring to the boil. Simmer until reduced a little. Stir in the redcurrant jelly and season. Strain the sauce and heat again and spoon over the steaks.

OSTRICH STEAKS
4 teaspoons butter
2 teaspoons sunflower oil
Salt and crushed peppercorns
350 g ostrich steaks (fillet or escalopes)

RED WINE SAUCE
1 tablespoon chopped onion
1 clove garlic, crushed
1 tablespoon butter
2 teaspoons flour
1 cup dry red wine
1 tablespoon redcurrant jelly
Salt and black pepper to taste
A pinch of sugar

PREPARATION TIME: 15 minutes

COOKING TIME: 5 minutes for steaks; 15 minutes for the sauce

SERVES: four

FROM BOOM TO DOOM AND BACK AGAIN

It was the fashion rage for ostrich feathers at the beginning of the 20th century which established large-scale ostrich farming, but the crash of the feather market at the outbreak of World War I sent the industry into the doldrums. However, in recent years the low-fat quality of ostrich meat has seen the popularity of ostrich farming rise once more.

Chicken Pie with Yellow Rice

Serve this old-fashioned 'hoenderpastei' with yellow rice. Start by making the pastry.

FOR THE PASTRY

500 g flour

3/4 teaspoon salt

250 g unsalted butter
(refrigerator temperature)

1 cup sour cream (smetena)

PREPARATION TIME: 15 minutes

STANDING TIME: 30 minutes

MAKES: pastry to cover two 850 ml-1 litre pie dishes, or to line and cover two 23 cm pie dishes

FOR THE PIE

2 chickens

2 teaspoons salt

1 teaspoon pepper

1 tablespoon chicken stock
powder

2 cups dry white wine

2 onions, peeled and quartered

1 cup water

Sour cream flaky pastry (see
above)

1 egg white beaten with
1/2 teaspoon salt

FOR THE SAUCE

125 g butter

4 tablespoons flour

1 cup stock from cooked
chickens

3 cups milk

200 g cooked ham, diced

1 teaspoon dry mustard

4 tablespoons chopped parsley

2 tablespoons fresh cream

PREPARATION TIME: 40 minutes

COOKING TIME: 2½ hours

SERVES: eight

FOR THE YELLOW RICE

1½ cups raw long-grained
rice, washed

2 teaspoons turmeric

2 cinnamon sticks

1 teaspoon salt

1½ cups boiling water

3/4 cup seedless raisins

2 teaspoons sugar

1 tablespoon butter

PREPARATION TIME: 5 minutes

COOKING TIME: 1 hour

SERVES: eight

SOUR CREAM FLAKY PASTRY

Sift the flour and salt together twice. Using a small, sharp knife or a food processor, cut the butter into the flour. Continue until the mixture resembles breadcrumbs. Form a well in the centre of the flour and pour in the sour cream, cutting it in with the knife until blended.

Gather the dough to form a ball and roll it out on a lightly floured board to form a rectangle 1 cm thick and 3 times as long as it is wide. With the short side of the rectangle in front of you, fold the lower third of the pastry up away from you and the upper third down towards you to form 3 layers. Turn the pastry half a turn so that the folded edges are on the sides and one of the open ends is facing you.

Roll the pastry again to a rectangle 1 cm thick. Fold the dough again and turn, then repeat the process of rolling and folding.

Place the pastry in a plastic bag and allow it to rest in the refrigerator for 30 minutes.

THE CHICKEN

Mix the salt, pepper and chicken stock and rub into the chickens. Preheat the oven to 180°C. Place the chickens in a roasting pan. Carefully pour in the wine on the side of the pan and scatter the onions around and between the chickens. Cover the pan with aluminium foil and bake at 180°C for 1¼ hours. Remove from the oven and allow to cool. Remove the skin and bones, and break the chicken flesh into smaller pieces. Arrange the pieces in a big pie dish.

Increase the heat to 220°C. Put the skin and bones back into the pan in which the chickens were roasted, add the water, and then bring to the boil to de-glaze the pan and extract all the flavours from the skin and bones. Strain the liquid and keep it for the sauce.

THE SAUCE

Melt the butter in a heavy-based saucepan, then draw the pan off the heat and mix in the flour until smooth with a wooden spoon or spatula. Stir continuously over a gentle heat for 2–3 minutes until it becomes a thick paste. Do not allow the roux to brown.

Remove the pan from the heat again and add the warm, strained stock and milk, stirring all the time. When the mixture is thoroughly blended, return the sauce to the heat and bring it to boiling point, stirring continuously. Cook gently for 5–7 minutes, stirring from time to time until the sauce is smooth and creamy. Add the ham, mustard, parsley and cream. Remove from the heat, adjust the seasoning and pour over the chicken.

TO MAKE UP THE PIE

Cover the pie dish loosely with the pastry (rolled out to a thickness of 3 mm).

Fold the edges back and place an extra strip of pastry – about 2 cm wide – right around the outer edge of the pie dish. Damp it down with a little water. Fold the large pastry covering back over the edge strip, push it down lightly with your fingertips and trim the pastry to fit the dish. This will be easier to scallop.

Cut a few vent holes and decorate the pie with pastry leaves. Glaze the pastry with the egg white just before baking.

Bake for 20 minutes at 220°C, then reduce the heat to 190°C and cook for a further 20 minutes (or until golden-brown and cooked).

FOR THE YELLOW RICE

Add the rice, turmeric, cinnamon and salt to the boiling water in a large saucepan and boil briskly until almost cooked. Drain the rice through a colander, stir in the raisins and steam in the colander over boiling water for 30 minutes or until the rice is tender and cooked. Transfer to a serving dish and stir in the sugar and butter.

FACING PAGE: *Chicken pie*

Coronation Chicken

This dish is good for entertaining because both the chicken and the sauce can be prepared ahead of time and then assembled just before serving.

FOR THE CHICKEN

6 boneless chicken breasts,
    each about 175 g, skinned
1¼ cups chicken stock (p.305)
1 bay leaf
6 black peppercorns
2 parsley stalks
2 fresh thyme sprigs
1 lemon slice

FOR THE SAUCE

1 tablespoon olive oil
1 small onion, peeled
    and chopped
4 teaspoons medium-hot curry
    powder
1 teaspoon tomato paste
4 tablespoons water
5 tablespoons red wine
Salt and freshly ground
    black pepper
1 tablespoon apricot jam
1 slice lemon
2 teaspoons lemon juice
¾ cup thick cream
⅔ cup mayonnaise, home-
    made (p.306) or bought
Fresh coriander sprigs or
    watercress, to garnish

PREPARATION TIME: 30 minutes
COOKING TIME: 40–50 minutes
SERVES: six

Put the chicken into a large, shallow saucepan and add the stock, bay leaf, peppercorns, parsley stalks, thyme and lemon slice. Bring to the boil, reduce the heat, cover and simmer on very low heat for about 15–20 minutes, or until the chicken is tender. Remove from the heat and allow the chicken to cool in the stock.

Meanwhile, to make the sauce, heat the oil in a saucepan, add the onion and cook gently for 7–10 minutes, or until softened but not browned. Mix in the curry powder and cook for 1 minute. Stir in the tomato paste, water, wine, some salt and pepper, the jam and the lemon slice and juice and simmer for a further 8 minutes. Remove from the heat and discard the lemon slice. Pass the sauce through a nylon sieve into a bowl, pushing through as much as possible with a wooden spoon. Cover and leave to cool.

Lightly whip the cream and stir it into the cold curry sauce with the mayonnaise to make a thin coating sauce. Drain the cold chicken breasts and slice them thickly. Add the sliced chicken to the curried mayonnaise and mix together lightly.

Spoon the mixture into a serving dish, garnish with the coriander or watercress and serve with a rice salad.

MARKING THE OCCASION

This medal was struck to commemorate the 1953 coronation of Elizabeth II at Westminster Abbey. In honour of the occasion, the cookery writer Constance Spry invented the Coronation Chicken recipe, which was served at the Queen's Coronation lunch. The dish is said to combine the flavours of the Commonwealth.

Chicken Pot Roast

Traditionally, pot-roasted chicken was cooked in a heavy black iron pot.
Any heavy-based casserole would be suitable.

Cut away all surplus fat from the chicken. Cook the gizzard, heart and neck with a little seasoned water and set aside to cool. (The srtained liquid will be added to the gravy later.) Wash and dry the chicken (inside and out). Lightly rub the inside of the carcass with salt and pepper and insert cloves. Truss the chicken.

Rub the bird all over with a mixture of 1/2 teaspoon salt, 1/4 teaspoon pepper and the flour.

Mix the oil and butter, and heat in a pot to just under smoking point. Brown the whole onions lightly and remove from the pot (they are later chopped finely and added to the gravy).

Place the chicken in the pot and brown the breast, sides and back. Turn it breast side up, add 1/4 of the boiling water, bring to the boil and simmer, uncovered, for 30 minutes. Turn the bird to cook each side, adding a little more boiling water if necessary. Finally turn it breast side down and brown further in the gravy. Test with a skewer, add the wine, turn up the heat and spoon over the gravy until the surface has developed a slight glaze.

Remove the chicken from the pot and keep warm. Add the onions, the strained liquid from the gizzard, heart and neck, and a little *buerre manié* (if used) to the gravy. Simmer with the lid on for a few minutes: this will dislodge the tasty deposits from the sides of the pot. Serve the gravy separately in a heated gravy boat.

1 chicken (1,5 -2 kg)
Salt and white pepper
2 cloves
1-2 teaspoons flour
2 tablespoons sunflower oil
1 tablespoon butter
2 small onions, peeled
2 cups boiling water
1/2 cup sweet wine, port or brown sherry
Beurre manié (a little flour and water mixed into a paste) (optional)

PREPARATION TIME: 15 minutes
COOKING TIME: 2 hours
SERVES: six

A medium-weight Chinese cleaver will make quick work of the slicing and chopping involved in preparing stir-fry dishes.

FOR THE CHICKEN

600 g chicken breast fillets

¼ teaspoon salt

2 tablespoons cornflour

1 egg white

1 teaspoon sesame oil

2 tablespoons Chinese wine or sweet sherry

Oil, for frying

½ cup blanched almonds

1 onion, peeled and cut into thin wedges

125 g button mushrooms, halved

1 small red pepper, seeded, quartered and thinly sliced on the diagonal

Hot cooked rice, to serve

Thinly sliced spring onions, to garnish

FOR THE SAUCE

3 teaspoons cornflour

½ teaspoon caster sugar

3 teaspoons soya sauce

¾ cup chicken stock (p.305)

PREPARATION TIME: 15 minutes

COOKING TIME: 20 minutes

SERVES: four

Chicken & Almonds

This was one of the first Chinese-style dishes to become popular and it is still a winner with diners of all ages.

Thinly slice the chicken breast fillets across the grain. Make a thin paste by mixing the salt, cornflour, egg white, sesame oil and Chinese wine or sweet sherry in a medium bowl until well combined. Add the chicken slices and stir so that they are well coated with the paste.

Heat a wok or a deep medium saucepan on high heat until very hot. Add 2 tablespoons of oil and the almonds and stir-fry for 1–2 minutes, or until the almonds are golden. Remove the almonds to a plate lined with paper towels to drain.

Heat enough oil on medium-high heat in the wok or saucepan for deep-frying – the oil is hot enough when a cube of bread dropped in begins to bubble immediately. Add the chicken, a few pieces at a time, and cook in batches until the chicken is golden. Remove

to a plate lined with paper towels to drain. Repeat until all the chicken pieces are cooked. Remove the oil from the wok or saucepan and wipe clean with paper towels.

To make the sauce, combine the cornflour, caster sugar, soya sauce and chicken stock in a jug and set aside.

Heat the wok or saucepan on high heat until hot. Add a little oil and the onion and stir-fry for 1 minute. Add the mushrooms and stir-fry for 1 minute more. Add the pepper and the sauce ingredients and cook, stirring occasionally, until the sauce comes to the boil. Add the chicken and stir to coat the chicken with the sauce. Cook for 1–2 minutes, or until the chicken is heated through. Add the almonds and toss well to combine.

Serve the chicken and almonds over hot cooked rice garnished with spring onions.

Chicken Peri-Peri

This spicy Portuguese dish was once all the rage.
For a milder dish, reduce the chilli content.

8 small portions chicken, or
   1 chicken cut into 8 small
   portions
2 tablespoons coarsely
   crumbled dried hot chillies
   or chilli flakes
3 large cloves garlic, crushed
1 teaspoon salt
1 cup sunflower oil

FOR THE SAUCE
70 g butter
¼ cup lemon juice

PREPARATION TIME: 20 minutes
MARINATING TIME: 2 hours
COOKING TIME: 15 minutes
SERVES: four

Wipe the chicken portions and set aside. Combine the chillies, garlic, salt and ½ cup of the oil in a liquidiser or food processor and blend thoroughly. Pour the mixture into a deep bowl and stir in the remaining oil. (If you wish to make the sauce by hand, pound the chillies and garlic to a paste in a small bowl and stir in the oil and salt.)

Add the chicken pieces to the chilli mixture and coat them evenly. Marinate at room temperature for about 2 hours, then place the chicken on a grill pan or baking sheet, and grill about 5 cm from the heat for about 7–8 minutes on each side (or until cooked through).

Keep the chicken warm while making the sauce as follows: melt the butter gently, stir in the lemon juice, and pour the sauce over the chicken. Serve with plain, boiled rice.

VARIATION
Prawns or fish can be marinated in the same mixture and grilled for 2–3 minutes.

THE MODERN FUEL
In the 1930s home owners were encouraged to switch over to electricity. Electrical kitchen appliances forced housewives to change their food purchasing and cooking habits. A refrigerator meant that foods could be bought days ahead and chilled desserts could be made with ease, while cooking times and methods had to be adjusted to suit electric stoves. In their booklet A New Art, General Electric describes electricity as giving the housewife 'new joyous hours of freedom'.

Roast Duck with Orange & Van der Hum Sauce

Van der Hum, a South African naartjie-flavoured liqueur, complements the duck perfectly.

1 duck (about 2 kg), cleaned and patted dry
1 teaspoon salt
1 clove garlic, crushed
4 black peppercorns
2 oranges, quartered (unpeeled)
2 sticks celery, sliced
1 onion, peeled and quartered
4 tablespoons Van der Hum liqueur
4 tablespoons orange marmalade

FOR THE ORANGE SAUCE

2 oranges
3 tablespoons butter
Duck liver
3 tablespoons brandy
1 clove garlic, crushed
2 tablespoons flour
2 teaspoons tomato sauce
1½ teaspoons soya sauce
A dash of white pepper
1 cup chicken stock (p.305)
4 tablespoons Van der Hum liqueur
4 tablespoons orange marmalade

PREPARATION TIME: 30-45 minutes
COOKING TIME: 2 hours
SERVES: four

Preheat the oven to 210°C. Sprinkle the inside of the duck with salt and rub with the crushed garlic. Stuff the duck with the peppercorns, oranges, celery and onion, and pour in the Van der Hum. Place the duck, breast side up, on the rack of the grilling pan and roast for 30 minutes, pricking the flesh from time to time to release the fat. Discard the fat and place the duck in a roasting pan with ½ cup water under the grill rack. Reduce the oven temperature to 185°C. Spread the duck with the marmalade and roast for 1½ hours.

THE ORANGE SAUCE

While the duck is roasting, make the orange sauce. Peel the rind of one orange and cut it into fine slivers. Squeeze the juice from both oranges and put on one side. Melt 2 tablespoons of butter and gently fry the duck liver until brown on both sides and pink inside. Remove from the heat.

In a small saucepan, heat the brandy and ignite. Pour the flaming brandy over the liver: when the flame subsides, remove the liver and add the remaining 1 tablespoon of butter, orange peel and garlic. Cook for 3 minutes, then remove from the heat and stir in the flour, tomato sauce, soya sauce and pepper until well mixed.

Gradually stir in the chicken stock, Van der Hum, marmalade and orange juice. Bring to the boil, then reduce the heat and simmer for 15 minutes. Chop the liver and add to the sauce. Pour the hot orange sauce into a heated gravy boat.

Place the duck on a heated serving platter and decorate with orange segments and watercress. Serve the roast duck with crisp roast potatoes and minted peas.

Duck with Cherries

Duck cooked this way requires little attention, and as carving is done beforehand, it presents no problems when brought to the table. The finished dish is also suitable for freezing.

2,5 kg duck
Salt and black pepper
30 g unsalted butter
120 ml Madeira or sweet sherry
1 tin (450 g) pitted morello or black cherries
Lemon juice
150 ml port
3 level teaspoons cornflour
3 tablespoons chopped parsley to garnish

PREPARATION TIME: 20 minutes
COOKING TIME: 1¼ hours
SERVES: four

Joint the duck into four equal portions and prick the skin thoroughly. Season with salt and freshly ground black pepper. Melt the butter in a large frying pan and fry the duck over low heat for about 20 minutes or until brown all over. Drain the fat from the pan and pour the Madeira and the juice from the cherries over the duck. Bring the contents to simmering point, cover the pan tightly with a lid and continue simmering the duck for 45–55 minutes.

Lift the duck portions from the pan, drain on crumpled paper towels and keep them warm in the warmer drawer. Skim as much fat as possible from the pan juices and stir in the lemon juice and port. Mix the cornflour with 2 tablespoons of cold water, and stir into the pan juices until thickened. Bring to the boil and adjust seasoning; add the cherries and heat through.

Arrange the duck portions, coated with the sauce, on a platter. Sprinkle with parsley and serve with a selection of vegetables.

FACING PAGE: *Roast duck with orange & Van der Hum sauce*

6 large portions of chicken

2 tablespoons olive oil

2 cloves garlic, crushed

Salt and freshly ground black
pepper

6 cinnamon sticks

4 tomatoes, skinned and
sliced

150 g black olives, stoned and
halved

6 slices lemon

½ cup dry white wine

¼ cup orange juice

PREPARATION TIME: 15 minutes

COOKING TIME: 1 hour

SERVES: six

Greek Chicken

This colourful chicken dish captures the flavours of the Mediterranean.

Preheat the oven to 190°C. Arrange the chicken pieces side by side in a shallow oven-proof dish. Brush with olive oil then smear all over with crushed garlic Sprinkle with the salt, pepper and olive oil. Place the cinnamon sticks under and around the chicken.

Arrange slices of tomato and halved olives around the chicken pieces, with slices of lemon on top. Pour over the wine and orange juice, and cover with aluminium foil.

Put in the oven and bake for about 1 hour, remove the cinnamon sticks, and serve.

This dish tastes good served with either buttered noodles or rice and a simple traditional Greek salad consisting of lettuce, cucumber and feta cheese.

VARIATION

Add chopped or crushed fresh ginger or a mixture of both in the place of the cinnamon.

MRS H.S. BALL'S CHUTNEY

It comes as a surprise to many people to hear that Mrs Ball was a real person. Amelia Ball lived in Fish Hoek, a seaside suburb of Cape Town, and started selling her homemade chutney based on a family recipe during World War I. The chutney proved so popular that Cape Town businessman Fred Metter was approached to market it and the familiar eight-sided bottle appeared. Amelia Ball died in 1962 aged 97. The secret recipe has since been sold, and the chutney is now coveted by South Africans all over the world.

Trim the excess skin from the neck of the chicken and tuck it under the skin covering the breast. This adds flavour to the meat and helps make the outer skin crispy.

Roasted Chicken with Herbs

For the proper old-fashioned flavour, buy a chicken that is free-range and perhaps organic and corn-fed as well.

In a small bowl, combine the parsley, basil, origanum, rosemary, salt and pepper. Stir in the lemon juice and olive oil to form a paste.

Preheat the oven to 190°C. Rinse the chicken; drain and pat dry. Truss the chicken (see p.309), and place it, breast side up, on a rack in a roasting pan. Rub the surface of the chicken with the herb mixture.

Roast the chicken, basting with the pan juices every 15 minutes, for 1–1¼ hours, or until the juices run clear, with no tinge of pink when a fine skewer is inserted into the thickest part of the flesh between the thigh and the leg.

Remove the chicken and allow it to rest while you make a clear gravy. Tilt the roasting pan, spoon off the fat from the juices and discard. Add the chicken stock to the juices and boil briskly, stirring and scraping any browned residue off the bottom of the pan, until the liquid has reduced by about half. Turn the heat to low and whisk in the butter, a little at a time. Adjust the seasoning and transfer the gravy to a heated gravy boat or jug.

Garnish the chicken with lemon wedges and rosemary sprigs and serve with the gravy and a selection of steamed vegetables.

3 tablespoons chopped fresh parsley
3 tablespoons chopped fresh basil
2 tablespoons chopped fresh origanum
3 tablespoons chopped fresh rosemary
¼ teaspoon each salt and freshly ground black pepper
1 tablespoon lemon juice
2 tablespoons olive oil
1 whole chicken (about 1,6kg)
1½ cups chicken stock (p.305)
20g butter
Lemon wedges and fresh rosemary sprigs, to garnish

PREPARATION TIME: 10 minutes
COOKING TIME: 1 hour
SERVES: four or five

A TASTE OF THE EAST

Chinese workers were brought to South Africa in 1904 to work on the gold mines, but had no influence on cooking trends in South Africa and were all subsequently repatriated. There has been a small permanent Chinese community in South Africa since about 1891, but it is only since World War II that Chinese restaurants have become commonplace. Adventurous Grandmas would have cooked Chinese dishes from recipe books such as The Chinese Cook Book, *published by the Culinary Arts Press, Pennsylvania, U.S.A.*

2 tablespoons vegetable oil

600 g boned and skinned chicken breasts, cut into bite-sized strips

2 sticks celery, trimmed and cut into 2 cm pieces

2 medium onions, peeled, halved and sliced

2 cloves garlic, peeled and crushed

1¼ cups chicken stock (p.305)

¼ cup soya sauce

2 tablespoons cornflour

1 tablespoon firmly packed brown sugar

400 g frozen mixed vegetables

1 x 230 g tin sliced water chestnuts, drained

3 cups cooked chow mein noodles (crisp noodles)

PREPARATION TIME: 20 minutes
COOKING TIME: 20 minutes
SERVES: four

Chicken Chow Mein

This quick and easy dish is a good one to have in your repertoire for a casual dinner at short notice.

Preheat the oven to 160°C. Heat 1 tablespoon of the oil in a wok or frying pan on medium-high heat. Add the chicken in three or four batches, stir-frying each batch for 3 minutes, or until cooked through. Using a slotted spoon, remove the chicken from the wok. Cover and keep warm.

Heat the remaining 1 tablespoon of oil in the wok. Add the celery, onions and garlic. Stir-fry for 2 minutes, or until almost tender.

Whisk the chicken stock in a small bowl with the soya sauce, cornflour and brown sugar. Add the mixture to the wok along with the mixed vegetables and sliced water chestnuts. Bring to the boil and cook for 1 minute, or until the sauce thickens and the vegetables are heated through. Make a bed of crisp noodles on a heatproof serving dish and warm in the oven.

Return the cooked chicken, along with any juices, to the wok. Bring to the boil and cook for 1 minute, or until heated through. Spoon the chicken mixture over the hot chow mein noodles and serve immediately.

Chicken Kiev

The original filling of Chicken Kiev was simply butter flavoured with chives. In this version, the butter filling is flavoured with lemon, herbs and garlic.

Trim any skin or gristle from the chicken breasts and place them 3–4 cm apart between two large sheets of greaseproof paper. Beat them with a meat pounder or wooden rolling pin until flat and large enough to hold a stick of butter about the diameter of your little finger (do not puncture the chicken meat).

To make the herb butter, blend the butter, lemon rind, juice, herbs and garlic (if used) with plenty of seasoning. Shape into a 6 cm-square cake on a sheet of greaseproof paper. Cover and chill or freeze until very firm. Then cut into 4 long sticks.

Place one stick in the centre of each piece of flattened chicken (the inner surface) and roll the chicken up around it, tucking in the ends to make a neat, sausage-shaped package that completely seals in the butter. Roll the chicken packages in seasoned flour, brush or dip them in the beaten egg mixture, then roll them in crumbs – pressing them firmly onto the chicken flesh.

Chill (uncovered) for at least 3 hours or overnight. You could also freeze them, but in this case you should allow them to thaw for about 6–7 hours in the refrigerator before cooking.

Heat the oil in a deep-fryer to 180°C (a cube of day-old bread should turn golden-brown in 1–1¹⁄4 minutes) and fry the chicken breasts, two at a time, until golden-brown (about 5 minutes). Drain on paper towels and keep hot in an oven (with the door ajar) for 5–10 minutes while frying the remaining chicken breasts.

Arrange the pieces side by side on a serving dish, and serve immediately with baked potatoes with sour cream and a salad.

4 large boned chicken breasts,
   skinless
Sunflower oil for deep frying

FOR THE HERB BUTTER
10 g butter
Grated rind and juice of
   1 lemon
1 tablespoon freshly chopped
   parsley
1 teaspoon chopped tarragon
1 teaspoon chopped chives
2 cloves garlic, very finely
   chopped (optional)
Salt and freshly ground black
   pepper

FOR THE COATING
50 g flour, seasoned with salt
   and pepper
1 extra-large egg, beaten with
   1 teaspoon sunflower oil and
   1 teaspoon water
75 g dry white breadcrumbs

PREPARATION TIME: 45 minutes
CHILLING TIME: at least 3 hours
COOKING TIME: 30 minutes
SERVES: four

FOR THE TURKEY
1 turkey (4-5 kg), defrosted
250 g butter
Salt and black pepper
8 rashers streaky bacon
2 cups chicken stock (p.305)
1 cup red wine

FOR THE NECK STUFFING
90 g butter, softened
250 g fresh mushrooms
6 rashers rindless streaky
   bacon
1 large onion, peeled
1 clove garlic, peeled
200 g cooked pork, minced
125 g chicken livers
4 anchovy fillets
125 g liver pâté
Grated rind of 1 lemon
2 tablespoons chopped parsley
½ teaspoon dried thyme
½ teaspoon dried marjoram
1 tablespoon brandy
Freshly ground black pepper

FOR THE BODY STUFFING
6 pork sausages
2 cups fresh white breadcrumbs
1 onion, peeled and grated
Grated rind of 2 lemons
1 teaspooon dried sage
1 teaspoon dried mixed herbs
3 tablespoons chopped parsley
1 egg
½ cup sour cream
Salt and black pepper

FOR THE GIBLET GRAVY
Turkey giblets
1 clove
2 onions, peeled
2 sprigs parsley
1 bay leaf
Salt and black pepper
4 cups water
90 g flour
½ cup red wine
2 tablespoons cranberry jelly

PREPARATION TIME: 2 hours
COOKING TIME: 3½ hours
SERVES: ten to twelve

Roast Turkey with Two Stuffings

This recipe ensures that the bird remains succulent and tastes good whether served hot or cold. The neck stuffing helps to keep the notoriously dry turkey breast moist.

PREPARING THE TURKEY
Thaw the turkey for 2–3 days in the refrigerator, depending on its size. Remove the wing tips, preen gland and excess fat around the cavity. Preheat the oven to 150°C. Wipe the turkey clean and remove the giblets, reserving the gizzard, heart and liver for the gravy stock.

NECK STUFFING
Melt 30g of the butter and sauté the mushrooms until they just start to soften. Chop the bacon coarsely, quarter the onions and slice the garlic. Then combine all the stuffing ingredients except the remaining butter and the pepper, and mince together.

Melt the rest of the butter and stir it into the stuffing, mixing well. Season with pepper. Starting at the neck, work your fingers carefully under the skin to about halfway down the breast, being careful not to pierce the skin with your nails. Stuff the neck cavity and insert the stuffing under the skin on the breast, pressing it evenly to give the bird a well-rounded appearance.

Tuck the loose neck skin under a wing and skewer it into place, or truss it to ensure that there will be no danger of the stuffing oozing out during the cooking.

STUFFING FOR BODY CAVITY
Press the meat out of the sausage skins and discard the skins. Mix all the ingredients together, adding extra breadcrumbs if the stuffing is too moist. Stuff the body cavity, sew it up and truss the legs.

COOKING THE TURKEY
Rub the turkey all over with butter, sprinkle with salt and pepper and place it (breast side up) in a roasting pan. Cover the breast with rashers of bacon. Combine the chicken stock and wine and pour the liquid over the bird.

Cover with buttered greaseproof paper and roast for 3 hours, basting from time to time.

While the turkey is cooking, make a stock with the giblets, clove, onions, parsley, bay leaf, salt, pepper and water. Simmer for an hour, then strain.

Remove the greaseproof paper and bacon from the turkey when the 3 hours are up, increase the temperature to 200°C and brown it for about 30 minutes.

When it is cooked, transfer the turkey to a warmed serving platter.

THE GIBLET GRAVY
Stir the flour into the pan juices to make a smooth paste, scraping all the crisp, tasty bits from the sides of the pan. Add the red wine and the prepared giblet stock and simmer, stirring until the mixture starts to thicken.

Add the jelly, and as soon as the gravy comes to the boil, turn down the heat and simmer for 2 minutes. Season to taste and strain into a heated sauceboat.

Turkey is traditionally served with bread sauce and cranberry jelly.

To make a bread sauce, stud an onion with 4 cloves and put it in a pan with ¼ teaspoon of mace, 4 peppercorns and 2 cups of milk. Bring this mixture to the boil, then remove the pan from the heat immediately and leave it to infuse (covered) for about 30 minutes.

Strain the milk into another pan and stir in ½ cup breadcrumbs. Return to the heat, stirring continuously, until the mixture boils and becomes quite thick. Season to taste and stir in 1½ teaspoons butter and 2 tablespoons cream. Serve warm, but do not reboil.

Garnish the turkey with green salad leaves and serve with a selection of festive vegetables (see p.189).

FACING PAGE: *Roast turkey with two stuffings*

FOR THE GUINEA FOWL

1 guinea fowl (about 1 kg), with giblets

1 large onion, peeled and sliced

2 carrots, scrubbed and sliced

2 leeks, trimmed, washed and sliced

Bunch of mixed fresh herbs or 1 teaspoon dried mixed herbs

Salt and pepper

8 thin rashers streaky bacon, rinds removed

FOR THE SAUCE

275-300 ml stock made from giblets

1 tablespoon butter

1 tablespoon flour

¼ cup thin cream

1 tablespoon chopped parsley

PREPARATION TIME: 30 minutes

COOKING TIME: 1½ hours

SERVES: four

Casseroled Guinea Fowl

This is an ideal way to cook older, tougher birds. This dish will improve if chilled overnight in the refrigerator and reheated the following day.

Preheat the oven to 180°C. Clean the bird and remove the giblets. Truss it and place in a deep casserole with the vegetables, herbs, salt and pepper to taste, and just enough water to cover. Bring to the boil, then place, tightly covered, in the preheated oven for 1 hour (or until the bird is tender). During this time prepare the giblet stock.

Put the giblets into a saucepan with a little salt and pepper and water to cover. Simmer for 1 hour to obtain a good stock, strain, then boil briskly until reduced to about 300 millilitres.

Take the casserole from the oven and strain off 275–300ml cooking liquid. Lower the oven heat to 130°C and put the casserole back. Strain the prepared stock into the cooking liquid and boil rapidly to reduce to about half the original amount.

Roll up the bacon rashers and thread on skewers. Grill for about 5 minutes, turning, until they are crisp. Keep warm

To make the sauce, heat the butter, stir in the flour and cook gently for 2–3 minutes. Pour on the hot stock, stirring all the time, until smooth and thickened. Taste for seasoning, then add the cream and parsley. Warm the sauce well, but do not allow to boil or it will curdle.

Carve the guinea fowl into serving portions. Place on a warmed serving dish, pour on the sauce and arrange the bacon rolls around it.

HELMETED GUINEA FOWL

The guinea fowl is found throughout South Africa and is one of the most familiar of our veld birds. They do sometimes invade suburbs, where their shrill early morning calls ensure that no-one sleeps late! Flocks can number in the hundreds, although there is some concern about rapidly dwindling numbers in certain areas.

Chicken Curry

Anglicised curries like this were popular long before we became as familiar with Asian food as we are today.

Heat the butter and oil in a large saucepan, add the chicken pieces and brown them all over. Remove from the saucepan and drain well on paper towels.

Add all the onions to the saucepan and cook on medium heat for 5 minutes or until soft. Mix in the curry powder and cook for 1 minute, then add the flour and cook for 1 minute more. Gradually pour in the stock and bring to the boil, stirring until thickened. Add the mango chutney, lemon juice and apples and mix well.

Return the chicken to the saucepan, reduce the heat, cover and simmer on low heat for 30–40 minutes, or until the chicken is tender. Using a slotted spoon, remove the chicken pieces from the sauce and arrange them on a serving dish.

Pour the curry sauce into a food processor and blend until smooth. Return it to the saucepan, stir in the sultanas and cream and season to taste. Reheat the sauce gently, but do not boil or it will curdle. Pour over the chicken pieces and serve with hot, cooked rice.

30 g butter

2 tablespoons vegetable oil

1,5 kg chicken, cut into small joints (p.309)

2 small onions, peeled and chopped

4 small onions, peeled, halved and sliced

1 tablespoon medium-hot curry powder

1 tablespoon plain flour

2 cups chicken stock (p.305)

2 tablespoons Indian-style mango chutney

Strained juice of 1 lemon

2 medium cooking apples, peeled, cored and chopped

1/3 cup sultanas

2/3 cup pouring cream

Salt and freshly ground black pepper

Hot, cooked long-grain rice to serve

PREPARATION TIME: 30 minutes
COOKING TIME: 50-60 minutes
SERVES: four

ROADSIDE STOP

In Grandma's day it was not unusual to pull over to the side of the road and start a little fire to heat some water for tea, or to have a braai. Wood was scrounged from the surrounding countryside, a few rocks were put in place to hold the pot or grid, the fire was lit and then the family would sit back and enjoy the day.

Honey & Soya Chicken Wings

These chicken wings can be served warm or cold and make excellent picnic fare.

12 chicken wings (about 1 kg)

½ cup soya sauce

Juice of 1 lemon

3 tablespoons bought
   tomato sauce

1 small piece fresh ginger,
   peeled and thinly sliced

Oil, for greasing

¼ cup honey

PREPARATION TIME:
   Day 1, 10 minutes
   Day 2, 10 minutes

MARINATING TIME: overnight

COOKING TIME: 35–40 minutes

MAKES: 12 chicken wings

Cut the wing tips from the chicken wings and discard. Place the chicken wings in an airtight container. Mix the soya sauce, lemon juice, tomato sauce and ginger in a bowl and pour it over the chicken wings. Toss the chicken wings so they are all well coated with the marinade. Cover the container and marinate the chicken in the refrigerator overnight.

The next day, preheat the oven to 180°C. Lightly grease a shallow baking tray with oil and line with a sheet of baking paper. Drain the chicken wings, reserving ¼ cup of the marinade. Combine the reserved marinade with the honey in a small saucepan. Heat for 1–2 minutes, or until the mixture is combined.

Place the chicken wings on the baking tray. Brush the warm honey mixture over both sides of the chicken and bake in the preheated oven for 30–40 minutes, or until the chicken wings are cooked through. Serve warm or cold.

Devilled Chicken

Grilled, devilled chicken or turkey was traditionally served on Boxing Day (now the Day of Goodwill), because it was a good way to use leftovers from the Christmas bird.

Preheat the grill. Remove the skin from the chicken pieces. Using a sharp knife, cut deep slits into the flesh and place each piece of chicken, cut side up, on a grill tray.

Beat the butter, mustard, curry powder, Worcestershire sauce, cayenne pepper and salt until light and fluffy. Add the fruit chutney and mix well. Spread the butter mixture evenly over the cut side of the chicken and cook under the preheated grill, basting with the melted butter mixture occasionally, until the chicken is heated through. Serve drizzled with any remaining melted butter mixture and a dressed green salad.

If there is time to refrigerate the chicken pieces for a few hours or overnight after spreading them with the butter mixture, the flavour will be even better. Allow them to return to room temperature before grilling.

VARIATION

Devilled Turkey: Simply substitute 8 pieces of cooked turkey for the chicken and proceed as directed for devilled chicken.

8 pieces cooked chicken

125 g butter

3 teaspoons English mustard

3 teaspoons curry powder

1 teaspoon Worcestershire sauce

Pinch of cayenne pepper

Salt

1 tablespoon sweet fruit chutney

PREPARATION TIME: 10 minutes

COOKING TIME: 10 minutes

SERVES: four

Steamed rice and one or two cool, fresh relishes — such as diced mango with a little salt and lemon juice, or chopped cucumber and mint in yoghurt — are good accompaniments for devilled chicken or turkey.

Vegetables
& Salads

4 small swedes, peeled
    and cut into 2–3 cm cubes
3 medium carrots, peeled
    and halved lengthways
3 medium parsnips, peeled
    and quartered lengthways
2 small turnips, peeled
    and cut into wedges
1 teaspoon salt
5 tablespoons olive oil
4 teaspoons fresh
    thyme leaves
4 teaspoons fresh
    marjoram leaves
4 teaspoons fresh
    rosemary leaves
4 teaspoons shredded
    fresh sage leaves

PREPARATION TIME: 20 minutes
COOKING TIME: 45 minutes
SERVES: four

Roasted Root Vegetables

Thyme, marjoram, rosemary and sage season this delicious dish.

Preheat the oven to 200°C. Put the prepared swedes, carrots, parsnips and turnips into a large saucepan. Sprinkle with salt and pour over enough boiling water to cover the vegetables completely. Bring them back to the boil and cook for 5 minutes.

Drain the vegetables thoroughly through a large colander. Put the olive oil into a large roasting pan and heat in the oven for 10 minutes. Take the pan out of the oven and carefully add the drained vegetables to the hot oil. Sprinkle with the herbs and baste well until the vegetables are evenly coated. Roast, turning once, in the centre of the oven for 40–45 minutes, or until tender and browned. Serve hot.

THE SWEDISH TURNIP

Developed in the 1600s, the swede, hybrid of the cabbage and turnip, is called 'neeps' by Scots and 'rutabaga' by Americans. Our name for this root vegetable is a contraction of 'Swedish turnip', which is what it was called when introduced to England in the 1700s.

CONTROL BOARDS

By 1967, almost every aspect of South African agriculture was under the control of 18 Agricultural Control Boards. These were established after the Depression to stabilise widely fluctuating prices. Most were abolished in 1998, with a few lasting to mid-2002. These boards produced recipe books expounding the uses of their particular agricultural product - beans, potatoes, meat, maize and so on. This particular recipe booklet was published by the Dairy Board.

Stuffed Butternuts

This dish is ideal for vegetarians, although meat-eaters will enjoy it too.

Preheat the oven to 160°C. Wash and halve the butternuts lengthways. Scoop out the seeds and boil the butternuts (cut side down) in salted water for about 30 minutes, or until tender. Take care that they do not break. If the butternuts are too large, you will have to use two saucepans.

While they are boiling, prepare the stuffing. Heat the oil and butter in a frying pan, add the onion, carrot, celery, rice and nuts, and toss over a medium heat until tender-crisp. Spoon the rice mixture into a bowl.

Carefully remove the flesh from the cooked butternuts, leaving a firm shell. Mix the pulp thoroughly with the rice mixture, season with the soya sauce and add the honey.

Place the shells in a buttered oven-proof dish and fill with the stuffing. Dot with butter and sprinkle with cinnamon, then bake them in the oven for 25 minutes.

VARIATION

Top the butternuts with buttered crumbs and paprika, and serve as part of a vegetarian meal (omit the cinnamon).

2-3 butternuts (1,2 kg)
Salt
2 tablespoons sunflower oil
30 g butter
1 medium onion, peeled and finely chopped
1 carrot, coarsely grated
1 stick celery, thinly sliced
1 cup cooked brown rice
3 tablespoons mixed nuts, chopped
1 tablespoon soya sauce
2 teaspoons honey

FOR THE TOPPING
Butter
Cinnamon

PREPARATION TIME: 55 minutes
COOKING TIME: 25 minutes
SERVES: four to six

THE BIG WELCOME

During World War II, the South African Women's Auxiliary Services (SAWAS) organised hospitality for visiting troops. In Cape Town and Durban convoys numbering up to 40 000 men were welcomed - sometimes at only an hour or two's notice. The troops in this picture are at the Victoria League Service Club, which was in Pine Street, Durban. Typically, a 3-course meal, bed, bath and morning coffee would cost a serviceman about 1/6.

25 g butter

2 medium onions, peeled and chopped

3 carrots, peeled and chopped

4 rashers bacon, rinds removed, chopped

4 cooking apples, peeled, cored and chopped

1 kg red cabbage, finely chopped

1 clove garlic, finely chopped

Salt and freshly ground black pepper

½ teaspoon freshly grated nutmeg

1 bay leaf

2 cloves

2 tablespoons port

2 tablespoons red wine vinegar

PREPARATION TIME: 20-25 minutes

COOKING TIME: 2½ –3 hours

SERVES: six

Stewed Red Cabbage

Apples, onions, spices, port and vinegar are all traditional ingredients to cook with red cabbage. The wine prevents the cabbage from losing its colour.

Preheat the oven to 150°C. Melt the butter in an oven-proof dish. Add the onions, carrots and bacon, and cook for 5 minutes until they are soft.

Remove them from the heat and add the chopped apples, cabbage and garlic. Season with salt, black pepper and nutmeg and add the bay leaf and cloves. Mix all these ingredients well together and then stir in the port and the red wine vinegar.

Cover the dish and bake in the preheated oven for 2½ to 3 hours. Serve it hot or cold as you wish.

Red cabbage goes well with duck, goose, venison and pork and is also good with ham and sausages. It can be served cold or re-heated with a little cooked bacon added to it.

Glazed Sweet Potatoes

This traditional sweet potato recipe is a perfect accompaniment to a roast. The sweet potato is not a real potato – in fact, it is not even related to the potato plant family, but is the tuber of a leafy vine which comes from Central America.

Wash, peel and slice the sweet potatoes, then rinse in salted water. Place the sliced sweet potatoes in a heavy-based saucepan with the butter and golden syrup or brown sugar), naartjie peel, cinnamon or ginger and water.

Cook on medium-low heat until the water has evaporated. Shake the saucepan instead of stirring the ingredients to prevent the sweet potatoes from breaking. Increase the heat and fry to a golden caramel colour, making sure that the sweet potatoes do not burn. Add the lemon juice.

Remove the naartjie peel and cinnamon or ginger before serving.

1 kg sweet potatoes (yellow type called 'borrie')
Salt
100 g butter
200 ml golden syrup or 200 g soft brown sugar
5 cm piece dried naartjie peel
2 cinnamon sticks, or a 5 cm piece of peeled, fresh ginger
200 ml water
1 tablespoon lemon juice

PREPARATION TIME: 30 minutes
COOKING TIME: 1 hour
SERVES: six

Instead of potatoes, bake whole sweet potatoes in the oven. When cooked, slit open and serve with butter.

Potato Soufflé

This light and delicious soufflé, flavoured with Parmesan cheese and chives, makes an impressive dish for any occasion.

4 small floury potatoes (about 500 g), peeled and quartered

30 g butter

4 eggs, separated

5-7 tablespoons milk

2 tablespoons snipped fresh chives

½ cup grated Parmesan cheese

Salt and freshly ground black pepper

Freshly grated nutmeg

Preparation time: 30 minutes

Cooking time: 25 minutes

Serves: two as a main course or four as an accompaniment

Preheat the oven to 220°C and butter a 6-cup soufflé dish. Steam the potatoes until soft and put them in a bowl with the butter and egg yolks. Mash together well, beating in enough milk to bring the mashed potato to a slightly soft, dropping consistency. Add the snipped chives and all but 1 tablespoon of the grated cheese. Season liberally with salt, pepper and freshly grated nutmeg.

Whisk the egg whites until stiff, but not dry. Fold a third of the whites into the potato mixture to loosen it, then very gently and carefully fold in the remainder. Pour the mixture into the buttered soufflé dish, sprinkle the remaining cheese over the top and bake in the centre of the oven for 25 minutes, or until well risen, golden brown and soft but firm to the touch. Serve immediately, as a main course with a tossed salad, or as a vegetable accompaniment to other cooked dishes, such as roast poultry, grilled meat or fish, casseroles or cold cooked meats.

VARIATION

Vegetable Soufflé: Use half sweet potato, pumpkin or parsnip and half potato, and replace the Parmesan cheese with a mild Cheddar or Edam cheese.

Potatoes Lyonnaise

This rich, buttery melange of potato and onion is splendid with grilled steak, hamburgers or sausages.

6 medium waxy potatoes

50 g butter

2 medium onions, thinly sliced and separated into rings

Salt and freshly ground black pepper

2 tablespoons chopped, fresh flat-leaf parsley

Preparation time: 15 minutes

Cooking time: 30 minutes

Serves: four

Cook the potatoes, in their skins, in salted water for 15 minutes, or until tender. Drain and leave them to cool.

Meanwhile, heat half the butter in a large frying pan and cook the onions gently until they are evenly golden. Remove the pan from the heat and set aside.

Skin the cooled potatoes and cut them into slices about 5 mm thick. Add the remaining butter to the pan with the onions and, when it is melted, turn the heat up a little and add the potato slices. Cook, stirring to ensure that the potato slices do not stick together, for a further 10 minutes, or until the potatoes are well coloured. Season to taste, stir in the chopped parsley and serve the potatoes at once with steak or other meat.

VARIATIONS

Herbed Potatoes: To make herbed potatoes, prepare as for Potatoes Lyonnaise, but sprinkle the potato and onion with ½ teaspoon dried origanum, ¼ teaspoon dried rosemary and 1 clove garlic, peeled and chopped, along with the salt and pepper.

Galette Lyonnaise: Prepare as for Potatoes Lyonnaise, but stir the potato with the onion for 5 minutes only, then transfer the mixture to a gratin dish and carefully smooth the top with the back of a spoon. Brush with a little more butter and cook under the grill until it is golden brown.

FACING PAGE: *Potato soufflé*

TOMATO BUTTER BEANS

350 g dried butter beans

2 medium onions, peeled and thinly sliced

1 medium carrot, sliced

2 fat cloves garlic, crushed

1 bay leaf

1 sprig rosemary

¼ cup sunflower oil

4 medium tomatoes, skinned and chopped

Salt and freshly ground black pepper

Chopped fresh basil or parsley

PREPARATION TIME: 20 minutes

SOAKING TIME: overnight

COOKING TIME: 2 hours

SERVES: six

SOUSBOONTJIES

500 g butter or sugar beans

2 cups water

½ cup wine vinegar

60 g sugar

¾ teaspoon salt

15 g butter

PREPARATION TIME: 5 minutes

SOAKING TIME: overnight

COOKING TIME: 1¼ hours

SERVES: ten to twelve

Tomato Butter Beans & Sousboontjies

Both of these bean dishes go well with a roast. Sousboontjies have the added advantage of keeping well in the refrigerator.

TOMATO BUTTER BEANS

Soak the beans overnight in cold water – or cover with water, boil, remove from the heat and leave covered for an hour.

Place the soaked beans plus the soaking liquid in a heavy saucepan (ensure that there is enough water to cover the beans) and bring to the boil with 1 sliced onion, the sliced carrot, 1 clove crushed garlic, the bay leaf and the rosemary. Reduce the heat and simmer for about an hour. Add half the oil and simmer until the beans are tender. Drain the beans (reserve the stock).

Gently heat the rest of the oil in a large frying pan. Add the remaining sliced onion and cook very gently until softened. Stir in the remaining clove of garlic and the tomatoes. Cook for 5–10 minutes, then add the drained beans and heat through, adding a little of the stock if necessary. Season and serve sprinkled with basil or parsley.

SOUSBOONTJIES

Soak the beans ovenight. Drain them and cook very slowly in the water until they are tender. Add the wine vinegar, sugar, salt and butter according to your own taste. Press a few of the beans to pulp stage to bind the sauce. Allow to cool.

Baked Beetroot

For perfect tenderness, bake the beetroot very slowly at a low temperature.

Preheat the oven to 150°C. Carefully wash the beetroot. Do not pierce or bruise the skins. Wrap each one in a square of buttered foil and put in a roasting pan. Bake in the oven for 3–3¹/₂ hours, or until the skins come away easily when rubbed gently.

Remove from the oven and, when cool enough to handle, peel and cut into quarters. Melt the butter in a frying pan, add the beetroot, spring onions and herbs and toss gently until coated with the butter. Remove the beetroot and put into a heated serving dish. Add the cream to the pan, bring to the boil, boil for a minute, then pour over the beetroot. Sprinkle the beetroot with the gherkin strips.

COOKING BEETROOT IN A MICROWAVE OVEN

For 6 medium beetroot – wash and trim (halve or quarter large beetroot). Place in a white plastic shopping bag. Add 1 tablespoon water. Tie the handles but leave a small opening for steam to escape. Place the bag on a large plate. Microwave at 100% power for 10 minutes or until soft when tested with a skewer. Leave bag to cool. Remove the beetroot and peel.

8 small beetroot

60 g butter

4 spring onions, trimmed, washed and finely sliced

1 tablespoon snipped fresh chives

2 teaspoons chopped fresh parsley

¹/₂ cup pouring cream

2 baby gherkins, cut into very fine strips

PREPARATION TIME: 20 minutes

COOKING TIME: 3¾ hours

SERVES: four

MAKING IT JELL

Before gelatine was manufactured, Grandma would have boiled down bones to create a stock. Part of this stock would form a jelly that she would then clarify to form gelatine. Today we simply purchase gelatine. This beetroot salad is from the Davis Dainty Dishes recipe booklet which was distributed from 1922 onwards and was a staple recipe book in kitchens for generations.

FOR THE STUFFED LEAVES

2 slices white bread

500 g lean beef mince (or beef and pork mixed)

1 egg

1 medium onion, finely chopped

1 tablespoon finely chopped parsley

½ teaspoon freshly grated nutmeg

Salt and freshly ground black pepper

1 head of cabbage

FOR THE COOKING SAUCE

1 tablespoon oil or butter

2 large onions, sliced

1 clove garlic, finely chopped

1 teaspoon finely chopped ginger

1 large ripe tomato, diced

1 teaspoon brown sugar

Salt and pepper

PREPARATION TIME: 30 minutes

COOKING TIME: 1 hour

SERVES: four (makes 8 'parcels')

Stuffed Cabbage Leaves

Cabbage-leaf 'parcels' stuffed with frikkadels and cooked in a savoury tomato sauce.

Soak the bread in cold water, squeeze out the excess and mash with a fork. Mix the bread with the rest of the frikkadel ingredients.

Discard the tough outer leaves of the cabbage. Pull eight large leaves from the cabbage and cook them in a large saucepan of boiling salted water for 1 minute until slightly softened. Drain and dry well with paper towels. Spoon a portion of the frikkadel mixture onto each cabbage leaf. Tuck the edges of each leaf around the filling, then roll it up to enclose the filling completely. Secure each 'parcel' with a toothpick and then set aside while the sauce is made.

In a large saucepan, heat the oil or butter and sauté the onions until soft and changing colour. Add the garlic, ginger, tomato, sugar and seasoning. Simmer for 5 minutes. Add ½ cup of boiling water, then pack the cabbage rolls on top of the onion mixture. Cover and braise slowly for about 45 minutes. Add a little hot water if required from time to time. Serve on white rice.

Potatoes should be firm and dry with no sprouts or green patches. Choose unwashed potatoes over washed ones, since the dirt protects them from deterioration.

Crisp & Creamy Potatoes

There's an appealing variation in flavours and textures in this dish –
it also looks most attractive.

Mash the cooked potatoes with the parsley and season to taste. Divide and shape into 12 small balls. Dip each ball in the beaten egg, then roll in breadcrumbs until evenly coated – reshape the balls after coating, if necessary. Put on a plate, cover and chill until required.

Boil the raw potatoes in salted water until cooked. Drain well, then mash with the butter and sour cream until smooth. Season with salt and pepper and mix in the snipped chives. Spoon the mashed potato into a mound in the centre of a heatproof serving dish and swirl it attractively with a palette knife, leaving a narrow border clear around the edge for the potato balls. Cover the dish loosely with foil and keep warm.

Deep-fry the chilled potato balls in hot oil for 3–4 minutes, or until lightly golden. Drain well on paper towels. Arrange the croquettes round the edge of the mashed potato mound and serve. Garnish with snipped chives or sprigs of mint, if desired.

5 small potatoes, peeled
  and cooked
1 tablespoon chopped
  fresh parsley
Salt and freshly ground
  black pepper
1 egg, beaten
1 cup soft white breadcrumbs
  (p.310)
6 medium potatoes, peeled
  and cut in quarters
30 g butter
5 tablespoons sour cream
  (smetana)
2 tablespoons snipped
  fresh chives
Oil, for deep-frying
Chives or fresh mint sprigs,
  to garnish (optional)

PREPARATION TIME: 1 hour
COOKING TIME: 20 minutes
SERVES: six

Savoury Stuffed Marrow

Stuffed marrow is an easily prepared and satisfying family meal.

1¾ cups vegetable stock (p.304)

½ cup long-grain white rice

1 marrow (about 2 kg)

½ cup pine nuts

60 g butter, softened

1 tablespoon olive oil

1 medium onion, peeled and chopped

1 stick celery, trimmed and chopped

1 clove garlic, peeled and crushed

4 teaspoons chopped fresh mint

2 tomatoes, peeled, seeded and chopped

½ teaspoon salt

Freshly ground black pepper

Fresh mint leaves to garnish

1¼ cups homemade tomato sauce (p.306), for serving (optional)

Preparation time: 25 minutes

Cooking time: 1¾ hour

Serves: four as a side dish or two as a main meal

Bring the stock to the boil and stir in the rice. Reduce the heat, cover and cook gently for 20–25 minutes, or until the rice is cooked and the stock is absorbed.

Meanwhile, preheat the oven to 200°C. Cut a slice about 3 cm thick from each end of the marrow and, with a dessertspoon, remove all the seeds to leave a hollow along its entire length. Set aside.

Heat the pine nuts gently in a dry, heavy-based frying pan until they are lightly browned, then remove from the pan and set aside. Melt half the butter with the oil in the frying pan, add the onion and cook until just soft. Stir in the celery and garlic and cook for 5 minutes. Remove from the heat and add the cooked rice, pine nuts, half the mint and the chopped tomatoes. Season well and mix together. Spoon this rice filling into the marrow, pressing it in well.

Spread the remaining butter over a piece of foil large enough to wrap around the marrow, then season it well. Place the marrow in the centre of the foil, wrap it up tightly and place it in a roasting pan. Bake in the oven for 1–1¼ hours, or until the marrow is tender.

Remove from the oven, unwrap and leave to stand for 5 minutes. Cut into 12 even slices and arrange on a serving dish or on individual plates. Garnish with fresh mint leaves and serve with homemade tomato sauce, if using.

Creamed Spinach

This is a good way to serve fresh spinach, but even frozen spinach can be given new life by mixing in cream, butter, salt and pepper.

1 kg spinach

⅓ cup cream or sour cream (smetena)

50 g butter

Salt and freshly ground black pepper

Freshly grated nutmeg

Preparation time: 20 minutes

Cooking time: 15 minutes

Serves: four

Tear the spinach leaves from the stalks, discarding any brown leaves. Wash in 2 or 3 changes of water, making sure the leaves are really clean. Put them in a large, heavy-based saucepan, cover and set over a low heat (do not add water).

After 1 minute, stir with a wooden spoon. Raise the heat and cook for about 10 minutes, stirring from time to time to prevent the leaves from sticking to the pan. Then drain very thoroughly, pressing out all the moisture.

Just before serving, chop the spinach roughly and drain again. Return it to a clean saucepan, stir in the cream or sour cream and reheat gently.

Add the butter, cut into flakes, and stir over a gentle heat until it has been absorbed into the creamed spinach. Season well with salt, pepper and nutmeg, and serve piping hot. Serve with boiled ham, roast beef, grilled steak or chops.

Alternatively use the spinach as a filling for omelettes or as a base for poached eggs, or in shortcrust tartlet cases topped with a sprinkling of grated cheese and served with roast lamb.

VARIATION

Final seasoning can include grated Parmesan cheese, a little lemon juice, crushed garlic and a teaspoon of vegetable extract.

FACING PAGE: *Savoury stuffed marrow*

FOR THE FILLING

60 g butter

1 small leek, trimmed,
    washed and thinly sliced

2 small carrots, peeled
    and diced

3 small peppers, 1 red,
    1 green and 1 yellow,
    seeded and diced

125 g field, flat or open-cup
    mushrooms, wiped
    and sliced

½ cup frozen peas

½ cup walnut pieces
    (optional)

½ cup plain flour

1 teaspoon ground coriander

⅔ cup pouring cream

⅔ cup milk

4 tablespoons chopped
    fresh dill

Salt and freshly ground
    black pepper

FOR THE PASTRY

4 cups plain flour

250 g butter

1 cup grated mature
    Cheddar cheese

½ teaspoon mustard powder

¼ teaspoon salt

¾ cup milk

1 egg, beaten

PREPARATION TIME: 1¼ hours

CHILLING TIME: 30 minutes

COOKING TIME: 40 minutes

MAKES: six pies

Vegetable Pies

*These pies can be frozen before baking and taken straight from
freezer to oven to provide a substantial, healthy snack.*

To make the filling, melt the butter in a large frying pan, add the leek and carrots and cook gently for 5 minutes. Mix in the peppers, mushrooms and peas and cook for a further 5 minutes. Add the walnuts, if used. Stir in the flour and coriander and cook, stirring, for 2 minutes. Gradually add the cream and the milk and cook on medium heat for 5 minutes, or until the mixture comes to the boil and thickens. Remove from the heat, stir in the dill, season to taste with salt and pepper and leave to cool.

To make the pastry, sift the flour into a mixing bowl and rub in the butter. Stir in three-quarters of the Cheddar cheese with the mustard powder and salt. Add the milk and mix to a soft but not sticky dough. Knead lightly on a floured surface until smooth.

Lightly grease six ovenproof saucers, or shallow pie tins, 15 cm in diameter. Cut the dough in half, roll out one half thinly and, using one of the saucers as a guide, cut out six rounds, each a little larger than the saucer. Line the saucers with the rounds and divide the filling equally among them, spreading it up to about 1 cm of the edges.

Roll out the remaining dough thinly and, using a 16 cm plate as a guide, cut out six more rounds. Brush the edges of the dough on the saucers with cold water, cover with the 'lids' and press the edges together well. Trim and decorate the edges. Make a small hole in the centre of each pie to allow the steam to escape, then chill for 30 minutes.

Preheat the oven to 200°C. Put the pies on two baking trays, brush with the beaten egg and sprinkle with the remaining Cheddar cheese. Bake for 30 minutes, then reverse the position of the trays and cook for a further 10 minutes, or until the pies are golden brown. If baking from frozen, check that the filling is heated through (insert a skewer through the hole in the crust, leave for 30 seconds and test on your hand). Bake a little longer, if necessary.

THE FIRST MENU

According to legend, menus can be traced back to the early 1500s. At the closing banquet of the Imperial Diet at Regensburg in Bavaria (now in Germany) the Duke of Brunswick did something which had apparently not been done before - he visited the kitchen and wrote down a list of the dishes which were going to be served, thus creating the first menu. Before long the menu card began to appear at the table all over Europe. The menu above was issued for a 1935 voyage of the Union Castle liner, Edinburgh Castle.

Glazed Carrots with Orange

The addition of orange to the carrots makes a different way of serving the highly adaptable carrot.

Put the baby carrots in a saucepan and add just enough water to cover. (If using larger carrots, cut them into finger-sized sticks.) Add the brown sugar, butter, orange rind and juice and bring to the boil. Boil rapidly for 12–15 minutes, or until the carrots are cooked and glazed with the juices (which should have reduced in volume and become syrupy).

Stir in the lemon juice or whisky and season to taste with salt and pepper. Garnish with chopped parsley and serve immediately.

- 12-16 baby carrots, scraped and washed
- 1 tablespoon brown sugar
- 30 g butter
- Finely grated rind and strained juice of 1 orange
- 1 tablespoon lemon juice or whisky
- Salt and freshly ground black pepper
- Parsley, chopped, to garnish

PREPARATION TIME: 5-10 minutes
COOKING TIME: 15 minutes
SERVES: four

An easier way to cook gem squash is to cut them in half and cook cut side down in a little salted water for 15 minutes. Serve with butter or a grating of nutmeg.

Stuffed Gem Squash

The delicate flavour of gem squash is brought out in this recipe.

4 large gem squash
Salt

FOR THE FILLING
30 g butter
2 tablespoons flour
200 ml milk
100 g mature Cheddar cheese, grated
Salt and freshly ground black pepper
3 egg yolks
4 egg whites

PREPARATION TIME: 45 minutes
COOKING TIME: 25 minutes
SERVES: four to six

Preheat the oven to 200°C. With the tip of a sharp knife, score a line around the middle of each squash. Cook the squash in salted boiling water for 15 to 20 minutes, or until the flesh is tender. Drain, cool and halve the squash and remove the seeds.

Slice a thin segment from the base of each shell so that they stand straight. Scoop out most of the flesh into a bowl.

To make the filling, melt the butter, stir in the flour and cook for 1–2 minutes without browning. Add the milk and bring to the boil, stirring continually to make a smooth sauce. Simmer for 2 minutes, then beat in the mashed or puréed flesh of the squash, together with the cheese and seasoning.

Remove from the heat and beat in the egg yolks one by one. Whisk the egg whites until stiff, fold into the mixture, and spoon into the hollowed squash shells. Place the squash on a baking sheet and cook for 20–25 minutes until puffed like a soufflé.

VARIATIONS
Cook, halve and fill the squash with a mixture of the squash flesh and a savoury beef mince, or with a mixture of the squash, rice, minced lamb and parsley.

For a different effect, sprinkle with grated cheese and bake at 180°C for 30 minutes (or until the tops are golden).

Samp and Beans & Stywe Pap

Be adventurous and try these dishes with a variety of combinations – samp (dried mealies) and beans with a bredie, or stywe pap (mealie meal porridge) with a curry.

SAMP AND BEANS

Drain the samp and beans. In a large saucepan, cover the samp and beans with cold water and bring slowly to the boil. Simmer gently for about 3 hours, stirring now and again and adding water when necessary. Add the salt towards the end of the cooking time. The dish is cooked when the beans are soft and the water absorbed. Serve with meat or vegetables – tomato bredie is also good.

STYWE PAP

Bring the water to the boil and add the salt. Lower the heat and gradually pour the maize meal into the water, whisking all the time to prevent lumps from forming. Cover the saucepan and simmer for 30 minutes or until cooked, stirring with a wooden spoon from time to time.

Serve plain as a porridge, with a braai, or as a starch in place of rice.

SAMP AND BEANS

500 g samp and beans, soaked overnight in water
1 teaspoons salt, or to taste

PREPARATION TIME: 5 minutes
SOAKING TIME: 24 hours
COOKING TIME: 3 hours
SERVES: six

STYWE PAP

6 cups water
1 teaspoon salt
2 cups maize meal

PREPARATION TIME: 5 minutes
COOKING TIME: 40 minutes
SERVES: four

DECIMAL DAN

On 14 February 1961 Decimal Dan 'the rand and cents man' introduced South Africans to their new decimal coinage. Metrification of weights and measures followed and housewives had to convert all their favourite recipes from pounds and ounces to kilograms and grams. This guide for housewives was published by the Metrification Department of the South African Bureau of Standards.

Stuffed Onions

*These nutty, fruity onions are particularly
good served with roast pork.*

4 large onions, each
    about 250 g, peeled
175 g Brie cheese, cubed
½ cup coarsely chopped
    walnuts, almonds or pecans
2 tablespoons seedless raisins
1 tablespoon chopped
    fresh sage
Salt and freshly ground
    black pepper
⅔ cup vegetable stock (p.304)
30 g butter, melted
2 teaspoons soft light
    brown sugar

PREPARATION TIME: 25 minutes
COOKING TIME: 45 minutes
SERVES: four

Preheat the oven to 180°C. Cook the onions in boiling water for 10 minutes, then drain well and rinse under cold water until cool enough to handle. Using a sharp knife, cut a thin slice from the top and remove the centre from each onion, making a hollow about 4 cm deep and 5 cm wide.

Chop the onion centres and tops finely and combine the chopped onions in a bowl with the cheese, nuts, raisins and sage. Season to taste. Pack the mixture into the centre of each onion, pressing it down firmly. Pile any leftover filling on top.

Arrange the stuffed onions in a shallow, heatproof dish that is large enough to hold them comfortably. Pour the vegetable stock over the onions. Brush the onions with the melted butter and sprinkle the light brown sugar over the top.

Cover the dish with foil, but do not let the foil touch the onions. Bake in the oven for 15 minutes, then remove the foil and bake for a further 20–30 minutes, or until the onions are lightly browned and tender and the top of the stuffing is crisp.

Remove the dish from the oven, baste the onions with the cooking juices and serve.

VARIATION

Ham-stuffed Onions: Prepare as for stuffed onions, but replace the cheese mixture with 200 g minced ham, mixed with a little sour cream and chopped celery. Serve with rice as a main course, or on their own as a light lunch.

Onions in a Sweet & Sour Sauce

*These onions are delicious either on their own as a starter, or when accompanying a main
course of meat. They can be kept in a covered container in the refrigerator.*

500 g pickling onions
Boiling water
2 tablespoons olive oil
2 tablespoons brown sugar
1 cup white wine
¼ cup white wine vinegar
2 tablespoons tomato paste
¾ teaspoon dried thyme
75 g currants
Salt and freshly ground black
    pepper
Finely chopped parsley to
    garnish

PREPARATION TIME: 30 minutes
COOKING TIME: 30 minutes
CHILLING TIME: 1 hour
SERVES: six

Put the onions in an ovenproof bowl and pour over enough boiling water to cover; leave to stand for 5 minutes. Drain in a colander and rinse with cold water, then peel and pat the onions dry.

Heat the olive oil in a saucepan and sauté the onions until they are very lightly browned. Sprinkle with the brown sugar and stir-fry until the sugar has melted and slightly caramelised.

Carefully add the white wine, white vinegar, tomato paste, dried thyme and currants and season lightly with the salt and freshly ground pepper.

Bring the mixture to the boil, then turn down the heat and simmer for 10–15 minutes, or until the sauce has thickened and the onions are tender but still crisp in the centre.

Spoon the onion mixture into a serving dish, cover with plastic wrap and chill for at least 1 hour before serving.

Just before serving, sprinkle over the finely chopped parsley.

FACING PAGE: *Stuffed onions*

10 medium boiling potatoes
100 g butter
Salt and freshly ground black
  pepper

PREPARATION TIME: 30 minutes
COOKING TIME: 25 minutes
SERVES: six

Potato Cake

Traditionally, this Swiss potato cake, known as rosti, is served with veal cooked in a cream sauce, but these days it is often served with smoked salmon or salmon trout with a dollop of sour cream. Grilled sausages, bacon, even fried eggs, all go well with rosti.

Scrub the potatoes and place them in a saucepan of cold water. Cover and boil for 10–15 minutes, or until they are barely tender. Drain and leave to cool, then peel the potatoes and grate on a fairly coarse blade of the grater.

Melt 1/2 the butter in a large, heavy-based frying pan. Add the grated potatoes and sprinkle with salt and pepper. Pat into a cake and fry over a medium heat for about 10 minutes until lightly brown. Then put a plate over the pan and invert the cake onto the plate.

Add the rest of the butter to the pan, if necessary, and slide the rosti back into the pan to cook on the other side for about 10 minutes until lightly brown.

Loosen with a spatula and invert the potato cake onto a large, round serving plate. Serve immediately.

VARIATIONS

Finely chopped cooked onion, chopped streaky bacon, ham or sausage can be added to the grated potato mixture before it is patted into a cake and fried.

Instead of making one large potato cake, make 6 smaller cakes for breakfast and top each one with a fried egg and a rasher of crisp bacon.

EVERYTHING AT THE O.K.
IS OK

'The greatest event in shopping history' happened, if the claims of the advertiser could be believed, on Saturday, 25 June 1927, when at 9 a.m. the doors of Sam Cohen and Michael Miller's O.K. Bazaars store in Johannesburg's Eloff Street opened for the first time. Goods fell into three price categories - 3d, 6d and 1/-. Sales were spectacular and police had to be brought in to control the crowds. For decades O.K. Bazaars was part of the South African shopping scene, until, sadly, the business declined and was sold.

Although the name has disappeared from shop fronts, it remains firmly lodged in the memories of generations of South Africans.

ONION LORE

Many myths and healing properties have been attached to the humble onion. Grandma may have put it into soup to clear up a bad complexion or cure a cold, used the juice to get rid of warts, and eaten it raw to clear the sinuses and to dull earache. If she was particularly superstitious, she may even have used the onion as a defence against evil.

Cheese, Potato & Onion Pie

You don't have to be a vegetarian to enjoy this wholesome dish.

Boil the potatoes in lightly salted water until cooked, drain well and mash with two-thirds of the butter and the milk. Mix in the Cheddar cheese and season to taste.

Preheat the oven to 200°C. Melt the remaining butter in a frying pan, add the onions and cook on medium heat for 10 minutes. Stir in the thyme and sugar and continue to cook until golden and caramelised.

Spread half the mashed potato in the bottom of a pie dish or ovenproof dish. Spread the onions on top and cover with the remaining potato. Arrange the tomato slices on top and sprinkle with the breadcrumbs and Parmesan cheese. Bake in the centre of the oven for 30 minutes, or until golden brown and piping hot. Serve with a crisp green salad or cooked green vegetables.

5 medium potatoes, peeled and quartered

Salt

90 g butter

3 tablespoons milk

1½ cups grated mature Cheddar cheese

Freshly ground black pepper

2 large onions, peeled and sliced

½–1 teaspoon dried thyme

1 tablespoon caster sugar

4 tomatoes, sliced

¼ cup dried white breadcrumbs (p.310)

1 tablespoon grated Parmesan cheese

PREPARATION TIME: 30 minutes
COOKING TIME: 55 minutes
SERVES: four

PUMPKIN FRITTERS

450 g peeled pumpkin

A pinch of salt and sugar

60 g flour

1 teaspoon baking powder

2 eggs

Milk (optional)

3 tablespoons sunflower oil

3 tablespoons butter

½ cup sugar mixed with
    1 teaspoon cinnamon

Lemon wedges for garnish

PREPARATION TIME: 25 minutes

COOKING TIME: 20 minutes

SERVES: six

SWEET CORN FRITTERS

2 extra-large eggs, separated

Salt and freshly ground black
    pepper

A pinch of sugar

1 tin (410 g) whole-kernel
    sweet corn (not creamed)
    or 2 cups fresh sweet corn,
    cooked

1 teaspoon baking powder

1 cup fresh breadcrumbs

Sunflower oil for frying

PREPARATION TIME: 10 minutes

COOKING TIME: 20 minutes

SERVES: six

Vegetable Fritters

Fritters are a delicious way to present vegetables - they can be dressed down for lunch or up for supper. In fact, they can even be served for breakfast.

PUMPKIN FRITTERS

Steam the pumpkin over boiling water in a vegetable steamer with a little salt and sugar until it is just done. Leave on paper towels to absorb excess liquid. Mash until smooth.

Mix the pumpkin, flour, baking powder and eggs to form a batter of dropping consistency. Add a little milk if it is too stiff.

Fry spoonfuls in the mixed, heated oil and butter in a large heavy-based frying pan. Drain the fritters on brown paper or paper towels.

Sprinkle them with cinnamon sugar and serve hot with wedges of lemon on the side.

VARIATION

Replace the pumpkin with sweet potatoes.

SWEET CORN FRITTERS

Beat the egg yolks with salt and pepper, then add the sugar and the sweet corn drained of all its liquid. Whisk the egg whites until stiff and fold into the yolk mixture, together with the baking powder and crumbs

Pour oil into a frying pan (to a depth of about 5 mm) and drop tablespoons of the mixture into the pan. Fry until golden-brown, then turn and fry the other side. Drain well and serve hot with crispy bacon.

VARIATION

To make the fritters more substantial, add finely chopped onion, diced ham or sliced cooked sausage to the basic mixture.

Red Cabbage & Orange

*Red cabbage, cooked slowly, improves with keeping and
any that is left over can be served with another meal.*

Put the cabbage in a large bowl. Finely grate the rind from 1 orange and squeeze the juice. Stir the rind and juice into the cabbage with the onion, garlic, sugar, vinegar, salt and pepper and the bay leaf. Cover and leave to stand overnight.

Melt the treacle and butter in a large, heavy-based, stainless-steel or enamel sauce-pan. Stir in the cabbage mixture and slowly bring to the boil, stirring occasionally. Reduce the heat, cover and simmer, stirring every 30 minutes, for 2 hours, or until the juices have almost evaporated and the cabbage is tender. Remove and discard the bay leaf.

Thinly pare the rind from the remaining orange and cut it into very fine shreds. Stir half the shreds into the cabbage, then spoon it into a serving dish and sprinkle with the remaining shreds. Serve with sausages or grilled meats and mashed potatoes.

1,5 kg red cabbage,
   finely shredded
2 medium oranges
1 small onion, peeled
   and finely chopped
1 clove garlic, peeled
   and crushed
3 tablespoons caster sugar
4 tablespoons red
   wine vinegar
Salt and freshly ground
   black pepper
1 bay leaf
1 tablespoon treacle
30 g butter

PREPARATION TIME:
   Day 1, 15 minutes
   Day 2, 10 minutes
STANDING TIME: overnight
COOKING TIME: 2 hours
SERVES: eight

To shred cabbage, use a long knife to cut the head in half through the stem, then halve again and slice out the core. With the cut side down, finely slice the quarters crosswise.

5 medium potatoes, peeled
   and quartered

500 g green cabbage, washed
   and shredded

4 tablespoons milk

¼ teaspoon salt

Pinch of freshly ground
   black pepper

Pinch of ground nutmeg

3 spring onions, trimmed
   and thinly sliced

60 g butter

Preparation time: 10 minutes
Cooking time: 25 minutes
Serves: four

Colcannon

*Colcannon is the glorious Irish version of bubble and squeak.
It is lovely dished up with sausages, ham or bacon.*

Preheat the oven to 160°C. Boil the quartered potatoes gently in salted water for 15 minutes, or until cooked. Drain well.

Meanwhile, put the shredded cabbage in another saucepan, cover with boiling water and simmer for 5 minutes, or until tender. Drain well.

Put a deep serving dish in the oven to warm. Mash the potatoes in the saucepan until smooth, add the milk, salt, pepper and nutmeg and mash again. Reserve 1 tablespoon of the green part of the sliced spring onions for garnish, then add the rest to the potatoes with the drained cabbage. Place the saucepan on low heat and continue to mash for 5 minutes, or until fluffy and heated through.

Spoon the colcannon into the heated serving dish, make a well in the centre, add the butter and return to the oven for 5 minutes, or until the butter has melted. Sprinkle with the reserved spring onion and serve piping hot.

UNDER PRESSURE

The term 'pressure cooker' first appeared in print in 1915 and 10-gallon aluminium pressure cookers were popular with those who did a lot of home canning. In 1939 National Presto Industries launched their new design with a locking lid and this method of cooking became very popular.

Use of pressure cookers has waned over the years, but new designs and safety features have resulted in renewed interest.

Festive Vegetables

These are the vegetables to serve with the Christmas turkey (see p.158).

BUTTERY ROAST POTATOES
Put the sliced potatoes in a large saucepan, cover with cold water, add the salt and bring to the boil. Drain.

Meanwhile, put the butter in a large, shallow, ovenproof dish or roasting pan, take 1–2 tablespoons of the fat from the turkey, add it to the butter and heat it in the oven, above the turkey, until it is sizzling hot. Add the potatoes to the hot fat and turn until evenly coated. Cook on the shelf above the turkey for 1–1½ hours, or until crisp and golden brown. If you have a double oven, it may be easier to bake the potatoes separately in the second oven, preheated to 180°C.

SWEDE & POTATO GRATIN
Steam or boil the swedes and potatoes together until tender, then drain well and mash. Beat in half the butter, season to taste with salt, pepper and nutmeg and spoon into an ovenproof dish. Melt the remaining butter in a frying pan, remove from the heat and stir in the breadcrumbs and the chopped parsley. Sprinkle the mixture over the mashed swede and potato and set aside.

When the turkey is removed from the oven, increase the temperature to 220°C. While making the gravy, put the gratin into the oven to cook until golden brown on top.

BRAISED CARROTS, PEAS & ONIONS IN CREAM SAUCE
Put the onions in a large saucepan and add the carrots. Sprinkle with the sugar, salt and pepper and pour in the stock – it will not cover the carrots, but they will cook in the steam. Cover the pan and bring to the boil, then reduce the heat and simmer for 5 minutes, or until the carrots are just tender.

Remove the lid from the pan and boil rapidly to reduce the stock by three-quarters. Add the peas and heat through. Stir in the cream and serve immediately.

BUTTERY ROAST POTATOES
6 medium potatoes, peeled and thickly sliced

½ teaspoon salt

30 g butter

1–2 tablespoons turkey fat

PREPARATION TIME: 15 minutes

COOKING TIME: 1–1½ hours

SERVES: six

SWEDE & POTATO GRATIN
5 small swedes, peeled and roughly chopped

3 medium potatoes, peeled and roughly chopped

30 g butter

¼ teaspoon salt

¼ teaspoon freshly ground black pepper

Pinch of ground nutmeg

½ cup soft white breadcrumbs (p.310)

2 teaspoons chopped fresh parsley

PREPARATION TIME: 30 minutes

COOKING TIME: 20 minutes

SERVES: six

BRAISED CARROTS, PEAS & ONIONS IN CREAM SAUCE
250 g baby onions, peeled, halved (if large)

6 small carrots, peeled and cut into long, thin strips

2 teaspoons brown sugar

Pinch each of salt and freshly ground black pepper

⅔ cup chicken stock (p.305)

2 cups (250 g) frozen peas, thawed and drained

2 tablespoons thick cream

PREPARATION TIME: 25 minutes

COOKING TIME: 15–20 minutes

SERVES: six

Onion, Apple & Sage Pie

Served cold, this pie is perfect company for cold picnic meats.

FOR THE PASTRY
2 cups plain flour
Pinch of salt
125 g butter
3 tablespoons cold water
1 small egg, beaten,
    or milk, to glaze

FOR THE FILLING
4 small onions, peeled,
    halved and thinly sliced
3 small cooking apples,
    peeled, cored and
    thinly sliced
2 teaspoons finely
    chopped fresh sage
    or 1 teaspoon dried sage
¼ teaspoon each salt
    and freshly ground
    black pepper
4 tablespoons sour cream
    (smetena)
Sage leaves, to garnish

PREPARATION TIME: 1 hour
CHILLING TIME: 1 hour
COOKING TIME: 40 minutes
SERVES: four

To make the pastry, sift the flour and salt into a mixing bowl. Rub in the butter until the mixture resembles fine breadcrumbs. Add the water and mix to a dough. Knead gently on a lightly floured surface for a few seconds until smooth, then wrap in plastic wrap and chill for at least 30 minutes.

On a lightly floured surface, roll out the chilled dough to a square a little larger than 30 cm, trim the edges to that size and place on a large baking tray. Put half the sliced onions, followed by half the apples, in the centre of the dough square and sprinkle with half the sage, salt and pepper. Add the remaining onion, apple and seasonings and spread the sour cream on top.

Brush some beaten egg or milk around the edges of the dough and fold the two opposite corners over the vegetable filling so that they meet and overlap slightly in the centre. Repeat with the other two corners to make an envelope. Press the joins together gently to seal. Use the trimmings to decorate the pie and chill for at least 30 minutes. Preheat the oven to 220°C.

Brush the chilled pie all over with the remaining beaten egg or milk and bake in the centre of the oven for 40 minutes, or until the pastry is crisp and golden brown. (If the pastry begins to brown too much, protect it by covering the pie loosely with greaseproof paper or aluminium foil.)

Carefully transfer the pie to a serving plate or board and garnish with the sage leaves. Serve hot or cold, on its own or with cold meats, sausages and cheese.

Game Chips

These chips are cut very thinly and cooked until crispy golden-brown. As the name implies, they are customarily served with game, but are good with any roast meats.

500 g potatoes
Sunflower oil for deep-frying
Salt and freshly ground black
    pepper

PREPARATION TIME: 10 minutes
SOAKING TIME: 30 minutes
COOKING TIME: 10 minutes
SERVES: four

Peel the potatoes and slice them very thinly with a cheese parer. Soak the slices in cold water for 30 minutes to remove excess starch. Drain them well and pat them dry on paper towels.

Pour the oil into a deep pan to a depth of 5 cm or more depending on the size of the pan and heat it to 200°C – a cube of bread dropped in it should turn golden-brown in about 45 seconds.

Put half the potato slices into a frying basket and lower it carefully into the oil. Move the slices around so that they do not stick together. Remove them after about 5 minutes when they are golden-brown. Drain them on paper towels. Keep the chips warm, uncovered, under a moderate grill while you cook the rest of the slices.

Sprinkle with salt and pepper.

FACING PAGE: *Onion, apple and sage pie*

THE BEAN SLICER
This aid to the busy cook enabled speedy slicing of green beans for the saucepan. It could also be used to slice peel for marmalade.

200 g fresh green beans, cut in 2,5 cm strips

400 g fresh unshelled peas or 200 g frozen peas

2 small aubergines, washed and cut into 2,5 cm cubes

1 large onion, peeled and chopped

1 teaspoon turmeric

1½ teaspoons salt

A 5 cm piece of fresh ginger, crushed to a paste

1 teaspoon red chilli powder

2 teaspoons coriander seeds, crushed

2 teaspoons cumin seeds, crushed

½ cup sunflower oil or ghee (p.313)

2 cinnamon sticks (each 7,5 cm long)

1 teaspoon lovage seeds (ajmo) or cumin

1 medium ripe tomato, chopped

2 tablespoons chopped coriander (dhania) leaves to garnish.

PREPARATION TIME: 20 minutes

COOKING TIME: 30 minutes

SERVES: six

Spicy Vegetables

This dish of Indian spiced vegetables can be served as a vegetarian meal, accompanied by warm chapati and pickles, or as a side dish with chicken, meat or fish.

Mix together the beans, shelled peas, aubergines, onion, turmeric, salt, ginger, chilli powder, coriander and cumin seeds in a bowl. Set the bowl aside.

Heat the oil or ghee in a saucepan, add the cinnamon sticks and lovage seeds (or cumin), and brown for a few seconds.

Add the mixture of spiced vegetables to the pot, stir and cover the saucepan. Simmer on a low heat for 20 minutes. Add the chopped tomato, and cook, covered, for a further 10 minutes.

Garnish with the chopped coriander leaves and serve.

Cauliflower Cheese

Smooth, rich and velvety cauliflower cheese is a perennial favourite.

Preheat the oven to 200°C. Trim the leaves and stalk from the cauliflower, and break it into large, even-sized florets (or leave whole if preferred). Cook in salted boiling water with the bay leaf for 5–7 minutes, or until just tender. Drain thoroughly and place in a shallow oven-proof dish.

To make the sauce, melt the first measure of butter and stir in the flour. Cook for 1 minute without browning. Slowly stir in the milk and bring to the boil, stirring continually, to make a smooth sauce. Reduce the heat and simmer (stirring) for 2 minutes. Season to taste with salt, pepper and nutmeg. Add the mustard and half the grated cheese.

Pour the sauce over the cauliflower. Sprinkle with the remaining cheese mixed with the breadcrumbs and melted butter. Bake for 30 minutes, or grill until golden-brown.

VARIATIONS

Add chopped hard-boiled eggs, diced ham or sautéed mushrooms to the sauce before spooning it over the cauliflower.

Alternatively, top with grilled bacon rashers just before serving.

1 medium cauliflower
Salt
1 bay leaf
60 g butter
4 tablespoons flour
2 cups milk
Fresh ground black pepper
Freshly grated nutmeg
1 teaspoon prepared English mustard
250 g mature Cheddar cheese, grated
50 g fresh breadcrumbs
1 tablespoon melted butter

PREPARATION TIME: 35 minutes
COOKING TIME: 30 minutes
SERVES: four to six

Avoid cooking cauliflower in an aluminium saucepan — a chemical reaction with aluminium can turn cauliflower yellow.

FOR THE ASPARAGUS

4 bunches fresh asparagus
(about 40 spears)

FOR THE LEMON BUTTER

90 g butter, chopped

Freshly ground white pepper

3 tablespoons lemon juice

1 tablespoon chopped
fresh parsley

PREPARATION TIME: 5 minutes

COOKING TIME: 8 minutes

SERVES: six

Asparagus with Lemon Butter

*Serve the dressed asparagus alone as a first course,
or as a luxurious vegetable accompaniment.*

Using a potato peeler, thinly peel the lower three-quarters of each spear of asparagus, and trim off the woody end. Wash and set aside.

For the best flavour, steam the asparagus in a tiered steamer for 6–8 minutes, or until tender, taking care not to overcook. Alternatively, place the spears in a single layer in lightly salted water in a frying pan and poach gently for 5–10 minutes, or until just tender. Lift out carefully with tongs and drain for a

few moments on paper towels. Arrange on a heated serving dish and keep warm.

Meanwhile, to prepare the lemon butter, melt the butter in a small saucepan, season with white pepper and stir in the lemon juice and parsley. Pour over the asparagus and serve immediately with crusty bread.

ASPARAGUS COLOURS

Asparagus spears come in three colours. White asparagus is grown underground so that it is not exposed to light. When harvested, it is cut below the surface before being lifted out of the soil. If the spears are allowed to grow in sunlight, they turn green. A newer purple variety is grown in the same way as green asparagus.

A WELL-TRAVELLED
WELSH DISH

*Wales has given the world a
number of well-known dishes -
this potato cake being one of the
most popular. Here a quartet of
Welsh ladies take tea in the
1930s. Their dress is based upon
countrywomen's clothes of the
1820s, while the hats were worn
by men at that time. The
ensemble was popularised as the
Welsh national costume by print
makers and photographers, and
with postcards, such as this one.*

Onion Cake

*In this dish, which originated in Wales, the layers of potatoes and onions
are drenched in butter and baked to a golden crispness. The cake is delicious
on its own or as an accompaniment to lamb or other meat.*

Preheat the oven to 220°C and line the base and sides of a greased 18 cm round cake tin with baking paper. Arrange a layer of overlapping potato slices in the bottom of the tin and sprinkle with some of the chopped onion. Season to taste with salt and pepper and pour on a little of the melted butter.

Continue to make layers of potatoes and chopped onion until the potatoes are used up and the tin is full. Pour any remaining butter over the top and bake in the centre of the oven for 1 hour, or until the potatoes are cooked.

Remove the potato cake from the oven and turn it out carefully onto an ovenproof dish. Return it to the oven for 10 minutes more, or until it is golden brown.

Cut the cake into wedges and serve as an accompaniment to casseroles, roast meats, cold meats or savoury pies.

8 medium baking potatoes,
  peeled and thinly sliced
1 medium onion, peeled
  and finely chopped
Salt and freshly ground
  black pepper
175 g butter, melted

PREPARATION TIME: 30 minutes
COOKING TIME: 1 hour 10 minutes
SERVES: six

Caesar Salad

Caesar salad is not named for a Roman emperor – Caesar Gardini, a restaurateur from Tijuana, Mexico created the salad in 1924. The classic Caesar salad should contain anchovies, croûtons, egg and lettuce leaves drenched in a creamy dressing. In this version, the anchovies and egg are combined with the dressing.

2 large garlic cloves

150 ml olive oil

2 anchovy fillets, finely chopped

2 tablespoons lemon juice

½ teaspoon dry English mustard

Freshly ground black pepper

1 egg

2 slices bread, cubed, crusts removed

1 cos lettuce

2 tablespoons freshly grated Parmesan cheese

PREPARATION TIME: 40 minutes
SERVES: four

Crush the garlic and mix with the olive oil. Leave to stand for 10 minutes. Strain off 3 tablespoons of the olive oil to make the salad dressing.

Add these 3 tablespoons of olive oil to the anchovy fillets, lemon juice, mustard, pepper and raw egg and blend in a liquidiser.

Pour the remaining oil and the garlic into a frying pan. Heat slowly. When the garlic shreds begin to sizzle, add the diced bread and fry, turning frequently until the croûtons are crisp and brown. With a perforated spoon, lift out the croûtons and drain and allow to cool on paper towels.

Separate the lettuce leaves, tear into bite-sized pieces and place in a salad bowl. Gently toss the lettuce in the dressing so as to coat all the leaves. Add the croûtons and Parmesan cheese and toss once more. Serve immediately.

Traditionally, Caesar salad was made in a wooden salad bowl, which was sprinkled with salt and rubbed with garlic.

Salad Nicoise

Salad Nicoise is thought to have originated in the areas around Nice in southern France. Follow tradition and serve this Mediterranean salad with a light, dry wine and crusty French bread.

500 g green beans, trimmed, washed and dried

1 butter lettuce, washed and patted dry

1 medium onion, peeled and finely sliced into rings

3 ripe medium tomatoes, cut into wedges

½ cup black olives

1 tin (55 g) anchovy fillets, drained

2 tins (200 g each) tuna, drained and broken into chunks

2 hard-boiled eggs, sliced

2 teaspoons chopped parsley

FOR THE DRESSING

½ cup olive oil

¼ cup sunflower oil

¼ cup red wine vinegar

1 clove garlic (optional)

Salt and freshly ground black pepper

PREPARATION TIME: 30 minutes
SERVES: six

Cook the green beans for 4 minutes or until tender in rapidly boiling water and then immediately cool under cold running water. Drain and reserve.

Arrange the lettuce leaves on a large, round platter. Overlap them with the beans, onion rings, tomato wedges, olives, anchovies, tuna and hard-boiled eggs. Sprinkle with the chopped parsley.

To make the salad dressing, blend the oils, vinegar, garlic (if used), salt and pepper in a liquidiser (or beat thoroughly) and pour over the salad.

VARIATION
Replace tinned tuna with 400 g fresh tuna steaks, brushed with oil and pan-fried over high heat for about 3 minutes on each side (the centre will still be pink). Cut into 3 cm chunks and add to the salad.

FACING PAGE: *Caesar salad*

A DAY OUTDOORS

In Grandma's day picnics were popular and albums of the time are filled with photographs of happy picnickers lounging on blankets with their flasks and other picnic paraphernalia.

POTATO SALAD WITH CRISPY BACON

1,5 kg baby new potatoes, washed

3 rashers lean bacon, rind removed, chopped

3/4 cup thick mayonnaise

2 tablespoons snipped fresh chives

Salt and freshly ground black pepper

PREPARATION TIME: 15 minutes

COOKING TIME: 25 minutes

SERVES: eight

TOMATO & ONION SALAD

4 ripe medium tomatoes, cores removed, sliced

1 small red onion, peeled and thinly sliced

6 spring onions, trimmed and finely chopped

3 tablespoons shredded fresh basil

Coarsely ground black pepper

7 tablespoons extra virgin olive oil, or to taste

PREPARATION TIME: 15 minutes

SERVES: eight

Picnic Salads

A good picnic salad is easy to transport, robust in flavour and not fussy about the temperature at which it is served – these two fill the bill perfectly.

POTATO SALAD WITH CRISPY BACON

Steam or boil the potatoes until cooked, drain well and allow to cool. Cook the bacon in a frying pan with no extra fat until very crisp and brown. Remove from the pan with a slotted spoon and leave to cool.

Halve the potatoes and put in a bowl, add the mayonnaise and chives and season to taste. Mix well and transfer to a serving dish.

Sprinkle the bacon over the top, cover the bowl with plastic wrap and refrigerate.

TOMATO & ONION SALAD

Arrange the tomato and onion slices in a serving dish. Sprinkle with the spring onions, basil and black pepper to taste. Drizzle with the olive oil.

Cover the dish with plastic wrap and refrigerate until packing time.

Cucumber Salad

The cucumbers are degorged of some of their juice before making this salad so that the fresh dill flavour of the dressing isn't diluted.

Scoop the seeds out of the cucumber and discard them. Thinly slice the cucumber and sprinkle with salt. Let stand for 30 minutes and drain well. Combine the cucumber with the spring onions and radishes in a small bowl.

To prepare the dressing, whisk the sour cream in a small bowl with the vinegar, dill, sugar, mustard and pepper. Pour the dressing over the cucumber mixture. Toss to coat. Cover and refrigerate for 1 hour.

FOR THE SALAD

1 medium green cucumber, halved lengthways

¼ teaspoon salt

2 large spring onions with tops, finely sliced

¼ cup thinly sliced radishes

FOR THE DRESSING

½ cup sour cream

2 tablespoons tarragon vinegar or white wine vinegar

1 tablespoon finely chopped fresh dill or 1 teaspoon dried dill

1 teaspoon sugar

1 teaspoon Dijon mustard

¼ teaspoon black pepper

PREPARATION TIME: 10 minutes

STANDING TIME: 30 minutes

CHILLING TIME: 1 hour

SERVES: four

Before preparing this salad, always taste a slice of the cucumber to ensure that it is not too bitter. If the skin is tough, you may want to peel the cucumber before slicing it.

MINTED NEW POTATOES

1,25 kg small new potatoes, well washed

1 large sprig mint

1 teaspoon salt

60 g butter

2 tablespoons chopped fresh parsley

Fresh mint and parsley sprigs, to garnish (optional)

PREPARATION TIME: 15 minutes

COOKING TIME: 20–25 minutes

SERVES: six

FOR THE WHITE WINE DRESSING

½ cup dry white wine

1 teaspoon lemon juice

1 clove garlic, peeled and thinly sliced

1 small onion, peeled and finely chopped

Pinch each of salt and caster sugar

FOR THE MIXED GREEN SALAD

½ crisp lettuce, such as iceberg, washed and dried

½ cos lettuce, washed and dried

4 sticks celery, trimmed and thinly sliced

½ bunch rocket, washed and drained (optional)

1 ripe avocado, halved, stoned, peeled and sliced

1 small cucumber, peeled, halved, seeded and sliced

4 tablespoons olive oil

Freshly ground black pepper

PREPARATION TIME:
Day 1, 5 minutes
Day 2, 20 minutes

STANDING TIME: overnight (for the dressing only)

SERVES: six

Summer Accompaniments

New potatoes in parsley butter and a mixed green salad tossed in white wine dressing demonstrate the charm of the fresh and simple.

MINTED NEW POTATOES

Cover the potatoes with boiling salted water in a large saucepan, add a sprig of mint and bring back to the boil. Reduce the heat, partly cover and simmer for 20–25 minutes, or until the potatoes are cooked. Drain well.

Melt the butter in the saucepan used to cook the potatoes and stir in the parsley. Return the potatoes to the saucepan and toss them gently in the hot parsley butter.

Transfer the potatoes to a heated serving dish, garnish with the sprigs of mint and parsley, if using, and serve immediately.

MIXED GREEN SALAD WITH WHITE WINE DRESSING

Make the dressing the day before serving. Put all the ingredients in a plastic container or a clean screwtop jar, cover with a tight-fitting lid and shake well. Refrigerate until required.

Next day, tear the lettuce leaves in small pieces and put in a salad bowl. Add the celery, rocket leaves (if used), avocado and cucumber slices. Pour the olive oil over the greens, season to taste with the pepper and toss well. Shake the dressing well just before straining it over the salad. Toss once more and serve.

FOR THE HOSTESS SALAD

4 cups mixed salad greens
2 yellow pattypan squash
  or 1 medium courgette
1 medium carrot
1 cup red and/or yellow
  cherry tomatoes or baby
  Roma tomatoes
1 cup small whole fresh
  button mushrooms
1 cup sliced cauliflower
  or broccoli florets

FOR THE HOSTESS DRESSING

¼ cup bought tomato sauce
2 tablespoons grated red
  onion
2 tablespoons olive oil
2 tablespoons lemon juice
  or wine vinegar
2 tablespoons water
1 teaspoon drained prepared
  horseradish
½ teaspoon sugar
½ teaspoon Worcestershire
  sauce
Pinch black pepper

PREPARATION TIME: 25 minutes
SERVES: four to six

Favourite Salads

Hostess salad with its piquant dressing could be served as a first course or as the perfect companion to cold roast beef. Coleslaw is the classic complement to corned beef, ham and frankfurters and other sausages.

HOSTESS SALAD

Tear the salad greens into bite-sized pieces; halve the squash lengthways and slice them 5 mm thick; cut the carrot into 3 cm x 5 mm sticks; and halve the tomatoes. Combine all the vegetables in a large salad bowl.

To prepare the dressing, combine all the ingredients in a screwtop jar, put the lid on and shake the jar well. The dressing will keep, refrigerated, for a week.

To serve, shake the dressing well, pour over the salad and toss lightly to coat.

COLESLAW

Cut the cabbage in half again, then shred. Measure 2½ cups shredded cabbage and discard the rest. Grate the carrots. Combine the cabbage, carrot and spring onion in a large bowl.

To prepare the dressing, whisk the mayonnaise in a small bowl with the sour cream and add the caraway or celery seeds, if used.

Fold the dressing through the vegetable mixture, season to taste with salt and black pepper and toss again. Cover and refrigerate the coleslaw for 1–2 hours. Alternatively, for a crisp coleslaw, refrigerate the prepared vegetables in a plastic bag and combine with the dressing just before serving.

You can make an eye-catching red coleslaw by substituting shredded red cabbage for the green cabbage and adding 1 small chopped Red Delicious apple.

FOR THE COLESLAW

½ small green cabbage
1 large carrot
6 spring onions with tops,
  finely sliced

FOR THE COLESLAW DRESSING

½ cup mayonnaise,
  homemade (p.306)
  or bought
½ cup sour cream (smetena)
1 teaspoon caraway seeds
  or ½ teaspoon celery seeds
  (optional)
Salt and freshly ground
  black pepper

PREPARATION TIME: 25 minutes
CHILLING TIME: 1–2 hours
SERVES: four to six

Boil or steam carrots, drain and mash, then drain again. Add butter, salt and pepper to taste and serve while still hot.

Carrot Salad

This colourful salad will make a fine addition to a buffet table.

5 medium carrots, grated

1 medium green pepper, seeded and finely chopped

1 stick celery, finely sliced

3 tablespoons finely chopped parsley

½ cup seedless raisins

Juice of 1 large orange

Juice of 1 lemon

2 tablespoons sunflower oil

PREPARATION TIME: 45 minutes

SERVES: four to six

Mix the carrots, green pepper, celery, parsley and raisins together and dress with the orange and lemon juices. Sprinkle the oil over the mixture and serve on a bed of lettuce with either cottage cheese or Ricotta cheese.

VARIATIONS

Omit the celery and pepper and add ¾ cup toasted sunflower seeds.

Alternatively, add ¾ cup chopped pineapple, grapefruit or green melon, and dress with natural yoghurt. Sprinkle the salad with chopped parsley or alfalfa sprouts.

Marinated Vegetable Salad

Self-sealing plastic bags weren't available in Grandma's day, but they are great for marinating salads.

Combine the broccoli in a large, heavy-duty plastic bag with the tomatoes, carrot, squash and celery. To prepare the marinade, combine the vinegar with the oil, parsley, sugar, dill, salt and pepper in a screwtop jar, put the lid on and shake well. Pour the marinade over the vegetables. Close the bag and refrigerate for 8 hours or overnight, turning the bag from time to time to ensure that all the vegetables absorb the flavours.

To serve, use a slotted spoon to transfer the vegetables to a serving bowl.

FOR THE SALAD

1 cup sliced broccoli and/or cauliflower florets
1 cup cherry tomatoes, halved
1 large carrot, cut into 3 cm x 5 mm sticks
2 yellow pattypan squash or 1 small courgette, cut into 5-mm-thick slices
¼ cup sliced celery

FOR THE MARINADE

½ cup vinegar
½ cup olive oil
¼ cup chopped fresh parsley or fresh coriander
1 tablespoon sugar
2 tablespoons finely chopped fresh dill or 2 teaspoons dried dill
½ teaspoon salt
¼ teaspoon black pepper

PREPARATION TIME: 25 minutes
CHILLING TIME: 8 hours or overnight
SERVES: four

FITTED KITCHEN

By the mid-1950s flat-dwelling had become commonplace and kitchen furnishings and equipment were scaled down accordingly. Food, crockery, knives, forks, spoons and saucepans were accommodated in kitchen cabinets as shown in this advertisement from Modern Homes Illustrated.

Desserts & Beverages

30 g butter, melted,
   for greasing
1¼ cups roughly chopped,
   ready-to-eat pitted prunes
1⅔ cups currants
1½ cups sultanas
1½ cups roughly chopped,
   seedless raisins
¾ cup mixed candied peel,
   homemade (p.289)
   or bought, chopped
¾ cup quartered glacé
   cherries
¾ cup ground almonds
2 teaspoons mixed spice
250 g packaged suet
1 cup brown sugar
3½ cups soft white or brown
   breadcrumbs (p.310)
1 cup cake flour
Finely grated rind
   of 2 oranges
Finely grated rind of 2 lemons
1 large carrot (about 175 g),
   peeled and grated
1 large potato (about 175 g),
   peeled and grated
1 cooking apple (about 175 g),
   peeled, cored and grated
5 eggs, beaten
⅔ cup brandy, whisky or rum
Sprigs of holly, for decoration
4–6 tablespoons brandy,
   whisky or rum, for flaming

PREPARATION TIME: 1 hour
STANDING TIME: overnight
COOKING TIME: 9 hours
REHEATING TIME: 2–3 hours
SERVES: twelve

Christmas Pudding

Serve this rich, moist pudding with custard or cream on any special occasion, but for Christmas choose one of the traditional butters or sauces. To follow Grandma's tradition of adding coins to the pudding, you can clean the coins by boiling them, then slip them in just before serving. Create slits for the coins with a thin, sharp knife.

Thoroughly grease a 10-cup pudding basin or heatproof mixing bowl with the melted butter. Line the bottom with a round of baking paper and grease the paper. Cut a round of baking paper large enough to cover the top of the basin or bowl and grease it well, too.

Put all the pudding ingredients in a very large mixing bowl and mix them thoroughly. Spoon the mixture into the prepared pudding basin or mixing bowl and smooth the surface. Cover the mixture with the greased paper, then cover the basin or bowl with heavy-duty cooking foil, pleated in the centre to allow for expansion. Using strong string, tie the foil securely in position under the rim of the bowl or basin and leave the pudding to stand in a cold place overnight.

To cook the pudding, stand it on a trivet, a small block of wood or a folded tea towel in a large saucepan and pour boiling water into the saucepan to come halfway up the side of the bowl or basin. Add some slices of lemon to prevent the saucepan from blackening during cooking, then cover and boil very gently for 9 hours. Replenish the water frequently with more boiling water. Do not use cold water as the pudding basin or bowl may crack.

Remove the pudding from the water and discard the foil. Leave to cool, then cover with fresh baking paper and foil. Store in the refrigerator for up to two months.

On Christmas Day, steam the pudding in the same way for a further 2–3 hours and then remove the basin or bowl from the saucepan. Pour the brandy, whisky or rum into a cup and stand the cup to heat in hot water.

Meanwhile, remove the foil and paper, loosen the sides of the pudding from the basin or bowl with a palette knife and turn the pudding out onto a heated serving plate. Decorate with the sprigs of holly.

Take the heated spirit to the table with the pudding. Before serving, remove the sprigs of holly, pour the spirit over the pudding and ignite. Alternatively, pour the spirit into a long-handled ladle, ignite it and, once flaming, pour it over the pudding. Serve with one or more traditional accompaniments.

Traditional Accompaniments

Some people enjoy these delicious butters and sauces even more than the Christmas pudding itself.

RUM OR BRANDY BUTTER

125 g unsalted butter
½ cup brown sugar
Finely grated rind
   of 1 large orange
½ cup rum or brandy

PREPARATION TIME: 10 minutes
CHILLING TIME: 2 hours
   or overnight
SERVES: twelve

RUM OR BRANDY BUTTER
Beat the butter, sugar and orange rind together in a mixing bowl, or with an electric mixer, until light and fluffy. Very gradually add the rum or brandy, a little at a time, beating well after each addition until smooth and creamy. Do not add the spirit too quickly or the mixture will curdle. Spoon the butter into a serving dish, cover and chill until required.

FROZEN BRANDY CREAM
Whisk all the ingredients together in a mixing bowl until smooth and slightly thickened, taking care not to overbeat or the mixture will curdle. Pour the cream into a 22 x 10 x 6 cm loaf tin lined with baking paper, then cover and freeze. Just before serving, remove the loaf tin from the freezer, dip it in warm water for 1 second and turn the brandy cream out onto

A TRADITIONAL CHRISTMAS

Christmas cards were an 1840s British initiative that rapidly spread to other parts of the world. The period 1900 to 1914 saw the world swept up in a postcard craze - millions were sent and avidly collected in return. Christmas postcards, such as this one, carried Christmas greetings all around the world.

FROZEN BRANDY CREAM

2½ cups thick cream

1 cup icing sugar, sifted

Finely grated rind of 1 lemon

4 tablespoons lemon juice, strained

⅔ cup brandy

4 tablespoons amaretto or cherry liqueur

1 teaspoon vanilla essence

PREPARATION TIME: 5 minutes

FREEZING TIME: overnight

SERVES: twelve

HOT RUM OR BRANDY SAUCE

45 g unsalted butter

⅓ cup cake flour

2½ cups milk

3–4 tablespoons caster sugar

1¼ cups pouring cream

½ cup rum or brandy

PREPARATION TIME: 10 minutes

SERVES: twelve

a flat serving dish. Cut into slices and serve with the hot Christmas pudding.

HOT RUM OR BRANDY SAUCE

Melt the butter in a saucepan, stir in the flour and cook for 1 minute, without browning, over low heat. Gradually add the milk and bring to the boil, stirring continuously until the sauce thickens. Reduce the heat and continue stirring for 1–2 minutes to remove all traces of raw flour. Add sugar to taste, then add the cream and rum or brandy. Stir the sauce over the heat for 1–2 minutes, or until hot but not boiling.

Pour into a hot serving jug and serve with the pudding. (The sauce can be made ahead and covered with plastic wrap to prevent a skin from forming.)

45 g butter
½ cup short-grain rice
½ cup caster sugar
1¼ cups pouring cream
2½ cups milk
Freshly grated nutmeg,
   for sprinkling

PREPARATION TIME: 5 minutes
COOKING TIME: 2–2¼ hours
SERVES: four

Rice Pudding

*Perhaps the ultimate comfort food, creamy rice pudding
can be served plain or topped with jam or fruit.*

Preheat the oven to 160°C and grease a 5-cup ovenproof dish lightly with a third of the butter. Put the rice and caster sugar in the prepared dish and stir in the cream and milk. Cut the remaining butter into tiny pieces and float them on the surface of the pudding. Grate the nutmeg over the top and cook on the centre shelf of the oven for 2 hours, or until the top is golden brown and the pudding is just set.

Take care not to overcook as the pudding will become dry. Remove from the oven and serve while still hot.

For a fruity rice pudding, try adding some sultanas to the rice before cooking.

A Famous Dessert

Australia and New Zealand have staked rival claims for the invention of the pavlova. Recipes for a fruit-filled meringue started appearing in New Zealand in 1926, when the acclaimed ballerina Anna Pavlova took the country by storm. Australia comes in a late second, with Bert Sachse, a chef at the Esplanade Hotel, Perth, claiming to have created the dessert in 1935, after Pavlova stayed at the hotel.

Pavlova

Claimed by both Australia and New Zealand, this classic dessert is easy to make. Once you have prepared the meringue mixture, bake it immediately, otherwise it will collapse and begin to weep.

Preheat the oven to 180°C. Line an oven tray with baking paper and mark a 23 cm circle as a guide for spreading the mixture.

Beat the egg whites on high speed in a large clean bowl with clean electric beaters until soft peaks form. Gradually add the caster sugar, beating continuously until the mixture is firm and glossy and all sugar has dissolved. Beat in the vanilla essence, then the vinegar and salt, and fold in the cornflour.

Using a spatula, spread the meringue mixture over the marked circle. Straighten the sides and make them higher than the centre. Bake for 10 minutes in the centre of the oven, then reduce the temperature to 120°C and bake for a further hour. Remove from the oven and allow to cool completely.

Just before serving, top the pavlova with whipped cream. Decorate with the strawberries and bananas, and drizzle with the granadilla pulp.

Alternatively, decorate the pavlova with 3 peeled and sliced kiwi fruit, arranged in rounds and drizzled with granadilla pulp.

FOR THE MERINGUE CASE
- 8 egg whites
- 1²/₃ cups caster sugar
- 2 teaspoons vanilla essence
- 2 teaspoons brown vinegar
- 2 pinches of salt
- 2 teaspoons sifted cornflour

FOR THE FILLING
- 1¼ cups cream, firmly whipped
- 1 punnet strawberries, hulled and halved
- 2 bananas, peeled and sliced
- ⅓ cup granadilla pulp

PREPARATION TIME: 20 minutes
COOKING TIME: 1 hour 10 minutes
SERVES: eight to ten

Pears in Red Wine

3 cups medium-dry,
　fruity red wine

4 tablespoons orange
　flower water

3/4 cup sugar

Strained juice of 1 orange
　and 1 lemon

10 cm cinnamon stick

4 cloves

3 cm piece fresh ginger,
　peeled and quartered

6 ripe Beurre Bosc or other
　firm pears

Preparation time: 15 minutes

Cooking time: 1 hour

Serves: six

This is a great dessert for entertaining as it looks dramatic but can be prepared ahead of time, even the day before. Be aware that some pears take a long time to become tender – test with a toothpick, which should slide in easily.

Gently heat all the ingredients, except the pears, in a large stainless-steel or enamel saucepan, stirring occasionally, until the sugar has dissolved. Bring the mixture to the boil and boil for 2 minutes.

Peel the pears carefully, without removing their stalks, and add them to the saucepan. Cover and cook on low heat for 30–40 minutes, or until tender, turning frequently to ensure that they cook and colour evenly to a deep pink. Using a slotted spoon, lift the pears from the saucepan and put them on a serving dish. Strain the juice through a nylon sieve and discard the spices. Return the juice to the pan and bring back to the boil. Reduce the heat and boil on low heat until the juice has reduced by half and is heavy and syrupy.

Pour the syrup over the pears and allow to cool. Serve with whipped cream flavoured with kirsch, if desired.

Lemon Meringue Pie

FOR THE CRUST
150 g Marie biscuits, crushed
2 tablespoons sugar
8 tablespoons melted butter

FOR THE
LEMON FILLING
1 tin (379 g) condensed milk
1/2 cup lemon juice
3 egg yolks
Finely grated rind of 1 lemon

FOR THE MERINGUE
3 egg whites
Pinch of cream of tartar
1/3 cup caster sugar

Preparation time: 15 minutes

Chilling time: about 2 hours

Cooking time: 10 minutes

Serves: eight

This old favourite contrasts the sweetness of the meringue with the tartness of lemons. It is a delicious teatime treat.

Make a biscuit-crumb crust by mixing the crushed biscuits, sugar and melted butter together. Press into a 22–24 cm loose-based flan tin and chill in the refrigerator.

Preheat the oven to 180°C. Whisk all the ingredients for the filling until thick and pour into the chilled crumb shell.

To make the meringue topping, whisk the egg whites in a bowl with the cream of tartar until soft peaks form. Gradually add the sugar, one spoonful at a time, beating well after each addition until the meringue has become thick and shiny.

Spread the meringue over the lemon filling, making sure that it seals to the crumb shell all around. Bake in the preheated oven for 10 minutes, or until the meringue is light golden. Allow to cool down and set before serving.

VARIATION
If preferred, a sweet shortcrust pastry crust (see p.213) may be used instead of the biscuit crust.

FACING PAGE: *Pears in red wine*

The pudding can be frozen and reheated again at a later date.

Cape Brandy Pudding

This traditional pudding, which is also known as tipsy tart, is really quite easy to make if you follow the instructions carefully.

FOR THE PUDDING
250 g dates, stoned
1 teaspoon bicarbonate of soda
1 cup boiling water
115 g butter
200 g sugar
2 eggs, beaten
240 g flour
1 teaspoon baking powder
½ teaspoon salt
1 cup chopped pecan nuts

FOR THE SYRUP
250 g sugar
15 g butter
¾ cup water
1 teaspoon vanilla essence
A pinch of salt
½ cup brandy

PREPARATION TIME: 30 minutes
COOKING TIME: 40-50 minutes
SERVES: six

Preheat the oven to 180°C. Cut up the dates and divide them into two equal portions. Add the bicarbonate of soda to one half and pour over the boiling water. Stir to mix, then leave to cool. Cream together the butter and sugar, add the beaten eggs and mix well.

Sift together the flour, baking powder and salt, and fold these into the butter mixture.

Add the second portion of dates and the nuts. Then stir in the bicarbonate and date mixture, and mix all the ingredients thoroughly.

Turn the batter into a large ovenproof dish and bake for 40–50 minutes. Or pour the batter into two 22 cm tart plates and bake for 35 minutes.

To make the syrup, heat the sugar, butter and water together and stir until the sugar has dissolved. Boil for 5 minutes. Remove from the heat and stir in the vanilla essence, salt and brandy. Pour the syrup over the hot pudding when it is taken from the oven. Serve hot or cold with whipped cream or ice ceam.

VARIATION
To make small individual puddings, butter 15 muffin tins or ramekins and line the bottoms with circles of greaseproof paper. Spoon the mixture into the tins and bake for 30 minutes or until done. Remove from the tins and pour the syrup over.

Apple Pie

The perfect apple pie is not too sweet, not too tart, and is delicately spiced.

Half-fill a bowl with cold water, add the lemon juice and sliced apples and set aside.

To make the pastry, follow the instructions for Shortcrust Pastry on page 311, adding the caster sugar to the flour with the salt.

Preheat the oven to 200°C. Simmer the apple peel in a covered saucepan with the cloves, cinnamon and cider for 20 minutes. Uncover and cook gently for 10 minutes, or until the liquid is reduced to 6 tablespoons.

Strain the liquid through a sieve, pressing down well with a spoon to extract all the juices. Discard the peel and spices. Stir the melted butter into the apple juice along with the lemon rind and sultanas or raisins.

Drain the apples, mix into the butter mixture and spoon into a 4-cup round or oval pie dish. Roll out the dough to 5 cm larger than the pie dish, then cut a 2–3 cm strip from around the edge. Brush the edge of the dish with cold water, press the strip onto it and brush with water again. Drape the remaining dough over the rolling pin and ease it into place over the pie. Press the edges together to seal, then trim and decorate the edge.

Make a small hole in the centre of the pie, then brush with the milk and sprinkle with the sugar. Bake in the centre of the oven for 20 minutes, then reduce the heat to 180°C and bake for a further 30–40 minutes, or until the pastry is golden and the apples are tender.

Test for tenderness by inserting a skewer into the pie through the hole in the centre. If the pie starts to brown too quickly, cover it loosely with foil.

FOR THE FILLING
Finely grated rind and strained juice of 1 lemon
6 large dessert apples, peeled, quartered, cored and sliced, peel reserved
2 cloves
8 cm cinnamon stick, broken into 3 pieces
1 cup medium-sweet cider
60 g butter, melted
3/4 cup sultanas or raisins
3 tablespoons milk
2 tablespoons sugar

FOR THE PASTRY
240 g cake flour
Pinch of salt
1 tablespoon caster sugar
125 g chilled butter, diced
1 teaspoon lemon juice
3 tablespoons iced water

PREPARATION TIME: 1 hour
CHILLING TIME: 30 minutes
COOKING TIME: 1½ hours
SERVES: four to six

THE JELLY TRADITION
The name Moir is familiar to South African cooks for a wide variety of baking ingredients, but is, perhaps, best known for jelly. Moir's Jelly was first manufactured by John Moir in Scotland in the 19th century. The first Moir's jelly produced in South Africa was made at a specially constructed factory in Woodstock, Cape Town just after World War I.

Sticky Sponge Pudding

A topping of thick cream or custard would add a luxurious touch to this pudding.

FOR THE PUDDING

200 g butter

3 tablespoons brown sugar

2 small oranges, rind finely grated and reserved, pith removed, flesh neatly sliced

3/4 cup caster sugar

3 eggs

1 1/2 cups self-raising flour

1/3 cup ground almonds

3 tablespoons warm water

FOR THE SAUCE

7 tablespoons marmalade, homemade (p.288) or bought

7 tablespoons water

1 tablespoon strained lemon juice

PREPARATION TIME: 20 minutes

COOKING TIME: 1 1/2–2 hours

SERVES: six

Put 1 tablespoon of the butter into the bottom of a well-buttered 6-cup pudding basin. Add the brown sugar and line the base with overlapping orange slices. Cream the remaining butter with the caster sugar and orange rind until light and fluffy. Beat in the eggs, one at a time, beating well after each addition, then fold in the flour, ground almonds and water.

Spoon the mixture into the basin on top of the oranges and smooth the surface. Cover the basin with buttered foil, pleated in the centre to allow for expansion and tied tightly under the rim of the basin with string. Cook in a steamer for 1 1/2–2 hours, or stand the basin on a trivet in a saucepan, add boiling water to come halfway up the side of the basin, cover and simmer on low heat for 1 1/2–2 hours, replenishing the water frequently with boiling water. The pudding is cooked when it is well risen and firm, and when a skewer inserted into the centre comes out clean.

Start making the sauce 5 minutes before the pudding is to be turned out. Combine all the ingredients in a small saucepan over medium heat until the marmalade blends with the water and lemon juice. Transfer to a jug and keep hot while turning the pudding out on a heated plate.

VARIATIONS

Golden Syrup or Jam Pudding: Make the pudding with 4 tablespoons of golden syrup or jam in place of the orange slices. Substitute syrup or jam for the marmalade in the sauce.

Chocolate Pudding: Substitute 1/3 cup of cocoa and 1/2 teaspoon of baking powder for 1/3 cup of the flour and serve the pudding with a homemade or bought chocolate sauce.

Creamy Custards

Baked custard can be cooked in one large dish or in individual small dishes. Pouring custard is the simple but perfect accompaniment to almost any hot pudding.

BAKED CUSTARD

1 3/4 cups milk

1/2 cup cream

3 large eggs

1/4 cup caster sugar

1 teaspoon vanilla essence

Grated nutmeg

Fresh seasonal fruit, to serve

PREPARATION TIME: 15 minutes

COOKING TIME: 1–1 1/4 hours

COOLING TIME: 2 hours

SERVES: four

POURING CUSTARD

1 1/2 cups milk

1/2 cup pouring cream

4 egg yolks

1/4 cup caster sugar

1 teaspoon vanilla essence

PREPARATION TIME: 5 minutes

COOKING TIME: 20 minutes

SERVES: four

BAKED CUSTARD

Preheat the oven to 160°C. Heat the milk and cream in a small saucepan over medium heat until hot. Do not boil.

Whisk the eggs, caster sugar and vanilla in a large bowl until light and fluffy. Whisking constantly, pour the warm milk mixture over the eggs. Strain the mixture through a sieve into a lightly greased 4-cup heatproof dish and sprinkle with grated nutmeg.

Place the dish in a large roasting pan. Pour enough warm water into the roasting pan to reach two-thirds of the way up the side of the dish. Bake for 1 hour, or until the surface is firm when touched lightly. Carefully remove the custard from the oven and stand at room temperature to cool. Spoon into serving bowls and serve with seasonal fruit.

POURING CUSTARD

Heat the milk and cream in a small saucepan over medium heat until hot, taking care not to let it boil.

Whisk the egg yolks and caster sugar in a medium bowl until light and fluffy. Whisking constantly, pour the warm milk and cream mixture over the eggs.

Cook the custard over very low heat, stirring constantly with a wooden spoon in a figure-of-eight movement, until it thickens and coats the wooden spoon.

Stir in the vanilla essence and strain the custard through a sieve into a serving jug. Serve the custard while it is warm.

FACING PAGE: *Sticky sponge pudding*

Lemon Delicious Pudding

As it bakes, the pudding separates into a delicate lemon sponge on top and a tangy lemon sauce underneath.

45 g unsalted butter, softened

¾ cup caster sugar

2 teaspoons finely grated lemon rind

3 eggs, separated

¼ cup self-raising flour

1 cup milk

¼ cup strained lemon juice

2 teaspoons icing sugar, for sifting

Rose petals, to decorate (optional)

Pouring cream, to serve

PREPARATION TIME: 30 minutes

COOKING TIME: 35-40 minutes

SERVES: four

Preheat the oven to 160°C. Grease four 1-cup gratin dishes. Beat the butter, sugar and lemon rind together until light and fluffy and almost white. Beat in the egg yolks, fold in the flour and gently mix in the milk and lemon juice. Whisk the egg whites until they hold soft peaks and fold carefully into the mixture.

Spoon the mixture into the prepared dishes and stand the dishes in a roasting pan. Pour hot tap water into the roasting pan to come halfway up the sides of the gratin dishes. Bake on the oven shelf below the centre for 1 hour, or until the cake topping is cooked when tested with a fine skewer.

Sift the icing sugar over the top of each pudding and decorate with the rose petals, if used. Serve the puddings hot or warm and pass the pouring cream separately.

Alternatively, pour the pudding into one dish which holds 1 litre or 4 cups and bake for 50 minutes.

ROYAL VISIT

In 1947 South Africa was swept up in royal fever as the Royal family - King George VI, Queen Elizabeth and the two princesses, Elizabeth and Margaret, toured Southern Africa for over two months. Banquets, garden parties and balls were the order of the day as local chefs outdid each other in their culinary presentations. This commemorative issue of CoffeeTearia was issued by Ellis Brown, coffee and tea manufacturers.

This adaptable dessert can be made with other fruits, such as pears, plums or apricots.

Fruit Crumble

Served with custard, cream or ice cream, this nourishing dessert is a great favourite in many families.

To make the crumble topping, sift the flour into a mixing bowl and rub in the butter until the mixture resembles fine breadcrumbs. Stir in the oats, ground almonds and sugar.

Preheat the oven to 190°C. Put the apples in a saucepan with the sugar and water. Cover and cook gently for 10 minutes, or until they begin to soften. Remove from the heat.

Peel and slice the banana and stir it into the apples, stir in the blackberries, then transfer to a 5-cup ovenproof dish and stand the dish on a baking tray.

Spoon the crumble mixture evenly over the fruit and press it down very lightly. Bake in the centre of the oven for 30–35 minutes, or until the crumble is golden brown and the juices from the filling begin to bubble up.

VARIATION

Apple and Rhubarb Crumble: Peel, core and thinly slice 2 cooking apples and toss with 2 cups of chopped rhubarb and 1/2 cup caster sugar. Put the fruit in an ovenproof dish, cover with the crumble topping and cook as above.

FOR THE TOPPING
1 cup plain flour
90 g butter
1/2 cup rolled oats
1/4 cup ground almonds
1/4 cup caster sugar

FOR THE FILLING
5 medium cooking apples, peeled, cored and sliced
1/2 cup caster sugar
5 tablespoons water
1 large banana
175 g berries such as blackberries, tayberries, boysenberries (thawed, if using frozen fruit)

PREPARATION TIME: 35 minutes
COOKING TIME: 40–45 minutes
SERVES: six

Fresh Fruit Fool

The dessert has nothing to do with foolishness: the name is derived from the French word 'fouler', meaning to crush.

500 g apples, rhubarb or
   plums
½ cup caster sugar
3 tablespoons water
⅔ cup pouring cream
1 egg
1 egg yolk
½ teaspoon vanilla essence
1¼ cups thickened cream
3 tablespoons chopped
   pistachio nuts, to
   decorate (optional)
Fresh or sugared flowers,
   to decorate (optional)

PREPARATION TIME: 30 minutes
COOKING TIME: 20 minutes
CHILLING TIME: 3 hours
SERVES: six

Prepare the fruit according to type – peel, core and slice apples; trim and chop rhubarb and halve and stone plums

Put the prepared fruit in a saucepan with three-quarters of the caster sugar and the water. Cover and cook over medium heat for 20 minutes, or until the fruit is very soft.

Meanwhile, to make the custard, bring the pouring cream almost to the boil. Lightly whisk the egg and egg yolk in a bowl with the remaining sugar. Stir in the hot cream and vanilla essence. Place the bowl over a saucepan of gently boiling water and stir the mixture until it thickens enough to hold a slight trail and thinly coat the back of the spoon. Take care not to overheat it or it may curdle. Remove the bowl from the saucepan and cover the surface closely with plastic wrap to prevent a skin from forming. Allow the custard to cool, then chill in the refrigerator.

Purée the cooked fruit in a food processor or blender, or pass it through a nylon sieve. Chill the purée for at least 1 hour. Whisk the cream in a large bowl until it holds soft peaks.

Combine the custard with the fruit purée and fold it gently into the whipped cream. Spoon the fool into glasses and chill for 2 hours. To serve, sprinkle with pistachio nuts or decorate with flowers. Serve with homemade shortbread fingers (see p.250).

VARIATION

Soft-Fruit Fool: To make the fool with soft fruits, you can use 2 punnets strawberries, raspberries, blackberries, mulberries or boysenberries; or 500 g skinned, stoned and sliced peaches or apricots; or 500 g pitted cherries.

Put the prepared fruit in a bowl and, depending on its sweetness, sprinkle with about ¼ cup of sugar and a squeeze of lemon juice. Leave to macerate for 30 minutes.

Purée the macerated soft fruit in a food processor or electric blender. If using a berry purée, pass it through a fine nylon sieve into a bowl to remove the seeds before mixing with the custard and whipped cream.

Serve with shortbread fingers (see p.250).

Lemon Sago

Some people have unhappy boarding-school memories of lemon sago, but it can be a delicate and delicious treat. It should be carefully cooked so that it has no lumps, is well flavoured, well chilled and presented in pretty bowls or dessert glasses, with a thin layer of cream poured over just before serving.

⅓ cup sago
4 cups water
Pinch of salt
Finely grated rind of 1 lemon
2 tablespoons lemon juice
1 tablespoon golden syrup
2 tablespoons brown sugar
Custard (p.214) or pouring
   cream, to serve

PREPARATION TIME: 5 minutes
STANDING TIME: 1 hour
COOKING TIME: 12–15 minutes
CHILLING TIME: overnight
SERVES: four

Place the sago in a bowl, cover with half the water and allow to stand for 1 hour. Drain.

Put the sago in a saucepan with the remaining water and add the salt. Cook over medium heat, stirring constantly, until the sago comes to the boil.

Reduce the heat to medium-low and simmer for 3 minutes, or until the sago is soft and transparent.

Remove the saucepan from the heat. Add the lemon rind and juice, the golden syrup and the brown sugar to the sago. Mix well to combine the ingredients.

Spoon the mixture into a 4-cup serving bowl or four small, pretty glass bowls. Cover with plastic wrap and place in the refrigerator overnight to chill.

Serve the chilled lemon sago with custard or drizzled with pouring cream.

FACING PAGE: *Fresh fruit fool*

Tate & Lyle

Both Henry Tate and Abram Lyle were sugar refiners in England in the 1800s - eventually they squeezed out all the other small refiners and, while Tate cornered the market on sugar cubes, Lyle handled the golden syrup trade. The two firms merged in 1921 to form Tate & Lyle. The famous Tate Gallery in London is named for Henry Tate, who bequeathed money to build it and donated his private collection of contemporary paintings to the gallery.

Golden Syrup Dumplings

Fluffy dumplings bathed in a rich golden syrup sauce have been a comforting family dessert for generations. Being economical and filling, they are also a good friend to the cook with a household budget to balance.

For the Dumplings
1½ cups self-raising flour
50 g butter, chopped
½ cup milk
1 egg
1 teaspoon vanilla essence
Cream or ice cream, to serve

For the Sauce
2 cups water
⅓ cup golden syrup
½ cup brown sugar
30 g butter
1 teaspoon lemon juice

Preparation time: 15 minutes
Cooking time: 20 minutes
Serves: four

Sift the flour into a mixing bowl. Add the butter and, using your fingertips, rub it into the flour until the mixture resembles fine breadcrumbs. Make a well in the centre. Beat the milk, egg and vanilla together with a fork until thoroughly combined and pour into the well in the dry ingredients. Mix gently from the centre, gradually drawing in the dry ingredients until the dough is just combined.

To make the golden syrup sauce, put the water, golden syrup, brown sugar, butter and lemon juice in a large saucepan. Cook over medium heat until the sugar dissolves. Increase the heat to high and bring to the boil. Reduce the heat to medium. Scoop up heaped tablespoons of the dough and drop them into the boiling syrup. Cover with a lid and cook for 10–15 minutes, or until a skewer inserted into the centre of a dumpling comes out clean. (Do not lift the lid during cooking. The time will depend on the size of the dumplings.)

Spoon the dumplings into serving bowls along with some of the golden syrup sauce and serve with cream or ice cream.

Granadilla Flummery

In the days when many people had a granadilla vine growing over the fence and kept a few chickens in the backyard, this luscious flummery would have been an economical pudding. It is still one of the best ways to use summer's bounty of fresh granadillas.

1 lemon
1 cup cold water
½ cup caster sugar
3 teaspoons gelatine
3 tablespoons boiling water
2 eggs, separated
½ cup granadilla pulp (about 4–6 granadillas)
Shortbread biscuits (p.250), to serve (optional)

PREPARATION TIME: 20 minutes
COOKING TIME: 8 minutes
CHILLING TIME: 8 hours
SERVES: four

Peel the rind from the lemon and then squeeze out the juice. Reserve 3 tablespoons of lemon juice. Combine the lemon rind, water and caster sugar in a medium saucepan. Cook, stirring occasionally, over medium heat until the sugar dissolves and the syrup comes to the boil. Remove from the heat. Remove and discard the lemon rind from the syrup.

Combine the gelatine and boiling water in a heatproof jug, following the manufacturer's instructions and stir until the gelatine dissolves and the liquid is clear. Add the lemon juice and mix well to combine. Put the egg yolks in a mixing bowl and whisk with a balloon whisk. Pour in the warm syrup in a thin stream, followed by the gelatine mixture, whisking constantly until well combined. Cover and refrigerate until the mixture thickens and begins to set around the edges.

Beat the egg whites in a clean bowl to the soft peak stage (so that they form a drooping peak when lifted on your beater). Fold the egg white and granadilla pulp into the lemon mixture. Spoon into four 1-cup serving glasses, cover with plastic wrap and place in the refrigerator for six hours, or until set. Serve with shortbread biscuits, if desired.

FREE COOKBOOKS
What better way to sell a product than suggest tasty ways of using it? For years food manufacturers have offered free copies of produce cookbooks. Often the 'price' of the book was a number of box tops or cards hidden in the boxes.

Sorbets

A refreshing sorbet is perfect to follow a rich main course.

FOR THE SUGAR SYRUP
1 cup sugar
2/3 cup water

RASPBERRY SORBET
500 g fresh raspberries
   or use frozen fruit, thawed
Strained juice of 1 lemon
Strained juice of 1 orange

PINEAPPLE SORBET
600 g prepared fresh
   pineapple flesh
Strained juice of 1 lemon
Strained juice of 1 orange

MELON SORBET
600 g spanspek or wintermelon
   flesh
1 tablespoon grated fresh
   ginger
Strained juice of 1 lemon

PREPARATION TIME: 35 minutes
COOKING TIME: 7 minutes
FREEZING TIME: 4 hours
SERVES: four to six

TO MAKE THE SYRUP

Dissolve the sugar in the water in a heavy-based stainless-steel or enamel saucepan by stirring over medium heat. Bring to the boil, boil for 2 minutes, then remove the mixture from the heat and set aside to cool while you prepare the chosen fruit.

RASPBERRY SORBET

Raspberries do not need to be cooked beforehand. Purée the raspberries in a food processor then pass the purée through a nylon sieve to remove the pips.

Stir the cooled syrup and the lemon and orange juices into the fruit purée. Pour the mixture into a shallow, plastic freezer container and freeze for 4 hours, whisking vigorously with a fork every hour to break up the ice crystals. Once frozen, the sorbet remains soft and creamy and can be scooped straight from the freezer.

Just before serving, spoon into chilled or frosted glasses. Sorbets can be served with brandy snaps (see p.266) or any light, crisp biscuits of your choice.

VARIATIONS

Raspberries can be replaced with any of the berries now locally available – loganberries, blackberries, boysenberries and tayberries. Frozen berries can also be used, if fresh berries are not available.

Berries with a skin, such as redcurrants or blackcurrants, which are now coming onto the market, should be simmered in 2 tablespoons of water for about 5 minutes or until just beginning to soften before the fruit is puréed.

PINEAPPLE SORBET

Process the pineapple flesh and follow the instructions as given for raspberry sorbet. It is not necessary to precook the fruit.

MELON SORBET

Purée all the ingredients with the sugar syrup in a blender until smooth. Pour the mixture into a shallow plastic freezer container and freeze for 4 hours. Whisk vigorously with a fork every hour to break up the ice crystals.

Fruit Soft Serve

Only more modern Grandmas would have been able to make this quick dessert as it needs a food processor to do the work.

FRUIT SOFT SERVE
2 cups soft fruit
   (strawberries, raspberries,
   mixed berries, bananas)
4 tablespoons caster sugar
1 cup thick cream

PREPARATION TIME: 10 minutes
FREEZING TIME: 2-3 hours
SERVES: four

Place the fruit on a baking tray lined with baking paper and freeze, uncovered until the fruit is frozen. (Cut large strawberries in half, and slice bananas.)

Cool the food processor bowl and blade in the freezer for 30 minutes before you start.

Process the frozen fruit in the processor with the sugar until almost smooth. With the machine running, add the cream in a slow stream until the consistency is thick and smooth. Spoon into tall glasses, garnish attractively and serve immediately.

The processing of the frozen fruit and sugar can be done after the main course, and the dessert then served immediately.

FACING PAGE: *Sorbets*

9 egg yolks

½ cup caster sugar

1 teaspoon cornflour

2½ cups thick cream

1 vanilla pod, split
    lengthways, or ¼ teaspoon
    vanilla essence

PREPARATION TIME: 20 minutes

COOKING TIME: 30–40 minutes

STANDING TIME: overnight
chilling, then 2 hours after
caramelising the top

SERVES: six

Crème Brûlée

*This is a simple but elegant pudding of rich
vanilla custard beneath a glassy toffee crust.*

Put the egg yolks in a mixing bowl with a third of the sugar. Add the cornflour and whisk very lightly together.

Pour the cream into a saucepan, add the vanilla pod, if using, and heat gently until almost boiling. Whisk the cream into the egg yolk mixture.

Place the bowl over a saucepan of gently simmering water, making sure that the bottom of the bowl does not touch the water, and cook, stirring, until the custard thickens enough to coat the back of the spoon. If using vanilla essence, stir it in now. As soon as the custard thickens, strain it through a nylon sieve into a shallow, flameproof serving dish about 20 cm in diameter and 3 cm deep. Stand the custard aside until completely cold, then cover the dish and refrigerate overnight.

About 2 hours before serving, take the custard out of the refrigerator and sprinkle the remaining sugar evenly over the surface to form a thin, even layer, adding a little extra sugar, if necessary. Leave to stand for about 10 minutes.

Meanwhile, heat the grill to high. Cook the custard under the hot grill until the sugar melts and turns a golden caramel colour. To ensure even browning, carefully turn the dish around as the sugar melts and becomes like thin toffee. Remove the dish from the grill and set it aside to cool, then chill in the refrigerator until ready to serve.

A STARCHY THICKENER

*In the 1850s, John Polson
patented a process to extract
starch from maize and preserve it
in a powdered form. He exported
this product, marketed as
cornflour, around the world.
Sauces, pie fillings and desserts
all benefit from the thickening
properties of cornflour.*

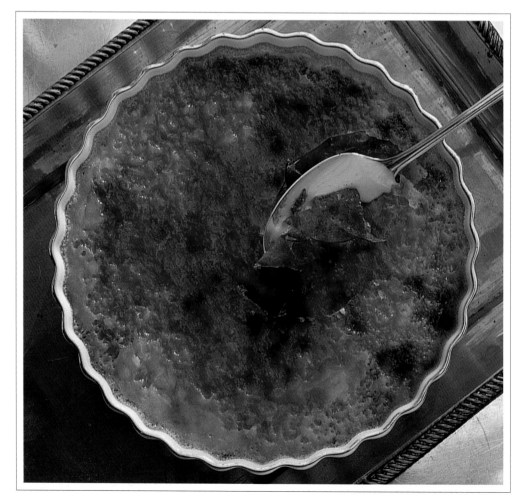

BEAT THAT

The familiar rotary whisk was patented in America in 1873, and its unique design has changed little since. Despite the popularity of electric beaters, hand-held whisks are still to be found among the utensils in most modern kitchens. The rotary whisk pictured here was purchased in 1932.

Bread & Butter Pudding

The homely appeal of bread baked in custard is timeless. In this version, fruit loaf is used for extra flavour.

Heat the milk and cream gently in a saucepan with the vanilla pod until almost boiling. Remove from the heat, cover and leave to infuse for 30 minutes.

Meanwhile, spread each slice of bread liberally with butter and cut it in half diagonally. Overlap the slices attractively in a buttered, shallow, ovenproof dish, scattering sultanas over the pieces as you go.

Whisk the egg yolks and caster sugar in a large bowl until pale and creamy. Strain the infused milk and cream onto the egg mixture and whisk well. Pour evenly over the buttered fruit bread and leave to soak for 20 minutes.

Meanwhile, preheat the oven to 180°C. Sprinkle the nutmeg and sugar evenly over the pudding and set the dish in a roasting pan.

Pour in enough boiling water to come halfway up the side of the dish and bake in the centre of the oven for 45 minutes, or until the custard is just set and the top is golden and crisp. Serve with pouring cream or hot custard.

VARIATIONS

Use slices of plain white bread. Spread with butter and apricot jam, marmalade or lemon curd, or put slices of banana between the layers.

FOR THE PUDDING

2 cups milk

1¼ cups thick cream

1 vanilla pod, split lengthways

1 day-old light fruit or raisin loaf, cut into slices 1 cm thick

90 g unsalted butter, softened

⅓ cup sultanas

6 egg yolks

½ cup caster sugar

1 tablespoon freshly grated nutmeg

⅓ cup demerara or brown sugar

PREPARATION TIME: 50 minutes

COOKING TIME: 45 minutes

SERVES: six

Melktert

Melktert accompanied by a platter of preserves or crystallised fruit makes an unusual and delicious dessert.

Puff pastry, homemade
(p.311) or bought

FOR THE FILLING
3 extra-large eggs, separated
50 g cake flour
3 tablespoons cornflour
50 g sugar
600 ml milk
1 cinnamon stick
15 g butter
Ground cinnamon for dusting

PREPARATION TIME: 40 minutes for the pastry; 30 minutes for the filling

CHILLING TIME: 30 minutes for the pastry

COOKING TIME: 25 minutes

SERVES: six

Preheat the oven to 230°C. Roll out the pastry until it is very thin, and line a pie plate of 25 cm diameter. Ease the pastry into the plate (don't stretch it) to counteract possible shrinkage when baking. Slightly dampen the rim of the pastry and put additional strips around the edge so that the filling will not run over.

Paint the inside edge of the pastry lining with 2 teaspoons of the egg whites. This will prevent the filling from pulling away from the crusts. Put the lined plate into the refrigerator while preparing the filling.

Mix the dry ingredients well (setting aside 1 tablespoon sugar), stir them into a paste with a little of the cold milk, and then add the rest of the milk and the cinnamon stick. Pour into a saucepan and bring this mixture to the boil, stirring continuously.

When the mixture is well thickened and cooked, add the butter. Remove from the heat, then carefully add the egg yolks, first adding a little of the hot mixture to the yolks. Return to the heat for a minute, cooking slowly. Remove from the heat and cool slightly.

Meanwhile, beat the egg whites and reserved sugar until the mixture holds soft peaks, then fold thoroughly into the cooled milk mixture.

Spoon the filling into the cold lined pastry case, dust the top very lightly with cinnamon and bake the tart in the middle of the preheated oven for 10–15 minutes. Reduce the temperature to 180°C so that the soufflé can rise well and cook through. When it is golden, turn off the heat and leave it for 5 minutes more.

If the tart is not to be served immediately, take it out before the final 5 minutes so that the soufflé can puff again when being reheated.

If the tart is to be served after being frozen, defrost it before reheating at 180°C.

Pancakes

The tradition of making pancakes on Shrove Tuesday (Pancake Day) has its origin in the need to use up perishable foods before the Lenten fast began.

100 g flour

A pinch of salt

3 eggs

1 cup milk or half milk and half water

1 tablespoon melted butter or sunflower oil (optional)

Butter for frying

Cinnamon and sugar or syrup for sprinkling

PREPARATION TIME: 10 minutes

CHILLING TIME: 1 hour

COOKING TIME: 15 minutes

MAKES: 12 pancakes

Sift together the flour and salt. Beat in the eggs and milk to make a smooth batter. Chill for at least 1 hour.

Just before making the pancakes, stir in the tablespoon melted butter or oil, if used.

Heat a frying pan (one with a non-stick surface is best) until very hot and swirl some butter around in it before pouring in a thin layer of batter. Once browned and set, flip the pancake over to lightly brown the other side. Keep warm over a bowl of boiling water while you cook the rest of the pancakes. Sprinkle with cinnamon and sugar or syrup and roll up and serve with lemon wedges.

VARIATIONS

The pancakes can also be served with ice cream topped with honey, maple syrup or orange liqueur, or raspberry or chocolate sauce. Alternatively, the pancakes can be filled with stewed fruits, such as apples or berries, and served with cream or even with a good jam.

Crêpes Suzette: Melt 75 g butter with 1 teaspoon grated orange rind and 4–6 teaspoons caster sugar. Add 175 ml strained orange juice and 2–3 tablespoons Van der Hum liqueur. Fold the 12 pancakes in quarters and arrange on an ovenproof dish. Heat the sauce and pour it over the pancakes. Cover the dish and bake at 180°C for about 15 minutes.

Warm 2 tablespoons brandy and light it as you pour it over the crêpes.

THE PASTEURISING PROCESS

In the old days, people would boil milk to kill the bacteria, but that gave the milk an unpleasant burnt taste. In 1860, Louis Pasteur was experimenting with wine and discovered that by heating it for a few moments, germs were killed without destroying the taste. When he applied this process to milk, he found that it kept longer and did not taste unpleasant. Many foods, including milk, are now routinely pasteurised.

VANILLA ICE CREAM

2 vanilla pods

1 cup sugar

1¼ cups milk

3 egg yolks

2½ cups thick cream

STRAWBERRY ICE CREAM

2 punnets fresh
  strawberries, hulled

340 g strawberry whole fruit
  jam

1¼ cups milk

¾ cup caster sugar

2½ cups thick cream

Strained juice of 2 lemons

BROWN BREAD ICE CREAM

4 tablespoons butter

250 g wholewheat rusk
  crumbs

½ cup soft brown sugar

½ teaspoon finely ground
  cinnamon (or to taste)

PEPPERMINT & CHOCOLATE-CHIP ICE CREAM

1 cup sugar

1¼ cups milk

3 egg yolks

2½ cups thick cream

1–2 teaspoons peppermint
  essence

200 g dark chocolate,
  finely chopped

Few drops of green food
  colouring (optional)

PREPARATION TIME: 15–20 minutes
  for each ice cream

COOKING TIME: 15 minutes for
  vanilla ice cream and for
  peppermint and chocolate-chip
  ice cream; 10 minutes for
  brown bread ice cream
  (no cooking required for
  strawberry ice cream)

FREEZING TIME: 8–10 hours in
  the freezer, 25–40 minutes
  in an ice-cream maker

MAKES: about 4 cups

Ice Creams

*No bought ice cream can compare with the richness and consistency
of the homemade version. The best flavours, however, demand the freshest,
juiciest ingredients and the patience to delay the first spoonful
until the ice cream begins to soften.*

VANILLA ICE CREAM

With a fine, sharp knife, cut the vanilla pods in half lengthways. Scoop out the insides with a teaspoon and put into a saucepan with the empty pods and the sugar.

Lightly whisk the milk with the egg yolks, pour into the saucepan and stir over low heat until the sugar has dissolved. Bring almost to the boil, stirring continuously. Remove the pan from the heat and leave until the custard is completely cold.

Strain the cold custard into a bowl, discard the vanilla pods and stir in the thick cream. (Note that the custard will be speckled with the vanilla seeds.)

Freeze the custard until it has frozen 2–3 cm around the edge. Remove from the freezer, whisk well and return to the freezer. Repeat this process four to six times more, then allow the ice cream to freeze completely. Alternatively, the mixture can be frozen in an electric ice-cream maker (follow the manufacturer's instructions).

VARIATION

Coffee Ice Cream: Add 125 g richly flavoured, finely ground coffee beans or 4 teaspoons of instant coffee granules to the milk with, or in the place of, the vanilla pods.

STRAWBERRY ICE CREAM

Process the strawberries and strawberry conserve in a food processor, then stir in the milk and pass the mixture through a nylon sieve to remove the seeds. Alternatively, mash the strawberries and jam together and whisk in the milk, then pass the mixture through a sieve to remove the seeds. Stir the caster sugar, cream and lemon juice into the strawberry mixture and freeze as for vanilla ice cream.

VARIATION

Raspberry Ice Cream: This can be made in the same way by substituting the same quantity of raspberry conserve and fresh raspberries for the strawberry jam and strawberries.

BROWN BREAD ICE CREAM

Use wholewheat rusk crumbs which are already crisp to make this delicious ice cream in a flash.

Melt the butter in a frying pan over low heat. Combine all the ingredients and fry in the pan slowly to develop the flavour and until the crumbs are crisp and lightly browned. Stir now and then with a wooden spoon. (It takes about 10 minutes). Cool and store in an airtight container in the refrigerator.

To make up the ice cream, alternate layers of vanilla ice cream with layers of the crumb mixture. Keep some of the crumbs back to sprinkle over the top of the ice cream when serving.

PEPPERMINT & CHOCOLATE-CHIP ICE CREAM

For peppermint and chocolate-chip ice cream, whisk the sugar, milk and egg yolks lightly together in a bowl.

Pour the mixture into a saucepan and stir over low heat until the sugar has dissolved. Stirring continuously, bring the mixture almost to the boil, then remove from the heat and allow to cool completely.

Stir the cream into the cooled custard mixture and add the peppermint essence to taste. Stir in the chocolate and add a few drops of the green food colouring, if used.

Freeze as for vanilla ice cream either in the freezer or in an electric ice-cream maker.

VARIATION

Rum and Raisin Ice Cream: To make rum and raisin ice cream, omit the peppermint essence, the chocolate and the green colouring. Soak 2/3 cup of seedless raisins in 4 tablespoons of dark rum for a few hours or overnight. Stir the raisins into the ice-cream mixture after adding the cream.

FACING PAGE: *Ice creams*

200 g sugar

2 eggs

1 tablespoon apricot jam

150 g flour

1 teaspoon bicarbonate of
soda

A pinch of salt

15 g butter

1 teaspoon vinegar

100 ml milk

FOR THE SAUCE

200 ml cream

100 g unsalted butter

150 g sugar

100 ml hot water

PREPARATION TIME: 35 minutes

COOKING TIME: 45 minutes

SERVES: six

Malva Pudding

*Redolent of childhood, this satisfying baked pudding
is always welcome on a chilly winter's day.*

Preheat oven to 180°C. Beat the sugar and eggs well in a food processor until thick and lemon-coloured, and add the jam.

Sieve together the flour, bicarbonate of soda and salt. In a separate bowl, melt the butter and add the vinegar. Add this butter and vinegar mixture and the milk to the egg mixture alternately with the flour. Beat well and bake in a covered ovenproof dish for 45 minutes.

To make the sauce, melt together the cream, butter, sugar and hot water. Pour the hot, melted sauce over the pudding as it comes out of the oven. Serve the pudding with custard or ice cream.

THE BOWL THAT BURPED

The creator of Tupperware was an American inventor Earl Silas Tupper, but Bonnie Wise became the marketing genius whose brainchild it was to sell via Tupperware parties - a marketing ploy which spread Tupperware around the world from the 1950s onwards. The patented containers 'burped' as air was expelled, thus keeping the food fresher for longer. Tupperware started with colourless plastic items, but soon introduced brightly coloured products.

Spiced Peaches

This version of an 18th century recipe is quick and simple to prepare and can be made well in advance of any dinner party.

Put the peaches in boiling water for 2–3 minutes. Drain and peel them carefully. Stud each peach with a clove.

Put the water, sugar, cinnamon stick and mace in a deep pan, and bring to the boil, stirring until the sugar has dissolved completely.

Add the peaches to this syrup and cook them gently for about 15–20 minutes, making sure that they are completely covered by the syrup during that time. The cooking ensures that the fruit will not discolour while it matures in the jar.

Lift the peaches carefully into a warm, clean, wide-mouthed, screw-top jar.

Remove the cinnamon stick from the syrup and stir in the brandy. Pour the syrup over the peaches and leave them to cool before covering tightly with the screw top. Stand in a cool place and keep for 3 days before using.

Serve the spiced peaches in individual glass bowls and pass around a jug of cream.

If you wish to keep the peaches for longer than 3 days, double the amount of brandy.

6 ripe peaches

6 cloves

450 ml water

350 g sugar

1 cinnamon stick (5 cm)

¼ teaspoon ground mace

100-125 ml brandy

Preparation time: 15 minutes

Cooking time: 20 minutes

Standing time: 3 days

Serves: six

FOR THE CRUMB CRUST

200 g dry biscuit crumbs, such as Marie biscuits

2 tablespoons sugar

75 g butter, melted, plus a little extra for brushing the pan

FOR THE FILLING

750 g cream cheese

1 cup sugar

3 eggs

1 teaspoon vanilla essence

250 ml sour cream (smetena)

FOR THE SAUCE

500 g raspberries, fresh or frozen

4 tablespoons caster sugar

PREPARATION TIME: 20 minutes

COOKING TIME: 1-1¼ hours

CHILLING TIME: 12 hours or overnight

SERVES: four

Cheesecake with Raspberry Sauce

Raspberry sauce complements this classic baked cheesecake perfectly.

Preheat the oven to 150°C. Brush a 23 cm springform pan generously with melted butter.

THE CRUMB CRUST

Mix the biscuit crumbs, sugar and melted butter together. Press the mixture firmly over the bottom and sides of the pan. Place in the refrigerator to chill while preparing the filling.

THE FILLING

In a food processor, pulse the cream cheese and sugar until smooth. With the motor running, add the eggs, one at a time. Scrape down the sides of the bowl, add the vanilla essence and sour cream and pulse until smooth.

Pour the filling onto the crumb crust and bake for 1–1¼ hours or until done. Turn the oven off, open the door slightly and leave the cake to cool for 1 hour. Transfer to the refrigerator and chill for at least 12 hours. Serve with raspberry sauce.

THE RASPBERRY SAUCE

Purée the raspberries (thaw first if frozen) with sugar in a blender or food processor. Strain through a sieve to remove the seeds. Taste, adding more caster sugar if necessary. Pour into a serving jug and keep cool in the refrigerator.

COLLECTING CRAZE

Just as children today collect stickers, cards and plastic tokens, so the children of the early 1930s had a collecting craze - picture stamps which were found in one penny tablets of Nestlé's chocolate. The series was called 'Wonders of the World' and the stamps could be pasted into special albums. Prizes were offered at the end of the promotion.

Chocolate Mousse

Chocolate mousse has been a popular dessert since the 1960s.

Place the chocolate in a heatproof bowl over a saucepan of simmering water (make sure the water does not touch the base of the bowl). Melt, stirring occasionally with a metal spoon until the chocolate is smooth. Remove from the heat. Stir in the egg yolks and mix well. Combine the instant coffee powder, water and brandy and add to the chocolate mixture.

Whisk the egg whites in a bowl until soft peaks form (so that when you lift some mixture on your beater, it forms a drooping peak). Add the sugar, a little at a time, beating well after each addition.

Fold a quarter of the egg-white mixture into the chocolate and mix well to combine, then gently fold in the remaining egg-white mixture. Beat the cream and vanilla to soft peaks and gently fold into the chocolate mixture. Spoon the mixture into six 1-cup glasses or 1 large bowl. Cover with plastic wrap and place in the refrigerator for three to four hours, or until the mousse is set.

If you wish, decorate each glass or bowl with a dollop of whipped cream and a colourful cherry.

250 g dark chocolate, chopped
4 eggs, separated
2 teaspoons instant coffee powder
1½ tablespoons warm water
1½ tablespoons brandy
3 tablespoons caster sugar
1 cup thickened cream
1 teaspoon vanilla essence
Whipped cream, to serve

PREPARATION TIME: 20 minutes
COOKING TIME: 5 minutes
CHILLING TIME: 4 hours
SERVES: six

3 oranges
1 pear
2 peaches
¼ honeydew melon
1 slice watermelon
¼ spanspek
½ mango
½ cup grapes (preferably seedless)
½ cup strawberries (optional)
1 tablespoon Kirsch
Caster sugar (optional)
Fresh mint to garnish

Preparation time: 30 minutes
Serves: six

Summer Fruit Bowl

Use the plentiful fruits of summer to create this fruit salad which is not only good to eat, but beautiful to look at.

Wash and dry the fruits where necessary. Squeeze the juice from 2 oranges and pour into a bowl. Peel and slice the pear and peaches and toss gently in the orange juice.

Use a small scoop to cut out balls from the melons (or slice them) and add to the bowl. Next peel the last orange and slice it into thin segments. Add to the bowl with cubes of mango, then add the grapes (halved and seeded if not the seedless variety) and the strawberries (if used).

Pour in the Kirsch and gently toss the fruit salad. If you think it necessary, add a light sprinkling of caster sugar (although the natural sweetness of the fruit should be sufficient).

Cover the bowl and chill until serving. Garnish with fresh mint and a few of the best strawberries (with their stalks) set aside for decoration.

Serve with a bowl of sweetened whipped cream.

VARIATION
Add stoned fresh cherries when available, or a sliced kiwi fruit.

BROOKE'S SQUASH
Oros and Lemos have been cooling South Africans on hot summer days for over 100 years. Charles Brooke patented his 'Brooke's Lemos' trademark in 1899 and it remains South Africa's oldest registered trademark. Initially Lemos was the bigger brand, but Oros has since taken over. Although the bottle design might have changed over the years, the squash recipe has remained basically the same.

AN IMPRESSIVE JELLY

In an effort to impress, Grandma may have used an elaborate jelly mould. Ceramic jelly moulds appeared in Britain in the 1770s, and were followed by copper, earthenware and pottery versions.

Real Lemon Jelly

Freshly squeezed lemon juice flavoured with cinnamon results in a truly memorable jelly.

Pour 2/3 cup of the water into a small bowl, sprinkle in the gelatine and set the bowl aside for 10 minutes, or until the gelatine is swollen and opaque.

Meanwhile, scald a large saucepan and a balloon whisk with boiling water. Line a large nylon sieve with a double thickness of muslin or a clean tea towel, place over a large bowl and scald to remove all traces of grease.

Put the remaining water in the saucepan, add the gelatine and all the remaining ingredients. Whisk over medium heat until the mixture forms a thick, heavy, white froth on the surface.

Stop whisking, increase the heat and allow the froth to rise almost to the top of the pan,

then immediately remove from the heat and allow the froth to settle back down. Repeat twice more and leave to stand for 5 minutes.

Taking care not to break up the froth, pour the jelly through the muslin-lined sieve into a 5-cup wetted jelly mould and refrigerate for 3–4 hours, or overnight, until firmly set.

To turn the jelly out, dip the mould up to the rim in very hot water for 5 seconds. Put a flat plate on top of the mould and, holding both together tightly, invert and give a good, sharp shake to free the jelly. Remove the mould. If the jelly does not come out of the mould the first time, dip briefly in hot water again and repeat the process.

Serve with whipped cream or yoghurt.

4 cups water

45 g gelatine

Finely grated rind of 2 lemons

1¼ cups freshly squeezed
   lemon juice (7 or 8 lemons)

¾ cup sugar

1 cinnamon stick

2 egg whites

2 egg shells, well washed in
   cold water and crushed

PREPARATION TIME: 15 minutes

COOKING TIME: 10 minutes

SETTING TIME: 3–4 hours
   or overnight

SERVES: six

1¼ cups milk

1¼ cups pouring cream

1 vanilla pod, split lengthways

5 eggs

2 teaspoons cornflour

¼ cup caster sugar

2 punnets small strawberries

4 tablespoons sweet sherry

6 tablespoons icing sugar,
   sifted

300 g Madeira cake

175 g strawberry jam,
   homemade (p.297)
   or bought

2 cups thick cream

½ teaspoon vanilla essence

¼ cup flaked almonds,
   lightly toasted

PREPARATION TIME: 20 minutes

COOKING TIME: 20 minutes

CHILLING TIME: 2 hours

SERVES: eight

Trifle

This frivolous confection looks wonderful on a buffet.

Pour the milk and the pouring cream into a saucepan, add the vanilla pod and bring slowly to the boil. Whisk the eggs, cornflour and sugar together in a bowl and stir in the hot milk and cream.

Place the bowl over a saucepan of gently simmering water, making sure the bottom of the bowl does not touch the water, and stir until the custard thickens enough to coat the back of the spoon. Strain through a nylon sieve into a clean bowl. Cover the surface of the custard closely with plastic wrap, to prevent a skin from forming, and leave to cool.

Reserve a few strawberries for decoration. Slice the remainder and put them in a bowl with the sherry and 3 tablespoons of the icing sugar. Mix together and set aside.

Cut the Madeira cake into three horizontal layers and sandwich together with the jam. Cut into thin slices and arrange in the bottom and slightly up the sides of a glass bowl. Cover with the strawberries and their juice. Pour in the custard, cover the bowl and leave in the refrigerator for at least 2 hours, or overnight.

Whisk the thick cream with the vanilla and the remaining icing sugar until it holds a soft peak. Spread on top of the trifle. Slice the reserved strawberries and use, with the toasted almonds, to decorate the top.

Chill the trifle until ready to serve.

THE GOLDEN FRUIT

The name 'Outspan' immediately brings to mind oranges from South Africa. Outspan export oranges actually had the name stamped on the skin of the fruit. Active publicity campaigns involving teams of 'Outspan Girls' who travelled far and wide promoting the product, made it a household name in 33 different countries around the world.

Two Cool Jellies

A jelly dessert is always popular. Here is a boozy jelly for adults and a healthy sweet jelly for children (and adults).

PORT JELLY
Soak the gelatine in ½ cup cold water. Heat the sugar, 4 tablespoons water, cinnamon sticks and cloves in a saucepan. Stir to dissolve the sugar and bring to the boil. Simmer for 5 minutes and remove from the heat. Dissolve the gelatine in the hot syrup. Stir in the port and pour a little into a flat bowl and the rest into 6 individual glasses to set. When the jelly has set firmly, break the jelly in the flat bowl up with a knife and spoon it on top of the jelly in the 6 tall glasses.

ORANGE JELLY
Soak the gelatine in ½ cup cold water. Heat the orange juice, sugar and the remaining water. Stir to dissolve the sugar. Add the gelatine and stir well until dissolved. When the mixture has cooled down, add the milk. Pour into a bowl and allow to set. Serve with fresh fruit.

VARIATION
Orange Cloud Pudding: Dissolve 1 tablespoon gelatine in ¼ cup hot water. Mix together in a bowl 1 cup milk, 1 cup orange juice, ¾ cup sugar and 2 egg yolks. Add the dissolved gelatine, pouring through a strainer to catch any gelatine pieces. Place the pudding in the refrigerator to thicken slightly. Then whisk the egg whites stiffly and fold into this mixture. Leave to set in the refrigerator.

This dessert contains raw eggs which some people are unable to eat.

PORT JELLY
2 tablespoons gelatine
(2 envelopes)
3/4 cup sugar
4 tablespoons water
2 cinamon sticks
2 cloves
1 bottle (750 ml) port (or
1 bottle of rosé wine)

PREPARATION TIME: 5 minutes
COOKING TIME: 15 minutes
SERVES: six

ORANGE JELLY
1 cup water
2 level tablespoons gelatine
1 cup orange juice
3/4 cup sugar
1 cup milk

PREPARATION TIME: 5 minutes
COOKING TIME: 15 minutes
SERVES: six

The fermentation creates strong pressure inside the bottles, so always store them where an exploding bottle will do no harm.

Ginger Beer

This fizzy and refreshing childhood treat is made by fermenting sugar syrup with a yeast mixture called the 'ginger beer mother' or 'ginger beer plant'.

FOR THE GINGER BEER MOTHER

½ teaspoon dried yeast

1 cup warm water

3 tablespoons sugar

3 tablespoons ground ginger

FOR THE SUGAR SYRUP

4 cups sugar

1,5 litres cold water

4,5 litres warm water

½ cup strained lemon juice

PREPARATION TIME: 8 days

FERMENTATION TIME: 3–5 days

MAKES: about 6 litres

For the ginger beer mother, place the yeast and ½ teaspoon of the sugar in a large jar and add the warm water and ½ teaspoon ginger. Mix well, cover the jar with a cloth and leave at room temperature for 8 days, mixing in ½ teaspoon each of sugar and ginger every day.

For the sugar syrup, put the sugar and cold water in a large saucepan and heat, stirring, just until the sugar has dissolved. Remove from the heat and add the warm water and the lemon juice. Stand, if necessary, until just comfortably hand-warm.

Strain the yeast mixture into the syrup, through a sieve lined with a double thickness of muslin, and stir well. Keep the sediment on the muslin for making further batches of

ginger beer. Stir the syrup mixture well and pour into clean, sturdy bottles, preferably fitted with clip-on seals, or else with screw-tops. Fill the bottles only to the base of the necks, and seal. Leave in a cool, safe place for about five days – in hot weather, the ginger beer will be ready in three or four days.

To make further batches of ginger beer, return half the ginger beer mother left on the muslin to the jar (discard the rest) with 1 teaspoon each of ground ginger and sugar and 1 cup of water (no more yeast is added).

Repeat the process as before, feeding the mother with ½ teaspoon each of ginger and sugar daily. After 8 days, mix with the sugar syrup and bottle as before.

Summer Drinks

These are wonderful, refreshing drinks for a party – the non-alcoholic fruit cup can be enjoyed by children and adults alike, while the Pimm's No.1 punch should be reserved for the grown-ups.

FRUIT CUP

Put the water and sugar in a medium saucepan. Cook, stirring every now and then, on high heat until the sugar dissolves and the syrup comes to the boil. Reduce the heat to medium-low and simmer for 20 minutes, or until the syrup thickens slightly. Set aside to cool. Juice the oranges and lemons and strain the juice into the sugar syrup. Add the granadilla pulp and mix well. Pour the syrup into sterilised bottles and chill in the refrigerator overnight. (The syrup will keep in a sterilised bottle in the refrigerator for a week.)

When you are almost ready to serve, peel, core and finely chop the pineapple and put the fruit in a punch bowl or jug. Add the granadilla syrup and lemonade. Stir well. Add some fresh mint leaves and ladle or pour into glasses half-filled with crushed ice.

PIMM'S NO.1 PUNCH

Just before your guests arrive, put the cucumber skin and all the sliced fruits into a very large punchbowl and add the ice cubes. Alternatively, make the punch in smaller bowls or large jugs, dividing the ingredients equally among them.

Pour the Pimm's into the bowl, add the lemon and lime juice and stir well. Add the tonic water, soda water, lemonade or ginger ale and stir again. Decorate the bowl with sprigs of mint and serve the punch ladled into glasses. If you wish, the glasses can be decorated with fruits and mint leaves.

FRUIT CUP

4 cups water
2½ cups white sugar
6 oranges
6 lemons
6 granadillas, pulped
1 large pineapple
2,5 litres lemonade, chilled
Fresh mint leaves,
    to decorate
Crushed ice to serve

PREPARATION TIME:
    Day 1, 15 minutes
    Day 2, 10 minutes
COOKING TIME: 25 minutes
CHILLING TIME: overnight
MAKES: 18 cups

PIMM'S NO.1 PUNCH

Thinly peeled skin from
    1 cucumber (reserve the
    cucumber for another use)
2 small lemons, sliced
1 small orange, sliced
2 limes, sliced
1 punnet strawberries,
    hulled, washed and sliced
2 small red apples, washed,
    quartered and thinly sliced
40 ice cubes
1,7 litres Pimm's No.1 Cup,
    chilled
Strained juice of 2 lemons
Strained juice of 2 limes
3,5 litres tonic water,
    soda water, lemonade
    or ginger ale, chilled
Fresh mint sprigs,
    to decorate (optional)

PREPARATION TIME: 20 minutes
MAKES: 20 cups

Lemon Drinks

Less sweet and heavy than most bought varieties, homemade lemon barley water and lemonade are free from artificial colourings and flavourings.

LEMON BARLEY WATER

2/3 cup pearl barley

60 g sugar cubes

2 lemons, washed

6 cups boiling water

Ice cubes and slices
    of lemon, to serve

PREPARATION TIME: 20 minutes

COOKING TIME: 5 minutes

COOLING AND CHILLING TIME:
    4 hours

SERVES: four

OLD-FASHIONED LEMONADE

9 large lemons, washed

1/2 cup caster sugar

6 cups boiling water

Ice cubes and mint leaves,
    to serve

PREPARATION TIME: 20 minutes

STANDING AND CHILLING TIME:
    2 1/2 hours

SERVES: eight

LEMON BARLEY WATER

Rinse the pearl barley in a sieve under cold, running water and drain well. Tip the rinsed barley into a saucepan, cover with cold water and bring to the boil, then reduce the heat and cook gently for 5 minutes. Pour the barley back into the sieve and rinse again.

Put the cooked barley into a large jug or bowl. Rub each sugar cube over the skins of the lemons to extract the oils, then add the cubes to the jug or bowl.

Pour in the boiling water and stir until the sugar has dissolved. Cover the jug or bowl with a clean tea towel and leave to infuse for 3 hours, or until cold.

Squeeze the juice from both lemons and add it to the barley water. Strain through a nylon sieve into a serving jug. Cover and chill for 1 hour. Put several ice cubes and one or two lemon slices in each of four tall glasses, pour in the lemon barley water and serve.

OLD-FASHIONED LEMONADE

Peel the rind from the lemons with a vegetable peeler, taking care to avoid including any of the white pith. Squeeze out and strain the juice to make 1 1/3 cups.

Put the lemon rind in a large, heatproof bowl and add the sugar and boiling water. Stir until the sugar dissolves, then cover and leave to stand for 30 minutes.

Strain the lemon liquid into a jug and stir in the lemon juice. Cover the jug and refrigerate for about 2 hours, or until the lemonade is well chilled.

Put several ice cubes in tall glasses, pour in the lemonade and decorate with the mint leaves. Alternatively, put a large block of ice in a serving jug, add some lemon slices, pour in the lemonade and decorate with mint.

The lemonade will keep in the refrigerator for up to a week, but do not add ice to the jug before storing or you will dilute the flavour.

Fruit Cordials

Homemade cordial using fresh fruit makes wholesome and inexpensive drinks for children and, with a measure of gin or vodka added, is also delicious for grown-ups!

LEMON CORDIAL

2 cups white sugar

1 1/2 cups water

2 cups fresh lemon juice

3 teaspoons citric acid

Iced water or soda water,
    to serve

LEMON & GRANADILLA CORDIAL

2 cups white sugar

1 1/2 cups water

1 cup fresh lemon juice

3 teaspoons citric acid

12 granadillas, pulped

PREPARATION TIME: 15 minutes

COOKING TIME: 25 minutes

COOLING TIME: 30 minutes

MAKES: 3 1/2 cups

LEMON CORDIAL

Place the sugar, water and lemon juice in a medium saucepan. Cook, stirring every now and then, over high heat until the sugar dissolves and the syrup comes to the boil. Reduce the heat to medium-low and simmer for 20 minutes, or until the syrup thickens slightly. Stir in the citric acid. Strain the cordial into a sterilised bottle. The cordial will keep, refrigerated, for up to one month.

To serve, pour the lemon syrup into glasses, top with iced water or soda water, stir well and serve immediately.

LEMON & GRANADILLA CORDIAL

Make as for lemon cordial, but pour the hot lemon syrup over the granadilla pulp and allow to stand for 30 minutes to cool. Strain the cordial into a sterilised bottle. The cordial will keep, refrigerated, for up to one month.

Pour the cordial into glasses, top with iced water or soda water, stir and serve at once.

FACING PAGE: *Lemon barley water and old-fashioned lemonade*

Tea & Coffee with a difference

Sip Irish coffee through whipped cream and iced tea through orange and lemon slices.

IRISH COFFEE

3 tablespoons ground coffee, freshly ground if possible

2 cups water

1 small orange

1 small lemon

3 whole cloves

3 cm cinnamon stick

2 teaspoons brown sugar

2/3 cup Irish whisky

1 tablespoon caster sugar

1/2 cup thick cream, whipped to soft peaks

PREPARATION TIME: 10 minutes

COOKING TIME: 10 minutes

SERVES: two

ROOIBOS ICED TEA

1-2 rooibos tea bags

Boiling water

3 teaspoons sugar (or to taste)

1 lemon, sliced

Ice cubes

Still mineral water or filtered water

Sprigs of mint

PREPARATION TIME: 10 minutes

SERVES: six

Don't let the leaves for the iced tea infuse for longer than 10 minutes — otherwise it will taste too strong.

IRISH COFFEE

Put the ground coffee into a large jug or coffee plunger. Bring the water to the boil, allow to stand for 20 seconds, then pour onto the coffee. Cover the jug or coffee plunger and leave the coffee to infuse for 10 minutes.

Meanwhile, peel the orange and lemon, taking care not to remove any of the white pith. Put the peel in a saucepan with the cloves, cinnamon and brown sugar and cook over very low heat, stirring occasionally, until the sugar has just melted.

Add the whisky to the spice mixture, remove from the heat and ignite. Swirl the pan gently until the flames die out. Return the pan to the heat and strain the coffee into it. (If using a jug, strain the coffee through a fine coffee strainer or a sieve lined with a paper towel.) Heat very gently for 5 minutes.

Meanwhile, cut the lemon in half and rub a cut side carefully around the rims of two heatproof 1-cup serving glasses. Dip the rim of each glass into the caster sugar, and shake gently to remove the excess. Strain the coffee into the glasses, stir well and top with the whipped cream. Serve immediately.

ROOIBOS ICED TEA

Make a fresh pot of tea with the teabags and boiling water. Put the sugar into a 2 litre glass jug. Pour about a cup of tea into the jug and stir to dissolve the sugar. Add 2 more cups of tea, then lemon slices and plenty of ice. Fill the jug with cold mineral or filtered water and stir with a wooden spoon, bruising the lemon slices a little. Add the mint sprigs and serve in tall glasses.

Traditional Christmas Drinks

Although Christmas comes in our summer, it can be pleasant to serve a traditional drink as a nightcap. Sack Posset is the forerunner of the egg nog.

CHAMPAGNE CUP
Put the prepared fruit into a large, glass jug. Pour in the brandy and Grand Marnier and stir well. Cover and chill for 1 hour. Just before serving, add the ice and pour in the champagne and the soda or mineral water. Decorate with the cucumber slices, add the cherries and serve immediately.

MULLED WINE
Pour the water into a large saucepan, add the sugar, the whole lemon and the spices and heat gently until the sugar has dissolved. Bring the mixture to the boil, then reduce the heat and simmer for 1 minute. Pour in the red wine and brandy or rum and heat gently for a few minutes until hot, but not boiling. Strain into a heatproof punch bowl, float the orange and lemon slices on top and serve immediately.

SACK POSSET
Put the egg yolks, egg whites, sherry and spices into a large mixing bowl and whisk until they are well blended. Place the bowl over a saucepan of gently boiling water and stir until warm. Take care not to let the egg mixture overheat or it will scramble.

Reserving 1 teaspoon of the caster sugar, heat the remainder with the cream in a saucepan until it rises to the boil. Pour the cream mixture immediately, in a steady stream from a height, onto the egg mixture, whisking as you pour to make it frothy.

Leave the posset to stand in a warm place for 5 minutes, then sprinkle the reserved sugar and a little nutmeg over the surface and serve in heatproof glasses. This drink goes well with mince pies and, because it is rich, one glass per person should be sufficient.

CHAMPAGNE CUP
½ cup each fresh pineapple pieces, seedless grapes, halved, and orange segments
⅓ cup brandy
½ cup Grand Marnier
12 ice cubes
1 bottle champagne, well chilled
1¼ cups soda water or sparkling mineral water, well chilled
A few cucumber slices
6 maraschino cherries

PREPARATION TIME: 15 minutes
CHILLING TIME: 1 hour
SERVES: four to six

MULLED WINE
2 cups water
¾ cup caster sugar
1 small lemon, washed
6 cloves
¼ teaspoon freshly grated nutmeg
2 cinnamon sticks
3 blades of mace
2 bottles fruity red wine
1 cup brandy or rum
Thin slices of orange and lemon, to decorate

PREPARATION TIME: 15 minutes
COOKING TIME: 10 minutes
SERVES: twelve

SACK POSSET
6 egg yolks
3 egg whites
1 cup sweet sherry
¼ teaspoon each ground cinnamon and mace
¼ teaspoon freshly grated nutmeg
⅔ cup caster sugar
4 cups pouring cream
Grated nutmeg, for sprinkling

PREPARATION TIME: 15 minutes
COOKING TIME: 10 minutes
SERVES: twelve

BREADS, CAKES & BISCUITS

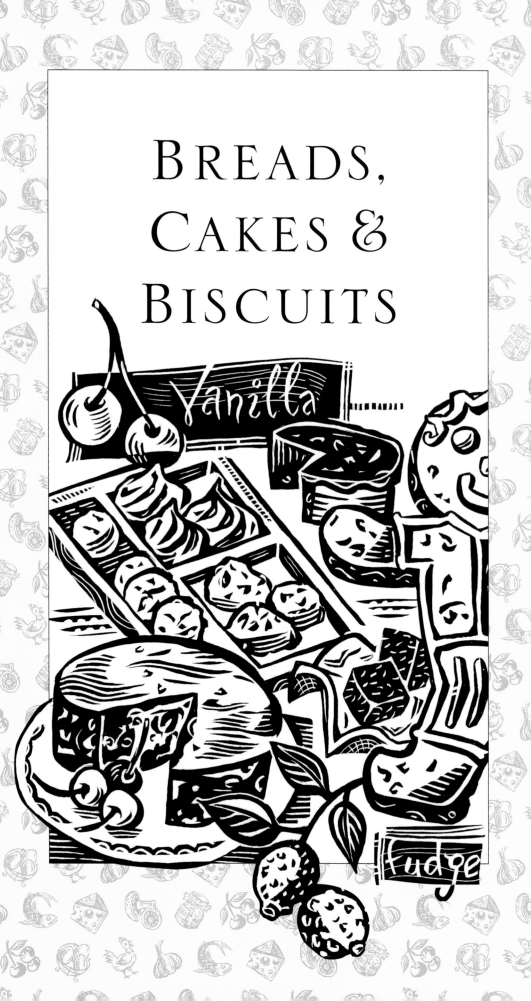

3 teaspoons fresh yeast or
  2 teaspoons dried yeast plus
  1 teaspoon caster sugar
2 cups lukewarm water
  (or half water and half
  milk for a softer texture)
6 cups white bread flour
  or wholewheat flour
  or a mixture of both
2 teaspoons salt
15 g lard, butter or margarine

PREPARATION TIME: 30 minutes

RISING TIME: up to 2 hours
depending on room
temperature

COOKING TIME: 20–40 minutes for
loaves, 15–20 minutes for rolls

Breads from the Baker

It is easy to fill your kitchen with the aroma of freshly baked bread – many breads sold at the bakery can be readily made at home.

If using fresh yeast, pour all the liquid into a bowl, add the yeast and stir with a fork until dissolved. If using dried yeast, stir the caster sugar into 2/3 cup of the water and whisk in the yeast. Cover the bowl and leave to stand in a warm place for 15 minutes, or until frothy, then stir in the remaining water.

Sift the flour and salt into a large mixing bowl and, using your fingertips, rub in the lard, butter or margarine. Make a well in the centre, pour in the yeast liquid and mix to a soft dough. Turn out on a lightly floured surface and knead well for 10 minutes, or until the dough is very smooth and elastic in texture and no longer sticky. Alternatively, mix for 3 minutes with an electric mixer, using a dough hook at low speed.

Put the dough in a lightly floured bowl, cover tightly with plastic wrap and leave to stand in a warm place for 1–1 1/2 hours, or until the dough has doubled in size. Turn the risen dough out on a lightly floured surface and, with clenched fists, punch it back to its original size. Continue to knead for a further 2–3 minutes, or until smooth.

PREPARING LOAVES

Tin Loaf: Put the dough into a large, well-greased loaf tin, or divide it equally between two smaller ones.
Cob Loaf: Shape the dough into a neat round. Place the round on a greased baking tray and mould in the bottom edge to plump up the shape of the loaf.
Coburg or Scofa Loaf: Shape the dough as for a cob loaf but, halfway through the proving time, cut a deep cross in the top.
Cottage Loaf: Cut off one-third of the dough and shape it into a ball. Shape the other piece of dough into a larger ball. Place the larger ball on a greased baking tray and lay the smaller ball on top. Lightly flour the handle of a wooden spoon and push it down through the centres of both balls to join them together. Twist the handle slightly and pull it out.
Plaited Loaf: Cut the dough into three equal pieces and roll each piece into a strand about 45 cm long. Lay the strands side by side on the work surface and, working from the centre of each strand, plait them together, then pinch the ends to seal. Carefully turn the strands around, from top to bottom, and plait the other ends. Place on a greased baking tray. If preferred, cut the dough in half and make two smaller plaits.

PREPARING ROLLS AND BAPS

Rolls: Cut the dough into pieces the size of an egg and shape into smooth balls by rolling firmly on the work surface with your cupped hand. Put the rolls on greased baking trays.
Baps: Shape as for rolls, then flatten each with a rolling pin.

PROVING THE DOUGH

The dough must be proved – left to rise – after it has been shaped. Loosely cover the tins or baking trays with lightly oiled plastic wrap and leave in a warm place for about 30 minutes, or until the dough has doubled in size and will retain a small dent when pressed lightly with your fingertip. When it has doubled in size, either leave the dough as it is or, for a soft-topped bread, sprinkle it lightly with flour. To give a delicious crusty finish to the bread, dissolve 1 teaspoon of salt in 1/2 cup of water and brush over the top of the dough. For a golden sheen, brush the top with milk.

Before baking, the dough can be sprinkled with cracked wheat, rolled oats, sesame seeds or poppy seeds.

Bake large loaves in a preheated oven at 220°C for 35–40 minutes, smaller ones for 20–25 minutes and rolls for 15–20 minutes. To check if the bread is done, tap the loaf on the bottom with your knuckles. It is done when it sounds hollow.

When the bread is cooked, remove the loaves or rolls from the tins or baking trays and cool on a wire rack.

It is no wonder that many housewives refused to replace their anthracite stoves with new electric stoves. Compare the 'modern' stove to the model above which provided a constant even temperature, burned continuously 24 hours a day, gave off no dirt, grime or soot and gave an ever ready supply of hot water.

FACING PAGE: *Breads from the baker*

QUICK BREAD

2 cups self-raising flour

Pinch of caster sugar

Pinch of salt

1 tablespoon butter
   or dripping

About 1 cup milk

Extra self-raising flour,
   for dusting

PREPARATION TIME: 15 minutes

COOKING TIME: 35–40 minutes

SERVES: four

WHOLEWHEAT YOGHURT BREAD

4 cups wholewheat flour

1 teaspoon salt

1 tablespoon brown sugar

1 tablespoons oil

1½ teaspoons bicarbonate of
   soda

500 ml natural drinking
   yoghurt or buttermilk

PREPARATION TIME: 10 minutes

COOKING TIME: 1 hour

MAKES: one loaf

No-Yeast Breads

*These two breads do not use yeast as a raising agent and are quick and easy to make.
If possible, serve your bread straight from the oven.*

QUICK BREAD

Preheat the oven to 200°C. Sift the flour, caster sugar and salt together in a large mixing bowl. Rub the butter or dripping into the flour mixture with your fingertips.

Make a well in the centre of the flour and gradually add the milk, using a round-bladed knife to mix it in. Continue adding milk until the mixture forms a soft dough.

Turn the dough out on a lightly floured surface and knead gently until the surface is smooth. Shape the dough into a round about 14 cm in diameter. Using a sharp knife, slash a cross in the dough about 1 cm deep.

Dust a baking tray generously with flour and place the bread on the tray. Dust the top of the bread with a little more flour and bake in the preheated oven for 20–25 minutes, or until it is golden and cooked through when tested with a skewer.

Serve hot with butter and golden syrup.

WHOLEWHEAT YOGHURT BREAD

Preheat the oven to 180°C. Mix the flour, salt and brown sugar together in a bowl. Add the oil. Mix the bicarbonate of soda in the yoghurt (or buttermilk) and stir into the dry ingredients until thoroughly mixed.

Pour into an oiled 23 x 8 x 7 cm loaf tin. Bake on the middle shelf of the preheated oven for about an hour. Remove from the oven and stand for 5 minutes then turn out and return to the oven to 5 minutes to crisp the sides.

Bread with Dried Fruit

*This mouthwatering fruit bread has a rich fruity texture
and a firm, nutty crust.*

Preheat the oven to 180°C. Sieve the flour and salt on to a working surface or into a large mixing bowl. Rub in the butter and make a well in the centre. Mix the sugar and spice together – reserving 1 teaspoon sugar if you are using dried yeast – and put into the well.

Combine the beaten egg with the warm water. If you are using dried yeast, dissolve the reserved sugar and the yeast in 100 ml of the egg and water mixture. If using fresh yeast, use 3 tablespoons of this mixture to blend the yeast to a smooth paste and allow to stand for 10 minutes.

Stir the rest of the egg/water mixture into the yeast mixture. Pour this over the sugar in the well, mix vigorously to blend, then knead well to a make a smooth, elastic dough. Mix together the currants, sultanas and mixed peel, and knead lightly in the dough.

Mould the dough into a round or long shape and put on a greased baking sheet or in a greased 900 g loaf tin. Cover with a sheet of greased plastic and put in a warm place to rise for 1½ hours. Bake in the preheated oven for 35 minutes.

275 g cake flour

1 teaspoon salt

20 g butter

25 g sugar

½ teaspoon ground mixed spice

1 large egg, beaten

150 ml warm water

½ teaspoons dried yeast, or 20 g fresh yeast

225 g currants

100-125 sultanas

25 g mixed peel, chopped

PREPARATION TIME: 30 minutes

RISING TIME: 1-1½ hours

COOKING TIME: 35 minutes

MAKES: one large loaf

TINS FOR TEA

Mazawattee Tea is no longer produced, and neither are tea tins. In the absence of cellophane and foil, tea could only be kept fresh in an airtight tin and all the major tea manufacturers had their own tins. In the 1930s a special Tea Market Expansion Bureau was established to 'convert the rural districts of the Union to tea'. Rural districts were perceived as being coffee-drinking strongholds.

Shortbread

Whether moulded as rounds or shaped as petticoat tails or fingers, the crumbly buttery texture of shortbread guarantees it a welcome at any morning or afternoon tea.

2½ cups cake flour

½ cup caster sugar

⅓ cup rice flour
   or fine semolina

250 g butter, chilled and
   cut into small cubes

Caster sugar, for sprinkling

PREPARATION TIME: 25 minutes

COOKING TIME: 20–30 minutes

CHILLING TIME: 1 hour

MAKES: two 18–20 cm moulded shortbreads, 16 petticoat tails or 20 fingers

Sift the flour, caster sugar and rice flour or semolina into a mixing bowl. Add the cubed butter and rub it in with your fingertips until the mixture clings together in heavy lumps. Gather the dough into a ball and then knead it on a lightly floured surface until smooth. Proceed according to how you wish the finished shortbread to be shaped.

Moulded Shortbread: Lightly sprinkle an 18–20 cm diameter shortbread mould with flour. Cut the dough in half, roll out each piece to a round a little smaller than the mould and press, smooth side down, into the mould to fit exactly. Carefully turn the dough out on a flat baking tray. The mixture can also be shaped in small moulds to produce biscuit-size shortbreads.

Petticoat Tails: Cut the dough in half and roll out two rounds each 18–20 cm in diameter. Flute the edges with your fingers, then prick all over with a fork. Alternatively, fit the rounds into two fluted flan tins and prick well.

Shortbread Fingers: Press the dough into a shallow, 28 x 18 cm tin, smooth with a palette knife, then prick well with a fork.

Having prepared the dough according to the shape chosen, chill it in the refrigerator for 1 hour and preheat the oven to 160°C. Bake the moulded shortbread and petticoat tails for 20–25 minutes and fingers for 25–30 minutes, or until cooked through, but not browned.

Remove from the oven and leave to cool and firm up for 5 minutes. Loosen the moulded shortbread and petticoat tails from the baking trays with a palette knife. Mark the petticoat tails into triangles. Cut fingers into 20 equal pieces while still in the tin. Sprinkle generously with caster sugar.

After 15 minutes, transfer the petticoat tails and moulded shortbread to wire racks to cool completely. Leave the shortbread fingers in the tin until cold.

The shortbread will keep well if stored in an airtight container.

Scones

Many grandmothers could whip up a batch of scones at a moment's notice.
To enjoy scones at their very best, eat them on the day they are made.

Preheat the oven to 230°C and lightly flour a baking tray.

Sift the flour, caster sugar, salt and baking powder into a bowl and rub in the butter. Add the milk and mix with a round-bladed knife, adding a little extra milk, if necessary, to make a soft dough. Turn out on a lightly floured surface and knead gently for a few seconds until smooth.

Roll out to about 2 cm thick, then, using a 5 cm round pastry cutter, stamp out as many rounds as possible. Reknead and reroll the trimmings and cut out more rounds, making about 12 scones in all. Place the scones, touching one another, on a greased baking tray and brush the tops lightly with milk.

Bake for 10 minutes, or until they are well risen, golden and sound hollow when tapped on the bottom. Transfer to a wire rack to cool slightly. Serve warm, with cream and jam.

VARIATIONS

Fruit Scones: Make as for basic scones, mixing in 2 tablespoons caster sugar, 1/3 cup sultanas and 1/4 cup chopped mixed peel before adding any of the milk.

Golden Syrup Scones: Make as for basic scones, sifting 1/2 teaspoon mixed spice and 2 tablespoons caster sugar in with the flour. Add 1 tablespoon golden syrup with the milk.

Cheese Scones: Make as for basic scones, adding 3/4 cup grated mature Cheddar cheese, 1/2 teaspoon mustard powder and a pinch of cayenne pepper before the milk. Sprinkle with a little cheese before baking.

Scone Round: Roll out the dough to an 18 cm round, put on the baking tray and mark into eight wedges. Brush with milk, sprinkle with sugar or cheese, as appropriate, and bake for 15–20 minutes, or until cooked.

3 cups self-raising flour
1 teaspoon caster sugar
Pinch of salt
1/2 teaspoon baking powder
60 g butter
1 cup milk
About 1–2 tablespoons milk, extra

PREPARATION TIME: 20 minutes
COOKING TIME: 10 minutes
MAKES: 12 scones

For a change, try substituting yoghurt, sour cream or buttermilk for the milk when you make your scones.

4 tablespoons water

125 g butter

3 cups caster sugar

3 tablespoons golden syrup

¾ cup sweetened
  condensed milk

½ teaspoon vanilla essence

PREPARATION TIME: 20 minutes
plus standing time

COOKING TIME: 30 minutes

MAKES: about 500 g

Vanilla Fudge

*Everyone loves rich, chewy fudge – a lovely, easy treat to make
for children, or to give, packed in a pretty box, to friends.*

Butter an 18 cm square, shallow tin. Pour the water into a heavy-based saucepan, add the butter, caster sugar and golden syrup and stir over low heat until all the sugar has dissolved. Brush down the sides of the pan with hot water from time to time. Add the condensed milk, bring to the boil and cook, stirring continuously, for about 10 minutes, or until the mixture reaches a temperature of 118°C on a sugar thermometer.

Alternatively, take the pan off the heat and test by dropping a teaspoon of the mixture into a bowl of cold water – if it does not form a soft ball when taken out, continue to boil for a little longer and retest as before.

When the fudge is ready, remove the pan from the heat and set aside until the bubbles subside. Stir in the vanilla essence and beat with a wooden spoon until the texture is thick and creamy and a heavy trail is formed when the mixture is allowed to fall from the spoon.

Immediately pour the mixture into the prepared tin and allow to cool. When almost set, mark the fudge into squares with an oiled knife. Cut when completely cold and firm and store in an airtight tin, interleaved with waxed paper or baking paper. The fudge will keep for up to four weeks.

VARIATIONS

Walnut Fudge: Stir ⅓ cup chopped walnuts into the mixture just before the fudge is poured into the tin.

Chocolate Fudge: Add 2 tablespoons sifted cocoa powder with the condensed milk.

Fruit and Nut Fudge: Stir ⅓ cup each of raisins and chopped, toasted hazelnuts into the fudge before pouring into the tin.

THE CONDENSED STORY

The origins of Nestlé, one of the world's biggest food multinationals can be traced back to one commodity - plentiful, good quality Swiss milk. In 1905, the Page brothers of the Anglo-Swiss Condensed Milk Company and Henri Nestlé, of Nestlé combined forces. The Swiss founders had both independently developed preserved milk in tins - the Pages a condensed milk and Nestlé an evaporated milk. After years of fierce competition, they decided to unite and formed one company - the company we all know today.

If you need to make gingerbread men ahead for a party, they will keep well if you wrap them individually in plastic wrap and store them in an airtight container.

Gingerbread Men

Children find these little edible men, with eyes and buttons of currants, quite irresistible.

Preheat the oven to 180°C. Sift the flour, ginger and bicarbonate of soda into a bowl and make a well in the centre. Heat the butter, sugar and golden syrup gently in a small saucepan until the butter is melted, then pour into the flour. Add the egg and mix to form a soft dough. Knead lightly on a floured surface for a few seconds until smooth, then roll out to about 5 mm thick.

Using a specially shaped 10 cm cutter, stamp out the gingerbread men and place them, spaced apart, on lightly greased baking trays. Reknead and reroll the trimmings – you should cut out 12 men in all.

Cut 12 currants in half and gently press two bits on each shape for the eyes. Use whole currants for the buttons. Bake the gingerbread men in the oven for 15–20 minutes, or until lightly browned.

Leave on the baking trays for 5 minutes, then, using a palette knife, carefully transfer to a wire cooling rack and cool completely.

2 cups cake flour

2 teaspoons ground ginger

1 teaspoon bicarbonate of soda

60 g butter

⅓ cup soft brown sugar

4 tablespoons golden syrup

1 egg, beaten

Currants, for decoration

PREPARATION TIME: 25 minutes
COOKING TIME: 15–20 minutes
MAKES: 12 gingerbread men

3 cups cake flour

1 teaspoon baking powder

250 g butter, at room temperature

1¼ cups caster sugar

4 eggs, beaten

4–5 tablespoons sweet sherry or milk

1½ cups currants

1½ cups sultanas

¾ cup glacé cherries, halved

4 tablespoons each candied orange, lemon and lime peel, chopped, or ¾ cup chopped mixed peel

¾ cup ground almonds

Finely grated rind of 1 orange

Finely grated rind of 1 lemon

1 cup whole almonds, blanched

PREPARATION TIME: 30 minutes

COOKING TIME: 2¼–2½ hours

SERVES: ten

Dundee Cake

Candied peel, dried fruit, ground almonds and sherry result in a cake that improves with keeping. The topping of blanched almonds is traditional.

Preheat the oven to 160°C. Lightly grease a 20-cm-diameter round cake tin and line the base and sides with nonstick baking paper.

Sift the flour and baking powder together into a bowl. In another bowl, beat the butter with the sugar until light and fluffy. Gradually beat in the eggs, a little at a time, beating well after each addition. Add a little of the flour if the mixture begins to curdle. Then add the remaining flour and fold in gently. Stir in enough sherry or milk to mix to a soft, dropping consistency. Fold in the fruit, peel, ground almonds and grated rinds. Spoon the mixture into the prepared tin and level the top with the back of a spoon. Arrange the blanched whole almonds in concentric circles on top of the cake, dropping, not pressing them, lightly in place.

Bake the cake in the centre of the oven for 2¼–2½ hours, or until it is firm to the touch and when a skewer inserted into the centre comes out clean. After 1 hour, cover the top with foil to prevent the almonds from overbrowning. Leave to cool in the tin and then store in an airtight container.

The Dundee cake will mature and develop in flavour if it is kept for two to three days before cutting and serving.

Banana Cake with Lemon Icing

This nourishing cake keeps well in a covered container for three or four days. A denser cake with a more pronounced banana flavour is obtained by using very ripe bananas.

FOR THE CAKE

140 g butter

¾ cup caster sugar

2 eggs, lightly beaten

½ cup milk

1 teaspoon vanilla essence

2 cups cake flour

2 teaspoons baking powder

½ teaspoon bicarbonate of soda

3 ripe, medium bananas, mashed well with a fork

FOR THE ICING

1½ cups icing sugar

Strained juice of 1–2 lemons

PREPARATION TIME: 20 minutes

COOKING TIME: 30 minutes

COOLING AND FINISHING OFF: 20 minutes

SERVES: ten to twelve

Preheat the oven to 175°C. Melt the butter gently in a small saucepan, then cool a little. Add the sugar, eggs, milk and vanilla essence. Sift the dry ingredients into a wide bowl and pour in the butter mixture. Stir everything together, adding the mashed bananas; do not overmix or beat the batter.

Turn the mixture into a lightly buttered 6-cup ring tin and bake for 30 minutes. The cake should be browned, slightly shrinking from the sides of the tin and a skewer inserted in the middle should come out clean.

To make the lemon icing, put the icing sugar in a bowl and add enough lemon juice to make it a barely pourable consistency. Spread over the cooled cake and leave to set.

To make a loaf, bake in a 28 x 11 x 7 cm loaf tin for 45 minutes.

VARIATIONS

Banana and Orange Cake: Add the grated zest of 1 large orange to the banana cake batter. Substitute the juice of 1–2 oranges for the lemon juice in the icing.

Banana and Coconut Cake: Add ½ cup desiccated coconut to the banana cake batter. Sprinkle the icing, before it sets, with toasted desiccated or shredded coconut.

Banana Muffins: The banana cake batter can also be used for muffins. Preheat the oven to 190°C. Lightly butter 12 deep muffin tins (or line with bought paper cases) and pour in the batter. Cook for 12–15 minutes. Cool for 10 minutes in the tin, then turn out on a wire rack. When cool, spread with lemon icing.

FACING PAGE: *Dundee cake*

2 cups cake flour

1 teaspoon baking powder

90 g butter, cut into small
  cubes

½ cup sugar

½ cup sultanas

2 tablespoons chopped mixed
  peel

1 egg, beaten

2 tablespoons milk

PREPARATION TIME: 45 minutes

COOKING TIME: 15 minutes

MAKES: twelve cakes

Rock Cakes

*Warm or cold, buttered or plain, rock cakes are great for picnics or lunch boxes,
as well as for morning or afternoon tea.*

Preheat the oven to 200°C. Grease a baking tray. Sift the flour and baking powder into a large mixing bowl, add the cubed butter and rub it into the flour with your fingertips until the mixture resembles breadcrumbs. Reserve 1 tablespoon of the sugar, then add rest with the sultanas and the mixed peel to the rubbed-in mixture in the bowl. Mix well.

Make a well in the centre of the mixture, put the egg and milk into the well and mix to form a stiff dough. Spoon 12 rocky heaps of dough onto the prepared baking tray, spacing them well apart.

Bake the cakes in the centre of the oven for 10–15 minutes, or until well risen and golden brown. Transfer them from the baking tray to a wire rack, sprinkle with the remaining sugar and leave to cool. When cold, store the cakes in an airtight container. Serve plain, buttered, or drizzled with lemon icing (see p.254).

LOSING THE LUMPS

If Grandma did not have a hand sifter, she would have used a mesh sieve. Sifting flour removes any lumps and also helps the flour absorb liquid, making the batter lighter and tastier.

Lemon Sponge

Vigorous whisking of the eggs and sugar ensures that this sponge rises perfectly.

Preheat the oven to 190°C. Grease and flour two sandwich tins, 22 cm in diameter, and line the bottoms with nonstick baking paper.

Whisk the eggs and caster sugar in a large mixing bowl or a food mixer until they are very thick, pale and creamy and will hold a ribbon trail of the mixture almost indefinitely.

Sift the flour over the mixture and fold it in carefully with a large metal spoon, then gently fold in the butter. Divide equally between the tins and tap gently to level the mixture. Bake in the oven for 20–25 minutes, or until well risen, firm and springy to the touch and slightly shrunk away from the sides of the tins.

Allow to cool in the tins for 1–2 minutes, then loosen the sides with a knife and transfer to a wire rack to cool completely.

For the filling, whisk the cream with the sugar and vanilla until thick but not buttery. Using a very sharp knife, carefully cut each sponge cake in half horizontally. Put 2 tablespoons of the lemon curd in a small paper piping bag and refrigerate.

Place one sponge layer on a flat serving dish and spread with a third of the remaining lemon curd followed by a layer of cream. Place another sponge layer on top and spread with more lemon curd and cream. Repeat with the third layer, then place the final layer on top and press together gently.

Spread cream around the side of the cake and coat with the flaked almonds, brushing away the excess nuts when the side is well covered. Put 2 tablespoons of the remaining cream into a piping bag fitted with a small star nozzle, then spread the rest evenly over the top of the cake, marking it decoratively with a palette knife. Pipe small rings of cream around the top of the cake, then fill each ring with the reserved lemon curd. Chill until required.

FOR THE SPONGE CAKE
5 eggs
⅔ cup caster sugar
1¼ cups cake flour
30 g unsalted butter,
    melted and cooled

FOR THE FILLING
2½ cups thick cream
1 tablespoon caster sugar
½ teaspoon vanilla essence
350 g lemon curd, homemade
    (p.301) or bought
¾ cup flaked almonds,
    lightly toasted

PREPARATION TIME: 1 hour
    (if making the lemon butter
    on the same day, allow
    extra time)
COOKING TIME: 20–25 minutes
SERVES: eight to ten

Lamingtons

The sponge cake will be firmer and easier to handle if you make it the day before you assemble the lamingtons. The finished lamingtons can be stored overnight, standing on baking paper, in airtight containers.

FOR THE SPONGE CAKE
3 tablespoons self-raising flour
¼ cup cake flour
3 tablespoons cornflour
3 eggs
Pinch of salt
½ cup caster sugar
3 teaspoons boiling water

FOR THE CHOCOLATE
ICING
2 cups icing sugar
⅓ cup cocoa powder
½ cup boiling water
1¾ cups desiccated coconut

PREPARATION TIME:
  Day 1, 15 minutes
  Day 2, 30 minutes
COOKING TIME: 18 minutes
MAKES: 15 lamingtons

Preheat the oven to 160°C. Lightly grease a deep 28 x 18 cm lamington pan with melted butter and line the base and sides of the pan with nonstick baking paper, allowing a 5 cm overhang (this makes it easier to remove the sponge from the pan).

Sift the two flours and cornflour together. Repeat the sifting process five times (this will aerate the flour thoroughly).

Using an electric mixer, whisk the eggs and salt in a large mixing bowl for 6 minutes, or until pale and thick. Gradually add the sugar, 1 tablespoon at a time, whisking until the mixture is thick and the sugar is dissolved.

Sift the combined flour mixture over the egg mixture. Add the boiling water and gently fold in until the batter is just combined. Pour the mixture into the prepared pan and bake in

the preheated oven for 15–18 minutes, or until cooked through when tested with a skewer. Allow the cake to cool completely in the pan. Cover with foil and stand overnight.

Lift the cake from the pan. Trim the edges and cut the sponge into 5 cm squares.

To make the chocolate icing, sift the icing sugar and cocoa powder into a medium heat-proof bowl. Stir in the boiling water and mix well to combine.

Place the coconut in a medium bowl. Using two forks, dip the sponge squares, one at a time, into the warm icing and then roll in the coconut. (If the icing begins to thicken, place the bowl over a saucepan of simmering water and stir until it is warm and thin again.)

Place the lamingtons on a wire rack lined with nonstick baking paper for 1 hour to set.

Crunchie Biscuits

Crunchies have become synonymous with school bazaars and church fêtes. Usually they are made in a square baking tin and then cut into squares when baked. Try this more sophisticated version – crunchie biscuits.

1 cup cake flour
Pinch of salt
1¼ cup rolled oats
⅔ cup caster sugar
¾ cup desiccated coconut
125 g butter, chopped
2 tablespoons water
2 tablespoons golden syrup
1 teaspoon bicarbonate
  of soda

PREPARATION TIME: 20 minutes
COOKING TIME: 30 minutes
MAKES: about 30 biscuits

Preheat the oven to 150°C. Lightly grease two baking trays with melted butter and line with a sheet of nonstick baking paper.

Sift the flour and salt into a medium mixing bowl. Add the rolled oats, caster sugar and desiccated coconut and mix well.

Combine the butter, water and golden syrup in a small saucepan. Cook over medium heat until the butter melts and the mixture is well combined. Remove from the heat and stir in the bicarbonate of soda (the mixture will begin to froth). Working quickly, add the butter mixture to the dry ingredients and mix well to combine.

Roll the mixture into balls and place on the prepared trays, allowing room for the biscuits

to spread. Flatten each biscuit slightly with your fingertips. Bake in the preheated oven for 8 minutes, then swap the trays and bake for a further 7–8 minutes, or until the biscuits are golden around the edges. Allow to stand on the trays for 5 minutes before transferring the biscuits to a wire rack to cool completely. Repeat with the remaining biscuit mixture.

FACING PAGE: *Lamingtons (foreground) and crunchie biscuits (centre)*

Mosbolletjies

It was once customary during the wine-making season at the Cape to use fresh must as a leavening agent for must buns, which became known as mosbolletjies.

250 g raisins with seeds

3 cups cold water

½ teaspoon dried yeast, or
   5 g fresh yeast

¼ cup warm water

2,5 kg cake flour, sifted

500 g sugar

1½ teaspoon salt

1 tablespoon aniseed

250 g butter, melted
   (margarine, vegetable fat
   or lard may be used
   instead)

3 cups lukewarm milk, or an
   equal mixture of milk and
   water

FOR THE GLAZE

1 egg yolk, beaten with a
   pinch of sugar and
   1 tablespoon milk

PREPARATION TIME: 1½ hours
STANDING TIME: 2 days
COOKING TIME: 1 hour
MAKES: fifty buns

Crush the raisins and place in a saucepan with the cold water. Boil for 10 minutes, then allow to cool until lukewarm. Pour into a glass jar or enamel container with a well-fitting lid.

Dissolve the yeast in the warm water and stir into the raisin mixture. Stir well together and leave in a warm place for 24–48 hours, or until the raisins have risen to the top. Strain the raisin liquid (must).

Stir 250 g of the flour into the must to form a smooth batter. Leave in a warm place for 3-4 hours, or until it is well fermented.

Sieve together the rest of the flour, the sugar and salt, and add the aniseed. Form into a stiff dough with the must and flour mixture, the melted butter and enough of the milk (or milk and water) to make a stiff dough. Knead very well together (it is ready when a piece of the dough cut with a knife shows evenly distributed air bubbles).

Cover well and leave in a warm place overnight, or until the dough doubles in bulk. It is not necessary to knead it again.

Carefully shape the dough into buns and pack into greased deep loaf pans. Lightly cover and allow to rise in a warm place until doubled in bulk.

Preheat the oven to 180°C. Brush with the egg yolk, sugar and milk glaze, bake for 1 hour, then turn out and break apart.

Serve hot, spread with butter. The buns can be toasted the next day. To keep them for a long time, make rusks by drying the buns out in a very slow oven (about 140°C). Store in an airtight container.

Buttermilk Rusks

This is a variation on the traditional yeast-based rusks and is much simpler to make. Do not substitute margarine for butter if you intend to keep the rusks for a long time.

375 g butter
500 g sugar
2 extra-large eggs
1,5 kg self-raising flour
2 tablespoons baking powder
2 cups buttermilk or plain drinking yoghurt

Preparation time: 40 minutes
Cooking time: 45-50 minutes
Drying time: 4-5 hours or overnight
Makes: thirty-six rusks

Preheat the oven to 180°C. Cream the butter and sugar together very well. Add the eggs, one at a time. Sift the flour and baking powder together, and add this to the creamed mixture, using a fork to mix. Add the buttermilk or yoghurt, using a little milk to rinse out the carton. Mix well with a fork and then knead lightly.

Pack lightly rolled, golfball-sized buns of the dough close together into greased bread pans, and bake for 45–55 minutes. Place the pans in the middle of the oven, with a sheet of brown paper on the top shelf to prevent the tops of the buns from becoming browned too quickly.

Remove the paper after the buns are well risen and cooked through, to brown the tops. Reduce the heat to the lowest possible setting. Turn out the buns onto cake racks, cool them and separate them, using 2 forks. Pack them on wire racks or on cooled oven racks – air must circulate. Dry out in a cool oven (100°C) for 4–5 hours.

If buttermilk or yoghurt is not available, fresh milk curdled with lemon juice or white vinegar may be used.

'Koffie en Beskuit'

Coffee and rusks, or 'koffie en beskuit' is a South African tradition, and when South Africans think of rusks, they think of 'Ouma'. Ouma Greyvensteyn from Molteno in the Eastern Cape started making her rusks during the Great Depression in the 1930s. Originally they were sold to raise money to sponsor mission work, but proved so popular that orders started flooding in and a factory was eventually set up on the farm to bake Outspan Rusks, as they were then called. Today it is estimated that over 1 000 million rusks are eaten in South Africa every year.

Meringues

Ring the changes by flavouring the filling with a selection of ingredients – coffee or orange and Van der Hum, for instance.

FOR THE MERINGUES
4 egg whites
1¼ cups caster sugar
⅔ cup thick cream, for filling
A little icing sugar, for sifting

FOR LEMON FLAVOURING
Finely grated rind of 1 lemon
1 tablespoon lemon juice
1 tablespoon icing sugar

FOR VANILLA FLAVOURING
¼ teaspoon vanilla essence
1 teaspoon icing sugar

FOR COFFEE FLAVOURING
1½ tablespoons strong black coffee
1 tablespoon icing sugar

FOR ORANGE LIQUEUR FLAVOURING
Finely grated rind of 1 small orange
1 tablespoon Van der Hum (Cointreau or Grand Marnier can also be used)
1 teaspoon icing sugar

PREPARATION TIME: 15 minutes

COOKING TIME: 2–3 hours (the time needed to dry the meringues will vary from oven to oven)

MAKES: eight meringues

IN THE MIX
Electric mixers were developed in the United States in the 1910s, but the form we know today was created by Ken Wood, a British engineer, in the 1950s. It revolutionised cooking and led to many a battle over who got to lick the beaters!

Preheat the oven to 110°C. Line two flat baking trays with nonstick baking paper. Make sure that the mixing bowl and whisk are perfectly clean and dry.

Whisk the egg whites until stiff but not dry. If using an electric whisk, add the sugar, a tablespoon at a time, until it is all incorporated and the mixture is thick and glossy. If whisking by hand, add half the sugar, a tablespoon at a time, then fold in the rest.

Using two tablespoons to make neat oval shapes, put 16 spoonfuls of the mixture on the baking trays, spacing them 2–3 cm apart. Bake in the preheated oven for 2–3 hours, or until the meringues are lightly coloured on the outside but still slightly soft, like a marshmallow, in the centre.

Remove the meringues from the oven, allow to cool on the baking trays, then store in an airtight container until ready to fill.

For the filling, whisk the chosen flavouring into the cream until thick but not buttery. Sandwich the meringues together with the cream, place on a large serving dish and sift the icing sugar lightly over them. Serve the meringues in paper cases, if you wish.

Chocolate Cake

This luscious chocolate-filled and chocolate-iced sponge is best made a day ahead because its flavour improves.

Preheat the oven to 190°C. Grease and flour two 23 cm sandwich tins and line the bottom of each with a round of nonstick baking paper. Sift the flour, bicarbonate of soda and both the caster and the brown sugar into a bowl and make a well in the centre.

Combine the water with the cocoa powder and butter in a small saucepan and stir over medium heat until the butter melts and the mixture becomes smooth. Do not allow it to boil. Remove from the heat and stir in the vanilla essence.

Stir the vinegar into the cream and pour it into the flour. Add the cocoa mixture and eggs and whisk the batter until smooth. Pour it into the prepared tins, dividing it equally. Bake for 20–25 minutes, or until the cakes have risen and are springy and firm to the touch. Remove from the oven, loosen the sides with a knife and turn out on wire racks to cool.

Meanwhile, to make the filling, heat the chocolate and water in a small saucepan, stirring over low heat until it is melted and smooth. Set aside.

Put the caster sugar, cream and butter in another saucepan and stir constantly over medium heat for 4–5 minutes, or until it becomes smooth and thick and will hold a trail. Take care not to let it burn. Remove from the heat and stir in the vanilla and chocolate. Cool, stirring occasionally, then chill until cold.

Sandwich the two cakes together with the filling and leave on a rack over a drip tray.

To make the icing, stir the chocolate with the butter and water in a small saucepan over low heat until the chocolate melts and the mixture becomes smooth and will coat the back of the spoon thickly. Do not overheat.

Pour the icing over the top of the cake, allowing it to trickle randomly down the sides, then chill until set. If you wish, you can pipe a decorative border around the top of the cake with warm icing, as shown in the picture.

FOR THE CAKE
2½ cups cake flour
1½ teaspoons bicarbonate of soda
¾ cup caster sugar
1 cup brown sugar
1 cup water
½ cup cocoa powder
125 g unsalted butter
1 teaspoon vanilla essence
1 teaspoon distilled malt vinegar
⅔ cup pouring cream
2 eggs, beaten

FOR THE FILLING
125 g dark plain chocolate, roughly chopped
4 tablespoons water
1 cup caster sugar
½ cup pouring cream
125 g unsalted butter
½ teaspoon vanilla essence

FOR THE ICING
125 g dark plain chocolate, roughly chopped
30 g unsalted butter
3 tablespoons water

PREPARATION TIME: 1 hour
COOKING TIME: 30 minutes
COOLING TIME: 1–1½ hours
SERVES: twelve

Perfect Sponge Cake

About 250 g butter, at room
    temperature
About 1½ cups caster sugar
4 eggs, at room temperature
½ teaspoon vanilla essence
About 2 cups self-raising flour
125 g strawberry jam,
    homemade (p.297)
    or bought
1¼ cups thick cream
3 tablespoons caster sugar,
    for sprinkling

PREPARATION TIME: 25 minutes
COOKING TIME: 30–40 minutes
SERVES: eight

*This classic sponge is made in an old, reliable way. The method of
weighing the ingredients ensures the right quantities for perfection.*

Preheat the oven to 190°C. Lightly grease two straight-sided, 23 cm sandwich tins and line with nonstick baking paper.

If you have balance scales, put the eggs on the weight side and weigh out the butter, sugar and flour each to the same weight as the eggs. If you have spring or digital scales, weigh the four eggs in their shells, then measure out the same weight of the other ingredients.

Beat the butter in a bowl until soft. Add the sugar and continue beating until the mixture is light and fluffy. Gradually beat in the eggs, one at a time, beating well after each addition, then beat in the vanilla essence.

Sift the flour into the bowl and, using a large metal spoon, carefully fold it into the creamed mixture. Divide the mixture equally between the two tins, spread evenly and bake in the oven for 30–40 minutes, or until well risen, springy to the touch and very slightly

shrunk away from the sides of the tins. Allow to cool in the tins for 5 minutes, then turn out on a wire rack and leave to cool completely.

When cold, place one of the cakes upside-down on a serving plate and spread evenly with the jam. Whisk the cream until it is just thick enough to hold its shape and spread it evenly over the jam, just up to the edge of the sponge. Place the second cake over the filling and sift the caster sugar evenly over the top.

VARIATION

Granadilla Cream Sponge: Omit the jam for the filling and the caster sugar for sprinkling. Whip the cream with 1 tablespoon of icing sugar until it holds its shape. Fold through 3 tablespoons of fresh granadilla pulp and use to fill and top the sponge sandwich. Cover the top with an additional 2 tablespoons of granadilla pulp.

Cinnamon Teacake

FOR THE TEACAKE
60 g butter, chopped
½ cup caster sugar
1 teaspoon vanilla essence
1 egg, lightly beaten
¾ cup self-raising flour
¼ cup cake flour
½ cup milk

FOR THE TOPPING
2 tablespoons caster sugar
1 teaspoon ground cinnamon
20 g butter, melted

PREPARATION TIME: 10 minutes
COOKING TIME: 30 minutes
SERVES: four or five

*This is an excellent, easy first cake for a young cook to make. It is always a hit,
whether served warm from the oven, or sliced and buttered, cold, for lunch boxes.*

Preheat the oven to 180°C. Lightly grease a 20 cm round cake pan with melted butter and cut out a round of nonstick baking paper to line the base of the pan.

Using an electric mixer, beat the butter, caster sugar and vanilla essence in a medium bowl until pale and creamy. Add the beaten egg gradually, mixing well after each addition.

Sift the self-raising flour and cake flour together. Mixing with a wooden spoon, add the flours to the butter and sugar mixture in two batches, alternately with the milk.

Spoon the cake batter into the prepared pan and smooth the surface with a spatula.

Bake for 30 minutes, or until cooked when tested with a skewer. Allow the cake to stand in the pan for 5 minutes before turning out on a wire rack.

Combine the caster sugar and ground cinnamon. While the cake is warm, brush the top with melted butter and sprinkle with the sugar and cinnamon mixture. Serve the cake warm or at room temperature.

Alternatively, this cake is delicious iced with lemon icing (see p.254).

FACING PAGE: *Perfect sponge cake*

MINERVA BISCUITS

Minerva Biscuits was a Durban-based company which tried to break into the biscuit market in 1935 by producing a bigger than normal biscuit. Other biscuit manufacturers were forced to follow suit, but Minerva Biscuits soon went insolvent. The large biscuits were of a cheap quality and intended for sale to the rural trade and to the poor. Before cellophane was invented all biscuits were stored in tins. This Minerva tin held 28 pounds of biscuits.

BRANDY SNAPS

125 g butter

½ cup caster sugar

125 g golden syrup

1 tablespoon lemon juice

2 tablespoons brandy

1 cup cake flour, sifted

1 teaspoon ground ginger

1¼ cups thick cream, whipped
   (if filling the brandy snaps)

PREPARATION TIME: 30 minutes

COOKING TIME: 8–10 minutes for
   each batch

MAKES: 36 biscuits

GINGER SNAPS

1 cup self-raising flour

1 teaspoon bicarbonate
   of soda

¼ teaspoon salt

1 teaspoon ground ginger

1 teaspoon mixed spice

¼ cup rice flour

60 g butter

¼ cup caster sugar

125 g golden syrup

PREPARATION TIME: 20 minutes

COOKING TIME: 20–25 minutes

MAKES: 24 biscuits

Brandy & Ginger Snaps

*These thin, crisp biscuits are elegant to serve with
coffee or tea, or to accompany a fruit dessert.*

BRANDY SNAPS

Heat the butter, sugar, syrup, lemon juice and brandy gently together in a saucepan until the butter melts and the sugar has dissolved. Remove the pan from the heat, mix in the flour and ginger and leave to cool.

Preheat the oven to 190°C. Line two baking trays with nonstick baking paper and place 6 teaspoons of the mixture, spaced well apart, on each. Bake for 8–10 minutes, or until lightly browned. To ensure enough time to roll the brandy snaps, put one tray into the oven 5 minutes before the other.

Remove the brandy snaps from the oven and cool on the baking tray for a few seconds, then lift the biscuits off with a palette knife and roll around wooden spoon handles. If they become too hard to roll, pop them back in the oven for a few seconds. When firm, remove from the spoon handles and cool on a wire rack. Repeat with the remaining mixture.

To fill the brandy snaps, spoon the cream into a piping bag fitted with a small star nozzle and pipe into each end of the biscuits. Serve as soon as they are filled.

GINGER SNAPS

Preheat the oven to 190°C. Sift the flour, bicarbonate of soda, salt, ginger and spice into a bowl. Stir in the rice flour, rub in the butter and mix in the sugar. Warm the syrup and stir it in, then knead lightly in the bowl to form a smooth dough. Shape the dough into walnut-sized balls and space well apart on greased baking trays. Bake each batch for 10–12 minutes, or until they are golden. Cool on the baking trays for 5 minutes, then transfer to a wire rack to cool completely.

Rich Nutty Biscuits

Both these biscuits can be stored in airtight containers for unexpected teatime guests.

WALNUT BUTTER BISCUITS

Preheat the oven to 160°C. Sift the flour and salt into a bowl and add the butter. Reserve 1 tablespoon of the sugar and add the rest to the bowl with the coffee.

Rub all the ingredients together until the mixture resembles large breadcrumbs, then mould into small balls about the size of a walnut. Roll each ball in the chopped walnuts.

Space the balls well apart on lightly greased baking trays and flatten them with the bottom of a glass tumbler dipped in the reserved sugar.

Bake in the oven for 20–30 minutes, or until the edges are lightly browned. Leave the biscuits to cool a little before lifting onto a wire rack to cool completely. Store in an airtight container.

The biscuits look most attractive if you arrange them on a plate and sift a little icing sugar over them just before serving.

MACAROONS

Combine the ground almonds, caster sugar and cornflour in a mixing bowl and mix well. Add the egg whites and vanilla essence and beat well to make a fairly stiff mixture.

Line two baking trays with rice paper and put teaspoons of the mixture, in round blobs, on the paper, spacing them well apart. Lightly press a split almond into the centre of each macaroon. Bake in the oven for 15–20 minutes, or until pale golden brown. Remove from the oven and leave to cool on the trays.

When cold, remove the macaroons from the trays and tear away the excess rice paper from each biscuit. (The rice paper is edible.) Store in an airtight container.

WALNUT BUTTER BISCUITS

1½ cups cake flour
¼ teaspoon salt
125 g butter, at room temperature, cut into small pieces
½ cup sugar
2 teaspoons instant coffee powder or granules
¼ cup chopped walnuts

PREPARATION TIME: 30 minutes
COOKING TIME: 20-30 minutes
MAKES: 24 biscuits

MACAROONS

1¼ cups ground almonds
¾ cup caster sugar
1 teaspoon cornflour
2 egg whites, lightly beaten
¼ teaspoon vanilla essence
Rice paper
split almonds

PREPARATION TIME: 15 minutes
COOKING TIME: 15-20 minutes
MAKES: 24 macaroons

If biscuits become soft, freshen them by heating for a few minutes in a 160°C oven, then cooling on a wire rack.

Butter Biscuits

This recipe can also be used to make jam or date squares or for a sweet pie crust.
The dough will keep in a refrigerator for up to two weeks,
wrapped in greaseproof paper.

250 g butter

375 g sugar

360 g cake flour

1 tablespoon baking powder

A pinch of salt

2 extra-large eggs, beaten

1 teaspoon vanilla essence

PREPARATION TIME: 30 minutes

CHILLING TIME: 1 hour

COOKING TIME: 10 minutes

MAKES: 80 biscuits

Preheat the oven to 200°C. Cream the butter and sugar together. Sift the dry ingredients and add them to the creamed mixture alternately with the beaten eggs, then add the vanilla essence. Allow this mixture to rest in the refrigerator for at least 1 hour before rolling it out (about 5 mm thick). Cut out desired shapes, place them on lightly greased biscuit trays and bake for 8–10 minutes.

VARIATION

These biscuits can be 'painted' for festive occasions or birthday parties. To make the 'paint', beat an egg yolk and blend in enough red, green or yellow food colouring to reach the colour intensity desired. Mix yellow and red to get orange. The mixture thickens on standing so beat in drops of water to maintain a good brushing consistency.

With a small paintbrush, brush the coloured egg yolk on to the unbaked biscuits. Brush the biscuits in one colour, or be imaginative and work out designs. After baking, you can accentuate the shapes with outlines of piped icing.

Bake the biscuits for about 8 minutes at 190°C until they are set but not browned. Baking for too long darkens and spoils the brightness of the baked colours.

Chocolate Brownies

These are chewy and fudgy and great with a short espresso or
long black coffee. Try the basic recipe using pecans in place of walnuts.
For a brilliant dessert, serve with whipped cream and strawberries.

125 g butter

125 g dark chocolate

2 eggs

1 cup caster sugar

1 teaspoon vanilla essence

½ cup cake flour

1 cup fresh walnuts or pecans,
   roughly chopped

PREPARATION TIME: 25 minutes

COOKING TIME: 30 minutes

MAKES: 20–24 squares

Preheat the oven to 180°C. Line a 20 cm square cake tin with baking paper. Carefully melt the butter and chocolate in a small saucepan over very low heat. Remove from the heat and let the mixture cool. Whisk the eggs in a bowl with an electric mixer.

Add the sugar, beating continuously, and continue beating until the mixture is thick and foamy and leaves a ribbon-like trail when dribbled off the upheld beaters. Add vanilla essence and the chocolate mixture and blend in thoroughly. Sift the flour over the mixture and scatter in the walnuts, then fold everything together with a large spoon. Pour the batter into the prepared tin and bake for about 30 minutes, or until the top is a rich brown (make sure the cake doesn't burn).

Allow the cake to cool slightly in the tin, then cut into squares. Cool the squares completely on a wire rack. The brownies will keep well in an airtight container for 3–4 days.

VARIATION

Iced Brownies: Ice the brownies with dark or white chocolate icing. Beat 125 g butter with ¾ cup icing sugar until creamy, then beat in 1 tablespoon water alternately with a further ¾ cup icing sugar. Finish by beating in a few drops of vanilla essence and 30 g melted dark or white chocolate.

BAKING POWDER

Baking powder was invented in 1843 by the Birmingham chemist Alfred Bird. The inspiration was his wife who found yeast-based products indigestible. Bird's Fermenting Powder actually resulted in cakes, bread and buns of a much lighter texture. In the United States William Ziegler improved on Bird's formula and called his product Royal Baking Powder, which is now owned by the huge Nabisco corporation. One marketing ploy was to offer free Royal recipe books - every kitchen had at least one.

Koeksisters

Koeksisters are fiddly to make, but the result is well worth the effort.

To make the syrup, put all the ingredients into a saucepan. Heat (stirring) until the sugar has competely dissolved. Cover the mixture and boil for 1 minute.

Remove the saucepan lid and boil the syrup for a further 5 minutes, but do not stir it.

Remove the syrup from the stove and allow it to cool for at least 2 hours in a refrigerator, or preferably overnight.

To make the dough, sieve together the dry ingredients and rub in the grated butter with your fingertips, or cut it in with a pastry cutter.

Beat the egg, add 1 cup of the milk or water and mix lightly with the dry ingredients to form a soft dough. Add more milk or water if the dough is too stiff. Knead well until small bubbles form under the surface of the dough. Cover with a damp cloth and allow to stand for 30 minutes–1 hour. Roll out the dough to a thickness of 1 cm, then form the koeksisters.

Cut strips 1 cm wide and twist 2 strips together, or plait 3 strips together, cutting the twisted or plaited lengths at 8 cm intervals and pinching the ends together.

Heat 7–8 cm deep oil to 180°–190°C – a cube of day-old bread should turn golden-brown in a minute. Fry the koeksisters for 1-2 minutes or until golden-brown, then turn them over with a fork, and fry until golden-brown on the other side.

Remove the koeksisters with a slotted spoon, drain them for a moment on paper towels and then plunge them into the ice cold syrup for 1–2 minutes. Stand the container of syrup in a bowl of ice so that the syrup will stay cold.

Remove the koeksister from the syrup with a slotted spoon, allowing the excess syrup to flow back into the basin, the drain them slightly on a wire rack.

FOR THE SYRUP
1 kg sugar
2 cups water
2 pieces fresh ginger (each 5 cm), peeled and crushed
½ teaspoon cream of tartar
A pinch of salt
Granted rind and juice of ½ lemon

FOR THE DOUGH
500 g flour
½ teaspoon salt
2 tablespoons baking powder
55 g butter, grated
1 egg
1-1½ cups milk or water
Sunflower oil for deep-frying

PREPARATION TIME: 1 hour
CHILLING TIME: 2 hours or overnight for the syrup
STANDING TIME: 30 minutes-1 hour
COOKING TIME: 50 minutes
MAKES: 40 koeksisters

Chelsea & Plain Buns

The same dough can make spicy, fruit-filled Chelsea buns,
or plain buns to be spread with cream and jam.

FOR THE CHELSEA
BUN DOUGH

3 teaspoons fresh yeast,
or 2 teaspoons dried yeast
(p.311), plus 1 teaspoon
caster sugar

1 cup lukewarm milk

4 cups white bread flour

1 teaspoon salt

¼ cup caster sugar

60 g butter

1 egg, beaten

FOR THE CHELSEA
BUN FILLING

1 cup mixed dried fruit

⅓ cup chopped mixed peel

¾ cup brown sugar

2 teaspoons ground cinnamon
or mixed spice

30 g butter, melted

2 tablespoons clear honey,
warmed

Sugar, for sprinkling

PREPARATION TIME: 35 minutes

RISING TIME: 1 hour 20 minutes

COOKING TIME: 30–35 minutes

MAKES: 15 buns

PLAIN BUNS

1 quantity of dough, made
and risen as for Chelsea
buns above

Icing sugar, for sifting

PREPARATION TIME: 30 minutes

RISING TIME: 1 hour 20 minutes

COOKING TIME: 10–15 minutes

MAKES: 15 buns

CHELSEA BUNS

To make the dough, dissolve the fresh yeast, if using, in the milk. If using dried yeast, follow the directions given on p.311, then stir in the rest of the milk.

Sift the flour, salt and sugar into a bowl and rub in the butter. Make a well in the centre, pour in the yeast liquid, add the beaten egg and mix to a soft dough. Knead the dough on a lightly floured surface for 5 minutes. Put into a bowl, cover and leave in a warm place for about an hour, or until doubled in size.

Combine the fruit, peel, sugar and spice. Grease a 30 x 23 cm baking or roasting tin. Turn the dough out on a floured surface and knead for 2–3 minutes, then roll out to about 50 x 25 cm. Brush with the melted butter, sprinkle evenly with the fruit mixture and roll up, like a Swiss roll, from one long side. Cut into 15 equal pieces and space evenly, cut sides up, in the greased tin. Cover loosely with plastic wrap and leave until doubled in size.

While the buns are rising, preheat the oven to 190°C. Bake for 30–35 minutes, or until well risen, golden brown and firm. Remove from the oven, brush immediately with the warmed honey and sprinkle with the sugar. Cool in the tin.

PLAIN BUNS

Divide the dough into 15 equal pieces, shape each piece into a smooth ball and place, spaced apart, on greased baking trays. Leave to rise as for Chelsea buns while preheating the oven to 220°C. Bake in the centre of the oven for 10–15 minutes, or until well risen, golden brown and hollow-sounding when tapped on the bottom. Cool on a wire rack, then sift lightly with the icing sugar. Serve split and filled with cream and jam or golden syrup.

FINER FLOUR

Metal rollers, part of a mechanical milling process developed at the end of the 19th century, introduced a more finely ground flour. Labels differentiated this 'superior' product from its rougher, stone-ground cousin. Golden Cloud, for example, advised that the flour needed 'no pushing' - it was so fine it passed easily through the sieve.

Drop Scones & Vetkoek

Both drop scones and vetkoek are versatile, quickly made standbys. They also make a handy substitute for bread, when none is available.

DROP SCONES

Sift the flour, salt, baking powder and caster sugar in a bowl. Stir in the egg and milk, and mix just enough to blend the ingredients, adding the melted butter just before cooking.

Fry spoonfuls of the mixture in a lightly oiled, flat, heavy-based frying pan until they are golden-brown on both sides.

Keep warm by wrapping them in a clean tea towel until serving. Serve with butter and jam, honey or syrup.

VETKOEK

Sift the flour and baking powder together, and add the sugar and salt. Mix together the beaten eggs and the water or milk, then gradually add this mixture to the dry ingredients. The batter should be fairly stiff.

Heat enough fat or oil for shallow- or deep-frying until it is hot, but not smoking. Dip a tablespoon into the hot oil and then use it to drop spoonfuls of the batter into the frying pan. Fry until the cakes brown on all sides. Allow the vetkoek to drain well on a wire rack over a bowl.

Serve with jam or honey for breakfast or supper. Vetkoek make a good alternative to bread.

DROP SCONES

125 g cake flour
A pinch of salt
2 teaspoons baking powder
1 tablespoon caster sugar
1 extra-large egg
150 ml milk
2 tablespoons melted butter

PREPARATION TIME: 5 minutes
COOKING TIME: 15 minutes
MAKES: about 15 drop scones

VETKOEK

240 g cake flour
2 teaspoons baking powder
1 tablespoon sugar
½ teaspoon salt
2 eggs, beaten
½ cup water or milk
Sunflower oil for frying

PREPARATION TIME: 40 minutes
COOKING TIME: 5-10 minutes
MAKES: about 20 vetkoek

Christmas Cake

Covered with almond paste and iced in a simple style, this rich fruit cake looks most impressive, but it is very easy to make. It should be prepared at least 1 month ahead to allow the flavours to develop, and will keep well in an airtight container for several months.

FOR THE CAKE

225 g butter

1½ cups brown sugar

6 eggs

2 cups cake flour, sifted

3 cups sultanas

2 cups currants

3 cups seedless raisins,
   roughly chopped

2 cups glacé cherries, halved

¾ cup mixed candied peel,
   homemade (p.289)
   or bought, chopped

¾ cup ground almonds

Finely grated rind
   of 1 large orange

Finely grated rind
   of 1 large lemon

5 tablespoons whisky, brandy
   or rum, for sprinkling over
   the cake before icing

PREPARATION TIME: 1 hour

COOKING TIME: 3½–4 hours

SERVES: twelve

FOR THE ALMOND PASTE

4½ cups ground almonds

1½ cups icing sugar, sifted

1½ cups caster sugar

8 egg yolks

1 teaspoon almond essence or
   1 teaspoon vanilla essence

4 tablespoons apricot jam,
   heated and sieved

PREPARATION AND APPLICATION
   TIME: 1 hour

DRYING TIME: 24 hours

FOR THE ROYAL ICING

3 cups icing sugar, sifted

4 egg whites

1½ tablespoons glycerine

2 teaspoons lemon juice

PREPARATION AND ICING TIME:
   1 hour

DRYING TIME: 24 hours

THE CAKE

Line the base and sides of a 23 cm round cake tin with a double thickness of greaseproof paper.

Preheat the oven to 150°C. Beat the butter and sugar together in a large mixing bowl until very light and fluffy. Beat in the eggs, one at a time, beating the mixture well after each addition. As there is a larger proportion than normal of eggs to the other ingredients in this recipe, the mixture will curdle a little, but do not worry.

Fold in the flour and mix in the dried fruit, glacé cherries, chopped peel, ground almonds and the grated orange and lemon rind.

Spoon the mixture into the prepared tin and smooth the top. Bake in the centre of the oven for 3½–4 hours, or until a warmed skewer, inserted into the centre of the cake, comes out clean.

Remove the cake from the oven and leave to cool in the tin for 1 hour, then carefully turn it out on a wire cooling rack and leave to cool completely.

Without removing the baking paper, wrap the cold cake in plastic wrap, then overwrap it in foil. Put the wrapped cake into an airtight container and store in a cool, dry, airy cupboard until you are ready to ice it.

THE ALMOND PASTE

Mix the ground almonds with the sifted icing sugar and the caster sugar, add the egg yolks and the almond or vanilla essence and mix together to form a soft, but not sticky, paste. Smooth the paste by kneading it very briefly on a work surface lightly which has been sifted with icing sugar.

Remove the cake from its wrappings and put it, upside-down, in the centre of a 30 cm round, silver or gold cake board, or on a cake stand, if preferred.

Using a fine, clean skewer, make several holes in the base of the cake, inserting the skewer to a depth of about 4 cm. Carefully spoon the whisky, brandy or rum over the base of the cake and allow it to gradually seep into the holes.

Roll out the almond paste to a neat round about 33 cm in diameter. Turn the cake right side up and brush all over with the warm, sieved apricot jam.

To cover the cake with the almond paste, carefully lift the paste onto the cake and smooth it evenly over the top and down the sides, pressing it gently but firmly into position. Trim away any excess paste from around the bottom edge of the cake. Finally, smooth it with a palette knife.

Leave the cake, uncovered, in a cool, dry place for 24 hours to allow the almond paste to dry thoroughly before icing.

THE ROYAL ICING

Put the sifted icing sugar and the egg whites into a large mixing bowl and beat together until they are smooth, white and fluffy. Beat the glycerine and lemon juice into the egg white mixture.

Spoon 4 tablespoons of the icing mixture onto the cake and spread it evenly over the top only. Using a clean, metal ruler, smooth the icing by pulling the ruler over the top of the cake. Trim the excess icing from around the edge of the cake and leave overnight to allow the icing to dry.

Put the remaining icing into a clean bowl, cover the surface closely with plastic wrap and refrigerate. Next day, beat the icing up again and give the top of the cake another coat, spreading it evenly and then smoothing with a ruler as before.

Spread the remaining icing around the side of the cake, letting a little overflow onto the top (see picture). Pull the icing up into attractive peaks and mark into swirls with a palette knife.

Allow the icing to dry once more overnight, then decorate with a traditional Christmas ornament of your choice.

RUM TRUFFLES

200 g plain dark chocolate, broken into small pieces

3 tablespoons rum

60 g unsalted butter, at room temperature

2 teaspoons pouring cream

1/4 cup ground almonds

3 tablespoons icing sugar, sifted

1/4 cup cocoa powder, sifted, for coating

PREPARATION TIME: 25 minutes

STANDING TIME: 10–20 minutes

COOKING TIME: 5 minutes

MAKES: about 24 truffles

MARZIPAN-FILLED FRUITS

1 1/4 cups ground almonds

1/4 cup caster sugar

1/4 cup icing sugar, plus a little extra for rolling out

A few drops almond essence

1/2 egg white

Natural green food colouring (optional)

125 g fresh dates, each slit along the top and stoned

125 g small, soft, ready-to-eat prunes, each slit and pitted

125 g each small, soft, ready-to-eat dried apricots and figs, each fruit sliced in half horizontally

1/4 cup sugar

PREPARATION TIME: 40 minutes

MAKES: about 48 filled fruits

Christmas Sweets

Delicious homemade truffles and marzipan-stuffed fruits are just the right thing to serve with the after-dinner coffee.

RUM TRUFFLES

Melt the chocolate in the rum in a heatproof bowl placed over a saucepan of simmering water. Do not allow the water to boil or the chocolate to become too hot. Remove the bowl from the heat and beat in the butter, a little at a time. Stir in the cream, ground almonds and icing sugar. Let the mixture cool, then chill for about 10 minutes, or until firm enough to handle.

With dampened fingertips, take teaspoons of the mixture and roll into small balls. Roll in the cocoa powder, spread on a baking tray lined with baking paper, and refrigerate until firm. Put the truffles in individual paper cases and store in an airtight container in the refrigerator – they will keep for up to 10 days. Serve after dinner with coffee.

VARIATIONS

Orange Truffles: Add orange juice instead of rum and 1/2 teaspoon finely grated orange rind.

Coffee Truffles: Use 1–2 tablespoons black coffee instead of the rum.

Hazelnut Truffles: Replace the ground almonds with 1/4 cup ground hazelnuts.

MARZIPAN-FILLED FRUITS

Put the ground almonds and sugars in a bowl. Add a few drops of almond essence and sufficient egg white to make a stiff paste. Blend in a few drops of green colouring, if used.

Sprinkle a board or work surface with a little sifted icing sugar and roll the marzipan into a sausage shape, about 25 cm long. Cut the roll into about 48 equal pieces.

Shape each piece of marzipan into a neat oval and insert one piece into the centre of each fruit, gently moulding the fruit flesh around the marzipan. Roll lightly in sugar and put into individual paper cases.

These marzipan-filled fruits will keep, refrigerated, in an airtight container, for up to four weeks. Serve at room temperature.

Iced Mince Pies

If you prefer to fill your pies with homemade fruit mincemeat, try to make it a month or two ahead to allow time for the flavours to blend and mature.

Sift the flour into a bowl and mix in the ground almonds, orange rind, caster sugar and a pinch of salt. Rub the butter into the flour until the mixture resembles fine breadcrumbs. Add the egg and mix into the flour with a round-bladed knife until the dough starts to come together, then gently gather it into a ball with your hands. Knead the dough swiftly on a lightly floured surface until smooth. Wrap in plastic wrap and chill for at least 30 minutes.

Preheat the oven to 200°C. Roll the dough out as thinly as possible and cut out 20 rounds, 6 cm in diameter, with a fluted biscuit cutter. Gather the trimmings together, roll again and cut out 20 rounds 8 cm in diameter.

Line 20 patty or tartlet tins with the larger rounds and spoon in just enough mincemeat to fill each pie. Put a teaspoon of the brandy butter on top of each portion of mincemeat.

Brush the pastry edges with a little milk and place a smaller round on top of each pie, pressing the edges together to seal.

Brush the tops with the milk and make a hole in the lid of each pie. Bake in the centre of the oven for 25 minutes, or until golden brown. Remove from the oven, leave to cool in the tins for 5 minutes, then lift out onto a wire rack to cool for 10 minutes.

For the icing, whisk the egg white until frothy, then beat in the sifted icing sugar. Spread a little icing over the top of the mince pies and arrange them on a baking tray. Bake at 200°C for 5–10 minutes, or until the icing has browned a little and the pies are heated through. Leave them to cool for about 5 minutes before serving.

1¾ cups cake flour
¾ cup ground almonds
Finely grated rind of 1 orange
2 tablespoons caster sugar
Salt
150 g butter, chilled and cut into small cubes
1 egg, beaten
About 550 g mincemeat, homemade (p.312) or bought
125 g brandy butter (p.206, half quantity)
3 tablespoons milk
1 egg white
1½ cups icing sugar, sifted

PREPARATION TIME: 40 minutes
CHILLING TIME: 30 minutes
COOKING TIME: 35 minutes
MAKES: about 20 pies

CHRISTMAS 'UP NORTH'

South African troops spending Christmas on the North African campaign during World War II received a tin of chocolates from General Smuts. The tin has Smuts's profile embossed on the lid. Many South African homes still have one tucked away somewhere and they often crop up in antique shops. Here the Officer-in-Charge of the Medical Unit passes the gift onto his men. Other gifts were also sent by the Gifts and Comforts Committee back home in South Africa.

JAMS, PICKLES & PRESERVES

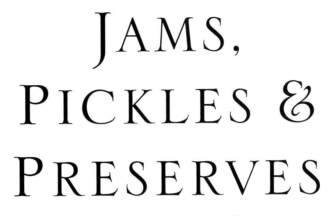

CHERRIES

Three Preserves

Preserves, or stukkonfyt, are a traditional South African delicacy consisting of whole fruit, or large segments of fruit, boiled in syrup until saturated. Instructions for the preparation of the jars can be found on page 309.

ORANGE PRESERVE

1 kg oranges (not too ripe)
Salt
2,5 litres (10 cups) water
1,25 kg sugar
4 teaspoons lemon juice
A 4 cm piece of fresh ginger
Peel of ½ a naartjie

PREPARATION TIME: 1 hour
STANDING TIME: 30 minutes
SOAKING TIME: overnight
COOKING TIME: 1½ hours
MAKES: four jars of 500 ml

GREEN FIG PRESERVE

1 kg green figs
1 tablespoon slaked lime
2,5 litres (10 cups) water
1,25 kg sugar
4 teaspoons lemon juice

PREPARATION TIME: 1 hour
SOAKING TIME: overnight
COOKING TIME: 1¼ hours
MAKES: four jars of 500 ml

SOUR FIG PRESERVE

1 kg dried sour figs
100 g salt
6 litres water
1 kg sugar
1 cinnamon stick

PREPARATION TIME: 2 hours
SOAKING TIME: overnight
COOKING TIME: 2 hours
MAKES: three jars of 500 ml

ORANGE PRESERVE

Grate the rind very thinly from the oranges (this helps the syrup to penetrate the fruit), then rub the oranges with salt to prevent discoloration. Leave to stand for 30 minutes. Place the oranges in a basin and pour boiling water over them. Leave to stand until the water has cooled, then rinse in cold water and leave to soak overnight in fresh, cold water to remove any bitter taste. Drain off the water.

Remove the pips by cutting a deep, narrow cross at the base of each orange. Roll the orange gently between your hands and squeeze out the pips. Place the oranges in boiling water and continue boiling until the skin is soft (about 20 minutes). Test by piercing with a matchstick – the skin must be soft. Then, either leave the oranges whole, or halve or quarter them.

Prepare the syrup by boiling the 2,5 litres water and pouring it over the sugar in a saucepan. Add the lemon juice, ginger and naartjie peel, and bring the syrup to the boil, stirring to dissolve the sugar. Add the fruit and boil until the oranges are translucent and the syrup thick (about 1 hour).

Skim the foam from the preserve. If the syrup is ready before the fruit, add some thin syrup and boil again. If the oranges are ready and the syrup is too thin, remove the fruit and boil only the syrup; add the fruit when the syrup is ready and bring back to the boil.

Pack the oranges into hot, dry, sterilised jars. Fill with syrup, covering the fruit completely, and seal immediately.

VARIATIONS

Naartjie Preserve: To make whole naartjie preserve, use 1 kg tight-skinned naartjies.
Grapefruit Preserve: To make grapefruit preserve, use 1 kg grapefruit with firm peel and follow the above recipe – leaving out the ginger and naartjie peel from the ingredients.

GREEN FIG PRESERVE

Scrape the figs with a knife and make a cross on the rounded bottom end of each fig. Make a lime solution by stirring the slaked lime in the 2,5 litres water and soak the figs in it overnight. This ensures that the preserve will be tender yet crisp. Rinse thoroughly in fresh water and leave to soak for 15 minutes.

Drain and then boil in a fresh batch of water (enough to cover the fruit) for about 15 minutes, or until just tender. Remove the figs (reserving the cooking water) and allow to drain and cool slightly in a colander.

Prepare the syrup by pouring 2,5 litres of the water in which the figs were boiled into a saucepan containing the sugar (make the liquid up to 2,5 litres by adding a little water if necessary). Add the lemon juice and bring the syrup to the boil, stirring to dissolve the sugar.

Squeeze the excess water from each fig. Place them, one at a time, in the boiling syrup, ensuring that the syrup does not stop boiling. Boil, uncovered, until the figs are tender and translucent and the syrup is thick. Spoon the figs and syrup into hot, dry, sterilised jars and seal immediately.

SOUR FIG PRESERVE

Top the sour figs, rinse well and soak overnight in a brine solution made from the salt and 5 litres of the water, to clean the fruit thoroughly. Drain and rinse again.

Make a syrup with the sugar, remaining 1 litre water and cinnamon. Bring to the boil and add the fruit. Boil until the fruit is shiny and the syrup is thick (1½–2 hours).

Bottle immediately in hot, dry, sterilised jars and seal.

FACING PAGE: Green fig preserve (foreground); orange preserve (middle); sour fig preserve (background)

SPICED VINEGAR

¼ cup caster sugar

1 tablespoon celery seeds

1 tablespoon each mustard seeds and green cardamom pods

2 teaspoons each cloves, coriander seeds and allspice berries

10 dried red chillies

1 tablespoon black peppercorns

Small piece fresh ginger

4 cloves garlic, peeled

5 cups cider or malt vinegar

PREPARATION TIME: 10 minutes

INFUSING TIME: 1–2 months (for first method only)

COOKING AND STANDING TIME: 2 hours (for second method only)

FRUIT VINEGAR

2 punnets fresh raspberries or blackberries, or 500 g frozen

2½ cups red wine vinegar

PREPARATION TIME: 10 minutes

INFUSING TIME: 5–7 days

HERB VINEGAR

5 cups white wine vinegar

4 bay leaves

6 cloves garlic, peeled

Sprigs of mixed fresh herbs

PREPARATION TIME: 10 minutes

INFUSING TIME: 2 weeks

HORSERADISH VINEGAR

100 g fresh horseradish, grated

1 golden shallot or small onion, peeled and chopped

1 tablespoon mixed whole peppercorns

¼ teaspoon cayenne pepper

5 cups vinegar

PREPARATION TIME: 10 minutes

INFUSING TIME: 1 week

Spiced Vinegars

Vinegars infused with spices, fruit, herbs or horseradish are easy to prepare at home and make delightful gifts.

SPICED VINEGAR

There are two methods; the first gives the best results as it allows the full flavours of the spices to be absorbed by the vinegar, but the second method is quick.

For the first method, put the sugar, celery seeds, mustard seeds, cardamom pods, cloves, coriander seeds, allspice berries and chillies in a bowl. Lightly crush the black peppercorns, peel and thinly slice the ginger and add them, with the garlic, to the bowl. Mix the spices together well, then put them in one or two clean, dry bottles and fill to the top with the vinegar. Seal and leave to stand for one to two months, shaking occasionally. Strain the vinegar before using.

For the second method, put all the ingredients in a bowl, cover with a plate and stand the bowl over a saucepan of water. Bring the water to the boil, remove the pan from the heat and leave the bowl over the pan for up to two hours, allowing the spices to steep in the warm vinegar. Strain, pour into a clean bottle and use within a short time.

FRUIT VINEGAR

Put all the ingredients in a bowl or plastic container, cover and leave to stand for five to seven days. Strain into clean, dry bottles, add a few whole berries, if desired, and seal well.

HERB OR HORSERADISH VINEGAR

Use the fruit vinegar method above, but allow the ingredients for the herb vinegar to stand for two weeks before straining, and the horseradish vinegar to stand for one week. For a decorative effect, add sprigs of fresh herbs and cloves of garlic to the bottles of herb vinegar before sealing, if desired.

Piccalilli

The name 'piccalilli' probably comes from its chief components – vegetable pickle and red-hot chilli. It is splendid served with cold meats.

Put the water in a large stainless-steel or enamel saucepan or preserving pan, add the salt and bring to the boil. Add the prepared vegetables and the red chillies and cook on low heat for 5 minutes. Pour into a colander, rinse well under cold water, then drain very well on paper towels or a clean tea towel.

Meanwhile, to make the sauce for the pickle, put the sugar, flour, allspice, ground ginger, curry powder, turmeric, mustard powder and cayenne pepper in a bowl. Add 3–4 tablespoons of the vinegar and mix to form a thick spicy paste.

Put the paste, the remaining vinegar and the peppercorns in a stainless-steel or enamel saucepan and bring to the boil, stirring continuously. Reduce the heat and continue to cook, stirring continuously, for 3–5 minutes, or until the sauce thickens. Remove the pan from the heat and leave to cool, stirring occasionally to prevent a skin from forming.

Put the drained vegetables in a bowl, add the sauce and mix together. Cover the bowl and leave to stand for 24 hours.

The following day, stir the piccalilli again to coat the vegetables evenly, then spoon into clean, dry jars and cover with vinegar-proof lids. Label and date the jars and store for two to three months in a cool, dark, airy cupboard to allow the flavours to develop before eating.

FOR THE VEGETABLES
5 cups water
1/3 cup salt
500 g button onions, peeled
675 g trimmed cauliflower, cut into small florets
500 g mini cucumbers, or standard cucumbers quartered lengthways, then cut into 1–2 cm pieces
500 g fine green beans, trimmed and cut in half
3 small fresh red chillies, cut in thin strips

FOR THE SAUCE
1 cup sugar
3/4 cup cake flour
2 teaspoons allspice
2 tablespoons ground ginger
3 tablespoons mild curry powder
2 teaspoons turmeric
2 tablespoons mustard powder
1/2 teaspoon cayenne pepper
5 cups white or cider vinegar
2 tablespoons black peppercorns

PREPARATION TIME: 30 minutes
COOKING TIME: 20 minutes
STANDING TIME: 24 hours
MAKES: about two jars of 500 ml

PRESERVING THE PENNIES
In Grandma's day, bottling the seasonal glut of produce was a sensible way of stretching the pennies and providing variety throughout the rest of the year. Fowler's Vacola Bottling Outfit would have been essential kitchen equipment.

Vegetable Chutneys

These appetising chutneys improve with keeping and are a good way to use unripe or misshapen vegetables from your garden. Always put the date the chutney was made on the label.

GREEN TOMATO CHUTNEY

1,75 kg green tomatoes, washed and chopped

750 g peeled, chopped onions

500 g peeled, cored and chopped cooking apples

600 ml vinegar

8 red chillies

25 g whole dried ginger, or 2 cm fresh ginger

250 g seedless raisins or chopped dates

2 teaspoons salt

500 g sugar

PREPARATION TIME: 30 minutes

COOKING TIME: 2 hours

MATURING TIME: 6 weeks

MAKES: four-five jars of 500 ml

RED TOMATO CHUTNEY

2,5 kg peeled and chopped ripe tomatoes

500 g peeled, chopped onions

2 tablespoons salt

2 teaspoons paprika

¼ teaspoon cayenne pepper

300 ml spiced distilled or malt vinegar

350 g sugar

PREPARATION TIME: 30-40 minutes

COOKING TIME: 1½-2 hours

MATURING TIME: 3-5 weeks

MAKES: four jars of 500 ml

BEETROOT CHUTNEY

6 medium raw beetroot

3 medium onions

5 large cooking apples

1 lemon

2½ cups distilled white vinegar

2 teaspoons ground ginger

½ teaspoon salt

1½ cups seedless raisins

1 cup sugar

PREPARATION TIME: 35 minutes

COOKING TIME: 3½ hours

MAKES: about two jars of 500 ml

GREEN TOMATO CHUTNEY

Put the chopped tomatoes, onions and apples in a large, heavy-based saucepan with half the vinegar. Bring to the boil, then simmer gently for about 30 minutes, or until everything is tender.

Tie the chillies and whole dried ginger in a muslin bag, bruise with a hammer, and add to the pan with the raisins or chopped dates. Simmer, stirring from time to time, until the mixture thickens (about 1 hour).

Add the salt, sugar and the rest of the vinegar, stirring well until the sugar dissolves. Continue cooking, pressing the bag of spices occasionally with a wooden spoon, until the mixture is very thick. Remove the muslin bag before potting and sealing (see. p.309). Leave to mature for 6 weeks in a cool, dark cupboard to allow the flavours to develop.

This chutney is a good way of using up green tomatoes and goes well with cold meats and cheeses. It can also be served with or added to curry dishes.

RED TOMATO CHUTNEY

Put the tomatoes and onions in a large, heavy-based saucepan. Bring to the boil, then simmer for 20–30 minutes until soft. Add the salt, spices and half the vinegar, and cook gently for about 45 minutes.

Add the sugar and the rest of the vinegar, stirring until the sugar dissolves. Continue simmering until thick, stirring occasionally. Pot and seal (see p.309). Leave the chutney to mature for about 3–5 weeks in a cool, dark cupboard to allow the flavours to develop.

BEETROOT CHUTNEY

Cut the leaves off the beetroot, leaving 3 cm of stalk and root attached. Put the beetroot in a saucepan and simmer for 1½–2 hours, or until tender, then drain and allow to cool. Remove the skin, stalks and roots, cut the beetroot in 1–2 cm dice and set aside.

To avoid staining your hands when peeling the cooked beetroot, slip the skins off under running water.

Alternatively, if you have a microwave oven, cook the beetroot in the microwave, following the instructions on p.173.

Once the beetroot is cooked, peel and chop the onions, peel, core and slice the apples, finely grate the rind from the lemon and squeeze out the juice. Put the onions, apples, lemon rind and juice, vinegar, ginger, salt, raisins and sugar in a large, heavy-based saucepan or preserving pan and bring to the boil. Reduce the heat and simmer for 30 minutes, then add the beetroot and simmer for 1 hour more, or until the chutney is thick and all excess liquid has evaporated.

Spoon the chutney into clean, warm, dry jars (see p.309) and cover them immediately with vinegar-proof lids. When the chutney is cold, label the jars and store them in a cool, dark cupboard for two to three months before using. This storage period allows the flavours of the chutney to develop well and mature before you eat it.

FACING PAGE: *Some of the ingredients needed to make beetroot chutney*

Preparing Dried Herbs

*If you grow your own herbs, drying them will provide
a year-round supply of wonderful flavours.*

Herbs are at their most pungent just before flowering and this is the best time to pick them for preserving. Choose a dry day and pick them early in the morning after the dew has dried and before the sun is fully on them. Seeds, such as coriander, dill and fennel, can also be preserved and these should be picked as soon as they have formed on the plants.

Drying Leaves
Lay a piece of muslin on a large wire cooling rack and put it in a warm, dry, airy place, out of direct sunlight. Lay the herbs on the muslin, spacing them apart, cover with a second piece of muslin and leave for one to four days, or until they are dry and brittle. Do not leave longer than necessary as they will lose their flavour. Crumble the leaves, or strip them from the stems and store in clean glass jars in a cool, dark cupboard. Label and date the jars.

Drying Seeds
Lay the stems on trays lined with paper towels and cover with more paper to keep off the dust. Leave the trays in a warm, dry, airy place for 10–14 days, or until the seeds are dry. Shake the seeds from the flower heads onto the paper, then pack in clean, dry jars. Alternatively, tie the stems in bunches and place them, heads down, in paper bags and hang until dry. Shake the seeds out into the bag, then pack in dry jars. Label and date the jars.

Dried herbs should always be stored in the dark — they deteriorate if exposed to light.

Herb Jellies

*Piquant herb jellies are versatile accompaniments to roast meats,
poultry and game, cold cuts, and raised pork or game pies.*

To make the basic apple juice stock, put the prepared apples and water in a stainless-steel or enamel preserving pan. Simmer for 45 minutes, or until soft and pulpy. Add the vinegar and cook for a further 5 minutes.

Meanwhile, prepare a jelly bag and stand (see p.312). Alternatively, you can line two large nylon sieves or colanders with several layers of scalded muslin or scalded tea towels and place them over two large bowls.

Pour the apples and all the liquid into the jelly bag or lined sieves and allow to drain for 2–3 hours, or overnight.

MINT OR SAGE JELLY
Dip the mint or sage leaves in boiling water for 2–3 seconds, then rinse them under cold water. Pat the leaves dry with paper towels and chop them finely – there should be about a tablespoon.

Pour the apple juice stock into a large, heavy-based saucepan, add the sugar and stir over low heat until all the sugar has dissolved. Bring the mixture to a full rolling boil and boil for 5–10 minutes. Remove the pan from

the heat and test if setting point has been reached (see p.309).

When the jelly will set, quickly skim the scum from the surface. Stir in the chopped mint or sage and a few drops of green colouring, if used. Pour into clean, warm jars (see p.309) and cover immediately with waxed paper discs and vinegar-proof screwtops or cellophane covers. When the jelly is cold, label and date the jars and store them in a cool, dark, airy cupboard.

ROSEMARY OR THYME JELLY
Dip the rosemary or thyme sprigs into boiling water for 2–3 seconds, rinse under cold water and pat them dry with paper towels. Set aside.

Make the jelly as for mint or sage jelly, adding the larger herb sprigs while dissolving the sugar. Remove the herbs and bring to a full rolling boil for 5–10 minutes. Remove the pan from the heat and test if setting point has been reached (see p.309). When the jelly will set, put the small herb sprigs into clean, warm jars, then pour in the jelly. Cover, label and date the jars, and store as for mint or sage jelly.

**FOR THE BASIC
APPLE JUICE STOCK**

25 large cooking apples
(about 5 kg), washed and
roughly cut up (including
the peel and cores)

10 cups water

10 cups distilled white vinegar

PREPARATION TIME: 25 minutes

COOKING TIME: 50 minutes

STRAINING TIME: 2–3 hours,
or overnight

MAKES: about 3,5–4 litres,
enough to make 1 batch each
of mint, sage, rosemary and
thyme jelly

**FOR MINT
OR SAGE JELLY**

3 tablespoons fresh mint
or sage leaves

4 cups basic apple juice stock

3 cups sugar

Natural green food colouring
(optional)

COOKING TIME: 20 minutes

MAKES: about four jars of 250 ml

**FOR ROSEMARY
OR THYME JELLY**

8–10 small fresh rosemary
or thyme sprigs

4 cups basic apple juice stock

3 cups sugar

2 large fresh rosemary or
thyme sprigs, washed

COOKING TIME: 20 minutes

MAKES: about four jars of 250 ml

A 500 ml jar requires
about 350 g prepared fruit
and 1 cup of sugar syrup
to cover the fruit.

Sugar Syrup
1 cup sugar
2 cups water

Makes: about 3 cups
Cooking time: 10 minutes

The following fruits are
suitable for bottling:

Soft Fruit
Blackberries
Boysenberries
Loganberries
Raspberries
Strawberries
Tayberries
Cape gooseberries

Stone Fruit
Plums
Cherries
Apricots
Peaches
Nectarines

Other Fruit
Rhubarb
Pineapple
Mango
Kiwi fruit
Apples
Pears
Guavas

Preparation and cooking time: varies according
to the type and amount
of fruit being bottled

Cooling time: several hours
or overnight

Bottled Fruits

*Boiling with sugar is an excellent way of preserving fruit.
It was practised long before home freezing became possible and remains popular
today. The bottled fruits can be used in cooking, on top of breakfast cereal, or, when
lightly chilled and served with cream or ice cream, as a quick and easy dessert.*

Thoroughly wash and dry the preserving jars and lids. Sterilise the rubber bands and screw-on lids belonging to the jars in boiling water.

Preparing the Fruit
Cherries: Stone the cherries, but leave the fruit unpeeled and whole. Wash and drain well.
Berries: Hull, and wash only if necessary.
Cape gooseberries: Remove the capes and stalks, then wash and drain well.
Plums: Remove the stalks, wash the fruit and leave whole.
Apricots, peaches, nectarines: Remove the skins, leave the fruit whole or halve and stone.
Rhubarb: Trim, wash and cut the stalks into 2–3 cm lengths.
Pineapple: Remove the skin and all the brown eyes. Cut into slices and remove the centre core. Leave in slices or cut into pieces.
Mangoes: Remove the peel, cut the flesh from the stone and slice the flesh.
Kiwi fruit: Peel and slice the fruit.
Apples, pears: Core, peel, halve or slice the fruit. Place in cold water with a little lemon juice added to prevent discoloration.
Guavas: Peel and halve the fruit.

Sugar Syrup
Preheat the oven to 150°C, leaving only the centre shelf in place. Stir the sugar and water in a saucepan over low heat until the sugar has dissolved completely. Bring to the boil, boil for 1 minute, then remove the pan from the heat.

Pack the fruit, as tightly as possible without damaging it, into clean, warm jars (see p.309). Stand the jars in a heavy roasting pan, lined with several layers of newspaper. Space the jars at least 5 cm apart and, to ensure even heating, process only one batch of jars at a time.

Bring the sugar syrup to the boil and pour into the filled jars to come within 3 cm of the top. With the rubber rings attached, place the lids on the jars, but do not seal with their rings or clips. If using screw-on lids, screw on very lightly so that they are just in position.

Preserving the Fruit
Put the jars in the oven and cook for the recommended time, according to the type of fruit. The cooking time is dependent on the number of jars being used and on how tightly the fruit is packed.

For four jars of up to 1 litre of soft fruit, allow 35–40 minutes. Allow from 40 minutes to 1 hour for five to ten jars of up to 1,5 litres of soft fruit. Stone and other fruits need 40–50 minutes for up to four jars, and 50 minutes to 1 hour 10 minutes for five or more jars.

Once the minimum time has been reached, check the oven frequently. Wear oven gloves to remove the jars as soon as bubbles are seen rising regularly.

Stand the jars on a wooden board – not on a cold surface, as they will crack. Quickly wipe the tops of the jars with a clean, damp cloth to remove any syrup. Immediately tighten the clips, screw on the sealing rings or tighten the screw-on lids. Leave for 2–3 minutes, then tighten again.

Leave the jars on the board until cold, preferably overnight.

Testing the Seal
When cold, test the jars to make sure they are vacuum sealed. Undo the clip or ring and carefully lift each jar a little by its lid – if the lid holds, a seal has been formed. Metal lids on screwtop jars become concave when a vacuum has been created. Use the contents of any unsealed jars immediately or reprocess them and test for a seal as before.

Wipe the outside of the jars with a clean, damp cloth to remove any stickiness, then label, date and store them in a cool, dark, airy cupboard. Check the jars often. If the fruit rises to the top and is no longer covered by the syrup, turn upside-down for a short time, but make sure that they don't leak.

Properly sealed, the contents of the jars will keep indefinitely. Once opened, they must be stored in the refrigerator.

The best time to make marmalade is during June, July and August, when citrus fruits are at their best and cheapest.

Marmalades

Homemade marmalade makes the perfect finish to a traditional breakfast.

OXFORD MARMALADE

6 small Seville oranges, well washed

3 lemons, well washed

10 cups water

3 cups sugar, warmed

2 cups brown sugar

60 g black treacle

PREPARATION TIME: 1 hour

COOKING TIME: about 2½ hours

STANDING TIME: 1 hour 10 minutes

MAKES: about 2½ jars of 500 ml

FOUR-FRUIT MARMALADE

1 large grapefruit, well washed

3 large Seville oranges, well washed

4 large lemons, well washed

1 lime, well washed

10 cups water

6 cups sugar, warmed

PREPARATION TIME: 1 hour

SOAKING TIME: about 24 hours

COOKING TIME: about 2½ hours

MAKES: a little more than two jars of 500 ml

OXFORD MARMALADE

Cut the oranges and lemons in half, squeeze the juice and strain it into a stainless-steel or enamel preserving pan. Using your fingers, remove all the flesh and pips from the squeezed fruit and tie the pips securely in a muslin square with the halves of lemon peel.

Cut the orange peel pieces in half, then crossways into strips about 5 mm thick. Add the strips and the muslin bag to the pan, pour in the water and bring to the boil. Reduce the heat and simmer for 2 hours, or until the peel is very soft and the liquid has been reduced by half.

Remove the muslin bag from the pan, put it in a bowl and leave until cool enough to handle. Squeeze the bag to remove as much juice as possible, then pour the juice back into the pan. Discard the bag.

Add the sugars and treacle to the pan and stir over medium heat until the sugar has dissolved. Bring to a full rolling boil and boil for 15–20 minutes. Remove from the heat and test if setting point has been reached (see p.309).

When the marmalade will set, skim any scum from the surface. Leave the marmalade to stand for 20 minutes to allow the peel to settle. Stir to disperse the peel evenly, then pour into clean, warm, dry jars (see p.309) and cover the jars with waxed paper discs and cellophane covers (see p.310). When cold, label and store in a cool, dark, airy cupboard.

FOUR-FRUIT MARMALADE

Using a sharp knife, cut a thin slice from each end of each fruit and set aside. Cut the grapefruit into eight wedges, each orange into six and the lemons and lime into four. Cutting across each segment, thinly slice all the fruit, removing and reserving any pips.

Put the end slices and pips into a square of muslin, tie securely to form a bag and place in a large bowl with the sliced fruit. Cover with the water and leave to soak for 24 hours.

Next day, transfer the contents of the bowl to a stainless-steel or enamel preserving pan and bring to the boil. Reduce the heat and simmer for 2 hours, or until the peel is very soft – test by pressing a piece, after cooling, between your thumb and forefinger.

Remove and discard the muslin bag and add the sugar to the pan. Stir over medium heat until the sugar has dissolved, then bring to a full rolling boil and continue boiling for about 20 minutes. Remove the pan from the heat and test if setting point has been reached (see p.309). Proceed as for Oxford marmalade.

Candying

Keep your candied fruit and peel in a wooden or cardboard box lined with nonstick baking paper. Mould may form in an airtight container.

CANDIED FRUIT

Put the fruit and boiling water into a saucepan and cook until just tender. Drain off the liquid, reserving 2 cups. Put the fruit in a heatproof bowl. Pour the liquid into a saucepan, add 1¼ cups of sugar and stir over low heat until dissolved. Bring to the boil and pour over the fruit. Cover and soak for 24 hours.

Days 2–7: Each day, strain the syrup into a heavy-based saucepan, leaving the fruit in the bowl. Add ¼ cup of sugar to the syrup and stir over low heat until dissolved completely. Bring to the boil and pour over the fruit, submerging it fully. Cover and leave for 24 hours.

Day 8: Strain the syrup into a saucepan, add ⅓ cup of the sugar to the syrup and stir over low heat until dissolved. Add the fruit, bring to the boil, then reduce the heat and simmer for 3 minutes. Return the fruit and syrup to the bowl, cover and leave for two days.

Day 10: Repeat Day 8, adding the remaining sugar, and leave for four days. By then, the syrup should be very thick and heavy – if not, repeat the last process.

Day 14: Drain the fruit, place on a wire rack and leave in a dry, warm place for several days, or until no longer sticky.

CANDIED PEEL

Cut the fruit in quarters and remove the flesh. Weigh the peel – there should be about 250 g. Put the peel in a large, stainless-steel or enamel saucepan, add the water and bring to the boil, then reduce the heat and simmer for about an hour, or until the peel is very tender.

Reserve 2 cups of the cooking water and put the drained peel in a bowl. Pour the water into a saucepan and add 2½ cups of the sugar. Stir over low heat until the sugar has dissolved completely, then bring to the boil and boil for 1 minute. Pour over the peel, cover and leave to stand for 24 hours.

Day 2: Strain the syrup into a saucepan and add the remaining sugar. Stir over low heat until dissolved, bring to the boil and boil for 1 minute. Pour back over the peel, cover and leave for 24 hours.

Day 3: Pour the peel and syrup into a heavy-based saucepan, bring to the boil, reduce the heat and simmer for 30 minutes, until the pith is transparent. Return to the bowl, cover and leave for four days.

Day 7: Drain the peel, place on a wire rack and leave in a dry, warm place for several days, or until no longer sticky.

Note that the quantity of sugar given is for candying 500 g of any single fruit. Candy fruits separately.

CANDIED FRUIT

500 g prepared, fresh, ripe but firm fruit, such as pineapple, peeled, sliced and cored; peaches, nectarines or apricots, halved, skinned and stoned; plums, halved and stoned; cherries, stoned, or figs

2½ cups boiling water

About 3½ cups sugar

PREPARATION AND COOKING TIME: 45 minutes, then 30 minutes each day for days 2–8, 10 and 14

SOAKING TIME: 13 days

DRYING TIME: several days

MAKES: about 250 g

CANDIED PEEL

4 large lemons, well washed, or 4 medium oranges, well washed

5 cups cold water

3½ cups sugar

PREPARATION AND COOKING TIME: 45 minutes, then 30 minutes each day for 2 days

SOAKING TIME: 6 days

DRYING TIME: several days

MAKES: about 250 g

FRESH APRICOT JAM

1,5 kg apricots, washed, halved and stoned (half the stones reserved)

Strained juice of 1 large lemon

1,5 kg sugar, warmed in the oven at 110°C for a few minutes

15 g unsalted butter

PREPARATION TIME: 45 minutes
COOKING TIME: 40 minutes
MAKES: 3½ jars of 500 ml

GRAPE JAM

1 kg black or green grapes

75 ml water

750 g sugar, warmed (see above)

4 teaspoons lemon juice

PREPARATION TIME: 20-30 minutes
COOKING TIME: 30-40 minutes
MAKES: three jars of 500 ml

FIG JAM

1,5 kg ripe figs

1 cup water

¼ cup lemon juice

750 g sugar, warmed (see above)

PREPARATION TIME: 10 minutes
COOKING TIME: 40 minutes
MAKES: two jars of 500 ml

PLUM JAM

1,5 kg plums, washed

3¾ cups (1.5kg) sugar, warmed (see above)

15 g unsalted butter

PREPARATION TIME: 15 minutes
COOKING TIME: 1½ hours
MAKES: about 2½ jars of 500 ml

Fruit Jams

Although few of us today may want to devote a day to jam-making as our grandmothers did, it is still a pleasure to take an hour or two to turn a favourite fruit into a delicious jam. For directions on preparing the jars and potting, covering and storing the jam, see p.309. Once you open a pot of homemade jam, store it in the refrigerator and use within a few weeks.

FRESH APRICOT JAM

Using nutcrackers or a hammer, crack open the reserved apricot stones. Remove the kernels and blanch them in boiling water for 1 minute, then drain and slip off the skins.

Put the apricot halves and kernels, the lemon juice and 1 cup of water in a large stainless-steel or enamel preserving pan and bring slowly to the boil, stirring occasionally. Reduce the heat and simmer for 15 minutes, or until the fruit is soft and the water has been reduced in volume.

Remove the pan from the heat, add the warmed sugar and stir until it has dissolved completely. Return the pan to the heat, add the butter and stir until melted.

Bring the jam to a full rolling boil and boil rapidly for 15 minutes, then test for a set (see p.309). If setting point has not been reached, boil for 5 minutes more, then test again. Pour into hot, sterilised jars and seal immediately.

GRAPE JAM

Remove the grapes from their stems, halve them and remove the seeds.

Place the grapes and the water in a heavy-based saucepan and simmer, covered, until the fruit is tender (about 5–10 minutes). Remove from the heat.

Add the sugar and lemon juice, and heat slowly, stirring occasionally, until all the sugar has dissolved. Boil rapidly, uncovered, until ready, testing the jam for setting point. Skim any foam from the surface.

Pour the jam into hot, sterilised bottles and seal immediately.

FIG JAM

Peel the figs, then place the fruit in a large saucepan with the water and simmer, covered, until tender (about 5–10 minutes). Remove from the heat.

Add the lemon juice and sugar and stir until the sugar has dissolved. Boil, uncovered, until ready, testing the jam for setting point.

Skim to remove the foam from the surface. Bottle the jam in hot, sterilised jars and seal immediately.

PLUM JAM

Put the plums in a large stainless-steel or enamel preserving pan with ⅔ cup of water and simmer for 1 hour, or until the fruit is very soft and the liquid has been reduced by about two-thirds. Reduce the heat, add the sugar and stir until it has dissolved completely. Increase the heat, then add the butter and stir until it has melted.

Bring the jam to a full rolling boil and boil rapidly for 15 minutes, then test for a set (see p.309). If setting point has not been reached, boil for 5 minutes more, then test again.

Remove the pan from the heat and, using a slotted spoon, remove and discard the stones. Skim any froth from the surface and pour the jam into hot, sterilised jars and seal immediately.

SLICED PEACH JAM

Halve, stone and peel the peaches. Mix the salt with 2,5 litres of the water and soak the peaches in this brine solution for 10–15 minutes to prevent discoloration. Drain well and rinse quickly in fresh water.

Slice the peaches 3–5 mm thick, then place in a heavy-based saucepan. Add the remaining 100 ml water and poach the fruit, covered, until the slices are just soft (about 5–10 minutes). Remove the saucepan from the heat.

Warm the sugar slightly in the oven so that it will dissolve more quickly, then add it to the peaches with the lemon juice. Stir until all the sugar has dissolved.

Boil, uncovered, over a medium heat until the peach slices are translucent and shiny, and the syrup is thick (this will take about 20–30 minutes). Test the jam for setting point.

Bottle in hot, dry sterilised jars and seal immediately.

GLASS BOTTLES

Jam - and all things sweet - were such an important part of the daily diet that Grandma would have bought or made jam in bulk. The distinctive shape of Consol glass bottles graced the shelves of many pantries. This picture comes from their publication The Consol Guide to Bottling and Preserving.

SLICED PEACH JAM

1 kg yellow cling peaches
5 teaspoons salt
2,6 litres water
1 kg sugar
4 teaspoons lemon juice

PREPARATION TIME: 40-50 minutes
COOKING TIME: 35 minutes
MAKES: two to three jars of 500 ml

VARIATION

If the peaches are ripe or slightly damaged you can make a smooth peach jam instead. Peel the peaches, remove the stones and cut into pieces. Calculate 750 g sugar per 1 kg fruit, and 4 teaspoons lemon juice per 1 kg fruit. Poach the fruit, covered in a little water until soft. Purée the fruit, add the sugar and stir until dissolved, then boil the mixture until it is ready, testing the jam for setting point and bottle in hot, dry sterilised jars.

You may add 2 teaspoons whisky to each jar of jam if you like.

TOMATO RELISH

6 medium tomatoes,
    roughly chopped
4 small cucumbers,
    peeled, seeded and
    cut into 1–2 cm pieces
¼ cup salt
2 large peppers, 1 red
    and 1 green, seeded and
    cut into 1–2 cm pieces
½ cup sugar
4 teaspoons mustard powder
¼ teaspoon freshly
    grated nutmeg
½ teaspoon mustard seeds
1¼ cups distilled white
    vinegar

PREPARATION TIME: 20 minutes
COOKING TIME: 35 minutes
STANDING TIME: 24 hours
MAKES: about three jars of 250 ml

RHUBARB RELISH

1 kg rhubarb, trimmed,
    washed and cut into
    2–3 cm pieces
3 medium onions,
    peeled and chopped
1½ cups sultanas
1½ cups brown sugar
2 teaspoons ground ginger
1 teaspoon mustard seeds
2 teaspoons salt
¼ teaspoon cayenne pepper
2½ cups distilled white
    vinegar

PREPARATION TIME: 20 minutes
COOKING TIME: 1½ hours
MAKES: about three jars of 250 ml

Relishes

*Juicy tomato relish brings out the best in burgers (fried or braaied),
while rhubarb relish goes well with pork.*

TOMATO RELISH

Layer the tomatoes and cucumber in a large bowl, salting each layer. Cover and leave to stand for 24 hours. Pour the salted cucumber and tomatoes into a colander, rinse under cold running water and drain well. Put them into a large stainless-steel or enamel preserving pan and add the peppers, sugar, mustard powder, grated nutmeg, mustard seeds and vinegar. Bring to the boil, then reduce the heat and simmer, stirring frequently, for 30 minutes, or until the tomatoes are softened and the mixture is reduced by a quarter.

Spoon the relish into clean, warm, dry jars (see p.309) and cover them immediately with vinegarproof lids. Label and date when cool.

Store in a cool, dark, airy cupboard and use within two months. Once opened, keep refrigerated and use within a week.

RHUBARB RELISH

Put all the ingredients in a large saucepan or stainless-steel or enamel preserving pan and simmer, stirring frequently, for about 1½ hours, or until the relish is thick and leaves a clear trail when a wooden spoon is pulled across the base of the pan. Do not allow the relish to cook too quickly or it will stick to the pan.

Spoon into clean, warm, dry jars (see p.309) and cover immediately with vinegar-proof lids. Label and date when cool. Store in a cool, dark, airy cupboard and use within two months.

Eggs should be stored in their carton in the refrigerator, but should be taken out and returned to room temperature before cooking.

Pickled Eggs

*Use these tasty eggs for quick snacks and packed lunches
or serve them as a side dish with curries and spicy rice dishes.*

Tie the spices in a small square of muslin and place in a saucepan with the vinegar. Cover the pan, bring to the boil and simmer for 3 minutes. Remove from the heat and leave to stand for 2 hours.

Meanwhile, put the eggs in a saucepan, cover them with cold water and bring to the boil. Reduce the heat slightly to maintain a steady boil. Boil hen eggs for 10 minutes, quail eggs for 3 minutes.

When the cooking time is up, remove the saucepan of eggs from the heat and pour off the water. Stand the saucepan in the sink and allow cold water to run onto the eggs for 2–3 minutes. Leave the eggs in the water until completely cold. Remove the shells.

Put the cold, hard-boiled eggs into clean, dry jars and pour the cold, spiced vinegar over to cover them completely. Add extra plain, cold vinegar, if necessary.

Cover the jars with vinegar-proof lids. Label and date the jars and store in a cool, dry, airy place for six weeks. The pickled eggs should be eaten within three months.

8 cloves
3 blades of mace
10 allspice berries
6 peppercorns
8 cm cinnamon stick
2½ cups distilled white
    vinegar
12 hen eggs or 36 quail eggs

PREPARATION TIME: 15–30 minutes

COOKING TIME:
    20 minutes for hen eggs,
    13 minutes for quail eggs

STANDING TIME: 6 weeks

MAKES: about three 2-cup jars
    or three 500g jars

PICKLED BEETROOT WITH HORSERADISH

2½ cups distilled white
    vinegar
2 teaspoons allspice berries
½ teaspoon salt
2 tablespoons brown sugar
9 medium raw beetroot
175 g fresh or bottled
    horseradish

PREPARATION TIME: 30 minutes
STANDING TIME: 2 hours
COOKING TIME: 1 hour 40 minutes
MAKES: about 5 jars of 250 ml

PICKLED ONIONS

2 kg small pickling onions
3 tablespoons white
    peppercorns
2 tablespoons allspice berries
6 cloves
10 cups white wine vinegar
    or distilled white vinegar
1½ tablespoons salt

PREPARATION TIME: 1 hour
COOKING TIME: 20 minutes
MAKES: about 5½ jars of 250 ml

MIXED PICKLED VEGETABLES

1 cucumber
2 large peppers, 1 red
    and 1 green
1 medium cauliflower
175 g fine green beans
175 g tiny onions
175 g baby carrots
2/3 cup plus 1½ teaspoons salt
7½ cups distilled white
    or cider vinegar
2½ cups sugar
1 teaspoon black peppercorns
1 teaspoon pickling spice

PREPARATION TIME: 50 minutes
STANDING TIME: 48 hours
COOKING TIME: 5 minutes
MAKES: about 5 jars of 250 ml

Vegetable Pickles

*Serve these pungent pickles with rye bread and corned
beef or with a selection of full-flavoured cheeses.*

PICKLED BEETROOT WITH HORSERADISH

Pour the vinegar into a stainless-steel or enamel saucepan and add the allspice berries, salt and brown sugar. Bring to the boil, then remove the pan from the heat, cover and leave to stand for 2 hours.

Meanwhile, wash the beetroot, taking care not to break the skin. Place it, unpeeled, in a saucepan and add enough water to cover. Bring to the boil, reduce the heat, cover and simmer for 1½ hours, or until it is tender. While the beetroot is cooking, scrub, peel and coarsely grate the horseradish.

When the beetroot is cooked, remove the pan from the heat and leave the beetroot in the water to cool completely. Drain, remove the skin and dice the flesh.

Pack the beetroot and horseradish, in alternate layers, in clean, warm, dry jars (see p.309). Bring the spiced vinegar to the boil and pour it into the jars to cover the beetroot and horseradish completely. Cover the jars with vinegar-proof lids and, when cold, label, date and store in a cool, dry, airy cupboard for one month before using. Use the pickled beetroot within three or four months.

PICKLED ONIONS

Put the onions in a large bowl and cover them with cold water. Using a stainless-steel knife, peel the onions under water – to prevent tears! Put the peeled onions in clean, cold water.

Tie up the peppercorns, allspice and cloves in a small square of muslin and put into a large stainless-steel or enamel saucepan with the vinegar and salt. Bring to the boil, reduce the heat and simmer for 3 minutes. Skim any scum from the surface and discard the spices.

Drain the onions and dry well with paper towels. Bring the vinegar to the boil, add the onions and cook for 5 minutes, or until they are translucent.

Strain the hot vinegar off the onions and reserve. Pack the hot onions tightly in clean, warm, dry jars (see p.309). Fill each jar with enough hot vinegar to cover the onions completely, then cover the jars with vinegar-proof lids. When the onions are cold, label and date the jars and store in a cool, dry, airy cupboard for one month before eating. Use within six months.

MIXED PICKLED VEGETABLES

Wash the cucumber, cut it in half lengthways and scoop out the seeds with a teaspoon. Cut the flesh into small dice and put in a very large bowl. Seed and wash the peppers, then cut each in half lengthways. Cut the halves into strips 1–2 cm wide, then cut the strips into squares and put them in the bowl.

Trim the cauliflower and cut into small florets. Wash the florets well, then drain and add to the bowl.

Top and tail the beans, peel and halve the tiny onions, if necessary, and peel the carrots. Add them all to the bowl.

Sprinkle the vegetable mixture with 2/3 cup of salt and mix well together. Cover the bowl and chill in the refrigerator for 48 hours.

Meanwhile, pour the white vinegar into a stainless-steel or enamel saucepan and add the sugar, peppercorns, pickling spice and remaining salt. Heat gently, stirring frequently, until the sugar has dissolved. Strain the vinegar through a muslin-lined sieve into a heatproof jug, cover and leave until cold.

Pour the salted vegetables into a colander and rinse under cold running water. Drain, dry well on paper towels, then pack into clean jars. Pour in enough spiced vinegar to cover the vegetables completely. Cover with vinegar-proof lids, label and date, and store in a cool, dry, airy cupboard for at least two weeks before using. Use within two or three months.

PICKLED RED CABBAGE

Remove any discoloured outer leaves and cut the cabbage in quarters. Remove the hard white core, shred the cabbage finely and put it, in layers, into one or two large bowls, sprinkling each layer with salt. Cover and leave for 24 hours.

Meanwhile, put the malt vinegar in a stainless-steel or enamel saucepan and add the cinnamon sticks, allspice berries, cloves, mace

A FINE PICKLE

The Pan Yan brand of pickle no longer exists. This promotional postcard encourages pickle eaters, who are unable to find the product at their local grocer, to let the company know so that the pickles could be despatched immediately.

PICKLED RED CABBAGE

1,5 kg firm red cabbage

4 tablespoons salt

6 cups malt vinegar

3 cinnamon sticks, each 8 cm long

4 teaspoons allspice berries

4 teaspoons cloves

6 blades of mace

1 teaspoon black peppercorns

PREPARATION TIME: 50 minutes

STANDING TIME: 24 hours

COOKING TIME: 5 minutes

MAKES: about three jars of 750 ml

and peppercorns. Bring to the boil, then remove the pan from the heat, cover and leave until cold. Strain the cold vinegar through a muslin-lined sieve into a mug or bowl and discard the spice. Cover the bowl and reserve until needed.

Next day, transfer the cabbage to a colander and rinse under cold running water. Drain on several layers of paper towels, then pack loosely in clean jars. Pour the cold vinegar into the jars to come at least 2 cm above the cabbage. Cover with vinega-rproof lids, label and date, and store in a cool, dark cupboard. Let it mature for one week before using, but use within two months as pickled cabbage loses its crispness after this time.

PICKLED PEARS OR PEACHES

Thinly peeled rind and juice
   of 1 small lemon

2 teaspoons cloves

2 teaspoons allspice berries

2 cinnamon sticks,
   each 5 cm long

1 small piece dried
   ginger, bruised

4 cups white wine vinegar
   or distilled white vinegar

2/3 cup water

5 cups caster sugar

10 medium ripe but firm
   pears, peeled, halved and
   cored, or 9 large ripe but
   firm peaches, halved,
   skinned and stoned

PREPARATION TIME: 1 hour

COOKING TIME: 45 minutes

STANDING TIME: 3 days

MAKES: about three 2-cup jars
   or three 500 g jars

PICKLED LEMONS

1 cup salt

10 cups water

12 unwaxed, thin-skinned
   lemons, well washed,
   halved, pips removed

7½ cups distilled
   white vinegar

2 tablespoons white
   mustard seeds

1 small piece dried
   ginger, bruised

3 teaspoons cloves

3 blades of mace

2 teaspoons dried red chilli

PREPARATION TIME: 40 minutes

STANDING TIME: 6 days

COOKING TIME: 20 minutes

MAKES: about six 3-cup jars
   or six 500 g jars

Pickled Fruit

Pears, peaches and lemons can all be pickled perfectly in richly spiced vinegar. Serve them with hot curries or cold meats.

PICKLED PEARS OR PEACHES

Tie the lemon rind and spices in a small square of muslin. Pour the vinegar and water into a stainless-steel or enamel preserving pan, add the lemon juice, spice bag and sugar and stir over medium heat until the sugar has dissolved. Add the fruit and simmer for 15 minutes, or until just tender. Using a slotted spoon, transfer the fruit to a colander set over a large bowl, to drain. Discard the spice bag.

Boil the syrup for 15 minutes, or until slightly thickened and reduced by about a third. Pack the fruit in clean, warm jars (see p.309) and cover with the syrup. Cover immediately with vinegar-proof lids and seal tightly. Refrigerate any leftover syrup.

After three days, open the jars, pour the syrup into a saucepan and add any reserved syrup. Bring to the boil, boil for 3 minutes, then pour back over the fruit, cover and seal immediately. When cold, label and date the jars and store in a cool, dark, airy cupboard for at least a month before using.

PICKLED LEMONS

Dissolve the salt in the cold water in a large bowl, add the lemon halves and place a clean plate on top to keep them submerged in the salted water. Cover the bowl and leave to stand for six days, stirring daily.

On the seventh day, rinse and drain the lemons. Put them in a saucepan, add enough boiling water to cover, and boil for 15 minutes. Pour into a colander, rinse under cold water, and drain well.

Meanwhile, pour the vinegar into a saucepan, add the spices, bring to the boil and boil for 3 minutes. Remove the pan from the heat and strain the vinegar through a sieve lined with muslin or a clean tea towel, into a heatproof jug.

Pack the lemons in clean, warm jars (see p.309) and pour the hot vinegar over them. Cover the jars immediately with vinegar proof lids. When the pickle is cold, label and date the jars and store in a cool, dry, airy cupboard for about three months before using.

Berry Jams

Stock the pantry with these juicy jams to spread liberally on warm crusty bread or fresh, hot scones or croissants.

Follow the instructions on pages 309-310.

STRAWBERRY JAM

Layer the strawberries with the sugar in a stainless-steel saucepan and leave overnight, or for several hours.

The next day, heat the fruit and sugar very slowly, stirring to ensure that all the sugar dissolves. Add the lemon juice. Boil rapidly, uncovered, stirring occasionally to prevent burning, for about 35 minutes until the jam is ready. Test the jam for setting point.

Skim the surface of the jam with a slotted spoon to remove the foam and pour into hot, dry, sterilised jars. Seal the jars immediately.

CAPE GOOSEBERRY JAM

Place the cape gooseberries in a large, wide saucepan, add the water and cook over medium heat for about 5–10 minutes until the gooseberries are just tender. Add the warmed sugar and lemon juice and stir until the sugar dissolves. Turn up the heat, bring the mixture to the boil and continue to cook rapidly until setting point is reached, about 20–30 minutes. (Stir constantly as the jam has a tendency to catch and burn.). Ladle the jam into warmed, sterilised jars and seal.

RASPBERRY JAM

Wash the berries if necessary, draining well. Place the fruit in a large, heavy-based saucepan and simmer gently for about 10 minutes or until the raspberries are tender and the juice is running.

Take the saucepan off the heat and stir in the warmed sugar until it is completely dissolved. This will take about 5 minutes.

Put the saucepan back on the heat, bring to the boil and cook rapidly for about 5 minutes, testing for setting point (p.309).

Cool for 3 minutes, stir to distribute the fruit, then bottle.

STRAWBERRY JAM

1 kg cleaned and hulled
   strawberries

750 g sugar, warmed in the
   oven at 110° C for 10
   minutes

2 tablespoons lemon juice

PREPARATION TIME: 10 minutes
STANDING TIME: overnight
COOKING TIME: 35 minutes
MAKES: two jars of 500 ml

CAPE GOOSEBERRY JAM

1 kg cape gooseberries,
   washed

1¼ cups water

900 g sugar, warmed in the
   oven at 110° C for 10
   minutes

Juice of ½ a lemon

PREPARATION TIME: 10 minutes
COOKING TIME: 45 minutes to
   1 hour
MAKES: about four jars of 250 ml

RASPBERRY JAM

2,75 kg raspberries

2,75 kg sugar, warmed in the
   oven at 110° C for 10
   minutes

PREPARATION TIME: 45 minutes
COOKING TIME: 20 minutes
MAKES: about nine jars of 500 ml

Warming the sugar in the oven beforehand helps it to dissolve more quickly and completely.

DATE, APRICOT & WALNUT CHUTNEY

3 cups dried apricots

1½ cups stoned dates

2 cups strong tea, strained

4 medium onions

4 small cooking apples

½ cup seedless raisins

1 cup walnuts

2 small dried red chillies

2 teaspoons coriander seeds

½ cup sultanas

3 cups brown sugar

Finely grated rind of 1 orange

Finely grated rind of 1 lemon

2½ cups white vinegar

PREPARATION TIME:
   Day 1, 20 minutes
   Day 2, 1 hour

STANDING TIME: overnight

COOKING TIME: 1¾–2 hours

MAKES: about four jars of 500 ml

APRICOT BLATJANG

2 kg ripe apricots

1 large onion, peeled and
   chopped

1 clove garlic, crushed

500 g seedless raisins

400 g sugar

¼ teaspoon cayenne pepper

1 teaspoon salt

2 teaspoons ground ginger

1 teaspoon dry mustard

2 cups vinegar

PREPARATION TIME: 15 minutes

COOKING TIME: 1¼ hours

MAKES: six jars of 500 ml

Fruit Chutneys

*Every larder should stock a selection of sweet chutneys like these;
for the ingredients, use fruits that are perfect or only slightly blemished.*

DATE, APRICOT & WALNUT CHUTNEY

This recipe takes two days to make. Chop the apricots and dates and put them in a large bowl. Pour over the hot, freshly made tea and stir well. Cover and leave to stand overnight.

Next day, peel and chop the onions; peel, core and finely chop the apples; chop the raisins and walnuts, and then put them all in a preserving pan. Add the soaked apricots and dates, including any soaking liquid.

Using a mortar and pestle or an electric grinder, finely grind the chillies and coriander seeds and add them to the preserving pan with the sultanas, brown sugar, grated orange and lemon rinds and the vinegar.

Heat the pan slowly, stirring occasionally, until the sugar has dissolved. Bring to the boil, then reduce the heat and simmer for 1½–1¾ hours, or until all the ingredients are soft and the mixture is thick and has reduced in volume by about a quarter. There should be no free liquid when a spoon is drawn across the bottom of the pan. Stir frequently to prevent the chutney from sticking to the pan.

Remove from the heat and spoon the chutney into sterilised, warm, dry jars (see p.309). Cover immediately with vinegar-proof lids. When cold, label and date the jars and store in a cool, dry, airy cupboard for two to three months before using.

APRICOT BLATJANG

Halve and stone the apricots. Mix all the ingredients in a stainless-steel saucepan and bring slowly to the boil. Simmer, uncovered, for 45 minutes–1 hour, stirring occasionally.

When thick and shiny, bottle in clean, hot jars and seal immediately.

VARIATION

Date chutney: Combine 1,5 kg stoned and chopped dates, 1 kg sugar, 2 teaspoons ground ginger, 1,25 litres vinegar, 250 g peeled and minced onions, 1 clove garlic, minced, 1 teaspoon cayenne pepper and ½ teaspoon salt, and boil together in a saucepan until the mixture is thick and shiny – about 30 minutes.

Bottle the chutney in clean, hot jars and seal. The yield will be about 4–5 jars of 500 ml.

LEMON CHUTNEY

This recipe takes two days to make. Wash and thinly slice the lemons and remove any pips. Peel and chop the onions. Layer the lemon slices and chopped onions in a large bowl, sprinkling each layer lightly with the salt. Cover and leave to stand for 24 hours.

Next day, pour the lemons and onions into a colander and rinse well under cold running water. Drain well, then put in a preserving pan with the vinegar, sugar, raisins, cayenne pepper and ground ginger. Wrap the mustard seeds in a small square of muslin and tie securely. Add the muslin bag to the preserving pan, making sure it is thoroughly immersed in the mixture.

Heat the mixture gently, stirring occasionally, until the sugar has dissolved completely. Bring slowly to the boil, then reduce the heat and simmer for 1½ hours, or until the lemons are tender and the chutney has been reduced in volume by a quarter and is thick and shiny.

Remove the pan from the heat, remove and discard the muslin bag and spoon the chutney into sterilised, warm, dry jars (see p.309). Cover immediately with vinegar-proof lids. When the chutney is cold, label and date the jars and store in a cool, dry, airy cupboard for two months. The chutney is just as good if made with sultanas instead of seedless raisins.

INDIAN-STYLE MANGO CHUTNEY

Combine the mangoes, apples, onion, brown sugar, vinegar, garlic, chilli and salt in a large, heavy-based saucepan over medium heat. Bring to the boil, stirring occasionally. Reduce the heat to medium-low and boil gently for 1 hour, or until the excess liquid evaporates and the chutney is thick. Stir in the sultanas and allow to stand for 15 minutes. Ladle the hot chutney into sterilised, warm, dry jars (see p.309). When cold, label and date the jars and store in a cool, dry, airy cupboard.

LEMON CHUTNEY

4 large lemons
3 medium onions
1½ tablespoons salt
2½ cups white vinegar
3 cups brown sugar
1 cup seedless raisins
½ teaspoon cayenne pepper
1 teaspoon ground ginger
3 teaspoons mustard seeds

PREPARATION TIME:
  Day 1, 20 minutes
  Day 2, 40 minutes
STANDING TIME: 24 hours
COOKING TIME: 1¾ hours
MAKES: about two jars of 500 ml

INDIAN-STYLE MANGO CHUTNEY

4 large mangoes, chopped
2 apples, peeled, cored
  and sliced
1 small onion, peeled
  and finely chopped
2 cups brown sugar
2 cups white wine vinegar
2 cloves garlic, crushed
1 small red chilli, chopped
¼ teaspoon salt
½ cup sultanas

PREPARATION TIME: 20 minutes
COOKING TIME: 1¼ hours
STANDING TIME: 15 minutes
MAKES: about 3 jars of 250 ml

MANGO ATJAR

1,5 kg peeled and stoned,
  green and hard mangoes
2 cups white vinegar
250 g sugar
200 g almonds, blanched and
  chopped
2 onions, peeled and sliced
¼ cup fresh ginger, peeled
  and chopped
1 teaspoon cayenne pepper
1 teaspoon mustard seeds
2 cloves garlic, crushed
5 peppercorns
1 teaspoon salt

PREPARATION TIME: 30 minutes
COOKING TIME: 45 minutes
MAKES: three jars of 500 ml

MANGO ATJAR

Atjar differs from chutney because the fruit and spices are boiled until soft but the fruit is kept in chunks, whereas chutney has the consistency of thick jam.

The harder and greener the mangoes, the better. Cut the mangoes into 2 cm chunks. (Be careful when cutting up the mangoes as they are very slippery and you could cut your fingers.)

Combine all the ingredients and boil until the mango chunks are soft, but still whole. Bottle in sterilised, hot jars and seal (see p.309).

This atjar flavour is mild so it can be served with many dishes, although it is particularly good with mutton curry.

8 large or 12 medium
ripe tomatoes

3 lemons

8 cups white sugar

4 tablespoons preserved
ginger, chopped or 2 pieces
dried ginger about 3 cm
each, chopped

PREPARATION TIME: 15 minutes

COOKING TIME: 2 hours

STANDING TIME: 15 minutes

MAKES: about four jars of 500 ml

Tomato Jam

*No commercial product can capture the old-fashioned,
not-too-sweet flavour of homemade tomato jam. The addition of
chopped preserved ginger gives a pleasant touch of sharpness.*

Wash, dry and roughly chop the tomatoes. Finely grate the rind from the lemons and then squeeze out the juice. Place the chopped tomatoes, lemon rind and juice, the sugar and the ginger in a large, heavy-based saucepan. Stir over medium heat for 30 minutes, or until the jam comes to the boil. Reduce the heat to medium-low and simmer, stirring frequently, for 1½ hours, or until the jam reaches setting point (see p.309). When setting point is reached, stir in the ginger and allow the jam to stand, off the heat, for 15 minutes. Remove any scum from the surface and ladle the hot jam into sterilised, warm jars (see p.309). Seal and set aside to cool completely. The jam will keep for up to one year in a cool, dark place.

VARIATION

Tomato & Granadilla Jam: Make as for basic tomato jam, omitting the ginger. Stir the pulp from 6 granadillas into the jam for the last 20 minutes of cooking.

A PRIMER OF BOTTLING TERMS

Consol preserving jars - still with the name moulded on the side - are available in supermarkets. In their promotional material the company explains the parts of a bottling jar - the preserving jar, the rubber ring, the glass disc and the metal cap.

Citrus fruits are often waxed for sale, so always wash the fruit under warm running water before grating the rind.

Fruit Curds

Fruit curds, or butters, consisting of fruit, butter and sugar, do not keep for long, but are quickly prepared at any time of year.

Put the rind and juice of the fruit into a double boiler or heatproof bowl set over a saucepan of gently simmering water. Take care not to let the bottom of the bowl touch the water. Add the butter and sugar and strain in the beaten eggs through a nylon sieve to remove any white threads.

Stirring the mixture continuously, cook over medium heat for 20–25 minutes, or until thick enough to coat the back of the spoon and hold a light ribbon trail. Do not let it boil or it will curdle.

Remove the pan from the heat and immediately pour the fruit curds through a fine nylon sieve into a sterilised, warm, dry jar (see p.309). Cover immediately with a waxed paper disc and leave until completely cold. When cold, cover the jar with cellophane, then label and date the jar and store in the refrigerator for up to six weeks.

LEMON CURD
Finely grated rind
   and strained juice
   of 2 large lemons
90 g unsalted butter,
   cut into small pieces
1¼ cups caster sugar
3 eggs, beaten

LIME CURD
Finely grated rind
   and strained juice
   of 4 large limes
90 g unsalted butter,
   cut into small pieces
3/4 cup caster sugar
3 eggs, beaten

ORANGE CURD
Finely grated rind and
   strained juice of 2 large
   oranges, preferably Seville
90 g unsalted butter,
   cut into small pieces
1/3 cup caster sugar – if using
   Seville oranges, add about
   1/4 cup more
3 eggs, beaten

PREPARATION TIME: 30 minutes

COOKING TIME: 25 minutes

MAKES: about just more than one jar of 250 ml

PEACHES IN RUM

1¾ cups sugar

1¼ cups water

2 cinnamon sticks, each 5 cm
long, broken in half

6 large ripe but firm
peaches, washed

¾ cup white or dark rum

CHERRIES IN KIRSCH

600 g dark red cherries,
washed, stalks left on

1¼ cups sugar

1¼ cups water

½ cup kirsch

PINEAPPLE IN CRÈME DE MENTHE

2 medium pineapples, skin
and 'eyes' removed

¾ cup sugar

¾ cup water

½ cup crème de menthe

ORANGES IN BRANDY

12 small oranges

1¾ cups sugar

1¼ cups water

2 teaspoons allspice berries

¾ cup brandy

PREPARATION TIME: 30 minutes,
plus cooling time (for
each fruit)

COOKING TIME: 15–20 minutes

Fruits Preserved in Alcohol

Fruits preserved in this way make very appealing presents, especially when packed in attractive airtight jars with decorative labels. Use the fruits to decorate a plain cheesecake or baked custards in individual pots, or spoon them over vanilla ice cream.

Preserving in alcohol is one of the oldest, simplest and most delicious ways of preserving fruit. These recipes use a syrup made with equal quantities of sugar syrup and alcohol. A different spirit is used with each kind of fruit, but you can, of course, use any spirit that you prefer.

The amount of syrup required varies according to the type and quantity of fruit, so it is best to prepare the fruits individually. Although the methods of preparing the fruits before cooking vary, the method of preserving is the same for each fruit.

BASIC METHOD

Put half the sugar and all the water specified in the recipe into a wide, shallow saucepan, adding any spices. Stir over low heat until the sugar has dissolved, then add the prepared fruit and poach it gently for the time given in the special instructions below.

Position a colander over a smaller saucepan and carefully spoon the fruit into it. Pour the poaching syrup into the saucepan. Leave the fruit to drain over the saucepan for 10 minutes, then transfer the colander to a plate and leave the fruit to become completely cold, covering the colander with muslin or gauze to protect against dust or insects.

Add all the remaining sugar to the syrup and stir over low heat until dissolved. Then increase the heat, bring the syrup to the boil and boil rapidly until the temperature rises to 110°C on a sugar thermometer.

Remove the saucepan from the heat and pour the syrup into a measuring jug – the amount should be equal to the quantity of alcohol given in the recipe. If you have more syrup than is needed, reserve some for poaching other fruits or for using in a fruit salad; if less, make up the amount with alcohol. Cover the jug and set aside until the syrup is completely cold, then stir in the alcohol you are using.

Pack the cool poached fruits into clean, dry jars, filling them almost to the top. Pour enough syrup into the jars to cover the fruit completely. Cover the jars with airtight, acidproof screw tops. Label and date, and store in a cool, dry, dark, airy cupboard for at least two months before using.

Check the jars often. If the fruit rises to the top and is no longer covered by the syrup, turn upside-down for a short time, but make sure that they don't leak.

Properly sealed, the contents of the jars will keep well for six months. Once opened, they must be stored in the refrigerator.

SPECIAL INSTRUCTIONS

Peaches in Rum: Cut the peaches in half and remove and discard the stones. When the syrup comes to the boil, poach the peaches in two batches for about 4 minutes each batch, turning them once. Drain as described in the basic method above, leave until cold, then remove the skins.

Cherries in Kirsch: Prick each cherry in two or three places with a clean darning needle, then poach for 4 minutes. The stalks can be left on the cherries if they are to be used to decorate cakes; otherwise, remove them before bottling, if preferred.

Pineapple in Crème de Menthe: Slice each pineapple, remove the woody core from the centre of each slice and cut each slice in half. Poach for 4 minutes.

Oranges in Brandy: With a potato peeler, peel the rind very thinly from three of the oranges, taking care not to include the white pith. Cut the rinds in fine strips and blanch in boiling water for 30 seconds, then drain and leave to cool.

Using a very sharp knife, cut away all the peel and white pith from all 12 oranges. Poach the oranges for 5 minutes, turning once. Add the blanched orange shreds to the syrup before pouring it over the fruit.

TECHNIQUES

MAKING BASIC STOCKS

A good stock will add richness and flavour to soups, casseroles, stews and sauces. Stock purchased from supermarkets can be good, but it is not as good as homemade. Stock cubes can be used, but may contain monosodium glutamate and other synthetic flavour enhancers. Bought stock or stock cubes usually contain salt. Stock is usually made by the long, slow cooking in water of meat and bones with aromatic vegetables and spices; for vegetable stock, only vegetables are used. Fish stock is made in a similar way, but has a much shorter cooking time. Rich stocks are made with meat and bones, and when cartilaginous cuts of veal and beef, such as knuckle and shin, are used, the stock will set to a rich jelly. Simple stocks can be made from bones alone. The quantities of the ingredients listed in the following recipes can be reduced.

Stock should have a good flavour and be almost crystal clear. To achieve this, you must keep skimming the scum from the surface.

Stock can be made in a pressure cooker. Place the ingredients in lightly salted water in the pressure cooker (it must not be more than two-thirds full). Bring to the boil, remove the scum from the surface and fix the lid. Lower the heat and bring to a pressure of 80 kPa.

Reduce the heat quickly and cook steadily for 35 minutes. Strain the stock and remove the fat.

BEEF STOCK

60 g beef dripping
　　or 3 tablespoons olive oil
2,5 kg beef bones, including a marrow
　　bone and a veal knuckle, if available,
　　chopped by your butcher
3 medium onions, peeled and quartered
1,5 kg shin of beef or stewing steak, cubed
1 kg mixture of chicken backbones,
　　wing tips, legs and feet, and giblets
　　(excluding livers), washed, or the
　　same weight in chicken pieces
7 litres water
2 medium carrots, peeled and sliced
2 small turnips, peeled and sliced
2 celery sticks, trimmed and chopped
1 medium leek, trimmed, washed
　　and sliced
1 large sprig parsley
1 sprig thyme
1 bay leaf
1 tablespoon black peppercorns

Heat the beef dripping or olive oil in a stockpot or very large saucepan. Add as many bones as will fit in a single layer in the bottom of the stockpot and cook them on low heat in batches until they are a rich brown all over. Take care not to let the fat burn. Remove each batch from the stockpot and set aside.

Add the onions to the stockpot and cook slowly until they are a rich brown. Return the bones to the pot and add the meat, chicken and water. Heat very slowly until the water comes close to the boil, then add a cup of cold water and reduce the heat. Skim any scum from the surface, then add the prepared vegetables, herbs and peppercorns. Partly cover the stockpot with a lid and simmer over low heat for 5–6 hours, skimming the scum frequently from the surface of the stock.

Remove the stockpot carefully from the heat. Line a large colander with a piece of muslin or a clean tea towel. Strain the stock through the prepared colander into a very large bowl or jug. Discard all the bones, meat and vegetables. Cover the stock with a piece of muslin or a net cover and allow to cool. Once cold, refrigerate overnight. Next day, carefully discard the solidified fat from the surface. The stock can be frozen in measured quantities for later use.

PREPARATION TIME: 40 minutes
COOKING TIME: 6–7 hours
CHILLING TIME: overnight
MAKES: about 6 litres

VEGETABLE STOCK

90 g butter
2 medium carrots, peeled and sliced
2 large onions, peeled and sliced
2 small turnips, peeled and sliced
2 large, ripe tomatoes, chopped
3 celery sticks, trimmed and chopped
1 medium leek, trimmed, washed
　　and sliced
1 soft round lettuce, washed
1 sprig each parsley, thyme, basil
　　and marjoram
1 bay leaf
12 black peppercorns
1 blade of mace
3,5 litres water

Melt the butter in a large stainless-steel or enamel saucepan. Add all the vegetables, except the lettuce, and stir until they glisten with butter, then cook over very low heat for about 15 minutes, or until the vegetables are just beginning to soften. Do not allow them to brown.

Add the lettuce, herbs, peppercorns, mace and water to the saucepan and bring slowly to the boil. Reduce the heat, skim any scum from the surface, partly cover the saucepan and cook on low heat for 2–3 hours.

Strain the stock as for beef stock (see facing page). Set aside until cold, then refrigerate overnight. Next day, carefully discard the solidified fat from the surface. The stock can be frozen in measured quantities for later use.

PREPARATION TIME: 30 minutes
COOKING TIME: 4 hours
CHILLING TIME: overnight
MAKES: about 2,5 litres

FISH STOCK

1,5 kg white fish trimmings (bones and heads with gills removed), washed
1 medium onion, peeled and thinly sliced
1 small carrot, peeled and thinly sliced
1 small lemon, thinly sliced
1 sprig each parsley and thyme
1 bay leaf
12 black peppercorns
300 ml dry white wine
1,75 litres water

Put all the fish trimmings into a large stainless-steel or enamel saucepan. Add the sliced vegetables and lemon, the herbs, peppercorns and wine. Pour in the water and bring slowly to the boil. Immediately turn down the heat and skim the scum from the surface of the liquid, then partly cover the pan and simmer for 30 minutes.

Strain as for beef stock (see facing page). Use at once or cover and set aside to cool. When cold, refrigerate the stock and use within one day. Alternatively, the stock can be frozen in measured quantities for later use.

PREPARATION TIME: 20 minutes
COOKING TIME: 40 minutes
COOLING TIME: 2–3 hours
MAKES: about 2 litres

CHICKEN STOCK

1 chicken, about 3 kg, washed and chopped, or the same weight of drumsticks and wing tips
1 kg chicken giblets (excluding livers), washed
6 litres water
3 medium onions, peeled and quartered
4 medium carrots, peeled and sliced
3 celery sticks, trimmed and chopped
1 leek, washed and sliced
1 large sprig each parsley, marjoram, origanum and basil
1 bay leaf
1 small sprig each thyme and rosemary
1 blade of mace
1 tablespoon black peppercorns

Put the chicken, giblets and water in a stockpot or saucepan and bring slowly to the boil. Proceed as for beef stock (see facing page), simmering for 5 hours.

PREPARATION TIME: 30 minutes
COOKING TIME: 6 hours
CHILLING TIME: overnight
MAKES: about 5 litres

GIBLET STOCK

500 g chicken, turkey or duck giblets (excluding livers)
1 litre water
1 small onion, peeled
1 medium carrot, peeled and sliced
1 celery stick, trimmed and sliced
1 sprig each thyme, rosemary and parsley
1 bay leaf
8 black peppercorns

Put the giblets in a large saucepan, add the water and bring slowly to the boil. Reduce the heat and skim the scum from the surface of the water. Add the vegetables, herbs and peppercorns. Partly cover the pan and cook on low heat for 1 hour. Strain through a fine sieve, discarding the contents of the

sieve. Use immediately or allow to cool and refrigerate for use within two days. The stock can be frozen in measured quantities for later use.

PREPARATION TIME: 20 minutes
COOKING TIME: 1¼ hours
MAKES: about 3 cups

HAM-BONE STOCK
Proceed as for giblet stock (see left), but using a roughly chopped ham bone. Add a little more water, if necessary. Ham-bone stock will be slightly salty, so allow for this when using.

VEAL STOCK

2,5 kg veal bones, including a knuckle, chopped by your butcher
1 kg stewing veal, cubed
1 kg mixture of chicken backbones, wing tips, legs and feet, and giblets (excluding livers), washed, or the same weight in chicken pieces
5 litres water
2 large carrots, peeled and sliced
1 medium leek, washed and sliced
2 large onions, peeled and quartered
1 large sprig parsley
1 sprig thyme
1 bay leaf
1 blade of mace
2 teaspoons white peppercorns

Put the bones, meat and chicken pieces in a stockpot or large saucepan. Add the water and bring slowly to the boil. Proceed as for beef stock (see facing page).

PREPARATION TIME: 30 minutes
COOKING TIME: 6 hours
CHILLING TIME: overnight
MAKES: about 4 litres

ASPIC JELLY

2½ cups cold, good stock (fish, meat,
  chicken or vegetable)
3 tablespoons dry white wine
3 tablespoons dry sherry
2 tablespoons red wine vinegar
30 g gelatine
½ teaspoon salt
2 egg whites
Shells from the eggs, washed

Put all the ingredients into a large, clean saucepan and whisk over low heat until the mixture forms a thick froth on the top and starts to come to the boil. Stop whisking immediately and let the mixture rise to the top of the saucepan, taking care not to let it boil over. As soon as it reaches the top, remove the saucepan from the heat and wait for the mixture to subside. Return the pan to the heat and allow the mixture to rise and subside once more in the same way. Repeat the process once more, then set aside for 5 minutes.

Meanwhile, scald a large bowl, a sieve and a large piece of muslin or a clean tea towel with boiling water. Drain both bowl and sieve well and wring out the muslin or tea towel. Line the sieve with the piece of muslin, folded double, or the tea towel, and place it over the bowl. Taking care not to break up the froth, pour the aspic jelly carefully into the sieve and leave undisturbed to strain into the bowl. Do not press or squeeze. Cool the aspic and use immediately. Alternatively, it can be refrigerated for up to 24 hours.

If you do not feel confident about making your own aspic jelly, you can buy packets of aspic jelly powder from grocers or supermarkets. Simply dissolve the powder in boiling water according to the manufacturer's instructions.

PREPARATION TIME: 5 minutes
COOKING TIME: 15 minutes
COOLING TIME: 2–3 hours or overnight
MAKES: 3 cups

SAUCES & DRESSINGS

MAYONNAISE

1 egg yolk
¼ teaspoon salt
½ teaspoon mustard powder
  or 1 teaspoon Dijon mustard
Freshly ground black pepper
2 teaspoons lemon juice
¾ cup olive oil, or vegetable oil,
  or a mixture of both
1–2 tablespoons warm water

The golden rule for making mayonnaise is to add the oil very slowly at first. Because it is made with raw egg yolk, mayonnaise must be kept refrigerated and used on the day it is made.

Put the egg yolk, salt, mustard and some pepper in a small mixing bowl. Stand the bowl on a damp cloth to prevent it from slipping, then whisk the yolk with a stainless-steel wire whisk or a hand-held electric mixer until it becomes lighter in colour. Gradually whisk in the lemon juice, then, whisking continuously, add the oil, a few drops at a time, until the mayonnaise begins to thicken. The oil can now be whisked in a little more quickly and can be poured into the mayonnaise in a fine, steady stream. If, midway through mixing, the mayonnaise becomes very thick, add another teaspoon of lemon juice. When all the oil has been added, stir in enough warm water to bring the mayonnaise to the required consistency.

PREPARATION TIME: 10 minutes
MAKES: 1 cup

TARTARE SAUCE

Roughly chop 2 small gherkins, 2 teaspoons of capers and 6 stuffed green olives and mix them into 1 quantity of mayonnaise (see previous recipe).

VINAIGRETTE DRESSING

½ teaspoon salt
Freshly ground black pepper
½ teaspoon mustard powder
  or 1 teaspoon Dijon mustard
¼ teaspoon caster sugar
1 tablespoon red or white wine vinegar
2–5 tablespoons virgin or extra
  virgin olive oil

Put the salt, pepper, mustard and sugar in a small bowl, add the vinegar and stir until the salt and sugar have dissolved. Gradually whisk in the olive oil, according to taste: for a smooth, mild dressing, add 4–5 tablespoons; for a sharper dressing, add just 2 tablespoons.

Freshly chopped herbs can be stirred into the finished dressing.

PREPARATION TIME: 5 minutes
MAKES: ¼–½ cup

TOMATO SAUCE

30 g butter or 2 tablespoons olive oil
1 large onion, peeled and finely chopped
1 clove garlic, peeled and crushed
1 sprig each fresh rosemary, thyme,
  origanum and parsley, tied together
  with fine string
2 large, fresh tomatoes, roughly chopped
1 tin (410 g) tomatoes
½ teaspoon sugar
Freshly ground black pepper

This sauce can be used immediately, refrigerated for a few days, or frozen.

Melt the butter or heat the oil in a stainless-steel or enamel saucepan. Add the onion and cook on low heat until softened but not browned. Add all the remaining ingredients to the saucepan and bring to the boil. Reduce the heat, partly cover and simmer, stirring frequently, for about an hour, or until the sauce has thickened and been reduced by about a third. Remove the saucepan from the heat and discard the herbs. Strain the sauce through a nylon sieve into a clean saucepan, season to taste with salt and pepper, and reheat.

PREPARATION TIME: 15 minutes
COOKING TIME: 1 hour 10 minutes
MAKES: about 2¼ cups

BÉCHAMEL SAUCE

1 cup milk
1 slice onion
8 black peppercorns
1 small piece celery, about 5 cm
30 g butter
1½ tablespoons plain flour
Salt and freshly ground white pepper
Freshly grated nutmeg

Heat the milk in a small saucepan with the onion, peppercorns and celery until bubbles appear round the edge. Remove from the heat, cover and stand for 10 minutes to allow the flavours to infuse, then strain into a jug. Wash out the saucepan, melt the butter in it, stir in the flour and cook, stirring, over low heat for 2 minutes. Remove from the heat, cool a little and stir in the warm milk, a little at a time. Return the saucepan to medium heat and stir constantly until the sauce boils. Lower the heat and cook, stirring frequently, on very low heat for 5 minutes. Season to taste with salt, pepper and nutmeg.
NOTE: This recipe makes a coating sauce, the right thickness for covering food in the dish in which it is to be served. For a flowing sauce to be served separately, use 1 tablespoon of flour per cup of milk. For a very thick sauce or panada (used to bind croquettes or as a soufflé base), use 3 tablespoons of flour per cup of milk.

PREPARATION TIME: 5 minutes
COOKING TIME: 10 minutes
MAKES: 1 cup

MORNAY SAUCE

Add 30 g Parmesan, Gruyère or tasty Cheddar cheese and ½ teaspoon of dry mustard to 1 quantity béchamel sauce (see previous recipe) and stir over low heat until the cheese has just melted.

HOLLANDAISE SAUCE (MADE WITH A WHISK)

225 g butter
3 egg yolks
1 tablespoon water
1 tablespoon lemon juice
Salt and pepper

Place all but 25 g of the butter in a heavy-based saucepan and melt over gentle heat.

Half-fill a large pot with water. Bring to the boil and remove from the heat. Put the egg yolks with the tablespoon of water in a bowl over the pot of hot water (do not use a metal bowl) and whisk for 1–2 minutes.

Put the pot of water back on low heat, add half the reserved cold butter to the egg/water mixture and whisk again for 1 minute.

Then whisk in the other half of the reserved butter, remove from the heat, but keep the bowl over the hot water. The mixture should look smooth and creamy. Gradually add the melted butter, whisking it in until the sauce is thick. Then beat in the lemon juice and season with salt and pepper to taste.

If the sauce curdles during cooking, remove it from the heat immediately. Put another egg yolk in a bowl and gradually beat the sauce into it. Then resume the cooking. If the sauce is too thick, add 1–2 teaspoons hot water.

PREPARATION TIME: 5 minutes
COOKING TIME: 10 to 15 minutes
MAKES: about 1½ cups

BARBECUE SAUCE

2 cloves garlic, peeled and crushed
1 onion, peeled and grated
1 tin (410 g) peeled tomatoes, chopped
½ cup sunflower oil
½ cup white wine
Juice and grated rind of 1 orange
½ cup lemon juice
2 tablespoons Worcestershire sauce
100 g brown sugar
Salt and freshly fround black pepper
A dash of Tabasco sauce

Combine all the ingredients, except the seasoning and Tabasco, in a saucepan and bring to the boil. Turn down the heat and simmer the mixture for 45 minutes until the tomato is completely cooked and the sauce has thickened. Season to taste with salt and pepper, add 6–9 drops Tabasco to taste. Strain the sauce.

The sauce can be thickened with the addition of 2 tablespoons cornflour mixed to a smooth paste with water. This should be added to the sauce when it is done, and then the sauce should be brought to the boil again.

PREPARATION TIME: 20 minutes
COOKING TIME: 45 minutes
MAKES: 3 cups

SAVOURY BUTTERS

Allow 25 g butter per person. Soften the butter in a bowl before blending in the flavouring ingredients. Herbs and vegetables must be finely chopped, pounded or thoroughly crushed. When all the ingredients are combined, roll the savoury butter flat between two sheets of damp greaseproof paper. Chill thoroughly in the refrigerator before cutting the butter into small fancy shapes.

LEMON BUTTER

Blend the grated rind of half a lemon with 100 g butter. Season to taste with salt and black pepper.

GARLIC BUTTER

Peel and crush 4 cloves of garlic and blend with 100 g butter.

PREPARING SHELLFISH

PRAWNS

Wash the prawns well if you have caught them yourself. To cook raw prawns, drop them into a large pan of briskly boiling seawater, or fresh water with 2 teaspoons of salt added for each 1 kg of prawns. Boil for a few minutes until the prawns rise to the surface, then immediately put them into fresh cold water. If you are not eating the prawns straight away, drain them again and mix them with crushed ice. If you have bought frozen prawns, defrost them thoroughly.

To shell prawns, hold the body of each prawn firmly and twist off the head, then hold it with the legs uppermost and, using your thumbs, break the shell away from the body, peel it off and discard the shell. Slit along the back and pull out the dark vein.

CRAYFISH

Kill the crayfish by putting it head-first into a bucket of cold, fresh water and leaving it for at least 1 hour, or until it stops moving. Place it in a large saucepan of fresh cold water and bring slowly to the boil. Simmer the crayfish for 10 minutes for the first 500 g of weight and an extra 7 minutes for each additional 500 g. Remove the crayfish from the water and chill until serving time.

To serve, carefully twist off the claws and the legs and set them aside.

Lay the crayfish, back uppermost, on a board. With a large, sharp knife, split the tail in half, starting where it meets the head and cutting down along the

back. If necessary, hit the back of the knife with a heavy kitchen weight to help the blade to penetrate the shell.

Split the head down the centre in the same way, starting where it meets the tail. Separate the halves.

Remove and discard the transparent stomach sac, then remove and discard the gills, which lie in the head near the tip. There may be parts of the stomach sac and gills in both halves of the crayfish. With the tip of a knife, remove the beige or grey intestinal vein that runs down the tail (some of this may also be in both halves).

Remove the flesh from the claws and legs. With a fine skewer, prise out the white flesh from the legs, With a kitchen weight or hammer, crack open all the joints, taking care not to hit too hard. Slice the leg meat and arrange it neatly on top of the meat in the crayfish shell. NOTE: If a recipe calls for green (uncooked) lobster, it should be killed, as described above, immediately before cooking, then proceed with the recipe.

OYSTERS

Hold each oyster firmly, flat side up, in a thick cloth to protect your hands and to prevent the oyster from slipping. Insert an oyster knife into the join between the halves of the shell, pushing it in near the middle of the straight edge. Slide the knife from end to end along the inside of the top shell to sever the muscle, then twist the knife to separate the shells. Run the knife gently under the oyster to loosen it from the lower shell, keeping the shell in a horizontal position to retain the juice.

MUSSELS

Fill a large bowl or sink with cold water, add the mussels and sort through them, discarding any that have damaged shells and those that are open and do not close up when their shells are tapped gently. Using a small knife, scrape off any barnacles from the shells, then pull

away the 'beards' (the thread-like strands on the shells by which the mussels attach themselves to rocks). Scrub the shells under cold running water until they are clean, then rinse well in several changes of clean water.

Mussels should be cooked only until

the shells open. Overcooking will make them tough. To open mussels in the oven, arrange them in a single layer in a baking pan and place in a preheated very hot oven (230°C) for 7–8 minutes, or until the shells have opened. Throw away any unopened mussels.

To open mussels by steaming, put them in a large saucepan with 1 cup of water or wine, cover the saucepan and cook on high heat, shaking the pan once or twice, for 5–6 minutes, or until the shells have opened. Throw away any shells that have not opened.

Before harvesting mussels check that there has not been a red tide in the area recently. Mussels which have been affected by a red tide can be fatal to eat.

POULTRY & GAME

The following methods for jointing or boning chicken also apply for duck, turkey, goose and all game birds.

JOINTING A CHICKEN

Place the chicken, breast side up, on a large chopping board and cut off the wing tips at the last joint. Pull one leg away from the body to stretch out the skin and, using a large, sharp knife, cut through the skin and flesh between the body and the thigh until the knife comes into contact with the ball and socket joint.

Holding the leg firmly, twist and bend it outwards until the ball of the thigh bone pops from its socket. Continue cutting through the flesh to free the leg completely from the body. Repeat with the other leg. Separate the drumstick from the thigh by cutting in half where the thigh bone joins the leg bone. Neaten the drumstick by removing any remaining piece of leg.

Next, hold the chicken firmly upright with the neck end on the board and cut halfway down through the ribs to separate the breast and wings from the back part of the carcass. Pull the breast away from the remaining part of the back and cut through the skin at the neck. (The back can be reserved for making stock.)

Lay the breast on the board, skin side up, and cut it in half lengthways. Tap the back of the knife with a heavy kitchen weight to make cutting through the bone easier. Cut each breast in half crossways through the flesh just behind the wing.

TRUSSING A CHICKEN

Shape the bird neatly with your hands, tucking the neck flap under the folded wings at the back. Place a piece of cotton string across the bird with the centre of the string just below the breastbone. Bring the string down over the wings to cross underneath, then bring the ends up to tie the legs and tail (the parson's nose) together. Remove the string before carving the cooked bird.

SKINNING CHICKEN JOINTS

Slip your fingers under the skin and ease the skin free of the flesh. Pull it off, using a small pointed knife as needed to cut through the underlying membrane.

BONING A CHCKEN

Hold the bird breast side down and slit through the skin along the backbone, scraping and easing the flesh away on either side and gradually exposing the rib cage.

When you get to the wings and legs, cut through the tendons close to the carcass at the joints. Leaving the wings and legs attached to the skin (not to the carcass). Work around the bird, taking care not to puncture the skin.

To bone the legs, work from the thicker end of the joint and ease out the bones, scraping off the flesh as you pull carefully.

Spread the boned chicken on the work surface, skin side down and lay stuffing down the middle.

JAMS & PRESERVES

PREPARING JARS FOR JAM

Any clean glass jars can be used for storing homemade jam, provided that they are free from cracks, chips or any other flaws. Wash the jars thoroughly in very hot water and drain well. Dry them in the oven, heated to 140°C, then turn the oven off and leave the jars in the oven until you are ready to pot the jam.

It is important to warm the jars in this way before filling them, as the boiling-hot jam would cause them to crack. Never stand the jars on a cold surface for the same reason.

TESTING JAM FOR A SET

When the sugar has dissolved completely, bring the jam to a full rolling boil (one that cannot be broken down when the jam is stirred with a wooden spoon). Boil the jam for the minimum time given in the recipe, then test for a set as follows.

Turn the heat off under the pan, or carefully remove the pan from the source of heat, and then put about 2 teaspoons of the jam onto a cold saucer. Allow it to cool, then push your fingertip across the centre of the jam. If the surface wrinkles well and the two halves remain separate, the jam has reached setting point. However, if it forms only a thin skin or remains runny, return the pan to the heat and bring the jam back to a full rolling boil. Boil for another 5 minutes and then test again in the same way.

It is important to turn the heat off, or to remove the pan from the heat, each time you test for a set, to prevent the jam from overcooking. When overcooked, jam can lose its bright colour and attractive clarity.

POTTING & COVERING JAM

Once setting point has been reached, the jam must be potted immediately. There are exceptions to this rule, however – strawberry or raspberry jam and all marmalades should be left to stand for 10–15 minutes to allow the fruit to settle, in order to prevent it from rising in the jar.

Carefully lift the preserving pan off the heat and put it on a wooden board. Remove the heated jars from the oven and stand them on another board – if they are put on a cold surface, they could crack. Using a ladle or a small jug, pour the jam into the jars. Fill them almost to the very top in order to leave no space in which bacteria could grow. A jam funnel makes filling easier and helps to prevent jam from dripping down the outside of the jars.

As soon as the jars are filled they must be covered to make them airtight. You can do this using the metal lids with nonreactive, vinegar-proof linings that are used on jars of commercially produced jam, but they must first be washed, rinsed and dried thoroughly.

Alternatively, you can make the jars airtight with traditional waxed paper discs and cellophane covers. Place the waxed discs, wax side down, on the hot jam, then cover the tops of the jars with dampened cellophane covers. Secure the covers with rubber bands.

STORING JAM

Set the jars of jam aside until completely cold, then label the jars, stating clearly the type of jam and the date on which it was made.

Store the jars in a cool, dark, dry, airy cupboard. Homemade jam keeps well for up to a year, but may deteriorate in colour and flavour if kept longer, so don't make more jam than you can use in that time.

OTHER ITEMS

DRIED BREADCRUMBS

These breadcrumbs are made from oven-dried bread – this is an excellent way to make use of stale bread that might otherwise be thrown out. The breadcrumbs can be used for coating boiled ham, croquettes and fish for frying; sprinkling over gratins; or adding a crispy finish to roast chicken.

Stale traditional white bread is best. Cut the bread, with or without the crusts, into thin slices and arrange them in a single layer on one or two large baking trays. Put the bread into a cool oven, preheated to about 140°C, and leave for about 2½ hours, or until it becomes very crisp and pale fawn in colour – it should not be allowed to become any darker.

Remove the bread from the oven and allow to cool, then put it into a strong plastic bag and crush it finely with a rolling pin. Alternatively, grind it finely in a food processor. Sift the crumbs through a wire sieve to remove any coarser pieces.

When stored in an airtight container, such as a jar with a screw-on lid or glass stopper, the crumbs will keep in a cool, dark, airy cupboard for three to four months.

SOFT BREADCRUMBS

Remove the crusts from two-day-old bread, cut the bread into cubes and process in a food processor or rub through a wire sieve. Use immediately, or freeze in an airtight container.

CROÛTONS

Cut day-old white bread into 1-cm-thick slices, remove the crusts and cut the bread into 1-cm-wide strips, then into cubes. Toss the cubes in a mixture of olive oil and melted butter, arrange in a single layer on a baking tray and bake at 150°C for 15 minutes, or until they are crisp and golden. Check frequently, turning the tray, if necessary, to ensure that the crotoûns colour evenly, and removing any that are done before the others. Cool on paper towels. Store in an airtight container for up to 1 week. When required, reheat for 2–3 minutes on a baking tray in a 200°C oven.

BOUQUET GARNI

A bouquet garni can be made from the traditional combination of a sprig each of fresh parsley and thyme with a bay leaf – or else it can consist of a wider selection of herbs along with a few aromatic vegetables, such as the white part of a leek and a celery stick. A strip of orange or lemon rind can be added to provide extra flavour.

The combination of herûbs used will vary according to the recipe, or can be selected to suit your personal preference.

Arrange the herbs in a neat bunch and tie them together tightly with clean, fine string. For easy removal during or after cooking, simply insert a fork through the string and lift the bouquet garni out of the saucepan or casserole.

STRAW POTATOES

Straw potatoes, as their name implies, resemble stalks of straw. The easiest way to make them is with a mandolin cutter, adjusting the blade to cut peeled potatoes into the thinnest, narrowest strips possible. Alternatively, slice peeled potatoes into the thinnest slices you can cut with a sharp knife, stack the slices and cut into strips about 3 mm wide.

Another method is to slice them on the wide cutting blade of a grater or in a food processor. Taking a few slices at a time, pile them on top of each other and cut them into very fine strips about 3 mm wide. Rinse the potato straws in cold water, drain very well and dry in a clean tea towel.

Deep-fry the potato straws in batches, in oil heated to 190°C, until golden brown and crisp, stirring with a slotted spoon to prevent them from sticking together. Using the slotted spoon, remove the straws from the hot oil and drain well on paper towels. Season lightly with salt and serve immediately.

PUFF PASTRY

225 g flour

½ teaspoon salt

225 g unsalted butter or firm margarine

60-100 ml cold water to mix

1 teaspoon lemon juice

Sift the flour and salt into a mixing bowl and rub in 30 g of the butter. Place the remaining butter between two sheets of nonstick baking paper or greaseproof paper and beat into a 15 cm square with a rolling pin.

Make a well in the centre of the flour, add the iced water and lemon juice and mix with a round-bladed knife to form a soft dough.

Turn the dough out on a lightly floured surface – a marble slab, if possible. Without kneading it, roll out the dough to a 25 cm square – use short, sharp strokes with the rolling pin to avoid squashing out the air trapped between the layers of dough.

Position the butter to look like a diamond in the centre of the square of dough. Bring the corners of the dough to the centre of the butter to enclose it, then turn the dough to square it up. Roll out to an oblong about 45 cm long. Fold the bottom third of the dough over the centre third, then bring the top third down over the bottom third, trapping as much air as possible between each layer. Seal the open edges of the dough with the rolling pin, then wrap in plastic wrap and chill for 30 minutes. Do not chill for longer, as the butter will become too hard and will break through the dough when it is rolled out.

Unwrap the chilled dough and place it on the floured surface with the short, sealed ends to the top and bottom. Roll out and fold as before, then wrap and chill for another 30 minutes. Repeat this process six times more. (Keep note of how many times you have folded the dough by making a small mark on a scrap of dough with your fingertip each time.)

When folded for the last time, wrap the dough in nonstick baking paper, put it into a plastic bag and refrigerate until required. It will keep well in the refrigerator for two or three days, or can be frozen for up to three months.

The pastry is usually baked at 220°C and is particularly suitable for pies which are to be served cold.

PREPARATION TIME: 4 hours (mostly unattended)

MAKES: enough to line two 23 cm flan rings or cover a litre pie dish

SHORTCRUST PASTRY

225 g flour

½ teaspoon salt

100 g chilled butter, diced

¼ cup cold water

Put the flour and salt in a large bowl, add the butter and rub into the flour between your thumbs and fingertips until the mixture resembles coarse breadcrumbs. Pour the water over the flour and butter mixture and stir in quickly with a round-ended knife. When the dough starts to cling together, discard the knife and use the fingers of both hands to press the mixture gently together into a ball. Knead the dough lightly by pressing and turning it in the bowl until fairly smooth, then place it on a sheet of plastic wrap, press it into a disc and wrap tightly to exclude the air. Rest the dough for 20 minutes in the refrigerator before rolling out. After rolling out and lining the pie plate or tin you are using, chill for 1 hour before baking.

The pastry is usually baked at 190–220°C depending on richness and size.

PREPARATION TIME: 10 minutes

RESTING TIME: 20 minutes

CHILLING TIME: 1 hour

MAKES: sufficient pastry to line a 20–23 cm pie plate or flan ring; to line and cover an 18 cm pie plate, or cover a litre pie dish

CLARIFIED BUTTER

This butter does not burn and blacken as readily as normal butter does and is easy to make at home. Warm the butter in a saucepan on low heat until melted, skimming off any surface scum that may form. Remove the butter from the heat and pour it through a muslin-lined sieve into a bowl. Allow the butter to cool, but not to set. Pour off the clear liquid into a clean bowl and discard the white solids left behind. The clarified butter can be used immediately or can be kept in the refrigerator for two or three days.

RECONSTITUTING DRIED YEAST

Pour ⅔ cup of lukewarm water (or milk, if specified in the recipe) into a small bowl. Add 1 teaspoon caster sugar and stir until the sugar has dissolved. Sprinkle the dried yeast into the sugared water and whisk well with a fork. Cover the bowl with plastic wrap and set aside in a warm place for 10–15 minutes, or until the yeast has become very frothy. Whisk the mixture again and use it as instructed in the recipe.

FRESH FRUIT PURÉE

Soft fruits do not need to be cooked before puréeing. They can be puréed as they are or macerated first with a little sugar, if preferred.

Firmer fruits, such as apples, apricots, gooseberries, peaches and plums, must be softened first by being cooked in a little water (just enough to prevent them from sticking) and a little sugar.

Fruits such as rhubarb and apples produce a lot of juice as they are cooked. This is best drained off before puréeing as it may make the purée too thin. Reserve the juice and use it, if necessary, to dilute the finished purée to the desired consistency.

Soft fruits and cooked fruits can be made into a purée by pressing them through a fine nylon sieve with the back of a wooden spoon, or by processing in a food processor.

After puréeing in a food processor, fruits with seeds, such as raspberries and blackberries, should be passed through a nylon sieve to remove the seeds. Always use a nylon sieve when puréeing fruit – metal, other than stainless steel, will react with the acid in the fruit, tainting and spoiling its flavour.

As a guide, 500 g of soft fruit will yield 450 ml of purée, and 500 g of cooked fruit will yield 300 ml of purée.

MELBA TOAST

Genuine Melba toast is traditionally served with soups, terrines and pâtés. It is very simple to prepare and can be stored for up to a month in an airtight container in a cool, dry, airy cupboard.

A traditional white, sliced sandwich loaf or tin loaf, one or two days old, is best for making Melba toast. Toast the bread lightly on both sides and, while it is still warm, cut off the crusts and, with a serrated knife, cut each slice through the middle to produce two very thin slices. Cut each very thin slice into four triangles and arrange these, soft sides up, on a baking tray. Bake in a preheated 120°C oven for 20 minutes, or until crisp. As they dry out, the toasted triangles will curl attractively. Remove the Melba toast from the oven and cool. Store in an airtight tin. Warm through just before serving, or serve cold.

FRUIT MINCEMEAT

Finely grated rind and strained juice of
  3 large lemons, empty shells reserved
4 large (800 g) cooking apples
3 cups (500 g) seedless raisins
3 cups (500 g) currants
500 g packaged suet
5 cups (1 kg) firmly packed brown sugar
2 tablespoons candied citron peel,
  finely diced
2 tablespoons candied lemon peel,
  homemade (p.289) or bought,
  finely diced
2 tablespoons candied orange peel,
  homemade (p.289) or bought,
  finely diced
2 tablespoons orange marmalade,
  homemade (p.288) or bought
2 cups brandy

Prepare the mincemeat at least two weeks before you wish to use it to allow time for it to mature. Preheat the oven to 180°C. Put the reserved lemon shells into a medium saucepan, cover with cold water and bring to the boil. Reduce the heat, partly cover and simmer for 45 minutes, or until very soft.

Meanwhile, core the apples and make a shallow cut, just through the skin, around the middle of each. Place on a baking tray in the oven for about 45 minutes, or until soft. Remove from the oven and cool.

Drain the lemon shells well and chop finely. Halve the apples and scoop out the pulp. Put the chopped lemon, apple pulp, lemon rind and juice into a very large ovenproof casserole and beat well. Stir in all the remaining ingredients and half the brandy. Leave in a cool place, covered, for 12 hours, or overnight, to allow the flavours to develop.

Preheat the oven to 110°C. Cook the mincemeat, covered, for 3 hours, then remove the casserole from the oven and take off the lid. Allow the mincemeat, which will be swimming in fat, to cool, stirring occasionally. The suet will coat the fruit and be evenly distributed throughout the mincemeat.

When cold, stir in the remaining brandy, spoon into clean jars and pack down to exclude any air. Seal with a little melted suet or in the usual way (see p.310). Store in a cool, dark place and use within a year.

Mincemeat is usually used for mince pies or mince tarts, but it can also be used in fruit slices or warmed gently and served as a topping for ice cream.

PREPARATION TIME: 1 hour
STANDING TIME: 12 hours
  or overnight
COOKING TIME: 3 hours
MAKES: 3,5–4 kg

STRAINING JELLY

Jelly bags can be purchased at some speciality kitchen shops, or can be made at home. Take a large square of coarse flannel and sew strong tape across each corner to make loops just large enough to slip over the legs of an upturned stool or chair. Invert the stool in a corner where it will be out of the way over-night, or fix the inverted chair firmly to the corner of a table, and slip the tapes firmly over the legs so that the flannel hangs down like a bag. Put a large bowl under the bag and pour boiling water through to scald and open the cloth. Empty and dry the bowl and replace under the bag. When the fruit has been cooked until pulpy, pour it with its cooking liquid into the bag and leave to drain, undisturbed, overnight. Do not press the fruit or squeeze the bag as this will make the jelly cloudy.

GHEE

This form of clarified butter is sometimes used in Indian cooking. Since it can be heated to a high temperature, ghee makes frying less troublesome. It can also be stored at room temperature for up to six months.

Use 500 g butter which will yield about 350–400 g ghee. Put the butter in a deep saucepan, place it on the stove and bring to a gentle boil. Keep at a medium to low temperature and boil the liquid butter slowly for 15–20 minutes. The butter will bubble audibly as the water evaporates. When all the water has evaporated this sound will stop. At this stage a layer of scum will rise to the surface, the salt will settle at the bottom and the clarified butter will settle in the middle.

Place a steel, enamel or glass container on a flat surface nearby. Remove the ghee from the heat and blow the scum to one side of the saucepan.

Pour the clarified butter into the container, leaving the salt at the bottom of the saucepan. The ghee should be crystal clear. Cool and store.

ADAPTING GRANDMA'S RECIPES FOR A LOW-FAT DIET

Our grandmothers' recipes quite often included rather generous amounts of fat, but we can still maintain our healthy modern way of eating while enjoying traditional dishes. One approach is to use the richer recipes as treats rather than as everyday fare; another is to reduce the amount of fat in the traditional recipes, whenever it is possible.

All fats have the same energy (kilojoule) value, so there is no point in substituting, for example, margarine or oil for butter to make the recipe more slimming. You may, of course, prefer one type of fat over another for reasons such as cholesterol content: soft table margarines are usually low in cholesterol, while oils vary from low-cholesterol polyunsaturated vegetable oils through monounsaturated olive oil to high-cholesterol palm and coconut oil. If you are following a medically advised health regimen, consult your doctor about which fats are right for you, and read the labels carefully before you buy.

MEAT, POULTRY, VEGETABLE & SOUP RECIPES

You can reduce the quantity of fat — butter, margarine, oil — in most meat and vegetable recipes by half, without affecting the way the recipe works – the difference will be that some richness of flavour will be lost.

You can also reduce the quantity of fat in most soup recipes by half. In cream soups, substitute low-fat milk for whole milk and cream. Some richness of flavour will be lost, but the recipes will work. A sprinkle of chopped parsley, chives or other herbs, or a spoonful of low-fat evaporated milk swirled through the soup at the last moment, will give added interest and flavour.

Cut off all visible fat from meat before you start the recipe. If the meat is cooked in a sauce or gravy, you can prepare the dish a day ahead, chill overnight, then remove the visible fat from the surface before reheating. Before beginning to grill or roast meat, lightly brush both the meat and the grill or roasting pan with oil, or spray with cooking spray, and brush or spray the meat again as needed during cooking, rather than basting with fat.

Remove the skin from chicken before serving (don't remove the skin before cooking – unless the recipe instructs you to do this – as the skin protects the flesh from drying out). Have some well-reduced chicken stock on hand and brush a little onto the skinned chicken just before serving, to give an appetising gloss and add colour.

DESSERTS, CAKES & BISCUITS

Dessert recipes that involve flour mixtures (pastry, dumplings, steamed and boiled puddings) should not be changed. Simply stick to desserts that do not include fat, such as fruits, water ices and jellies. For the accompaniment, use low-fat ice cream or chilled, whipped, low-fat evaporated milk, or make custard using low-fat milk only instead of the mixture of whole milk and cream given in the recipes on p.214.

Cake and biscuit recipes should not be changed, as the proportion of fat to the other ingredients is crucial to the texture and the way the mixture sets when cooked. Scones, breads, pancakes and muffins have very little fat, but be careful of what you spread on them – try spreadable, light cream cheese or the soft, low-fat cheese called quark, instead of butter. Use a nonstick frying pan for pancakes and muffins and, rather than heating fat in the pan to grease it, brush very lightly with oil or melted butter, or spray with cooking spray.

INDEX

The index for the historical
anecdotes is on the
following page.

ACKNOWLEDGMENTS

The publishers wish to thank the following for their assistance:
Marina Searle-Tripp, Blackie Swart (Joubert House Museum, Montagu), John Kramer, Henrique Wilding, Suzette Wilding, Engela Schultz, Patty Pan (Somerset West).

The following photographs of the recipes in this book are Reader's Digest copyright.

MARTIN BRIGDALE 22, 41, 47, 53, 60, 62, 63, 108, 122, 131, 148, 161, 177, 178, 189, 195, 198, 207, 227, 243, 252, 255, 263, 265, 270, 273, 274, 275, 283, 288, 295, 297.
LAURIE EVANS 17, 32, 37, 46, 56, 61, 66, 87, 90, 113, 116, 118, 121, 126, 159, 166, 175, 185, 208, 213, 216, 217, 225, 241, 250, 253, 271, 285, 287, 296.
HOWARD JONES 209.
GREGORY MCBEAN 14, 19, 20, 21, 23, 24, 25, 27, 28, 33, 39, 45, 73, 75, 76, 78, 79, 80, 89, 93, 111, 119, 129, 145, 150, 155, 156, 162, 163, 167, 199, 201, 203, 220, 221, 239, 259, 300.
VERNON MORGAN, *home economist* Kathy Man 126, 236.
PIA TRYDE 35, 36, 40, 52, 139, 140, 173, 183, 191, 194, 200, 219, 224, 229, 242, 251, 256, 262, 266, 280, 284, 291, 293, 303.
PETER WILLIAMS 12, 16, 43, 55, 57, 59, 67, 70, 71, 77, 86, 99, 115, 125, 132, 133, 135, 136, 137, 171, 179, 187, 188, 211, 215, 235, 238, 247, 257, 267, 281, 289, 292, 301.

Copyright in the photographs as described and appearing on the pages referred to below, subsists in Heritage Publishing (Pty) Ltd:

HENRIQUE WILDING 15, 29, 30, 31, 44, 65, 72, 81, 85, 91, 97, 100, 101, 107, 109, 112, 123, 141, 144, 145, 149, 151, 169, 174, 180, 181, 186, 196, 212, 223, 226, 230, 232, 233, 237, 260, 269, 279, 291, 299
ALAIN PROUST, ROGER BELL, JAC DE VILLIERS, FRANZ LAUINGER, ANTHONY JOHNSON 15, 38, 48, 49, 67, 84, 94, 95, 96, 117, 130, 147, 153, 154, 157, 160, 167, 172, 184, 168, 192, 193, 202, 231, 234, 248, 249, 261

The editors have made every attempt to trace the holders of copyright. The persons or organisations listed below are not necessarily the copyright holders — they are listed because that particular item is in their collection.

PICTURE CREDITS

22 *left* John Kramer/Joubert House Museum, Montagu. **25** *right* Patricia Kramer. **28** *left* South African Library. **30** *left* South African Library. **32** *left* Heritage Publishing. **38** *left* John Kramer/Joubert House Museum, Montagu. **41** *right* Patricia Kramer. **61** *right* State Library of New South Wales. **71** *right* John Kramer/Joubert House Museum, Montagu. **94** *left* Heritage Publishing. **95** *right* South African Library. **96** *left* South African Library. **97** *right* John Kramer/Joubert House Museum, Montagu. **109** *right* John Kramer/Joubert House Museum, Montagu. **113** *right* John Kramer. **123** *right* National Museum, Bloemfontein. **130** *left* South African Library. **141** *right* State Library of Victoria. **145** *right* John Kramer. **156** *left* Patricia Kramer. **148** *left* J.B. Eaton Collection/by permission of the National Library of Australia. **160** *left* Heritage Publishing. **162** *left* John Kramer. **167** *right* Patricia Kramer. **168** *left* Killie Campbell Africana Library. **179** *right* Patricia Kramer. **181** *right* Patricia Kramer. **188** *left* Patricia Kramer. **192** *left* National Museum of Victoria. **195** *right* John Kramer. **198** *left* John Kramer. **203** *right* Patricia Kramer. **207** *right* John Kramer. **209** *right* Alexander Turnbull Library/National Library of New Zealand, Te Puna Mātauranga o Aotearoa. **213** *right* Alexander Turnbull Library/National Library of New Zealand, Te Puna Mātauranga o Aotearoa. **216** *left* Patricia Kramer. **220** *left* Patricia Kramer. **224** *left* South African Library. **225** *right* Heritage Publishing. **227** *right* New Zealand Ministry of Health/Alexander Turnbull Library/ National Library of New Zealand, Te Puna Mātauranga o Aotearoa. **230** *left* Heritage Publishing. **233** *right* Heritage Publishing. **237** *right* Heritage Publishing. **250** *left* Heritage Publishing. .**262** *left* Powerhouse Museum, Sydney. **266** *left* John Kramer/Joubert House Museum, Montagu. **269** *right* Patricia Kramer. **271** *right* John Kramer. **281** *right* State Library of New South Wales. **291** *right* Patricia Kramer. **295** *right* John Kramer. **300** *left* Patricia Kramer.

Endpapers: Patricia Kramer
Page 2: Pia Tryde
Cover photograph: Henrique Wilding; Stylist: Patricia Fraser.

ROYAL HOSTESS RECIPE-FOR-SUCCESS

Cookery Expert's choice for the month ... tested in Royal's own kitchen

CHRISTMAS CAROL CAKE

Royal Hostess says: Something
to sing about! You don't
need to be an icing expert to
decorate this prettiest-ever Christmas
cake by Royal

Make Food
go Further!

NOTES.

Minestrone (F)

2 tablespoons butter; 4 slices
smoked bacon, chopped; 375 g
potatoes, peeled and diced;
carrots, diced; 2 leeks, diced;
handful of chopped spinach; 1
litre chicken stock or 2 chicken
stock cubes dissolved in 1 litre
of boiling water; 1 bayleaf; 1
clove garlic, crushed; 125 g
small haricot beans, soaked overnight; one 120-g tin tomato
purée; one 410-g tin tomatoes,
sieved; salt and freshly ground
black pepper to taste; 125 g
broken pasta or rice; ½ medium
cabbage, finely shredded; 125 g
parmesan cheese or mature
cheddar, grated. Serves 6 - 8.
☐ Melt butter in a large saucepan. Fry bacon for a few minutes. Add potatoes, carrots,
leeks and spinach. Cover tightly
and cook over a gentle heat
for 15 - 20 minutes until soft but
not coloured. Add stock, bayleaf, garlic, beans, tomato purée,
sieved tomatoes, salt and pepper. Bring to the boil and simmer for an hour. Add pasta or
rice and cabbage. Simmer for a
further half hour. Remove from
heat. Remove bayleaf.* Add half
the grated parmesan to soup. Stir
well for a few minutes then serve
with remaining cheese in a
separate bowl. TOTAL KILO-
JOULE COUNT: 9 210 kJ (2 200
Cal). Per portion: 1 315 kJ (315

DOUBLING HALF-POUND BUTTER

USE LEFT-OVER VEGETABLES

AND NOW THIS FAVOURITE

SPANISH CREAM

GRANADILLA CHIFFON PIE.

2 cups crushed biscuits, (1pt Lennis)
3 oz shortening melted,
1 packet lemon jelly crystals,
1 cup boiling water,
1 cup Carnation Evaporated Milk, Chilled icy cold, — put in fridge over night.
one 4 oz can Nor-Jax granadillas,
whipped carnation.

Combine the crushed biscuits and melted shortening. Press over the base and
sides of an 8" by 9" pie plate. Chill. Dissolve the jelly crystals in the
boiling water. Cool. Whip the chilled Carnation Milk until thick. Blend
in Mixture. Fold in granadillas. Place in biscuit crust. Refrigerate.
completely cover with whipped carnation and decorate with extra
... if necessary.
... chilled to thickness of white of an egg or just a little

DAVIS GEL

NAME

DEPOSIT ON

Bottles	Wire	Malt
Issues		
Returns		48

00675 - 48 Received by